REDISCOVERING FIRE

REDISCOVERING FIRE

BASIC ECONOMIC LESSONS
FROM THE SOVIET EXPERIMENT

Guinevere Liberty Nell

Algora Publishing
New York

Library of Congress Cataloging-in-Publication Data —

Nell, Guinevere Liberty, 1976-
    Rediscovering fire: basic economic lessons from the Soviet experiment to eliminate
the market / Guinevere Liberty Nell.
        p. cm.
    Includes bibliographical references and index.
    ISBN 978-0-87586-747-2 (trade paper: alk. paper) — ISBN 978-0-87586-748-9 (case
laminate: alk. paper) — ISBN 978-0-87586-749-6 (ebook) 1. Mixed economy—Soviet
Union. 2. Soviet Union—Economic conditions. 3. Central planning—Soviet Union. 4.
Soviet Union—Economic policy. I. Title.
    HC336.26.N46 2010
    330.947'084—dc22
                        2010009328

Cover design by John Cox © 2010.

Printed in the United States

To my mother for raising me with confidence in my own creativity and ability, and my father for infusing me with the economics "bug."

To some, the future still unknown beckons
The shouts heard from the streets that wind
Through our imaginations
And time itself is a pause between two worlds
The known and the unknown
Impatiently we call out to time

Let us try!
We know how to bring Heaven to Earth
We can be the upheaval of history
Destroy illusion
Rewrite the human soul
So, electricity cracks across the sky
Shattering faith in the past
Thundering change
Emancipating anger

Bloody whispers crawl the halls
As the new Cabinet takes its place
The thinkers become the new order
Rearranging the structure
Of the new institutions

Putting into practice
The vision, the dream, the ideal
Rain beats the pavement
Washing the ruin
So that its fresh face
Looks almost innocent
The bright morning sun
Announcing a new day

The day of theory
Today we wipe the slate clean
And wear our workday
Inside out
Today what you own
Is owned by all
And we all own
What was once
The property of single men

You may vote on how to wield our common property
The thinkers shall ensure your verdict stands
And men stand tall on platforms and exclaim
Today we put into place
A fair system
A safe system
An eternal system
That shall reward all equally
And bring about a new kind of man

The shimmer of the sun on the newly erected order
Blinds the exuberant youth
The aging old buildings decay with disuse
And the old are incredulous
And time and men
March

Neither willing to submit
To the wisdom of the past

And the burning rays of the fierce new order
Crack the pavement under our feet
As we trod along implementing this ambitious system

The crumbling beneath us gives some pause
But not wanting to lose hope
Not willing to admit defeat
We are determined, unshakable, steadfast
And as the foundation of our world
Turns to dust
We plod along resolute
We are in the right
It is reality which has betrayed us
Abandoned us to this cruel hoax
This grey imitation of a new world.

Acknowledgments

In researching and writing this book, I am indebted to the Marxist Internet Archive (www.marxists.org), The Mises Institute (www.mises.org), and The Library of Economics and Liberty (www.econlib.org), in addition to the vast literature of Sovietology. I also wish to thank the professors at George Mason University who helped to shape my approach to economic theory, introduced me to many Austrian works as well as theories and ideas from other economic schools, debated with me for hours in person or online, and challenged and inspired me; I especially thank Peter Leeson for offering me so much of his scarce time, and Peter Boettke for his support and confidence. The Heritage Foundation, and especially William Beach of the Center for Data Analysis, offered their continued belief in me and support and flexibility as I completed this book.

Several people contributed to the effort by reading draft chapters, without which help I could never have completed the final manuscript. So, thank you to: Dain Fitzgerald, Ken Myers MSW, Kirk Dameron, Cameron Weber from the New School for Social Research, John Higgins, Slavisa Tasic, who was especially helpful, and Alexander Volokh, who also helped me fine tune my own theories and ideas; and my eternal gratitude to Jon Rodeback for helping to edit and copyedit the whole manuscript and Jessica Lowther for last-minute final proofreading and copyediting. Of course I am grateful for Algora Publishing's decision to take the chance on my book, and for the efforts of Claudiu A. Secara and the editors.

I also thank my brother Jacob for introducing me to Alec Nove's work, which was the inspiration for writing this book. I also must thank Thomas W. Moore IV for endless intellectual battles that helped me challenge the beliefs I was raised with, and my sister Miranda for then debating with me endlessly from the other side.

TABLE OF CONTENTS

Introduction

"Tell me about the life of capitalists. I've never been abroad. All I've heard and read is that ordinary people are starving while the bourgeois live well. I can see you don't come from a poor family—you've probably been to the university."

They were obviously impressed by the idea, so I went along with it. "I went to the university in Warsaw," I said confidently. "Two years. I wanted to be a writer."

"So tell us how you lived in the great capital of Poland," the *pakhan* prodded.

"In Warsaw I was a student, so I didn't live in opulence. But my family lived well. I wouldn't consider us rich, but we had seven rooms with two porches, a stable, a large garden with fruit trees, and two dogs."

"What are you talking about?" a jowly man asked with his mouth full. "Seven rooms for one family?"

"My father had his office there, and my brother, sister and I each had our own room. I also had a horse, and when I was fifteen my father bought me a motorcycle."

"Bullshit," the men leaning against the wall grumbled. "Nobody lives like that."

"Your father was a millionaire," said the *pakhan*, who was called Riaboj, or "Pockmarked."

"No, he was a simple dentist in Wlodzimierz-Wolynski. We lived ordinary lives."

..."Not everyone lived like we did. But hardly anyone was starving." I paused for a moment, not wanting to stir up envy in the group. "There was poverty. There were rich and poor. But I've seen the same or worse in this country."

...At the station in Kurgan, as in all the stations, dozens of women, young and old, sold boiled eggs, raw potatoes, and chunks of lard to the regular passengers through the train windows. Their faces were lined and deeply tanned, their teeth missing, their coats and shawls shaggy and torn. ...[M]en walked about in worn-out coats and hats, hardly looking up or noticing one another as they scurried down the street. The place hardly resembled what I had imagined a Soviet city to be—vital and clean with durable buildings and clothing. After all, wealth was being distributed equally; the workers were in power; they were in charge of their lives. The cities were so different from the picture that had been painted by the *politruks* and propaganda in the Red Army.[1]

This memoir, written by Janusz Bardach, a survivor of the Soviet Gulag and renowned surgeon, raises a simple but important question: Why did the Soviet system, which allowed the workers to own the means of production and held the hopes of so many for so long, fail to produce the promised prosperity and freedom?

Was it hijacked and turned on its face—or was it the system itself which failed the people? A dispassionate analysis must carefully analyze the economic and political theories of the Soviet leaders, determine whether the policies they enacted were in fact those suggested by their theories, and then proceed to analyze why the results of the system did not measure up to the promise.

There is no shortage of documentation on Marxist theory leading up to the revolution. "Without revolutionary theory there can be no revolutionary movement," Lenin wrote in 1901. This was the year he first used the pseudonym "Lenin" and 16 years before his sudden rise to power amidst the turmoil of revolution in 1917.

Lenin's revolutionary theory for that year is covered in volumes 4 and 5 of the 45-volume *Collected Works of V. I. Lenin*. Almost 9,000 works and documents are contained in the 45 volumes, including a huge number of articles relating to economic policy, political science, and the building of socialism. Yet many view Lenin as an impatient revolutionary, or see him as a dictator who exploited the peoples of the Soviet Union, betraying the hopes and dreams of socialism for his own benefit. Yet, if Lenin did make a true attempt at implementing Marxist theory, there are important lessons that could be lost to history if it is assumed that he was ill-intentioned.

Lenin built his theory and policy on Marxist economics and a powerful belief in the superiority of socialism: a belief in the superiority of a system built upon social ownership of the means of production to a system based on private property. However, the lessons from the experiment of the Soviet system extend beyond the question of which of the two systems is superior. If anything is fundamental to the discipline of economics, it is the distinction between public and private ownership.

Whether the profit motive is seen as immoral or useful or a necessary evil, economic theory must come to understand its effects and build them into economic models. As economists study public provision of core necessities, regulations, subsidies, and other economic policies, the distinction between private ownership and public ownership—the institutions of the society under study—must be well defined and well understood. The Soviet experiment presents a core body of evidence to researchers seeking to understand the full range of effects that institutions create. Yet the Soviet experiment with eliminating markets and installing a system of social ownership of production has not been closely analyzed by economists.

What is Socialism?

Before considering further how to learn from the Soviet experiment, some basic terminology should be cleared up. When I refer to socialism, I am using the term to mean something very specific: social ownership over the means of production. This is the definition of the word "socialism" used by economists during the period under discussion and today, including both advocates and skeptics of such a system. In popular policy debate, the term "socialism" is often used to describe economies without complete social ownership over all production: Sweden, France, and other European countries are sometimes called socialist, for example. Some political parties also call themselves "socialist" or "social-democratic" even if they do not advocate full-fledged socialism as defined above.

This casual usage can cause some confusion. These countries and political parties may be called "socialist" because they advocate greater social ownership in the economy, but if they do not advocate social ownership over all production in the economy they are not socialist in the sense used by economists at least since Karl Marx.[2] Furthermore, in casual usage, the economies that have implemented complete social ownership of the means of production are often referred to as "communist"—this is also misleading.

Marx used the terms "socialism" and "communism" interchangeably, but he distinguished the lower and higher phases of communism. Lenin then coined the lower phase as "socialism" and the higher phase, "communism." Thus, the Communist Party (Bolshevik) brought socialism to Russia in hopes of one day ushering in communism. This has been the way the two words have been defined ever since by economists debating the merits of social ownership, by Soviet economists and political leaders, and by public experts, including both advocates and skeptics of the socialist program. This is why some say that communism has never been attempted—what they mean is that we have never experienced communism because socialism has never ushered it in. In fact, the attempt has been made—the promise never materialized.

Marx defined socialism as an economic system in which the means of production are commonly owned. The means of production is a vague phrase, but it should not be understood to mean just the natural resources, major capital and land. The "commanding heights" were defined by the Bolshevik leader Nikolai Bukharin as the most critical sectors, which included land, transportation and primary industry. He argued these critical sectors might be a good start for the transition to socialism, but that they were not enough.

Socialism was to have common ownership of *all* means of production—all industry, even "petty production" or small business. Under socialism, all private property was to be outlawed, except consumer goods once in private use. Production was to be "for use," not for trade. Although it would take a "dictatorship of the proletariat" to implement the system, production, as well as administration of government, would become slowly more democratic until every individual became so personally involved that no hierarchy would be necessary in either economic or political affairs.

1   Socialism, as defined by Marx and Engels, abolished markets and replaced them with centralized allocation of resources, or central planning. Although some advocates of socialism or communism argue that Marx did not advocate planning, Marx and Engels recognized that common ownership, until the day that commu-

nism emerged from the socialist system, would require central planning. As Engels described it, "The social anarchy of production gives place to a social regulation of production upon a definite plan, according to the needs of the community and of each individual,"[3] "Anarchy in social production is replaced by systematic, definite organization."[4] Marx said, "The life-process of society, which is based on the process of material production, does not strip off its mystical veil until it is treated as production by freely associated men, and is consciously regulated by them in accordance with a settled plan."[5]

Communism—the final goal to which the system of socialism would lead—would be a society with no "commodity production": all production would be for use not for trade. Marxists believed that once socialism was in place, and the people became accustomed to it, scarcity would be eliminated. Furthermore, the people would so enjoy their new freedom from want, and their shared ownership and management of the economy, that the state would wither away and the system would function without any kind of enforcement mechanism. There would be no need for government because the workers would manage the economy in the shared interest of all people. This would be communism.

Lenin took on the task of implementing this Marxist vision.[6] Using Lenin's terminology,[7] socialism represents the theory and the system which Marx advocated. Communism was the resulting society that this theory predicted would come, once human nature had changed under socialism. Hence, the system to study is the socialist system, and analysis can help to determine what it looks like in practice, whether human nature would be changed by it, and why it did not seem to lead to communism during the Soviet period.

Marx also popularized the word "capitalism." Because Marx defined capitalism within his theoretical model, it means something more particular than simply a market system. In fact, it is a system in which business can depend upon the state—it is not a free market system. The term "capitalism" is confusing because it allows arguments against markets and arguments against a combined power of business and state to be conflated. For example, many political commentators blamed the 2007-2008 financial crash on free markets, arguing that excessive deregulation had allowed banks too much free reign. However, some of these same commentators also blamed the crisis on explicit and implicit bailout guarantees by the government, loose monetary policy, and corporate handouts and protection that allowed the banks to become so large in the first place. However, these are the opposite of free market policy. If these policies were in place and are partly to blame, it is inconsistent to argue that the free market is to blame. One can argue that "deregulation" in certain areas exacerbated problems (problems of deregulation will be discussed in Chapter 8), or that the wrong policies and regulations were in place—but one cannot say that the market was too free, while simultaneously blaming policies of intervention in the market. This will be discussed further in Chapter 10.

The Dream of Planning

The hopes and dreams of socialism were also Lenin's hopes and dreams. Although Marx was banned in Russia and many of his works were not translated in his lifetime, Lenin studied them in French or the original German and laboriously translated many of them into Russian. He wrote academic articles on the Russian economy, debating other Marxists and "bourgeois" economists and carefully defending his theoretical arguments with passages from the works of Marx and Engels.

The development of the theory of socialist economics did not stop once Lenin succeeded in rising to power. After Lenin came to power, Marxist theory continued to be developed, and Soviet economists studied planned-economy theory extensively. Optimal planning theory led one Soviet economist to win a Nobel Prize. In his 1975 Nobel speech, Leonid Kantorovich described the need for economic theory in the planned economy and the progress made to that point:

> [T]he main purpose of economic theory was altered. There appeared a necessity to shift from study and observation of economic processes and from isolated policy measures to systematic control of the economy.... This planning must be so detailed as to include specific tasks to individual enterprises for specific periods and to that common consistency of the whole this giant set of decisions was guaranteed.[8]

Kantorovich explained that while "[t]he economic theory of Karl Marx became the methodological background of the new created Soviet economic science and of the new control system," Marx alone was not enough,[9] the theory must continue to develop. "A practical use of Marx' ideas needed serious theoretical research" because there had been no practical economic experience of such a system during Marx's time.[10] The development of socialist economics in the Soviet Union went on for nearly 75 years.

Despite the wealth of information available on the theory and reality of the socialist experiment in the Soviet Union, few writers have chosen to analyze why it produced results so different from those intended and what these lessons might mean for market economies. If the theories were mistaken, then like the theories of the hard sciences, we should modify theory based on practical experience. At one time, science had nothing negative to say about using unwashed knives in surgery, but practical experience did.

Consensus has come nearly full circle on the merits of central planning. Before the popular rise of "scientific" socialist ideology in the 1870s, few argued for economic planning. At the peak of belief in planning, one-third of the world's land mass and half the world's population was under socialist rule, and many of the remaining states made extensive use of planning. For a time, the consensus was that allocation by central planning was economically[11] and morally superior to use of markets. However, the tide turned again, and the crumbling of the empires of socialism has worn down the fabric of this ideology.

In economics, the mainstream is no longer captured by belief in a centralized order. Yet the faith in planning has not been replaced by a return to the classical belief in markets. The profession remains ambiguous, partly appreciating and partly castigating markets. While some of the failures of planning are recognized, economists often advocate the use of planning to overcome perceived problems with markets. Perhaps this mixture of planning and market forces is best, but this has yet to be proven.

A recent *New York Times* article discussing US President Barack Obama's economic policy perspective summarizes this ambiguity. It argues that the President was influenced by the University of Chicago, where he was educated, but that he was skeptical of some of the stronger claims made there about the efficiency of markets. The author describes the Chicago School's view of the power of market decentralization:

> The Chicago School promotes the idea that markets—that is, millions of individuals making separate decisions—almost always function better than economies that are managed by governments. In a market system, prices adjust whenever there is a shortage or a glut, and the problem soon resolves itself. Just as important, companies constantly compete with each other, which helps bring down prices, improves the quality of goods and ultimately lifts living standards.[12]

Then, the author points out places where the market may prove insufficient:

> In its more extreme forms, the Chicago School's ideas have some obvious flaws. History has shown that free markets aren't so good at, say, preventing pollution or the issuance of fantastically unrealistic mortgages. But over the last few decades, as Europe's regulated economies have struggled and Asia's move toward capitalism has spurred its fabulous boom, many liberals have also come to appreciate the virtues of markets.[13]

The author identifies two supposed "market failures," but what he fails to address, and even worse, what many economists fail to examine, is the alternative to the market in these cases. For example, do we know for sure that government can prevent pollution better than the market or what the cost of prevention would be? Why do markets fail at pollution control if they succeed at increasing safety standards for automobiles? Can the answer to this question provide insight into ways to enable the market to succeed where it currently does not? How would the results in that case compare with a government solution?

Similarly, in regard to the "fantastically unrealistic mortgages," what caused the market to fail? Was it a market failure or was it really a failure of government intervention? Very often if any market exists—even if it is one that is heavily regulated by government—any perceived failure is assumed to be a market failure. Yet would the failure be less or more severe if the government was not regulating the price, stimulating demand, ensuring competition, or preventing collapse in that market? Mainstream economics has surprisingly little to say on this subject, but the answers to some of these questions may be hidden in the lessons of the Soviet experiment with socialism.

Economics as a discipline has yet to acknowledge the problems with planning and the lessons unveiled by socialist governments. Economists may personally acknowledge some of the lessons, but they continue to use models that ignore them. In fact, many models still used today in the economics classroom and by professional economists implicitly assume an omniscient and omnipotent government which can enact the policy solution to fix a "market failure." Although economists using these models are not advocating for full central planning, the models are incapable of revealing any of the problems that occurred under central planning. The models are inherently biased to show that planning is superior to markets.

Policymakers tend not to ask whether the failures of planning may also imply failure of their own policies or programs. At the dinner table, many people casually recognize economic problems of planning. In fact, many policies and programs suffer from the same failures that occurred in the Soviet Union, but as a society we shrug and wonder why. This is why it is so important to explicitly recall the arguments made for socialism,[14] the lessons learned when the experiment was undertaken, and the ways in which these lessons apply to policies undertaken in market economies. It was a failure of theory, so we must update our theory and learn from these mistakes.

There may be a limit to how much intervention can be exerted efficiently and how much of the economy can be publicly run. Entirely centralized economies may not be the only type of economic system that suffers from the inefficiency of centralization. Some interventions, even in an otherwise free market system, may create ripple effects or backfire. The interconnectedness of the Soviet economy is visible in their struggle with pricing policies, and the same pricing difficulties arise when only a single price is controlled by the state.

Common wisdom still fails to appreciate all of the major reasons for the failure of planning, concentrating on the problem of incentives and omitting the difficulties of *coordination* and *calculation*. For example, how is it that when you go to the store you find the bread, cheese, and cereal that you want and in the desired quantities, even if you live 100 miles from the nearest wheat field and maybe thousands of miles from where the cheese was made? How is it that the factory that makes pencils can obtain all of the tiny metal parts, the wood, the paint, and the stenciling and then deliver the finished pencil to the shops?[15] This is a matter of *coordination*.

The problem of calculation is related. In a market economy, calculation is something that individual firms (businesses) do when they count their costs and their profit and when they determine the cheapest assortment of inputs with which to produce their output. It is also something that consumers do when they choose where to shop. Until the experiment with socialism, few economists worried about this problem. However, with the introduction of central planning in a socialist economy came the need for centralized calculation. The central planner needed to calculate the cheapest way to produce the goods in the economy. Yet this posed a problem. In the market economy, firms can base their calculations on prices. In the socialist economy, there is no market and so there are no market prices. This is the problem of *calculation*.

These problems of calculation and coordination exist in any economy. Both problems can be resolved by the market but are unresolved in a planned economy. This is because the solution depends upon decentralized actions—individuals privately making exchanges and choices—in the market, which produces market prices. Because they depend upon the market, calculation and coordination are affected any time that market prices and market activity (exchange and entrepreneurship) are affected by a regulation or other government policy. Hence, in between the two extremes of *plan* and *market* exists an economy in which policies may affect calculation and coordination (in addition to the well known problem of incentives) and produce unintended results. Yet these two features of the market are rarely discussed, and it is even more rare that lessons about them are taken from the socialist experience.

This book attempts to address this gap by offering 10 lessons taken from the Soviet experience. For each lesson, I outline:

- The economic theory that socialists offered;

- The Soviet implementation of the socialist theory and the outcome and lessons that the Soviet policymakers learned; and

- The particular lessons that economists, policymakers, and others should take away from the experience of the Soviet Union and examples of their use in analyzing current policy questions.

THE IMPORTANCE OF THE SOCIALIST EXPERIMENT

Given the brutality and famine during the Stalin period,[16] it is tempting to conclude that the Bolsheviks simply used Marxist writings as a convenient justification to seize power and exploit the masses. Extensive writings and other evidence force historians to reject this claim. The Bolshevik party was probably acting in earnest, with good intentions. In general, famine in Stalinist Russia was the result of eliminating markets, not the result of malice.[17]

Many prominent intellectuals of the day were behind these ideas and actively supported socialist movements. Prominent economists at Oxford, Cambridge, and Harvard; writers including George Bernard Shaw; scientists including Albert Einstein; and even many prominent businessmen adopted these beliefs in part or in whole. Many of these intellectuals subsequently became disillusioned by Stalinism, but a good number of them retained their belief in socialism, believing that Stalin hijacked the movement and maliciously turned it against the people. In my own family, I saw a microcosm of this phenomenon. My maternal grandmother escaped the Bolsheviks in Russia, but she maintained belief in the socialist ideal afterward. My father learned Marxist theory from the economist Joan Robinson, later moderating his views but always sympathetic to his own mother's strong socialist beliefs.

One Marxist used the following metaphor to make the case:

> Like mushrooms, you go out and pick the right kind and you can cook a tasty dish. But if you gather up the kind commonly known as toadstools and call them mushrooms, you will poison yourself. Stalinist "socialism" is about as close to the real thing as a toadstool is to an edible mushroom.[18]

Yet was Stalin's socialism different from that suggested by Marx? Lenin and Stalin were not just ambitious men conniving to push through their schemes; they were attempting to implement the theories of socialism, based on Marx.[19] They had a specific set of institutions that they believed would bring prosperity and happiness. The 1918 and 1936 constitutions outlined rules that enforced collective property rights, the duty to contribute, and the right to social proceeds.

The wonderful contribution that the Soviet experiment can offer is its near-perfect laboratory testing of socialist theory[20] and of the economic laws of the market. Marxists literally did not believe that economic laws—immutable regularities that arise from scarcity of resources on the one hand and unlimited human wants on the other—would apply under socialism.[21] Hence, they wiped out the system by which prices emerge and through which these laws of economics direct production. Marxists believed that those laws only existed due to the capitalist system and thus were irrelevant under socialism. They did not realize that the laws would remain and that abolishing the system would therefore pit the laws against their new system.

Nikolai Bukharin, one of the Bolsheviks who came to power with Lenin, described the Marxist position in *The Economics of the Transition Period*:

> As soon as we take an organized social economy, all the basic "problems" of political economy disappear: the problem of value, price, profit, and the like. Here "relations between people" are not expressed in "relations between things," and social economy is regulated not by the blind forces of the market and competition, but consciously by a...*plan*. Therefore here there can be a certain descriptive system on the one hand, a system of norms on the other. But there can be no place for a science studying "the blind laws of the market" since there will be no market. Thus the end of the capitalist commodity society will be the end of political economy.[22]

The belief was that a planned society would not require economics as we know it, and economics, based as it was on the market system, could also not tell what the planned society would look like. Economic science was a science of the laws of commodity production and commodity relations—a science of the market. Without the market, the problems created by the market would disappear. The government could simply take rational control over resources and solve the problems experienced under capitalism.

Similarly, when economists and policymakers see market failures—situations where the market appears to allocate resources inefficiently—they sometimes assume that government intervention or provision will make these problems disappear. This is often referred to as the Nirvana fallacy, because it makes the logical error of comparing the performance of an *existing* market with a *hypothetically perfect* government. However, the laws of economics still apply even when government allocates the resources. They just apply to new institutional arrangements. This de-romanticizing of government action was the foundation of the "public choice" school of economics.

As the quote from Nikolai Bukharin illustrates, Marxist theory indicated that the laws of "bourgeois economics" would not apply under socialism. However, Marx also believed it was not possible to predict what laws, if any, would apply in the new system. He claimed such pretensions were hubristic and "unscientific." The bourgeois economic laws resulted from specific relations of production and applied only to those relations and to that specific period in history. Under new conditions, in a new historical period, new laws would apply. This was the belief of German "historicists," not just Marxists.

Soviet economists and policymakers living in the new society initially claimed that *no* economic laws applied under socialism, that the only law was the "law of the plan." Later, Soviet economists and planners characterized new "laws of socialist exchange." This was consistent with Marxist theory because they no longer had to predict the laws of the new society—they were living in it.

Sovietologist Alec Nove quotes a Soviet economist who explains that "[a]t one time it was fashionable among us to deny the existence of any objective economic laws in our society" because the plan was law.[23] However, reality forced planners to admit objective economic laws:

> Economic laws also do not lack an enforcement mechanism, even though it is not laid down in any code.... Economic sanctions operate independently, without the help of any kind of coercive apparatus, as a result of the very breach of (economic) law. To put it another way, economic laws take their own revenge on those who break them.[24]

Alec Nove adds that "when [planners] ignore [economic laws], the chickens come home to roost, things go wrong." However, "the fact that they do so provides us with material for study as economists."[25] This is where the lessons for market economies lie. The institutions within which economic actions took place were the opposite of those of Western market economies, yet the economic laws themselves, based upon human nature, remained:

> Economists should be interested in the fate of economic laws and economic theory in a philosophic and institutional setting quite different to the one to which they are accustomed. For example, what happens to resource allocation when there is no interest and no rent? Can market forces be replaced by administrative decision, or do they climb in through the window when driven out of the door? How far is centralized planning in practice consistent with any economic theory at all, Marxist or non-Marxist? What happens in their system to wage-determination, consumer choice, and so on? An examination of the Soviet economic scene can help us to see our own economic concepts more clearly, to see how far they depend on western institutions or apply to all systems, albeit in altered or distorted forms.[26]

In 1951, Stalin argued that it was a mistake to think that economic laws could be changed at will. Economic laws were real and were due to economic conditions. (Only later would Soviet economists question the historical basis for economic laws.) In his treatise *Economic Problems of Socialism in the U.S.S.R.*, Stalin said:

> Some comrades deny the objective character of laws of science, and of laws of political economy particularly, under socialism. They deny that the laws of political economy reflect law-governed processes which operate independently of the will of man. They believe that in view of the specific role assigned to the Soviet state by history, the Soviet state and its leaders can abolish existing laws of political economy and can "form," "create," new laws.[27]

Russian emigre economist Constantin A. Krylov described this shift. In 1979, he explained: "Whatever may be said or written to the contrary in the USSR, the economic theories of Marx have been found bankrupt in practice and have been debunked in theory in the Soviet Union."[28] He then described the discussion at the July 1955 Plenum of the Central Committee:

> One has to begin a discussion of economics by reestablishing the elementary concepts, by turning them right side up again. Thus, as a counterforce to the dogmas, it was established that an economic law objectively exists outside our consciousness and acts automatically, independent of the desires of the participants of the economic activity.[29]

Yet at this time, these laws were still believed to be historically based and thus different under socialism than under capitalism. During the debate preceding the 1965 reform, and in later years, many of the laws assumed to apply only under capitalism were rediscovered within the failures of the planned economy. When the Soviet experiment finally ended, the same economists who had advised the Soviet government on optimal planning theory were now to advise the new administration on how to create a limited government that would protect, rather than stamp out, markets.

These ex-Soviet economists were starting from scratch, recreating their economy and their economic science. One early market-reform paper[30] on the subject of taxation, published in 1989, illustrates this well. The authors discussed the basic functions of the tax system and listed the potential options for taxation of enterprises. Options spanned from appropriation of all profits except for a fixed sum (as under socialism) to simply taxing the firms a fixed lump-sum amount. A series of tax rates were presented in between the two extremes. The references in the paper are especially revealing: a few early Soviet economic papers, one recent paper, and one Western textbook on the principles of economics.

With the market economy wiped clean away, the government and the people were forced to rediscover fire: to relearn the basic laws of economics and rebuild civilization out of the ashes of ruin. This outlines the scope of the Soviet experiment with socialism. All of economics was put to the test, from the very elementary concept of whether or not economic laws exist objectively, to the relearning of these laws through crisis and reform, to the rediscovery of the institutions necessary for a market economy to function. All economics was relearned from scratch.

Valuable lessons emerge from these policy actions and reforms:

- The replacement of competition with public provision led to a sellers' market unresponsive to the consumer, revealing the power of even one potential rival and the process by which competition drives efficient and high-quality production.

- The attempt to eliminate unemployment and direct labor led to the difficulty of matching workers to appropriate jobs and to massive waste, revealing the fluid nature of a healthy labor market and the danger of "protecting jobs."

- The elimination of profit as a motive and loss as a constraint led to an assortment of unwanted products and an irrational allocation of resources across the economy, revealing the critical importance of these often-disparaged phenomena in both the microeconomic and macroeconomic spheres.

- The elimination of the supposedly wasteful capitalist "middleman" left socialist firms completely unable to obtain intermediate goods, and new socialist middlemen began to emerge to take over the role, offering insight into the efficiency of the market supply system.

- The eradication of the price system left planners with no information with which to direct the economy, and attempts to set prices centrally failed to help, revealing the power of the price signal and the folly of altering the prices that emerge in markets.

- The nationalization of banking and elimination of interest rates led to confusion over the value of investment, and the reintroduction of interest rates set centrally was of little help, revealing the danger of controlling this ubiquitous price signal.

- The attempt to command compliance with a plan rather than setting up institutions that would offer appropriate incentives led to unceasing frustration and additional decrees, along with an extensive enforcement apparatus, revealing the dominance of the underlying incentives over any regulatory regime.

- The replacement of free exchange ("negative liberty") with free goods ("positive liberty") led to central direction over nearly every aspect of life, revealing the true freedom inherent in the free market.

- Finally, attacking the market for ills connected to state involvement with business led to an enhancement of those ills as the state took control over all production, revealing the mistaken conflation between pro-business and free market systems.

These lessons are easily found within the experiment of socialism, if one takes the time to look for them. It would be a tragic waste to avoid seeing them and to repeat the mistakes of the past. The lessons are also an enjoyable romp through a fascinating bit of history and history of thought. However, before delving into them, it is important to remember why understanding economics and making good policy is important and to consider the appropriateness of taking lessons from such a different kind of system from the one in which those of us in the West live today.

THE GOAL OF ECONOMIC POLICY

This book does not intend to address morally or philosophically whether a policy is by nature right or good. The lessons we can learn from socialism speak to whether a given policy *achieves its aims* and *at what cost*. For example, if the goal is to lift the living standard of a certain group of workers, the policy should be judged first on whether it achieves the goal of raising the living standards of those particular workers and second on whether it achieves this goal at a reasonable cost.

When a policy has "unintended consequences," a rational policymaker or voter may still deem it the appropriate method to achieve a certain end. At one end of the spectrum, the unintended side effects of a policy may act as a counterforce and actually harm those the policy aimed to help, exceeding any potential benefit. At the other end, the unintended consequences may actually be positive. In between, the side effects of a policy, although harmful to society or to certain groups, may be seen as acceptable costs. A January 2010 article by economist Paul Krugman suggested that, although the egalitarian policies of Europe may have slowed the economic growth in those countries somewhat, one need only look at the relative stability and success in those countries, along with the (in his opinion) obvious better position of the poor, to see that the trade-off is worthwhile.[31]

This judgment is not for the economist to make, but economics can help to shed light on the indirect and dynamic[32] effects of policy proposals. If the unintended consequences are known and avoidable, the policy may be modified to reduce negative effects or better provide the benefits. Knowledge of the likely indirect consequences offers the citizen, voter, and policymaker the chance to weigh costs and benefits and make an informed decision. If the consequences are simply ignored or dismissed, the policy will be less likely to achieve its aims in the most effective way.

One indicator of the success of a policy might be whether it increases or decreases the standard of living of the people. Some will argue that there are things more important than gross domestic product (GDP) or economic growth. Instead, we should care about the broader consequences of economic policy, including its social aspects and humanity.[33] Perhaps policies should aim to reduce inequality, or foster a sense of community and the building of a shared future.

Policies aimed at these other goals should be judged based upon whether their aims are achieved. Although today we can consider these other goals, one should recall that it is a privileged perspective to even separate them from the material affects of policy. Many underdeveloped economies struggle at a level that developed nations surpassed a few hundred years ago.[34] It is meaningless to admonish a mother of hungry children living at subsistence level to put the social aspects of economic policy above the material. As one prominent anti-socialist economist said in 1949:

> In calling a rise in the masses' standard of living progress and improvement, economists do not espouse a mean materialism. They simply establish the fact that people are motivated by the urge to improve the material conditions of their existence. They judge policies from the point of view of the aims men want to attain. He who disdains the fall in infant mortality and the gradual disappearance of famines and plagues may cast the first stone upon the materialism of the economists.[35]

Today we often imagine that economic growth is no longer important. That we can think such a thought is only due to the incredible growth produced by the market economy over the last few hundred years. Yet even in the wealthiest countries, economic growth is a shorthand indicator for the phenomenon of technological and material advancement that means finding cures for disease, lifting the poorest members out of difficult circumstances, and making leisure and comfort more possible for everyone.

Again, this book does not intend to answer the question of tradeoffs. Sometimes a policy helps the least advantaged and causes a slight reduction in overall growth. A policy may hinder the economy in such a way that the least advantaged find fewer opportunities. Economic analysis can only shed light on the facts of this trade-off; it cannot determine whether it is worthwhile. If the goal is to reduce inequality, the economist may estimate the cost to different groups in society and indicate whether inequality is likely to be reduced, but it is not up to the economist to state whether the policy is worthwhile.

Similarly, when economists speak of efficiency, they are sometimes accused of ignoring more important factors. Yet when an economist argues that a policy is inefficient, it means that the policy is not achieving its aims at the least cost. Whatever the goals of the policy are, these are what concern the economist. If the goal is to feed hungry children, and the economist argues that the policy is inefficient, he is only saying that there is a way to feed the hungry children just as well at a lower cost, which means that more children can be fed. This is what is meant by understanding the trade-offs and aiming for efficient policies.

Soviet planners wanted to raise the living standards of the workers, and their other aims were, they realized, bound to this goal. For example, speaking of the aims of the 1971–1975 five-year plan, Soviet Premier Aleksei Kosygin said:

> The main task of the five-year plan is to ensure a considerable rise in the people's material and cultural level on the basis of a high rate of development of socialist production, enhancement of its efficiency, scientific and technical progress and acceleration of the growth of labor productivity.[36]

Socialism, in the Soviet Union, was intended and expected to produce a high level of growth and technological advancement. While growth in the early years impressed many in the West, by the 1980s it became clear that they had fallen behind in many areas. That a strictly planned economy is less dynamic than a free market is common knowledge. It is even common to hear claims that this was always obvious,[37] that no one ever thought that the Soviet Union could surpass the West in output or in technological advancement. Yet there was a time when the common wisdom was the opposite. Rational economic planning was thought to be clearly superior to the "anarchy of the market."

Many mainstream economists also believed that a planned economy, by eliminating unemployment, could make better use of all resources. Socialists had many arguments about the perceived inefficiencies of capitalism and benefits of central planning. The famous socialist writer Joseph Bellamy had a protagonist Doctor Leete who named the "four great wastes" of market economies: "waste by mistaken undertakings," "waste from competition and mutual hostility of those in industry," "waste by 'periodic gluts and crises,'" and "waste from idle capital and labor, at all times."[38] These supposed wastes had an elaborate theoretical foundation and the possibility of eliminating these wastes through planning was tested in the real world economy of the Soviet Union.

They were also tested elsewhere, although not always with a complete turn to socialism. In 1933, in his book *Looking Forward*, President Franklin D. Roosevelt argued, "The country needs, and unless I mistake its temper, the country demands, bold persistent experimentation. It is common sense to take a method and try it; if it fails, admit it frankly and try another. But above all, try something."[39]

Planning and government action are alluring because trying to "do something" always feels safer and more hopeful than appearing to do nothing to resolve a problem.[40] It seems natural that when the economy is in a downturn, rational central direction of the economy is appropriate to correct the problem. Thus, some of the theories of the socialists were also tested in the United States.

President Roosevelt was a strong believer that the chaos of the market was wasteful and that planning would be required to resolve the tendency to recession. Roosevelt's close confidant and cabinet member, the public intellectual Stuart Chase, wrote that "A planless national economy if it is to avoid disaster must give way to a planned economy."[41] In *Looking Forward*, Roosevelt described what he believed to be the causes of the downturn and made a case for the appropriate strategy to reverse it.

In the chapter entitled "Need for Economic Planning," he made the case that the chaos and lack of a plan had led many industries to inadequately prepare for the future. There were too many lawyers and teachers, he argued, because no one had warned students of the oversupply in time. Roosevelt then argued:

> In the same way we cannot carefully review the history of our industrial advance without being struck by its haphazardness, with the gigantic waste with which it has been accomplished—with the superfluous duplication of productive facilities, the continual scrapping of still useful equipment, the tremendous mortality in industrial and commercial undertakings, the thousands of dead-end trails in which enterprise has been lured, the profligate waste of natural resources.[42]

This description of the "wastes" of capitalism is reminiscent of Joseph Bellamy. Roosevelt goes on to make another familiar socialist argument, that "vast sums of capital or credit...in the past decade have been devoted to unjust enterprises—to the development of unessentials and to the multiplication of many products far beyond the capacity of the nation to absorb." Overproduction and production of useless, non-essential products in place of more important products were both common socialist criticisms of capitalism.

Economists debated the merits and potential performance of an economic system with common ownership of the means of production in the 1920s–1940s in what is referred to as "the socialist calculation debate."[43] This was a debate between economists who argued that a socialist economy could outperform a market economy because the central planner could mimic a perfect market system and economists who argued that the problems of economic calculation and coordination would prevent the socialist economy from functioning well.

The arguments that explain the problems of calculation and coordination under planning are not especially difficult to understand, but they did not convince economists of the time (and so the socialists are said to have "won" the debate). This was perhaps because many economists were influenced by moral arguments for socialism.[44] However, the moral reality of planning all economic life, in the undiluted fundamentalist way this was done in the Soviet Union, with its stifling commands, lower output, and lack of innovation may not have appealed to so many liberal-minded economists and intellectuals. Ideological sympathy had blinded them.

The most compelling moral arguments in favor of socialism, such as the ability of the system to raise the living standards of the poor to a more civilized level, depended on the efficiency of the system. "From each according to his ability, to each according to his need" takes on a sinister meaning when it boils down to extracting the maximum work and providing the barest subsistence to workers. The supposed Utopia where the worker can take from the common pot as much as he needs depends upon an end to scarcity. Yet, this limitless abundance proved as chimerical as the future for which the Soviet citizen was constantly working.

Extracting the Lessons from Socialism

The Soviet Union wiped out the market and with it the basis for all economic knowledge. Planners then instituted policies based on each of their socialist economic hypotheses. They tested their beliefs with the full confidence and backing of the state—a one-party state completely committed with ideological fervor to their success. When each Marxist policy failed, the state reorganized as necessary to better implement it, tried modified versions, and only when absolutely necessary pulled back on any one of them. Despite severe ideological objections, each belief in turn was found to be incorrect, and the classical[45] economists' reasoning was proven correct.

Finally, the Soviet state learned that individual policies could not be reversed in isolation. This sheds light on the interconnectedness of the economy and the way in which each intervention and public provision in a market economy affects not only the given sector but also the other sectors with which it interacts.

Some might object that this interconnectedness means that the outcome of policies will differ between the two economic systems—that the lessons that planners learned may not apply to policymakers in a market system. A given policy produces behavioral effects that directly result from the change in economic incentives that the policy creates. There are features of a planned economy that result from the total use of planning, but these features can be distinguished from behavioral responses that will be the same in any system. These behavioral effects are predictable according to the economic laws that the Soviet government denied. This is what makes the Soviet experiment such a useful case study.

One might also wonder whether it is possible to outline a particular "experiment with socialism" in the Soviet Union. Many Sovietologists distinguish between different periods of socialism in the USSR, calling the Stalin period "classical socialism," the early period "revolutionary-transitional," and the later period (and the New Economic Policy period) "reform-socialism."[46] This distinction is not necessary for the purposes of this book. The early period was an early attempt at instituting planning,[47] the Stalin period was a concerted effort, and the periods of reform were periods when planners recognized the failings of the system and took measures to correct them. I try to avoid sweeping statements about Soviet policies and provide dates where policies changed considerably over the period. Most important, the book is about the lessons that planners learned from enacting policies that did not work, so attention is paid to particular policies and reforms, not to the model of socialism at a given moment in time.

Although some might wonder whether the Soviet case is too extreme, and the lessons may not apply in a mixed economy, the "extreme" purity of the Soviet experiment is exactly what makes it such a good learning tool. Recent Nobel Prize winner Elenor Ostrom made a similar case for her research in economics. Comparing it to the laboratory work of biologists, she said:

> The biologists' scientific strategy involves identifying the simplest possible organism in which the process under investigation occurs in a clarified, or even exaggerated, form. The organism is not chosen because it is representative of all organisms. Rather, the organism is chosen because particular processes can be studied more effectively using this organism than using another. These cases are in no sense a "random" sample of cases. Rather, these are cases that provide clear information about the processes involved.[48]

The Soviet experiment is a pure case study that can be used to isolate behavioral effects that certain institutions produce. The total outcome may differ in a Soviet firm compared with a firm in a market economy, but the response to a given policy or a change in policy follows the same predictable pattern. Soviet man was no different than the "economic man" of capitalism and was just as ill-informed and imperfect as the real consumer. Although socialists had hoped to change human nature, the Soviet citizen had no better or worse moral character than the citizens of any society and responded in the same way to economic incentives. The purpose here is to isolate the behavioral effects of each policy, seen in its extreme form, and then determine whether these same behavioral responses will cause problems if they occur in a market economy situation.

The economic system as a whole is a product of the legal and informal structure of the system—the economic institutions that guide the behavior of individuals. The study of economic institutions is a relatively recent area of economics. "Lack of institutions" has become a popular culprit for the reason for underdevelopment in some countries. "Institutions matter" is a common refrain, but outside development economics few study institutions and their effects.

Classical economists, such as Adam Smith and his contemporaries, built theories around the assumption of a relatively free market because that was what they saw around them,[49] although they debated the merits of tariffs and certain other interventions. However, by World War I this was no longer the case. Government intervention into the economy in the West was a large enough factor by 1917 that, even if the Bolsheviks had not taken over Russia, it should have been factored into economic models.

Yet in the 1930s and 1940s, models that ignored the institutional structure of the economy being studied became increasingly popular. In the "socialist calculation debate," a model of "perfect competition" was used by the socialist side to represent the market. This model represents the outcome in a market after competition has driven down prices. Depending on this model, Oskar Lange argued that "market socialism" could perform even better than free markets because "market failures" could be avoided.[50] He argued that a planner could tell firms to set their prices to the "perfectly competitive" level—the level that the model indicated prices would be if markets were perfect. In this way, market socialism could have all the advantages of the market, and none of its flaws.

Yet the assumptions in this model that lead to this result of a "perfect" competition, if realistic at all, are based on certain institutions. The model assumes that firms compete away all their profit, but firms compete in a market economy to survive and earn profit, something neither necessary nor possible in an economy without private property. Market socialists argued that a central planner could mimic this by telling firms to set their prices. However, if prices fall to the "perfectly competitive" level in a market because of competition it is not clear that having a planner set them at that level will produce all of the same benefits. Because the assumptions of the model replace any modeling of institutions, it is unable to realistically compare the two systems or to determine relative efficiency.

In 1936, Keynes introduced his book *The General Theory of Employment Interest and Money*. In it he modeled the economy's fluctuations using society-wide aggregate measurements of economic activity. These aggregates, by their very nature, ignored whether transactions were government or private. Institutions and incentives were ignored. In this model, demand contributed to aggregate totals the same whether it was government demand or private demand. Spending was considered the same, whether it was private spending or government spending. Based on these assumptions, using equations of aggregates, Keynes argued that government could "stimulate" aggregate demand during a recession to help the economy recover.

Many other economists also ignored this distinction. In 1956, Robert Solow introduced a growth model, for which he was later awarded a Nobel Prize, that treated government and private savings and investment the same. His "exogenous growth model" took technological innovation for granted, as exogenous to the model, and attributed economic growth to savings. In fact, his model indicated that the level of savings was *the* key factor in long-term growth. (This is an interesting contrast to Keynes's preference for consumption over savings, at least for short-term stimulation of the economy.)

However, a model that ignores whether government or the private sector is purchasing and producing goods glosses over a major distinction. If it truly makes no difference whether government or the private sector is the major producer, and only the level of savings matters, then the Soviet Union should have succeeded marvelously. Taking technological change for granted also more or less assumes away the problem: Economic growth is an outcome of the innovation and entrepreneurship that produces technological change. How can one model differences in economic growth while taking its causal factors as givens?

Economists advanced beyond these simple aggregated macro models, and microeconomics also advanced. Yet models too often still rely on aggregates like Keynes or on assumptions of static ends rather than process, as with Oskar Lange. The lessons we can extract from the socialist experiment can inform the economists' models by showing where institutional structure is important, where aggregating does not make any sense, and where a model must allow for dynamic changes.

Recently, Keynesian ideas about spurring consumption through government spending have become increasingly popular. This makes inquiry into potential weaknesses in the Keynesian model even more important.

The study of behavioral effects of the Soviet experiment—its changing of each of the market institutions to its opposite and then reforming them one by one as the new institutions failed—sheds light on potential consequences of Western governmental attempts to guide the market using similar tools. The interrelationship of the policies provides insight into reform attempts in market economies, including attempts to deregulate. The dynamic consequences of rigid planning and the errors caused by use of aggregation provide valuable insight for improving economic modeling. In short, the Soviet experiment with socialism is a rich resource for better understanding economic laws and the behavior of individuals faced with different kinds of incentives.

Endnotes

1. Janusz Bardach, *Man is Wolf to Man: Surviving Stalin's Gulag* (Berkeley: University of California, 1998), pp. 151–155.
2. Prior to Marx's time, socialism was defined more by the ends that socialists sought such as equality, democracy, and an end to poverty and oppression than by the means. Most socialists still advocated a change in property relations, but there were a wider variety of proposed systems that all fell under the single name "socialism." A passage in John Stuart Mills's book *On Socialism* provides an idea of the usage during Marx's time. (Mill wrote the book in 1869.) "It is in France, Germany and Switzerland that anti-property doctrines in the widest sense have drawn large bodies of working men to rally round them. In these countries nearly all those who aim at reforming society in the interest of the working classes profess themselves Socialists, a designation under which schemes of very diverse character are comprehended and confounded, but which implies at least a remodelling generally approaching to the abolition of the institution of private property. And it would probably be found that even in England the more prominent and active leaders of the working classes are usually in their private creed Socialists of one order or another, though...they direct their practical efforts toward ends which seem within easier

reach." John Stuart Mill, *On Socialism* (Amherst, NY: Prometheus Books, 1987), pp. 60–61.

3.   Friedrich Engels, "Socialism: Utopian and Scientific," *Marx/Engels Selected Works*, Vol. 3 (Moscow: Progress Publishers, 1880), pp. 95–151, at http://www.marxists.org/archive/marx/works/1880/soc-utop/ch03.htm.

4.   *Ibid.*

5.   Karl Marx, *Das Kapital*, Vol. 1 (Chicago: Charles H. Kerr and Co., 1906 [1867]), chap. I, par. I.I.135, p. 92, at http://www.econlib.org/library/YPDBooks/Marx/mrxCpA1.html.

6.   This will be shown throughout the book. On the subject of definitions, it is worth noting here that the word "soviet" means council, and the use of soviets to govern, in place of a more traditional "bourgeois" parliament, was an attempt at bringing about the democratc administration by the people of the economic and political life of the new society.

7.   At Lenin's time, the term "social democracy" was also used differently than it often is in common use today. The Bolsheviks were formed from a split within the Social-Democratic party of Russia. The name was based on the idea of a democratic political system combined with a democratic economic system. This would be achieved by socializing the means of production. After coming to power, the Bolsheviks changed their name to the Communist Party, and the third international, run by the Bolsheviks was known as the Communist International. Social-democratic parties in line with the Bolsheviks changed their name to "communist." The remaining parties labeled social-democratic were sometimes more reformist and less revolutionary parties, but many were parties which had disagreements with the Bolsheviks on minor points, did not like the way socialism was being implemented in Russia, or had personal or political reasons for not wanting to be associated with Soviet communism. Reformist Marxist parties based their ideas on the same theoretical foundations but differed on the best way to implement the system, or the best time to take the more radical steps. In a multi-party system, compromise is necessary, hence many of these parties later made compromises which brought them away from the goal of implementing complete socialization of the means of production.

8.   Leonid Vitaliyevich Kantorovich, "Mathematics in Economics: Achievements, Difficulties, Perspectives," Nobel Prize Lecture, December 11, 1975, at http://nobelprize.org/nobel_prizes/economics/laureates/1975/kantorovich-lecture.html (November 17, 2009).

9.   Some might argue that Marx was not truly the inspiration for the Soviet planned economy. Because Marx was often vague about his specific vision, many people are under the impression that he was not even an advocate of planning. This is a false impression. For example, economist Morris Bernstein explains, "[A]lthough Marx and Engels, understandably, never attempted to define in detail the organization and operation of the post-revolutionary society, they did refer to a number of its features at various places in their writings, most conspicuously in *The Communist Manifesto* and *A Critique of the Gotha Programme*. Diligent searchers of the vast Marxian literature have assembled quotations to document, among others, such elements of the post-capitalist economy as (1) nationalization of the means of production and exchange, (2) planning in place of the 'anarchy' of the market, (3) valuation of goods according to their labour content, (4) abolition of money, (5) liability of all to labour, and (6) distribution according to contribution in socialism, according to need in communism." These six features are enough to pin the results of policy described in this book upon the theories of Marx and Engels. Morris Bernstein, "Ideology and the Soviet Economy," *Soviet Studies*, Vol. 18, No. 1 (July 1966), pp. 74–80.

10.   Kantorovich, "Mathematics in Economics: Achievements, Difficulties, Perspectives."

11.   The "political interpretation" of the Soviet five-year plan by G. F. Grinko was cited in an *American Economic Review* article in 1929 as one piece of evidence that Western economists were taken with the idea of planning. The article described the Soviet planned economy and then stated, "If socialists can demonstrate the feasibility of a centrally planned and coordinated industrial system, we may well question whether capitalism must not find a way to incorporate this feature into its economy, if it is not to give way to socialism." Grigorii Fedorovich Grinko, *The Five-Year Plan of the Soviet Union: A Political Interpretation* (London: Martin Lawrence Limited, [1930?]), p. 12.

12.   David Leonhardt, "Obamanomics," *The New York Times*, August 20, 2008, at http://www.nytimes.com/2008/08/24/magazine/24Obamanomics-t.html (March 6, 2009).

13.   *Ibid.*

14. The Soviet Union based its theory on Marxism. After the revolution it was transformed into Marxism-Leninism and then Marxism-Leninism-Stalinism because many of the theories addressed after the revolution were never addressed by Marx directly. It is clear that Lenin and other social democrats of his day based their theory on Marx's work. The primary source of the "theories of socialism" in this book will be pre-revolutionary Marxist writings (e.g., writings by Marx and Engels, Lenin, and other writers from Marxist political parties) and post-revolution Party writings, especially *The ABC of Communism*. However, I will also supplement these Marxist works with analysis by sympathetic economists and with other socialist writings, even those "Utopian socialists" for whom Marx had some contempt. They are included because their understanding of capitalism was often the same, and their writings were often more readable.

15. There is a wonderful story titled "I Pencil," which is told from the point of view of a pencil and discusses the problems of coordination and calculation. Leonard Reed, "I Pencil," December 1958, at http://www.econlib.org/library/Essays/rdPncl1.html (November 17, 2009).

16. Some estimates are even higher, but it is reported that Stalin confided to Winston Churchill at Yalta in 1945 that 10 million people had died in the course of collectivization. See Helen Rappaport, *Joseph Stalin: A Biographical Companion* (Oxford: ABC-CLIO, 1999), p. 53. For alternate estimates, see Leonard E. Hubbard, *The Economics of Soviet Agriculture* (New York: Macmillan Company, 1939), pp. 117–118; Robert Conquest, *The Harvest of Sorrow: Soviet Collectivization and the Terror-Famine* (Oxford: Oxford University Press, 1986); Mark Kramer *et al.*, *The Black Book of Communism: Crimes, Terror, Repression* (Cambridge, MA: Harvard University Press, 1999).

17. Based on archival materials, R. W. Davies makes a compelling case that Stalin, the Politburo, and the planning agencies scrambled to try to stop the famine in Russia, although the causes of the famine in Ukraine may have had a large malicious component. The problem was that towns and cities were on the edge of starvation as well, and Stalin made the choice to expropriate the countryside in order to save the cities. This is not to let Stalin off the hook, but rather to show that he may have had good intentions and to understand how the policy choices could fail even if he did. The question of intentional starvation of the Ukrainian population is outside the scope of this book. R. W. Davis, "Making Economic Policy," in Paul Gregory, ed., *Behind the Facade of Stalin's Command Economy: Evidence from the Soviet State and Party Archives* (Stanford, CA: Hoover Institution Press, 2001).

18. James P. Cannon, "Socialism and Democracy," at http://www.marxists.org/archive/cannon/works/1957/socialism.htm (November 17, 2009).

19. "The practical task of a reconstruction of society may be correctly solved by the application of a scientific policy of the working class, i.e., a policy based on scientific theory; this scientific theory, in the case of the proletarian, is the theory founded by Karl Marx." Nikolai Bukharin, *Introduction to Historical Materialism: A System of Sociology* (1921). When speaking specifically of Marx and Marxist thought, I will use the term "Marxist." More generally, I will refer to the theories of the Soviet Union as "socialist" because many were held outside Marxist circles and because some Marxists may not agree that certain theories were held by Marx or are consistent with Marxist thought.

20. The rejection of markets and replacement of them with social ownership of the means of production was perfectly tested. This is where the lessons lie. Marxist theory arguably was less well tested because Russia was not as highly capitalistic as some Marxists argued that it needed to be. However, as Trotsky pointed out, the Russia of 1917 was as advanced as the Germany of 1848, which Marx argued was ready for socialism: "The Soviet Union, to be sure, even now excels, in productive forces, the most advanced countries of the epoch of Marx." Leon Trotsky, *The Revolution Betrayed*, trans. by Max Eastman (1936), chap. 3, at http://www.marxists.org/archive/trotsky/1936/revbet/index.htm (November 18, 2009). — One might also argue that even this test cannot serve as a "laboratory experiment" because there was no control sample and that North and South Korea or East and West Germany serve as better examples. Those also make excellent case studies, and the "control" in those cases is invaluable. One disadvantage of those case studies is that both South Korea and West Germany had assistance from the West. In addition, the advantage of the Soviet Union is that it was an earnest and long experiment in testing the socialist theories in relative isolation, and there is extensive documentation about the

results of the policies and reforms.

21. Yves Guyot wrote in 1894 about this phenomenon. Speaking of the law of supply and demand, he said: "One day, at an electoral assembly, someone bitterly reproached me with being a supporter of this law. He imagined, honest man, that this law is inscribed in the Statute Book, and that I had voted for it. I thought that he was alone in this idea until lately, when in talking about this law to several Socialists, one of them said to me: Well, then, you decline to repeal this abominable law! — "From these two cases I am obliged to conclude that not only ignorance of economic principles, but even of the idea of a scientific law, is much greater than I had imagined it to be; a discovery which should make us full of indulgence towards the mistakes which we hear uttered every day, but which gives us at the same time the right to invite those who speak with such contempt of 'vile economists,' and advocate with so much assurance plans for social upheaval, to begin by learning the A B C of the questions with which they deal. — "The Law of Supply and Demand was not promulgated in any code. Its power comes from elsewhere. It imposes itself upon mankind in as implacable a way as hunger and thirst. We furnish fresh demonstrations of its truth, whether willingly or not, even while we imagine ourselves to be violating it. If the Socialist excommunicates and abuses the economist, who formulates this law, he should also hold Newton responsible for all the tiles that fall on the heads of passers-by, and should declare that if some poor wretch, in throwing himself from a window, kills himself, it is the fault of those physicists who have discovered and taught the law of gravitation." Yves Guyot, *The Tyranny of Socialism*, J.H. Levy, ed. (London: Swan Sonnenschein and Co., 1894), at http://oll.libertyfund.org/ index.php?option=com_staticxt&staticfile=show.php%3Ftitle=91&layout=html#chapter_21209.

22. Nikolai Bukharin, "Economics of the Transition Period," quoted in Stephen F. Cohen, *Bukharin and the Bolshevik Revolution* (Oxford: Oxford University Press, 1980), p. 93.

23. Alec Nove, *The Soviet Economic System* (London: Unwin Hyman, Inc, 1986) pp. 15, 18.

24. *Ibid.*

25. *Ibid.*, p. 18.

26. *Ibid.*, p. 15.

27. J. V. Stalin, *Economic Problems of Socialism in the U.S.S.R.* (Peking: Foreign Languages Press, 1972), pp. 1–2, at http://www.marx2mao.com/Stalin/EPS52.html (November 17, 2009). Stalin goes on to describe how they are historically contingent. "One of the distinguishing features of political economy is that its laws, unlike those of natural science, are impermanent, that they, or at least the majority of them, operate for a definite historical period, after which they give place to new laws. However, these laws are not abolished, but lose their validity owing to the new economic conditions and depart from the scene in order to give place to new laws, laws which are not created by the will of man, but which arise from the new economic conditions." *Ibid.*, p. 4.

28. Constantin A. Krylov, *The Soviet Economy* (Lexington, Mass.: Lexington Books, 1979).

29. *Ibid.*, p. 18.

30. S. V. Aleksashchenko *et al.*, "Tax Schedules: Functions, Properties, and Control Methods," in *Ekonomika i matematicheskiye metody* (Economics and mathematical methods), 1989, cited in Michael Alexeev, Clifford Gaddy, and Jim Leitzel, "Economics in the Former Soviet Union," *Journal of Economic Perspectives*, Vol. 6, No. 2 (Spring 1992), p. 146.

31. Paul Krugman, "Learning From Europe," *The New York Times*, January 10, 2010, at http://www. nytimes.com/2010/01/11/opinion/11krugman.html?th&emc=th.

32. Imagine taking a picture of the economy at a single moment in time, such as right when a policy is enacted. This is the "static" effect of a policy. For example, if a minimum wage is increased, the static result would be higher wages for all workers who had lower wages prior to the policy. The "dynamic" effects of the policy are those that result once that picture becomes just one frame in a longer film. For example, the firms that hire low-wage workers may not hire as many workers, may not have profit to invest in new equipment or to open new branches, etc.

33. Alternatively, some might argue that national security is more important than standard of living or equality. However, national security is of little use if the people are starving—North Korea is a case in point. A society which cares only for national security and not the people resembles a private country for the dictator only.

34. Hall and Leeson discuss whether labor laws pushed by the International Labour Organization

(ILO) are appropriate for developing nations, given the necessary tradeoff between growth and higher labor standards. They find that many countries that the ILO would like to see adopt these policies have not reached the level of development that Western nations had reached when they passed similar laws. For example, Ethiopia and Kenya have reached approximately the level of development that the United States had reached in 1820, well before the first national-level labor laws were passed in the U.S. and when child labor was still widely used. Joshua C. Hall and Peter T. Leeson, "Good for the Goose, Bad for the Gander: International Labor Standards and Comparative Development," *Journal of Labor Research*, Vol. 28, No. 4 (September 2007), pp. 658–676.

35. Ludwig von Mises, *Human Action: A Treatise on Economics*, 4th revised ed. (San Francisco: Fox & Wilkes, 1996), p. 193, at http://mises.org/resources/3250 (November 19, 2009). For more on this subject, see Benjamin M. Friedman, *The Moral Consequences of Economic Growth* (New York: Knopf, 2005).

36. Aleksei Kosygin, quoted in "Voices of Tomorrow: The 24th Congress of the Communist Party of the Soviet Union," p. 92.

37. If we think that it is well known after the fall of communism that Soviet-style central planning does not work, we would also be wise to recognize that others have thought we knew this in the past: "No one would dare to say today that the production or consumption of potatoes or rice must be regulated by the parliament of the German People's State (Volksstaat) at Berlin. These insipid things are no longer said." Peter Kropotkin, "Communism and Anarchy," *Freedom*, July and August 1901, at http://www.marxists.org/reference/archive/kropotkin-peter/1900s/01_07_x01.htm (December 6, 2009). Ideologies change, but the underlying belief in planning seems to persist.

38. Brink Lindsey, *Against the Dead Hand: The Uncertain Struggle for Global Capitalism* (New York: Wiley 2002), p. 19.

39. Franklin D. Roosevelt, *Looking Forward* (New York: Touchstone, 2009 [1933]), p. 33

40. It is interesting that in a republican democracy such as the United States, voters would feel that the only way to "do something" is through the government. For example, if the majority of voters were deciding whether to help the poorest in the society with an income supplement, they could "do something" by voting to institute a new program, or they could vote against the program, walk out of the voting booth and over to the local community center, and "do something" by volunteering and sharing the supplies of their own kitchen. Of course, if there is a problem of free-riding with individual charitable giving (everyone expects others to do the work) or if there is a need to invest large sums that the government can borrow, then voters may reasonably determine that government can do the job better.

41. Stuart Chase, "Society Adrift," in Harry W. Laidler, *Socialist Planning and a Socialist Program* (Falcon Press, 1932), p. 3.

42. Franklin D. Roosevelt, *Looking Forward*, p. 27.

43. A good overview of this debate can be found in Peter Boettke, "Economic Calculation: The Austrian Contribution to Political Economy," *Advances in Austrian Economics*, vol. 5 (1999), at http://economics.gmu.edu/pboettke/pubs/pdf/Economic_Calculation.pdf (December 6, 2009).

44. One "market socialist" writer, an economist sympathetic to socialism but with a belief in the promise of the market system, recently wrote: "While the ambition of socialists has often been the promotion of a system that is morally and ethically superior to capitalism, for most socialists (though certainly not for all), the principle mechanism for achieving this superior form of social organization has been a reconstituted economy." Christopher Pierson, *Socialism After Communism: The New Market Socialism* (University Park, Pa.: Pennsylvania State Press, 1995), p. 25. But he laments, "Whilst Marxists have frequently laid claim to the superiority of scientific socialism over its moralizing forerunners, it has long been argued that even Marxian socialism is replete with moral invocations.... Indeed many of socialism's critics have insisted that it is above all a *moral* theory concerned with the realization of 'social justice,' and lacking even the most basic rudiments of a coherent *economics*." *Ibid.*, p. 223, note 1.

45. By "classical," I mean the "bourgeois" economists against whom Marx argued. They may include thinkers from Adam Smith to contemporaries of Marx such as Eugen von Böhm-Bawerk. Usually

"neoclassical" economics is reserved for economists of a later period, starting about the 1930s. They include the socialist-sympathizing economists who debated for socialism in the socialist calculation debate, such as Oskar Lange. However, the economists on the other side of the debate also considered themselves neoclassical at the time. In large part due to the disagreements that arose during that debate, they began to call themselves "Austrian" instead of "neoclassical" to distinguish themselves.

46. For a good analysis on this basis, see János Kornai, *The Socialist System: The Political Economy of Communism* (Princeton, N.J.: Princeton University Press, 1992).

47. Although dubbed "war communism," the early period was a real concerted effort to institute the socialist economic system in Russia. As the historian Richard Pipes explains, "The notion that War Communism was 'dictated' by circumstances, however, does violence to the historical record.... While some of its measures were indeed taken to meet emergencies, War Communism as a whole was not a 'temporary measure' but an ambitious and, as it turned out, premature attempt to introduce full-blown communism." This is also clear from reading Lenin's writings from the time, including his description of the repeal of war communism and the introduction of the New Economic Policy as a "temporary retreat." See Richard Pipes, *The Russian Revolution* (Vintage Books, 1990), pp. 671-672.

48. Quoted in Paul Dragos Aligica and Peter Boettke, *Challenging Institutional Analysis and Development: The Bloomington School* (Routledge 2009), pp. 158-159.

49. Hutchison, *The Politics and Philosophy of Economics*.

50. Oskar Lange and Fred M. Taylor, *On the Economic Theory of Socialism*, reprinted (Minneapolis, MN: University of Minnesota Press, 1938).

Chapter 1. The Real Benefits of Competition

Introduction[1]

People often speak of the benefits of economic competition. Competition keeps prices low and prevents firms from taking advantage of the consumer. It offers consumers a choice and leads to higher quality goods and innovation. Because of these benefits, government enforces competition with anti-monopoly laws and regulations—known in the US as antitrust laws—when a firm has too much "market power." Competition is the core feature of markets and is generally loved by all, but it is often misunderstood or misrepresented.

Competition is obviously a process or activity: businesses compete with each other. However, economists model it as a state: They look at an industry and ask, "How competitive is it?" To answer this, they model competition as a fixed and static state in which the results that they would expect from a competitive market already exist. However, a process is *ongoing*, and modeling some imagined end-state may not be realistic. These models cannot capture the *process* of competition. Yet it is the process, not some final outcome, that is important to the market. The Soviet government learned what happens when this process is prevented from working.

As long as economists fail to fully understand and model competition, they will fail to understand the market system and its alternatives. A misunderstanding may also lead to policies, based implicitly or explicitly on models that misrepresent competition, that are actually likely to impede competition and economic progress.

The Socialist Argument

Economists recognize competition as fundamental to economic science. Many of the biggest names in economics have indicated that competition is the basis of economic science and that without it nothing can be said of economics. Economist John Hicks said that without competition "the basis on which economic laws can be constructed is ... shorn away."[2] Similarly, economist Francis Edgeworth said that under conditions of monopoly, rather than competition, theoretical economists "would be deprived of their occupation."[3] John Stuart Mill said, "Only through the principle of competition has political economy any pretension to the character of a science."[4]

Art Young — The Masses, Marxists.org

"I Like a Little Competition"—J. P. Morgan

These economists regarded market competition as the basis for the science of economics. Without it, the science could not answer basic queries about production, allocation of resources, efficiency, or any other economic subject. Marx agreed with this. As discussed in the Introduction, Marx argued that the "bourgeois" science would be dead. However, he also believed that this science would not be necessary because the bourgeois economic laws would no longer apply. Yet denying the laws of economics and everything economists have learned from them could not erase the laws. As the economist Ludwig von Mises passionately argued:

> The body of economic knowledge is an essential element in the structure of human civilization; it is the foundation upon which modern industrialism and all the moral, intellectual, technological, and therapeutical achievements of the last centuries have been built. It rests with men whether they will make the proper use of the rich treasure with which this knowledge provides them or whether they will leave it unused. But if they fail to take the best advantage of it and disregard its teachings and warnings, they will not annul economics; they will stamp out society and the human race.[5]

While competition is the basis of our models of economics, economic laws do not disappear when competition is suppressed. Socialists might have been concerned that the economic system that they proposed would have no use of the mechanism on which, to that point, all modeling and all economic understanding had rested. Instead, they maintained faith that there would simply be a new economics built on the foundation of planning.

The experience of an economic system entirely without competition but still with the same universal economic laws provides insight into what competition offers and how it performs its magic. These insights may allow more realistic and useful models and a greater understanding of what market competition really is, what it looks like, and what value it offers. This may then allow better analysis of whether systems such as market socialism and policies such as antitrust laws can improve competition successfully.

Socialists made two major arguments against competition: Competition is ruthless and wasteful, and competition under a system of private property must ultimately lead to concentration of market power.

Marx tied the argument together, arguing that the wastefulness of competition drove concentration of industry. This, he argued, was good except that capitalists exploited this position for private gain at the expense of the consumer and the worker. Hence, if socialists could take control over concentrated industry, the economy would perform better and serve the people. The idea that competition is wasteful or leads to low-quality goods is rarely heard today,[6] but the argument that there is not enough competition is widespread.

The concentration of industry was seen as advantageous because it was efficient, but the higher prices that often resulted from cartels and trusts were seen as harmful. Hence, nationalization appeared to be the best solution. With nationalization, large-scale production could be combined with mandated low prices. The disparate duplication of many goods in small inefficient shops would be replaced by distribution through large, rationalized state stores. They would have huge economies of scale, orderly and appropriate distribution techniques, and low prices. Socialist production would end the wasteful competition and the theft of profits. Socialist distribution would end the wasteful and unfair provision of luxury goods to the rich at the expense of cheap consumer products for the masses.[7]

Socialists considered advertising an obvious waste.[8] Given that many resources are used in advertising, they argued that there was a potential for incredible savings. For example, in 1903, it was argued that there was a "tremendous waste of labour which goes on to-day. All the labour employed in advertising, canvassing, travelling for orders, all the printing, railway, warehouse and other work connected with this."[9] Many people today still argue that one advantage of government provision is that it can eliminate the costs of advertising, marketing, and branding. Sylvia Pankhurst offered an even more extreme description of this waste.

> Any system by which the buying and selling system is retained means the employment of vast sections of the population in unproductive work. It leaves the productive work to be done by one portion of the people whilst the other portion is spending its energies in keeping shop, banking, making advertisements and all the various developments of commerce which, in fact, employ more than two-thirds of the people today.[10]

Finally, socialists recognized some benefits of market competition, but argued that socialism could reap those benefits and more by ensuring that the resources to compete were spread more evenly across the population. Just after assuming power, Lenin described how common ownership over resources would expand competition:

> Among the absurdities which the bourgeoisie are fond of spreading about socialism is the allegation that socialists deny the importance of competition. In fact, it is only socialism which, by abolishing classes, and, consequently, by abolishing the enslavement of the people, for the first time opens the way for competition on a really mass scale. And it is precisely the Soviet form of organisation, by ensuring transition from the formal democracy of the bourgeois republic to real participation of the mass of working people in administration, that for the first time puts competition on a broad basis. It is much easier to organise this in the political field than in the economic field; but for the success of socialism, it is the economic field that matters.
>
> Take, for example, a means of organising competition such as publicity. The bourgeois republic ensures publicity only formally; in practice, it subordinates the press to capital, entertains the "mob" with sensationalist political trash and conceals what takes place in the workshops, in commercial transactions, contracts, etc., behind a veil of "trade secrets," which protect "the sacred right of property." The Soviet government has abolished trade secrets; it has taken a new path; but we have done hardly anything to utilise publicity for the purpose of encouraging economic competition. While ruthlessly suppressing the thoroughly mendacious and insolently slanderous bourgeois press, we must set to work systematically to create a press that will not entertain and fool the people with political sensation and trivialities, but which will submit the questions of everyday economic life to the people's judgment and assist in the serious study of these questions.
>
> ...We have scarcely yet started on the enormous, difficult but rewarding task of organising competition between communes, of introducing accounting and publicity in the process of the production of grain, clothes and other things, of transforming dry, dead, bureaucratic accounts into living examples, some repulsive, others attractive.[11]

Lenin envisioned a "socialist competition" to replace the vicious market competition of capitalism. The negative view of market competition and markets did not persist among some later proponents of socialism. Instead, they argued that socialism could offer a more perfect environment for market competition. These socialist-leaning economists who value market competition are known as "market socialists."

More sophisticated models of competition were introduced and used by economists, yet they still do not capture the real benefits of competition. The neoclassical "perfect competition" model, used by Oskar Lange during the "socialist calculation debate,"[12] is still in use today and underlies the rationale behind modern antitrust legislation. The model characterizes competition as a state in which numerous identical firms exist, offering homogeneous products at prices that they receive from the market. The prices are set in the market, not by any one firm, because competition has driven the price down to cost and has reduced profits to nothing. (There is said to be no "economic profit," meaning that once all costs, including the opportunity cost, or wages, of the business owner are deducted, no profit remains.) The price is said to be the "equilibrium price" and this equilibrium state is said to be optimal. Any market that is in "disequilibrium" for any length of time may be classified as an "imperfectly competitive" market in which "excess profits" are being made at the expense of the consumer.

Oskar Lange used the model to show that socialist ownership could coexist with markets in a market socialist economy and produce better results than the "imperfect" competition of the capitalist market economy. Planners could require firm managers to set the price at the perfectly competitive level,[13] thereby eliminating the imperfections of the market. Rather than leave profits in the hands of a few capitalists, planning could achieve the optimal outcome by setting prices according to what the theoretically perfect market looks like. The planners could also ensure that production was directed toward socially optimal ends.[14] Finally, taxation could be used afterward[15] to provide a social safety net and to redistribute for greater equality.

This depiction of competition still underlies many of the policy recommendations of economists today. Firms are said to have "market power" if they set their price above or below that of other firms or make large profits. Industries that have only a few firms are said to have little competition on this basis. Commodity markets are considered the most competitive markets because the product is homogeneous and all sellers tend to offer the same price.

Yet many of the benefits of competition—such as choice, higher quality goods, and innovation—may require firms to charge different prices or offer differentiated products. Is "perfect competition" really the ideal? Does modeling competition in this way really make sense for economists or for policymakers? The Soviet experience can shed some light on the real nature of competition and the competitive process.

The Soviet Experience

The Soviet authorities wanted to replace the traditional private commercial culture, which involved "haggling over prices" and "haranguing customers to enter shops and make purchases" along with "selling shoddy goods at exorbitant prices."[16] Instead, socialist distribution would offer a centralized system of state retailing, supported by rural retail cooperatives. This rational distribution structure would be more efficient and make use of economies of scale and scope. It would allow government to ensure equal availability and affordability of consumer goods.

The Soviet government appropriated the major successful department stores of the pre-revolutionary era, complete with their existing reputation, facilities, and supply links. Experts advised on the standardization of equipment, procedures, and work routines. The large stores would offer the easiest route to socialist efficiency, and the socialization of distribution would allow streamlining that would eliminate the wastes of market competition. The elimination of profit would make possible affordable, high-quality goods for all consumers. The largest Soviet store was called GUM and was to be the ideal socialist retail store.

The Soviet state infused the new stores with inspiring artwork and industrial design aimed at transforming the shopping experience from the materialistic consumerism of the bourgeois society into an elevated, refined sense of taste. With many of the large shopping centers located in former palaces, now owned by "the people" and decorated by elite artists in the new constructivist style, the goal was to cultivate proletariat culture through the "democratization of consumption."[17]

In addition to nationalizing banks, foreign trade, large factories, and joint stock companies, in 1918, the famous department store Muir and Mirrielees was national-ized, along with some small and mid-scale retailers. That same year all private trade was decreed illegal. Cooperative and state stores were to perform distribution in its place. However, this new vision failed to materialize. By 1919, the 3,409 retail stores in Moscow that had been shut down by the government had been replaced by only 133 new socialist stores, and only private illegal trade kept goods flowing to the consumer.[18]

By 1923, there were already reports of problems. One report characterized the stores as "depressing" and complained that they had wasted their funds on merchan-dise that was inappropriate and unpopular. Inspectors and consumers complained that the stores were dirty and inefficient, that the sales staff was rude or inattentive, and that the most popular and necessary products were in chronic short supply. Pric-ing irregularities, bribe-taking, and favoritism were also reported.

The concessions of the New Economic Policy (NEP) included a limited legaliza-tion of private trade. At the same time, the state began to rationally plan distribution through state stores that, for the early period, would compete with private sellers. The Bolshevik theory was that the state could outcompete private traders and slowly take over retail. One Marxist later explained:

> It was a retreat from the position of [War] Communism — but it was neces-sary in order to make rapid headway. The *dictatorship of the proletariat* was as strong as ever. The *strategic positions* in the entire economic system were retained in the hands of the dictatorship of the proletariat; private industry and private trading were only to serve as a stimulus to socialist industry and socialist commerce to improve in quantity and quality so as to be able to compete with private business men. With the Soviet [government] giving protection to its own industries and commerce in preference to private industry and commerce, it was not difficult to predict that the former would ultimately triumph over the latter.[19]

State funding gave the state stores a significant advantage, but only restrictions on private retail allowed the state to finally win the battle. "Within the mixed NEP retail economy, the state sought a place for itself, becoming a competitor that tried to gradually eliminate private manufacturers and retailers, even as it tolerated them as a temporary, necessary means."[20] State stores did not win over the consumer through better or more efficient practices. Nor did the state enterprises enhance competition. The Bolsheviks had argued in fact that the private Nepmen would stimulate newly socialized enterprises, not the other way around. State advantage and restrictions on trade stifled private business. When they were lifted, there was a natural blossoming of market activity. Writer Mikhail Bulgakov described the change that NEP brought like this:

> On Kuznetskii Most, the painted faces of toy figures made by artel craftsmen smile. In the former Shanks store, ladies' hats, stockings, boots, and furs gaze out

at the clouds.... On Petrovka, windows sparkle with ready-to-wear clothing....
Waves of fabric, lace, rows of boxes of face powder.... There is a confectioners shop
at every step. And all day until closing, they are full of people (*narod*). The shelves
are full of white bread, wheatmeal loaves, French rolls. Countless rows of *pirozh-
ki* cover the counters.... The luxurious displays at the gastronomes are startling.
Mounds of crates with canned goods, black caviar, salmon, smoked fish, oranges.[21]

The Soviet state found that private markets flourished when the laws against
trade were relaxed. This was a boon to the economy but Bolsheviks worried that the
"building of socialism" was threatened by the "Nepman"—a new middle class com-
prised of the people who prospered under the new (but limited) economic freedom of
NEP. Yet the state stores did not flourish even when restrictions on private trade and
advantages to the state were great enough to quash the markets. The state stores did
not blossom naturally as the socialists had expected. In contrast, markets seemed to
pop up spontaneously and required heavy-handed laws to keep them down.[22]

Finally, the end of NEP brought the harsh laws banning all private trade. This
natural flourishing of markets and individual exchange was stamped out.

The Moscow Committee of the Party declared for the liquidation of the Nepmen along with the *kulaki*. The shops of the Nepmen were closed all over Moscow.
By the end of February it was said that not one private clothing shop remained
open in all Moscow. Restaurants, hardware shops, and practically all private
enterprises were closed. Food markets operated by private merchants were also
closed, although they had not completely disappeared by the time the change of
policy occurred. The peasants who had always been accustomed to sell their products on the streets or from door to door almost disappeared.[23]

However, customers preferred the private retailers even when they charged more
for products. Black markets remained popular until the end of the Soviet era, even
though their prices were almost always higher than state store prices. State stores
were inefficient, suffered from constant shortages, and could not serve the customer
well.

In 1960, an article described some of the inefficiencies still evident in Soviet state
stores. In most stores, the customer was required to line up three times to make a
purchase, and shop workers still used an abacus instead of a cash register. The article
explained that, "On the whole, it appears that trade in the Soviet Union is cumber-
some and service is poor. Largely due to the inattention devoted to marketing in the
past, Russian consumers must suffer numerous inconveniences in making even the
simplest purchase."[24]

Socialist production promised a rational plan of resource use without embitter-
ing competition between producing firms.[25] However, under socialism, the planning
of production led to a perpetual "sellers' market," meaning that the customer had to
make do with what he was offered:

For the enterprise which stands in the weak position of purchaser in one relationship stands later in the strong position of seller in another relationship. If
the prevailing sellers' market forces him to accept subquality materials and therefore causes his own production to suffer in quality, he can later hope to dispose
of his poor-quality output because of his strong position as a seller. The general
knowledge that "a customer will be found" motivates the enterprise as producer to

reduce the quality of its output and weakens its resistance as customer to purchasing the subquality output of other enterprises.[26]

In the perpetual sellers' market of the Soviet Union, even in business-to-business transactions the customer was stuck with whatever the seller offered. Often the seller, who was not concerned with losing customers, refused to offer even minimal additional services, such as shipping the product. Purchasing enterprises would need to travel to pick up the purchased goods or bribe the selling firm to ship them.[27] Customers also accepted low-quality goods, including those rejected by the state's department of quality control, because buyers "were in no position to be choosers."[28]

Modern economic theory has much to learn from this: The "neoclassical" model used by economists describes an "efficient" market in a way very similar to the Soviet nonmarket economy. The model describes an ideal market as one with a large number of firms selling identical products at the same price. This is theoretically the result of true competition. Firms are "price-takers" because they will fare worse to sell the product at any other price than the market price. Although the Soviet system achieved this state of "perfect competition" by a different route than the one the theoretical model prescribes (but one very like the proposal by Oskar Lange for market socialism), the experience of the Soviet economy offers many insights into the validity of such a model.

The Soviet government required all socialist enterprises to sell the same products at the same price—the stores were all price-takers. They were not allowed to retain economic profit, and the state could set the price at whatever level it desired.[29] The Soviet system was not designed to eliminate competition, but to obtain the result that Lange proposed.

The Soviet firms looked like perfectly competitive firms, but they were clearly not engaged in real competition. They were not engaged in any economic competition at all, nor were they supposed to compete. With planners instituting these results of "perfect competition," could the system achieve the benefits expected from competition? What does this imply about how competition is perceived?

Innovation, creating new products, and reducing costs are generally considered vital parts of an economy with robust competition, but if the Soviet firms had done any of these things, they would have violated both the Soviet plan and the conditions of "perfect competition." Differentiating a product requires incurring a cost. To offset the risk of differentiation, the price must be allowed to be (temporarily) reduced to attract customers, or increased to offset the higher cost and the excess profit kept in case the new product attracts lower demand. Similarly, creating new products requires the firm to be able to set its own price. This was a lesson that Soviet planners came to learn. Soviet firms were later encouraged to innovate and add new products to their line, for which they could obtain a higher but still state-controlled price.[30]

Cost reductions allow a firm to make additional profit and to further reduce the price of its products to attract new customers. However, Soviet firms could not do this and stay within this "perfect" system. If any Soviet firm lowered its cost *without* reducing its price, it would obtain economic profit. This would violate perfect competition and was also not allowed under Soviet law—the new profits were seized by the Soviet state in such cases. If the firm *did* lower its price, it would also be in violation of "perfect competition" because it would not be a price-taker; and unilaterally lowering prices was illegal in the Soviet system. Either way, a firm that lowers its costs forces the market out of "equilibrium" and also violates Soviet law.

Yet cost reduction is an important benefit of market competition. This was another lesson that Soviet planners came to learn. They had assumed that costs were fixed and equal among firms, and they had ignored the ongoing innovations in cost that occur in a market system, but these cannot be taken for granted. Cost reduction became a regular target of reforms and campaigns in the Soviet Union.[31]

Differentiated products, new products, and falling costs are among the cited benefits of competition. Yet if the Soviet firms had innovated in these ways, they would have been forced to violate both the terms of the Soviet plan and the conditions of "perfect competition." Firms cannot be price-takers if they are to continue the process of competition. Prices fall as firms innovate in cost reduction and then lower their prices to gain new customers: This is how competition raises efficiency. New products must be introduced, and old ones improved, or the economy stagnates. At no point in time do these processes stop—unless they are forced to stop by the government, as happened in the Soviet Union.

The American law student Logan Robinson recounted an experience he had in a Soviet shop. Having been forced to wait in line several times for each purchase, and having frequently encountered failure in attempting to purchase a large range of simple household goods, Robinson was asked by the store manager how her store compared with American supermarkets. "There was simply no way in which her little store compared favorably with a typical American supermarket. This was not her fault. Prices, product availability, location, and the size of staff were all determined by the state. Her function was to use the givens as best she could. She was helpless to improve things very much."[32]

Even in the simplest market, such as a commodity market for wheat, some firms may find a better and cheaper way to produce large quantities of the product and thus will make a profit. However, such homogeneous product markets offer few ways to innovate and technology changes slowly. This almost complete absence of innovation is why commodity markets look like the perfect competition model. In more complex markets— such as shoe sales, with the constant rhythm of new firms, new products, new technologies, fashions, and differentiated product lines—many firms would be expected to constantly make profits. When economists and advocates for antitrust laws point to commodity markets as nearly "perfect" markets and argue that other markets should look the same, what they are really saying is that they wish for less innovation and differentiation in other markets.

Complex markets are highly competitive—as anyone in business knows—but there is still opportunity for profit. Even as the profit from one new idea is quickly competed away, as the "perfect competition" model predicts, the next idea is already earning other firms profit, and still other firms are profiting from an innovative cost-reduction technique. At no moment are all of these profits simultaneously competed away; they are always overlapping and ongoing, like waves in the vast ocean of retail trade.

Advertising is often associated with "imperfect" competition, monopolistic markets, and waste. Yet, Soviet planners learned the benefit of brand names, marketing, and advertising, as they were forced to reintroduce them as part of trying to introduce competition into their economy. Getting feedback from consumers, when it was desired, was a huge problem in the Soviet system. Knowing the rate of demand is important to fulfilling it, and knowing which products were poorly made is critical to improving efficiency and the quality of products. Yet without brand names to tell them where the better or worse products were produced, how could consumers choose and how could they provide feedback (even if by questionnaire)?

Hence, the Soviet authorities introduced trademarks that varied plant by plant in hopes that consumers would purchase from the better plants and boycott the worst ones.[33] Unfortunately, production was too low to fulfill demand. The shortages throughout the economy forced consumers to purchase whatever they could obtain. This, combined with the relative uniformity and low quality at all the firms, made the introduction of this market technique far less useful in the socialist economy.

Soviet planners learned that marketing and advertising were still important, even in the socialist system, if they wanted to fulfill the demands of the people. One economist explained in the journal *Kommunist*, "To ensure success in the management of the national economy, it is essential to conduct market research for practical purposes."[34] In *Komsomolskaya Pravda*, the journal for communist youth, another wrote:

> Advertising, by influencing the taste of purchasers, is capable of easing the planning of production and the study of consumer demand.... Proper advertising accelerates commodity turnover....
>
> We all have an interest in good advertising. But improvement of its artistic and technical level will require an increase in the money spent on it.... Such expenditure will pay for themselves with interest.[35]

Advertising, Soviet planners learned, is part of the process of learning consumer demand. It could help to differentiate one supplier from another, and highlight differences between products. Consumers able to distinguish suppliers and products could then offer better feedback about how well their demands were satisfied. Other uses for advertising were also recognized. One article in *Pravda* argued, "Good advertising not only creates favourable conditions for a product or service, but also moulds rational needs on the part of the consumer."[36] Of course, these needs would be "molded" only by the state, not by competing private individuals, because the state would still decide what to produce.

Although advertising was used from nearly the start, when it was "socialized" during the New Economic Policy, it developed considerably over the course of the socialist experiment:

> Two other more radical (one would think a good Marxist would say reactionary) developments are the formation of a State advertising agency, Torgreklama, and the introduction of installment credit. Organizations are aided in preparing their advertising copy, making their window displays and preparing attractive packaging with the purpose of making their commodities or stores more attractive or differentiated. Television commercials are also prepared. Installment sales are as yet on a limited basis. This is partially because the Marxist theoreticians have suddenly been given the task of justifying a practice they condemned as late as 1959, and partially because most consumer goods are still in short supply. Installment sales would only worsen the situation.[37]

Hence, Soviet planners discovered that the tools of the market—seen as wasteful and an indicator of a lack of competition—were actually necessary and vital parts of a competitive economy. The Soviet experience with stagnation, poor customer service, and lack of innovation teaches us the keys to dynamic competition and the mistake of seeing some kind of static "equilibrium" as the ideal of competition.

Without free and different prices, heterogeneous goods and services, brand names and advertising, and the ability to make profit, there was no economic competition in the Soviet Union. Yet any of these things would have disturbed the "perfect" competition that was enforced in the Soviet Union. The Soviet "perfect" outcome of price-taking firms, no profit wasted on parasite capitalists, and uniform product lines across all firms was a static and dead economy.[38] It lacked the lifeblood of a truly competitive economy, which is carried in the "imperfections" of profit, price, product differentiation, and innovation.

Finally, Soviet economists and planners came to realize that profit, in the context of competition, is useful for guiding production so that it adjusts to changes in demand. For this, non-equilibrium pricing and non-equilibrium conditions are necessary: Firms must be able to change their prices and to seek and retain profit. For example, the Soviet economist Petrakov argued for prices that reflect supply and demand, specifically because only those made sense in a disequilibrium situation in which disproportions (changes in supply and demand) may develop. Then, when prices and profits rise, he explained, "thereby are created the conditions for the liquidation of the shortage and the restoration of proportionality."[39] In other words, prices that allow a firm to make profit are good because then those other firms and entrepreneurs that seek profit will be induced to increase supply, eliminating the original "disproportion."

Although Oskar Lange had argued that shortage and surplus would provide planners with this information, these indicators could not replace the signals created by profit and loss.[40] The Soviet economy was riddled with inefficient allocation of labor, capital goods, transport resources, and supply lines.[41] The rigid price and profit structure, which ensured the approximation of perfect competition, prevented local adjustment of prices to fix these errors.

LESSONS

The socialist argument was that competition is wasteful and that great savings can be realized by replacing competition with large-scale production. Economists endeared to socialism argued that perfect competition may be efficient, but market economies never reach this ideal. A socialist economy could actually replicate the conditions of perfect competition and would therefore be much more efficient than existing capitalist economies. Even Western non-socialist economists believed this. Speaking of the "socialist calculation debate" and of economic discussion in the inter-war and postwar periods, economist Andrei Schleifer recounted:

> A remarkable aspect of this debate is that even many of the laissez-faire economists focused overwhelmingly on the goal of achieving competitive prices, even at the cost of accepting government ownership in non-competitive industries. Thus Henry Simons (1934, p. 51), in "A Positive Program for Laissez Faire," writes: "The state should face the necessity of actually taking over, owning, and managing directly, both the railroads and the utilities, and all other industries in which it is impossible to maintain effectively competitive conditions."[42]

Today, similar arguments are used to make the case for regulation and even nationalization of certain industries. Yet those economists that call any market in which profits are available for some firms "imperfect" misunderstand competition. The state that they consider an ideal has little to do with the activity of competition, which produces the benefits for which we value competition.

In the perfect competition model, a large number of firms sell identical products at the same price. Competition has driven down the prices at all firms that tried to sell at a higher price, forcing all firms to sell at a price that just pays their costs and wages, leaving them no additional economic profit. This is how the equilibrium price is reached; perfect competition always means *no economic profit*.

Based on this model, economists have argued that real world market economies have little competition. It is obvious that many industries have firms making large profits. Thus, many economists conclude that market imperfections have allowed some firms to gain market power, and that these firms then keep prices higher than the equilibrium price and obtain profits *at the expense of the consumer*. They are acting monopolistically and therefore should be restrained, broken up, or regulated by the state.

However, the problem is with the model, not with these markets. The Soviet experience was negative for the same reasons that the model is incorrect. If all firms sell at a single price and obtain no profits, they are in a static state. Any change in this state would offer a firm profit or loss. Yet a static state is not desirable and does not represent a competitive market. The "imperfections" that economists and policymakers want to quash actually underlie the innovation and differentiation that make competition so beneficial. They drive growth.[43] They are also an integral part of the firm's experimentation process, and the ability to respond to changing desires of the consumer. They help to create a more dynamic market—with more entrepreneurship, growth, and creative destruction.

Economists using the perfect competition model argue that government should regulate or nationalize firms that monopolize a market. Similarly, socialists argued that the state would be able to create, for example, a Wal-Mart-type supermarket or department store much more easily and less wastefully than Wal-Mart itself. The "public sector Wal-Mart" would be able to offer the same kinds of products, but better quality ones with less wasteful multiplication of products across brands. By offering it through the public sector, the prices would be even lower than Wal-Mart prices.[44] This was what socialists in the Soviet Union attempted to do with their GUM superstore.

Common wisdom recognizes that publicly owned entities such as the U.S. Postal Service (USPS) or state departments of motor vehicles suffer from one flaw rarely seen in the private sector: dreary, slow, and miserable customer service. However, this would not be the only difference between a public-sector Wal-Mart and the actual Wal-Mart. Although economies of scale are a major cost-reducer for Wal-Mart, it is not the primary reason for its success. This assumption is based on a misunderstanding of the role that profit and imperfect competition play in the advancement of innovation and technology.

The profit motive led Wal-Mart to innovate and reduce costs, beginning when it was just a small store. Competitors copied many of its techniques and kept it on its toes, leading Wal-Mart to find new and different ways to further reduce costs and differentiate its store. As Wal-Mart continued to succeed and expand, competition by other stores constantly pressured Wal-Mart to keep prices low, leading Wal-Mart to seek innovative technologies to stay ahead. The fear of losing customers to other stores kept the pressure constant, even as Wal-Mart kept expanding both its stock and its locations. The economies of scale that Wal-Mart created were more a *result* of its innovation and success than its *cause*.

Once it gained its prominent position, it was able to take advantage of these economies of scale to further reduce costs, but the economies of scale were not a privilege granted to the store. Alone, they could not have produced the amazing efficiencies that characterize the chain. The constant competitive pressure still keeps prices low and continues to spur innovation to better serve the customer. The drive to serve the customer works at every level in the Wal-Mart decentralized and flexible management structure. A recent undercover reporter discovered that workers at the lowest rungs are encouraged to check prices, inventory, and markup on every product with a special Wal-Mart technology and, at their own discretion, to discount a product or to increase the stock of products that earn profit.[45]

Although Wal-Mart is a huge retail chain, this is essentially the same method used by local grocery stores. Recently, my local grocer told me about his daily ritual: he carefully documents the prices charged by his suppliers that deliver him fresh vegetables in morning, and then he recalculates the price he will charge customers and changes the price tags. This flexibility is critically important for each rung in the supply chain—from the farmer to the wholesaler to the retailer.

The massive Soviet department store GUM kept its prices low as socialists had imagined: by command. Yet it did not innovate to create new cost-reducing techniques. It had no incentive to serve the customer well, nor any ability to creatively expand product lines, increase inventory of popular products, or reduce prices to move merchandise more quickly. This lack of flexibility prevented the Soviet store from achieving the kind of performance that actually led to Wal-Mart's success. The Soviet government mimicked the *size* of big private businesses like Wal-Mart, but they did not reproduce their efficiency. The absence of competitive pressure meant that the Soviet stores stagnated at a constant level of productivity, merely performing the duty of allowing customers, who had no other choice, to obtain whatever products were available.

Although critics claim that Wal-Mart's size means that it fears no real competition, in fact it faces constant pressure from customers going to direct-substitute stores and from customers spending their money on indirect substitutes or simply reducing their purchases. Soviet stores did not have this pressure because there were no direct or indirect competitors, and the stores could not enjoy the profits of success or suffer the punishments of failure. Even the largest private firms with the most market share feel the pressure of competition much more than a firm that is subsidized, protected, or regulated by government.

When firms are subsidized by government, they may actually reduce competition in the market. Not only do they feel no need to innovate and cut costs, but they make it more difficult for other firms to survive, leading to fewer choices and less competition. Just as the publicly funded retailers during the New Economic Policy could not outcompete the private firms by offering better products or service, but could squeeze them out through subsidies and legal action, public firms in market economies can force out the private choices. U.S. President Barack Obama recently admitted that his public health care option could pose a similar problem in the United States.

> I think there can be some legitimate concerns on the part of private insurers that if any public plan is simply being subsidized by taxpayers, endlessly, that over time they can't compete with the government just printing money, so there are going to be some, I think, legitimate debates to be had about how this [public option] plan takes shape.[46]

Although the Obama administration has stressed that it wants to create competition in the health insurance industry by introducing a public option,[47] it is not clear that a public option would do this. Another way US lawmakers try to "increase competition" is through antitrust laws; however, these laws may also be misguided.

Antitrust policy has been moving away from some of the more extreme expectations about perfect competition. More recent variations of the neoclassical economic models explain how practices previously considered "anti-competitive" are actually beneficial to the consumer and competition in the marketplace. Other practices are still punished but far less often—and with weak theoretical justification. A recent article in *The Economist* explains that, for economists and judges, "Discounting that promotes competition is hard to distinguish from predatory pricing."[48] The evidence used to distinguish predatory pricing from justified and legal price-cutting tends to be based on motivation or "sinister intent." It is not based on the benefit to the customer or on whether the pricing has actually reduced competition in the market. *The Economist* article explains:

> The Sherman Antitrust Act of 1890, the foundation of America's competition policy, was partly a response to complaints by small firms that larger rivals wanted to drive them out of business. Trustbusters need to be wary of such claims. Low prices are one of the fruits of competition: penalising business giants for price cuts would be perverse. But in rare circumstances, a big firm with cash in reserve may cut prices below costs in order to starve smaller rivals of revenue. The profits sacrificed in the short term can be recouped by higher prices once competitors are out of the way.
>
> Establishing that a firm is guilty of predation is difficult. If rivals stumble or fail, that may be down to their own inefficiency or poor products, and not because they were preyed upon. Proving that a firm is pricing below its costs is tricky in practice. Even where a reliable price-cost or profit-sacrifice test is feasible, failing it need not imply sinister intent. There are often pro-competitive reasons to forgo short-term profits. Firms with a new product, or a new version of an existing one, may wish to pick a loss making price to defray the cost to consumers of switching, or because they expect their own costs to fall as they perfect the production process (video-game consoles are a classic example). Losses would then be a licit investment in future profits.[49]

Taking a loss when costs are expected to fall or when consumers need a price cut to make a switch is considered legitimate, but taking a loss to try to outcompete others in the market, expecting that profits will exceed the losses taken in the short term, is not. Yet firms frequently take losses as part of the competitive process. Some firms, such as gas stations, price certain products (such as gas) below cost and make a profit from other products (such as convenience store items). They may do this in hopes of "starving out" other convenience stores or gas stations. Yet few would call these gas stations anti-competitive.

Many times a "sale" is a short-term loss maker where price is below cost.[50] Special sales are explicitly for the purpose of getting new customers—usually by taking them away from rival stores. Any time a firm takes out a loan, rather than price existing products high enough to pay for all investments and existing costs outright, it is "pricing below cost," whether it is doing so just to survive (in which case it is likely less efficient than its rivals) or is doing so to "starve out" its competitors (in which case it is likely more efficient). Small and large firms, efficient and inefficient firms, all sometimes sell products at a loss in the short term.

It is wise business practice to invest profits and to borrow against future ones in order to compete on price with other firms. It is a part of competition, and if a firm succeeds in squeezing out its rivals in this way, it has helped the consumer in the short run and proven its own relative efficiency. If the firm is not significantly more efficient than other firms, then an investor likely knows this and will invest either in keeping another firm alive or in creating a new firm that can compete. In this case, the consumer need not wait long for fresh price competition. Very little empirical evidence shows that any firm using "predatory pricing" has succeeded in squeezing out all its rivals, taken a monopoly position, and kept prices high in the long term. Most economists believe that predatory pricing is also unlikely to be an effective strategy for firms.[51] Yet firms are still prosecuted for it every year, and this is costly to consumers.

German authorities accused Wal-Mart of predatory pricing[52] even though Wal-Mart's business strategy does not seem to include ever raising its prices, regardless of its market share. Although Target stores could match Wal-Mart on the low-prescription drug prices they offer in the United States, eight states considered them "predatory" and banned both stores from selling at those prices.[53] A law in France banned Amazon.com from offering free delivery. A union of French booksellers successfully sued Amazon, but the retailer chose to pay the fines rather than discontinue the service. If the law was intended to help consumers, they did not appear to be thankful. At least 120,000 customers signed a petition to allow Amazon to keep the discount.[54]

According to *The Economist*, a recent antitrust finding against the computer chip maker Intel resulted in a 524-page verdict in which the European Union fined Intel 1.06 billion Euros for illegally attempting to price out its rival AMD, even though AMD was still competing when the verdict was handed down. As of this time, Intel plans to appeal the case.[55]

Charging "too high" a price is also suspect. There is a long history of ethical arguments against businesses that charge more than the expected "fair" price. In 1639 in colonial America, Reverend John Cotton preached the values of the fair trader following a successful case against a man named Robert Keane for charging an extortionate markup on British imports.[56] Cotton described as "false" principles of the market when a man believes that it is alright to "sell as dear as he can, and buy as cheap as he can" and that he may raise his price if he loses some of his commodities "by casualty of sea." He follows this with the "true" principles, which include that "A man may not sell above the current price, i.e., such a price as is usual in the time and place," and that if he "loseth in his commodity for want of skill, etc., he must look at it as his own fault or cross, and therefore must not lay it upon another."[57]

What if we followed these commandments to the letter? This would be the "perfect competition" that theory has constructed, yet it would only provide the best result for consumers in a given instant and only in a static world. Instead, if sellers are able to charge a higher price, whether because their costs are higher, their produce is different and new, or because they have lost some of the product at sea (which was a risk they chose to take perhaps because they could offset losses with a higher price), this would drive new entrepreneurs into the market because they would realize that they would be able to underbid, capture some of the market, and earn a profit. If it is not luck and there is a reason for the loss of merchandise, such as poor equipment in the industry, then the price acts as an important signal. An entrepreneur may see the price charged by the merchants using the faulty equipment and think, "I can do better." However, if the price is held ethically low, the entrepreneur may not be enticed into the market.

Induced by the profit available due to the higher price, the entrepreneur may be driven to invent a new technology, device, or technique to reduce his own costs. With the new technology bringing lower costs, competition may then force the price to a new, lower level. In fact, how can market prices ever fall if all merchants and firms are always expected to sell at "the current price"? If every firm must take the losses for its mistakes and never raise prices, then this also implies that the customer must prefer a firm to go out of business than to raise its prices.

Even if no other competitors are in a market and apparently no others can exist—as in cases of perfect "natural monopolies," such as highways, utilities, and so forth—regulation or nationalization may still prevent the benefits of the market system of competition. A private company, without regulation or aid from government, will always face potential competition. Even if at a given moment it faces no competitors, if it takes advantage of this market dominance to raise its prices or reduce its quality, an entrepreneur can enter the market and steal away customers. Economists call this a "contestable market."

Although it was once assumed that cable television providers had a natural monopoly in their areas and were therefore heavily regulated, we now know that a new technology—satellite television—can compete in the same space. During the period of greatest regulation in the United States, service was very poor and there was little innovation. After deregulation, cable companies began to offer more services and choices. The introduction of satellite television also followed the deregulation of that industry, once cable companies were allowed to make some profit. In other words, once the regulations were lifted competition returned and the consumer benefited.[58]

Telephone companies were also given monopoly rights and were heavily regulated under the assumption that they had a natural monopoly. Once again, new technology has proven this assumption to be false. Today, "voice over IP" technologies allow Internet users to make phone calls, and cell phones offer the user a distinct service. The opportunity for profit in the land-line market may not have been necessary to induce this innovation as long as it was not banned for the new competitors.

Competition by these other technologies calls into question the idea of natural monopoly and the wisdom of protecting and regulating these markets. Highways are assumed to be a natural monopoly, yet if they were not nationalized or protected from competition, would a new technology have entered this market? If a private company provided the roads in a city and was not regulated or protected from competition, would some entrepreneur introduce competing jet highways, light-rails, or something else even more unexpected?

This lesson is key when considering policies that attempt to affect competition or regulate businesses based on ideals of the competitive market. Profit, differentiation, innovation, and flexible pricing are part of the "activity we call competition,"[59] and should not be understood as indicators that a market is broken, failing, or imperfect. Policies that aim for perfection may actually be detrimental to competition.

Economist Israel Kirzner describes competition as the "driving force of the market" and argues that competition is present even when monopolies exist. He argues that "the only situation in which competition can be said to be absent is one in which markets do not operate. Such a situation presumes, as in the centrally planned economy, the existence of institutional prohibitions on market exchanges."[60]

As we saw, the Soviet Union was able to destroy competition and with it this driving force and the customer-centered production, innovation, differentiation, and cost-cutting that come with it. János Kornai, invoking the similar description by the economist Joseph Schumpeter, described socialist systems in this way:

> [T]he "life or death" of a firm as a collective organization or organism is determined not by the "natural selection" of market competition but by the bureaucracy. There is a complete absence of what Schumpeter considered the most important driving force behind healthy economic development: the appearance of entrepreneurs who introduce new products or new technologies, establish new organizations, and conquer new markets, while obsolete organizations are squeezed out. In other words, the system leaves no room for what Schumpeter called the revolutionary effect of "creative destruction."[61]

The Soviet sellers' market, with poor service and little growth or change, was a direct result of eliminating this "driving force of the economy." It would serve the economist, policymaker, and consumer well to avoid stamping out this driving force in our own markets, in pursuit of some kind of "perfection."

Even a large amount of advertising does not necessarily signal that the market is not efficient (although too much advertising may be undesirable for other reasons). Money spent on marketing and promotion is not a pure waste or a pure cost for the consumer. Brands and marketing have at least two important uses. First, brand names help consumers remember which firms produce the products of the best quality. In the Soviet Union, brand names were reintroduced for this purpose because otherwise tracking which firms were producing the best products was difficult. Hence, it was discovered that brand names *increase the efficiency* of competition. In addition, marketing and advertising help to inform consumers about new products and innovations, and aid firms in distinguishing consumer tastes. The Soviet Union discovered that this was necessary even when the state was the only advertiser.

Both of these tools have another use. Both brand names and marketing are a form of "costly specific investment." They are both a form of "credible commitment" used by firms to show the customer that they are serious about their undertaking.[62] Firms that want to prove to their customers that they are serious about producing a good product will invest in these two expensive signaling activities. By spending money on establishing a brand name, customers see that the firm wants to be remembered and that it plans on building a good reputation. If the products associated with that reputation are low quality, there is no reason to invest in being recognized. Similarly, if a firm spends money on marketing and advertising, it must be planning to invest in the product for a long time.

The ability to use these signals is important for firms that need to invest heavily in a product, because the firm needs to gain the trust of the customer base to recoup its investment. These signals build trust between the firm and the customer. (For example: Would McDonald's spend millions of dollars on huge billboards and television commercials and then alter the type or quality of its food unexpectedly? Customers rely on McDonald's to consistently offer the product they expect because of their enormous investment in advertising. Many readers may remember when Coca-Cola tried to change its product, to New Coke, with disastrous results—it had to rebuild its brand all over again.) This, in turn, may improve the quality of the competing products by driving out untrustworthy competitors and allow for growth in the market because firms may be more willing and able to invest large amounts in their product lines.

Hence, advertising and brand names can actually help to create a strong competitive environment. Firms in the Soviet Union and publicly funded firms in general do not invest their own money. They cannot make a credible commitment because they produce according to the wishes of the state and they spend the state's money. The state, of course, does not face the same competitive pressures that private firms face.

The socialist system was unable to replace the market system of brand names, marketing, and advertising with a more efficient way of ensuring quality. They could not replace competition with streamlined production, nor could they replace these tools of competition. Even the highly concentrated, state-monopolized industries of the Soviet Union required marketing and brand name advertising to distinguish the various state-supplying firms. Unfortunately, these tools were unable to serve the full function that they serve in free market economies because the better firms could not innovate or adjust prices to associate something of higher value with their brand name. Nor did they have much incentive to do so because they had nothing to gain by doing so. In a market economy, better firms get to keep any additional profit created. Soviet firms could not make credible commitments and had little freedom to associate their brand name with a unique or trustworthy product.

These tools, planners learned, are a vital part of competition, not a waste of resources. Markets that display a great deal of advertising, have just a few firms, or have firms making profit, are not "imperfect." They are actively engaged in competition. The policies used to force these markets toward "perfection" may actually be detrimental to competition. If the attributes of "imperfect" markets are actually a critical part of the process of competition, then policies that act against them may hinder this process.

CONCLUSION

Economists and policymakers have focused on an unrealistic and static model of competition for the past several decades. Socialists used this model to argue that socialism could produce outcomes that only an ideal market could produce. The actual market is derided as "imperfect" and "uncompetitive" because it does not live up to this idealized "perfect competition." Yet this ideal is actually a static model of an outcome that is theoretically the result of rigorous competition, but it omits what causes competition in the first place.

The Soviet Union attempted to implement this perfect ideal with the result that competition was eliminated and the economy was static—responsiveness, growth, and change became difficult. Far from an idealized "perfect competition," the model represents an economy devoid of economic competition. Yet comparison to this ideal drives much of our regulatory and antitrust policy and forms the rationale for some of the subsidies and protections that businesses receive. By eliminating "imperfections," policymakers may actually hinder competition, slow innovation, and reduce growth in the economy. The Soviet experiment with eliminating competition should be viewed as a warning and as a lesson in what competition actually looks like.

Endnotes

1. Much of this chapter has been reprinted from Guinevere Liberty Nell, "Competition as Market Progress: An Austrian Rationale for Agent-Based Modeling," *Review of Austrian Economics*, published online June 23, 2009.
2. John Hicks, *Value and Capital*, 2nd ed. (Oxford: Oxford University Press, 1939), pp. 83–84.
3. Francis Ysidro Edgeworth, *Papers Relating to Political Economy*, Vol. 1 (1925), pp. 138–139, at http://homepage.newschool.edu/het//texts/edgeworth/edgepapers.htm (November 18, 2009).
4. John Stuart Mill, *Principles of Political Economy with Some of Their Applications to Social Philosophy*, ed. and abridged by Stephen Nathanson (Indianapolis, IN: Hackett Publishing, 2004), p. 113.
5. Mises, *Human Action*, p. 885.
6. There are a few exceptions, such as the popular notion that some firms are forced to lower the quality of their product to compete. However, in a market consumers may choose to purchase from competitors who do not reduce quality, but instead reduce cost. It is sometimes heard that "they don't make cars like they used to," or "everything is disposable these days," even incorporating "planned obsolescence" to force consumers to purchase the product again and again. According to the Federal Reserve Bank of Dallas, this popular notion about vehicles is incorrect. "Today's vehicles last longer. They require less maintenance, with some 1997 models traveling 100,000 miles before their first tune-up. They're more comfortable because of air-conditioning, power seats and adjustable steering columns. They often include such extras as power windows, sunroofs, tinted glass, cruise control and compact disc players"; and " They're safer with the addition of air bags and antilock brakes." Federal Reserve Bank of Dallas, *Time Well Spent: The Declining Real Cost of Living in America*, 1997 Annual Report, at http://www.dallasfed.org/fed/annual/1999p/ar97.pdf (February 12, 2010). The argument that competition may reduce quality is similar to the idea that greed and the profit motive induce corruption on Wall Street. This will be addressed in Chapter 8.
7. Franklin D. Roosevelt also made this argument, as noted in the Introduction.
8. John Ure, "The Waste of Competitive Advertising," *International Socialism*, No. 80 (July/August 1975), at http://search.marxists.org/history/etol/newspape/isj/1975/no080/ure.htm (November 18, 2009).
9. Belfort Bax and H. Quelch, *A New Catechism of Socialism*, 6th ed. (London: 20th Century Press, 1909), p. 44, at http://www.marxists.org/history/international/social-democracy/catechism.htm (November 18, 2009).

10. E. Sylvia Pankhurst, "Future Society," first published in *One Big Union Bulletin*, August 2, 1923, at https://www.marxists.org/archive/pankhurst-sylvia/1923/future-society.htm (November 18, 2009).

11. V. I. Lenin, "The Immediate Tasks of the Soviet Government," *Lenin's Collected Works*, Vol. 27, 4th English Edition, (Moscow: Progress Publishers, 1972) pp. 235-277, at http://www.marxists.org/archive/lenin/works/1918/mar/x03.htm#sec6.

12. Lange and Taylor, *On the Economic Theory of Socialism*.

13. The perfect level was argued to be the marginal cost of a product, the cost of producing the next unit of the product in question. The price should be equal to this cost because then no profit (or loss) is made for each product produced, no matter how many or how few are produced. In a "perfectly competitive" market, firms would be forced down to this level and would sell as much as they could at this price, just covering their costs. In "market socialism," planners would set this price.

14. Social direction of production will be addressed in Chapter 4.

15. With a static model, one can imagine an "afterward." In an ongoing process there cannot be an "afterward" because the policy may affect decisions made going forward. For example, even a tax on inheritance, which some argue cannot affect the behavior of the individual taxed because it takes place after her death, may affect behavior going forward if the individual works in part in order to raise funds to give to her children.

16. Marjorie L. Hilton, "Retailing the Revolution: The State Department Store (GUM) and Soviet Society in the 1920s," *Journal of Social History*, Vol. 37, No. 4 (Summer 2004), pp. 939–964.

17. *Ibid.*

18. *Ibid.*

19. Moissaye J. Olgin, *Trotskyism: Counter-Revolution in Disguise* (New York: Workers Library Publishers, 1935), at http://www.marxists.org/archive/olgin/1935/trotskyism/07.htm (November 18, 2009).

20. Hilton, *Retailing the Revolution*, p. 944.

21. *Ibid.*

22. For some discussion of the different periods and policies of NEP, see Alan Ball, "Nep's Second Wind: 'The New Trade Practice,'" *Soviet Studies*, Vol. 37, No. 3 (July 1985), pp. 371–385.

23. Calvin B. Hoover, "The Fate of the New Economic Policy of the Soviet Union," *Economic Journal*, Vol. 40, No. 158 (June 1930), p. 187.

24. Marshall I. Goldman, "Retailing in the Soviet Union," *The Journal of Marketing*, Vol. 24, No. 4 (April 1960), pp. 9–15.

25. Market competition was considered very crass and unsocialist, but Marxists including Lenin had argued that a new kind of socialist competition would emerge. In practice, "socialist competition" or "socialist emulation" was introduced, but it did not replicate the benefits of market competition. This is discussed further in Chapter 2.

26. Joseph Berliner, *Factory and Manager in the USSR* (Cambridge, MA: Harvard University Press, 1957), p. 151.

27. *Ibid.*, p. 190.

28. *Ibid.*, p. 219.

29. Although marginal cost was suggested during the 1965 reforms, Soviet planners based most prices on average cost for the industry, or sometimes ignored costs for entire industries that were "socially necessary" on the one hand, or "socially undesirable" on the other. For an overview of prices and costs in the Soviet Union, see Lynn Turgeon, "Cost-Price Relationships in Basic Industries during the Soviet Planning Era," *Soviet Studies*, Vol. 9, No. 2 (October 1957), pp. 143–177. See also Morris Bornstein, "The Soviet Price System," *American Economic Review*, Vol. 52, No. 1 (March 1962), pp. 64–103, and Morris Bornstein, "The Soviet Price Reform Discussion," *Quarterly Journal of Economics*, Vol. 78, No. 1 (February 1964), pp. 15–48. For more on Soviet pricing, see Chapter 6.

30. Berliner, *Factory and Manager in the USSR*, and M. Harrison, "Prices, Planners, and Producers: An Agency Problem in Soviet Industry, 1928–1950," *Journal of Economic History*, Vol. 58, No. 4 (December 1998), pp. 1032–1062. This policy was an attempt at a reform that would better mimic the results of the market economy, once it was seen that the competitive-level price setting alone

could not achieve the full benefits of market competition. Yet, this policy also could not achieve these results, and Soviet enterprises took advantage of the policy to raise their prices even when the product was not truly different or innovative. (This is also discussed in Chapter 6.)

31. Berliner, *Factory and Manager in the USSR*.

32. Logan Robinson, *An American in Leningrad* (New York/London: W. W. Norton & Company, 1982), p. 179. Robinson adds, "I could see, however, that she was in no mood for a lecture on comparative economics," and so he talked about cheese with her instead.

33. Peter Rutland, *The Myth of the Plan: Lessons of the Soviet Planning Experience* (Essex: Open Court, 1985).

34. L. Gatovsky, "Unity of Plan and Cost Accounting," in *Kommunist*, No. 15 (1965), in Myron E. Sharpe, ed., *Problems of Economics*, Vol. 2, *Reform of Soviet Economic Management* (White Plains, N.Y.: International Arts & Science Press, 1966), p. 88.

35. L. Pekarsky and S. Anufrienko, "The Wings of an Experiment," *Komsomolskaya Pravda*, June 3, 1965, in Sharpe, *Problems of Economics*, Vol. 1, *The Liberman Discussion: A New Phase in Soviet Economic Thought*, p. 299.

36. Y. Kanevsky, "The Effect of Advertising," *Pravda*, April 1, 1972, in Thomas V. Greer, *Marketing in the Soviet Union* (New York: Praeger, 1973), p. 100.

37. Marshall Goldman, *Retailing in the Soviet Union*.

38. Economist Ludwig von Mises noted this in his book criticizing socialism when he said that the tendency toward a kind of equilibrium in the economy "can never attain its goal in a universe not perfectly rigid and immutable, that is, in a universe which is living and not dead." Mises, *Human Action*, p. 250.

39. Nove, *The Soviet Economic System*, p. 177.

40. This is covered in more detail in Chapter 4 and Chapter 6.

41. Rutland, *The Myth of the Plan*, p. 110 and note 20; Constantin A. Krylov, *The Soviet Economy*, pp. 133–134; and Berliner, *Factory and Manager in the USSR*, pp. 210–214. These inefficiencies are discussed further in other chapters.

42. Andrei Shleifer, "State Versus Private Ownership," *Journal of Economic Perspectives*, Vol. 12, No. 4 (Fall 1998), p. 134, at http://www.economics.harvard.edu/faculty/shleifer/files/state_vs_private.pdf (December 7, 2009).

43. An interesting paper presented to the U.S. Department of Commerce in May 2007 makes the case that "competitive innovation" drives growth and that a metric of innovation should be used to measure GDP growth. The paper also explains, "The need to renew profits eroded by competition drives innovation in firms." Chris J. Farrell, "How to Measure Innovation in the Products and Services of Firms and Use It to Explain GDP Growth for the Second Half of the 20th Century," U.S. Department of Commerce, at http://www.techmatt.com/techmatt/Farrell0308.pdf (November 18, 2009).

44. I would encourage those inclined to dismiss the efficiencies of Wal-Mart to reconsider. Studies show that grocery prices drop an average of 10 to 15 percent in markets that Wal-Mart has entered, and their new offerings of low-price generic pharmaceuticals may drive medical costs to a small fraction of their previous levels. This may be a significant boost to the living standard of those households that survive on tight budgets and spend much of their income on food and medicine. Although some have tried to argue that this comes at the expense of the workers (as if the low prices were simply a result of paying workers less) or of the small businesses that cannot compete with Wal-Mart, these arguments do not stand up to scrutiny. Wal-Mart pays competitive hourly rates, generally more than the small businesses with which they compete, and offers advancement in the company. Some small businesses cannot compete with Wal-Mart because it is in fact more efficient; however, studies show that Wal-Mart has not driven out the "mom and pop" shops. Instead, many of them have been forced to offer better and more differentiated products and services to survive. In other words, Wal-Mart has boosted competition, not stifled it. For more on this, see Katherine Kersten, "Wal-Mart Means Low-Priced Goods and Good Jobs," *Star Tribune*, July 13, 2008, at http://www.startribune.com/local/25130494.html (November 18, 2009). For more discussion of scholarly work on Wal-Mart, see Art Carden, "Walmart's Bottom Line," *The Freeman*, Vol. 60, No. 1 (January/February 2010), at http://www.thefreemanonline.org/featured/walmarts-bottom-line/#.

45. Charles Platt, "Fly on the Wal," *The New York Post*, February 7, 2009, at http://www.nypost.com/seven/02072009/postopinion/opedcolumnists/fly_on_the_wal_154007.htm (November 18, 2009).

46. Barack Obama, news conference, transcript, June 23, 2009, at http://latimesblogs.latimes.com/washington/2009/06/barack-obama-news-conference-transcript.html (November 18, 2009).

47. Associated Press, "Obama: Public Option Helps Health Care Competition," *Seattle Times*, September 12, 2009, at http://seattletimes.nwsource.com/html/politics/2009854197_apusobamapublicoption.html (December 7, 2009).

48. "The Unkindest Cuts," *The Economist*, August 20, 2009, at http://www.economist.com/businessfinance/economicsfocus/PrinterFriendly.cfm?story_id=14258678 (November 18, 2009).

49. *Ibid.*

50. Although most Americans and British consumers would find it odd, sales are or have been restricted in many European countries (allegedly) for this reason. For example, sales are restricted in some countries to fixed time periods during the year, and the price reductions may also be regulated. Consumers are told that this is a benefit to them because the consumer is protected from false advertising about price reduction and can be assured that he can get a sale price—however this sort of regulation may reduce competition between firms or make it easier for them to keep prices higher throughout the rest of the year.

51. Donald J. Boudreaux, "Comments Before the Department of Transportation on the Statement of Enforcement Policy Regarding Unfair Exclusionary Conduct," Competitive Enterprise Institute, July 24, 1998, at http://cei.org/gencon/027,01529.cfm (December 7, 2009).

52. "Germany Says Wal-Mart Must Raise Prices," *The New York Times*, September 8, 2000, at http://www.nytimes.com/2000/09/09/business/09SHOP.html (November 18, 2009).

53. Associated Press, "Target Matches Walmart's Drug Cuts: State Law Limits Discounts," KXNet, September 29, 2007, at http://www.kxmc.com/t/minnesota/166862.asp (November 18, 2009).

54. Victoria Shannon, "Amazon.com Is Challenging French Competition Law," *The New York Times*, January 14, 2008, at http://www.nytimes.com/2008/01/14/technology/14iht-amazon.4.9204272.html (November 18, 2009).

55. "The Unkindest Cuts."

56. Hugh Rockoff, *Drastic Measures: A History of Wage and Price Controls in the United States* (Cambridge: Cambridge University Press, 1984), p. 21.

57. "John Cotton on the Just Price," 1639, at http://www.swarthmore.edu/SocSci/bdorsey1/41docs/20-cot.html (November 18, 2009).

58. U.S. General Accounting Office, "Issues Related to Competition and Subscriber Rates in the Cable Television Industry," October 2003, at http://www.gao.gov/new.items/d048.pdf (December 7, 2009). For a discussion of this report, see Adam Thierer, "GAO's Cable Report Smacks Down A La Carte Regulation," Cato Institute, October 28, 2003, at http://www.cato.org/tech/tk/031028-tk.html (December 7, 2009). There is not complete agreement on this. The federation of state Public Interest Research Groups (U.S. PIRG) argued that the GAO report overstated the new competition, and that satellite television "is popular primarily at two edges of the market—in rural areas where there is no cable service at all, and among the minority of consumers that are willing to pay stiff premiums to receive large numbers of sports channels." However, shortly after the release of that report the price of satellite television fell in most areas below the price of cable television. U.S. PIRG also argued that cable providers should be forced to offer "a la carte" channel packages (rather than pre-selected packages); satellite television also began to offer such deals without mandate. U.S. Public Interest Research Group, "A Blueprint for Creating a Competitive, Pro-Consumer Cable Television Marketplace," August 2003, at http://www.uspirg.org/media-internet/reports/media--the-internet-reports/the-failure-of-cable-deregulation-a-blueprint-for-creating-a-competitive-pro-consumer-cable-television-marketplace (December 7, 2009).

59. Economist F. A. Hayek made this point, saying the model described "a *state* that theory curiously designates as perfect competition, even though the opportunity for the *activity* we call competition no longer exists." F. A. Hayek, "Competition as a Discovery Procedure," *Quarterly Journal of Austrian Economics*, Vol. 5, No. 3 (Fall 2002), p. 13, at http://mises.org/journals/qjae/pdf/QJAE5_3_3.pdf (November 19, 2009).

60. Israel Kirzner, *The Driving Force of the Market: Essays in Austrian Economics* (New York: Routledge, 2000).

61. János Kornai, *The Socialist System: The Political Economy of Communism* (Princeton, N.J.: Princeton University Press, 1992), p. 115.

62. Oliver E. Williamson, "Credible Commitments: Using Hostages to Support Exchange," *The American Economic Review*, Vol. 73, No. 4 (September 1983), pp. 519–540.

INTRODUCTION

CNN reported on February 4, 2009, that the U.S. President had warned of a dire emergency which required the federal government to create and save jobs:

> President Obama warned Wednesday that failure to act immediately on his economic aid plan "will turn crisis into a catastrophe and guarantee a longer recession."
>
> "Millions more jobs will be lost. More businesses will be shuttered. More dreams will be deferred," Obama said, as Senate debate continued on amendments to the stimulus package.[1]

Many would agree that it is government's role to save the people from a dire emergency. If the economy is collapsing and government can act fast to alleviate the situation, such action would broadly appeal to the public. Yet can government "save" jobs? What would this require government to do? Are there other effects, perhaps unintended ones, which might come from such actions? These are some questions that economists must answer. CNN went on to report that "Obama says his plan would create or save up to 4 million jobs."[2] How was this figure calculated, and would these jobs be saved forever?

One view is that secondary effects might have forced businesses to close and that the government's actions could prevent this loss, helping the rest of the economy to recover. Even if the businesses later failed, the action would forestall a crisis. An alternative explanation might be that the action only prevents a necessary transition and that the action itself causes undesirable secondary effects. What is the cost of preventing the job losses? Who will bear the burden of this cost? CNN reported:

> Sen. Chuck Grassley, R-Iowa, said Wednesday that a preliminary analysis by the Congressional Budget Office shows that the jobs created by the plan being debated in the Senate would cost taxpayers between $100,000 and $300,000 each...

[which] indicates the cost of each stimulus job could be up to three times more than jobs created without the stimulus bill.[3]

More recently, the Obama administration reported that the stimulus package had been proven a success because, by September 2009, it had "saved" one million jobs.[4] The model used to estimate this number may itself be called into question, as should the wisdom of saving jobs at all, but at face value that would mean that a $780 billion package had saved one million jobs at a cost of $780,000 to the taxpayer for each job saved. Some economists have argued that this cost would outweigh the benefit.[5] If the job losses are part of a natural adjustment, the direct costs borne by the taxpayer may not be the whole cost to the economy. Rather than forestalling a crisis, the stimulus may prolong adjustment and slow recovery. Private-sector entrepreneurship might be stifled by government's actions.

As of January 2010, the economy was still losing jobs. Although in early 2009 the Obama administration projected that the stimulus package would create 3.5 million jobs by autumn 2010, employment actually fell by about 3.3 million jobs during 2009.[6] In January 2010, the White House stopped tracking jobs "created or saved" and began to count all jobs *funded* by the stimulus, whether they were ever in danger or not.[7] However, some economists felt that the government had simply not done enough. As of late November 2009, Nobel Laureate economist Paul Krugman was still suggesting that government soak up the excess unemployment by creating a jobs program. He argued, "The federal government could provide jobs by...providing jobs. It's time for at least a small-scale version of the New Deal's Works Progress Administration, one that would offer relatively low-paying (but much better than nothing) public-service employment."[8] In December, President Obama began to discuss a new round of spending designed to "accelerate job growth."[9]

Socialists long critiqued the "periodic crises" of capitalism and the problem of unemployment in capitalist economies. The unplanned market system was said to be inefficient and prone to excessive poverty because it could not keep workers employed. In the best of times a "reserve army of unemployed" was still necessary for capitalism to function. In periods of recession the unemployment problem was disastrous. Capitalists, in seeking profit, would frequently lay off workers, and the reserve of unemployed would put downward pressure on wages, tending to keep the standard of living from rising and the workers impoverished.

Socialists argued that rational planning of the economy could solve this. Every citizen of the Soviet Union would be promised a job with the right to work at a fair wage enshrined in the constitution. In this way, the whole of the productive resources of the country would be employed, and poverty would be eliminated. Although a policy of "saving jobs" in a market economy is distinct from the socialist program of full employment, there are important lessons in the socialist attempt that can help to inform economic models and better judge policies that attempt to save jobs.

THE SOCIALIST ARGUMENT

Marx argued that the nature of the capitalist system ensured that workers were always in danger of losing their jobs because capitalists were driven to use the fewest workers possible and to pay them as little as possible. "It is the absolute interest of every capitalist to press a given quantity of labour out of a smaller, rather than a greater number of labourers, if the cost is about the same."[10] He did not see competition as resolving this problem. In fact, capitalism ensured that there would always be unemployed workers at the beck and call of the capitalist. A "reserve army of unemployed" always kept wages low:

> Taking them as a whole, the general movements of wages are exclusively regulated by the expansion and contraction of the industrial reserve army, and these again correspond to the periodic changes of the industrial cycle.[11]

Not only were workers kept unemployed for the purpose of being available for capitalists when needed and to keep wages low, but workers were kept at the poverty line—at the barest subsistence level—to ensure that they would be willing to do the most terrible and unnecessary labor as virtual slaves to the capitalist class.

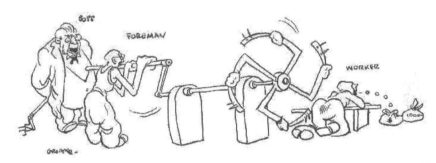

Worker beaten to produce, William Gropper — *The Revolutionary Age*, Vol 2. No. 4, 1919

> To this competition of the workers there is but one limit; no worker will work for less than he needs to subsist. If he must starve, he will prefer to starve in idleness rather than in toil. True, this limit is relative; one needs more than another, one is accustomed to more comfort than another; the Englishman, who is still somewhat civilised, needs more than the Irishman, who goes in rags, eats potatoes, and sleeps in a pig-sty. But that does not hinder the Irishman's competing with the Englishman, and gradually forcing the rate of wages, and with it the Englishman's level of civilisation, down to the Irishman's level.[12]

This is the same concern oft-repeated today, that the Indian or Chinese worker, who is paid less than the American or British worker, will drag down his wages. For socialists, this was merely the exploitation of the worker, which would ultimately leave him at the barest subsistence level.

The level at which the worker should be paid, socialists argued, was determined by the labor theory of value. In short, the value of a product is determined by the amount of labor put into it (or the average "socially necessary" amount of labor). The capitalist added nothing to this, and so the worker deserved the full amount:

> The capitalist class performs no manner of productive work. This is done by the wage-worker.... The proletarian, the wage worker, employed by the capitalist, is the wealth producer. Out of the heap of wealth brought into life by the wage-worker himself, the capitalist takes a part.... The rest of the wealth produced by the wage-worker...over and above what was necessary to enable him to restore the forces he expended in production [is the surplus]. That surplus the capitalist keeps to himself; he calls it *profits*; it constitutes his income. Industrial capital, accordingly, hatches its profits by exploiting the propertiless wage-workers.[13]

To Marx, the basic unit of value was labor. When comparing two material items to be exchanged, he found that work was involved to produce them and thus they were made up of labor. A person exchanges things of equal value because one is more useful to him than the other, so he exchanges things that are of equal *value* because one has a greater *use-value* to him.

Marx conceded that, "Every owner of a commodity wishes to part with it in exchange only for those commodities whose use-value satisfies some want of his," but he did not believe that the use-value determines the actual value of the product. He concluded, "If then we leave out of consideration the use-value of commodities, they have only one common property left, that of being products of labour."[14] This is the basis for his labor theory of value on which Marxist economics and the official economics of the Soviet system rested.[15]

Since commodities are exchanged for one another at their value, Marx asked how it is possible to make a profit. He explained that *commerce* on its own cannot generate new value, but can only distribute value around. Both parties to an exchange gain in the sense that they both *get what they want*, but neither profits because each gives in exchange a commodity of *equal value*.[16]

Marx drew the conclusion that profit can be made only by the purchase of labor and its exploitation. The capitalist creates a product only worth its labor-based value. He then underpays the labor and extracts the surplus value as profits. For socialists, *labor alone*, not capital and not demand, could determine the value. Under the bourgeois capitalist regime, the worker does not receive the value of his work. As one Marxist writer explained:

> It is a common delusion that wages are a payment for work done. If they were this, then to the worker would go the full market price of his product. To the miner would go the full selling price of the coal less only the cost of maintaining the railwaymen, transport workers and others incidental to the transfer of coal from pit to grate or furnace. To the engineer would go the price of his product—to the agricultural labourer his. To the worker would go the whole produce of his toil, and there would be none left for profits, dividends or other forms of outdoor relief to parasite idlers. The fact that the workers are a class—clearly identified under that name—establishes the fact that the shirkers also are a class—even though it be "bad form" so to describe them.[17]

Under communism he would receive this full value. "The worker in the future communist society would receive a certificate from society that he has furnished such and such an amount of labour (after deducting from his labour something for the common funds). With this certificate he would draw from the social stock of means of consumption as much as costs the same amount of labour. The same amount which he has given to society in one form he receives back in another." [18]

This would also lead to the time when labor would become "life's prime want," and society, in an age of abundance, could provide according to need, rather than according to work performed.[19] First, having taken control of his own productive powers and freed from capitalist exploitation, the worker would increase his productive potential and become more skilled and developed all around. Then the division of labor would be overcome and scarcity eliminated. Finally, the distribution of resources could be based on need only, not on labor effort.

Socialists were also concerned that modern production in the capitalist society would lead to an increase in unemployment. The accumulation of capital would lead to the creation of more and more labor-saving devices—machines that could replace workers—which would lead to more and more unemployment. They saw this as an inherent contradiction and cause of increased suffering for workers. Engels pointed to this contradiction:

> But the perfecting of machinery is making human labour superfluous. If the introduction and increase of machinery means the displacement of millions of manual by a few machine-workers, improvement in machinery means the displacement of more and more of the machine-workers themselves. It means, in the last instance...the formation of a complete industrial reserve army, as I called it in 1845, available at the times when industry is working at high pressure, to be cast out upon the street when the inevitable crash comes...a regulator for the keeping of wages down to the low level that suits the interests of capital.
>
> [The] very product of the worker is turned into an instrument for his subjugation.[20]

Revolutionary Marxists were not the only ones who believed this. In the United States in the 1930s, the National Recovery Administration (NRA) regulated labor-saving machinery for this reason. The NRA controlled the rate of speed of machinery and the hours per week it could be used, along with output and the hours and wages of workers. "We've got to have a showdown with the machine," argued the governor of Pennsylvania.[21]

Socialists explained that a planned economy would also require machinery, but the attendant evils could be controlled. Labor-saving machinery could be used, but the worker-controlled government would ensure that all the workers who lost their jobs got new ones. In fact, socialists argued that they could take better advantage of labor-saving machinery than a capitalist government could:

> All *economic obstacles* to development will be abolished under the new system. Thus, the application of machinery, which under capitalism is determined by considerations of *profit*, under the new system will depend entirely upon *productivity*. As we have seen, machinery which may be very useful for saving labour is very frequently useless from the standpoint of capitalist profits. In socialist society such a point of view will not prevail and there will therefore be no obstacles to the application of labour-saving machinery.[22]

Planners would also be able to avoid the periodic panics and slumps of capitalism, which cause unemployment. Economist Barbara Wootton argued that socialism could indeed do this.

> We have now to ask whether a planned economy can hope to escape the peculiar type of breakdown which makes the capitalist world look so foolish; whether it can avoid the paradox of unemployed labour side by side with unused resources; whether, in fact, it is capable of a smooth and steady march toward ever higher standards of living without the continual setbacks which have chequered the progress of the rival system.
>
> It is the firm faith of the Russian Communists that their planned economy has this power. There is, I suppose, no point on which the Russians are more emphatic than in this matter of the alleged immunity of that system from "overproduction" crises and their attendant unemployment.[23]

Today, it is difficult not to joke that they indeed prevented overproduction. In any case, Wootton further claimed that she did not "think it can be denied that a planned economy, which desired above anything to avoid this particular form of inefficiency, could do so." According to her reasoning:

> [I]f we suppose that a planning authority finds itself faced with growing figures of unemployment.... The immediate necessity is to find something these workers can do.... [T]here are always in any community a vast number of things which it would be in some degree useful to be done...[which is better] than that [the workers]...should be at the street corner doing nothing at all.
>
> ...[E]verybody realizes that to set people to dig holes and fill them up again is a wasteful and futile proceeding....
>
> [But] The practical issue is not between making stockings and making, let us say, handkerchiefs, but between making stockings and making nothing at all.... [W]e have, I think, good grounds for reckoning the superior ability of a planned system to eliminate prolonged and general unemployment.[24]

Wootton argues here that the choice facing the economy is not whether government work is better than other projects but whether government-created work is better than no work at all. The government can always find some work for the citizens to do and can employ them to do it. Of course, for this argument to hold, the workers must be unemployed when hired by government, *and the state's action must not prevent a private employer who would have hired them from doing so.* In other words, government hiring must not "crowd out" the private sector.

The socialist argument, which was accepted by many, was that government has the power to employ the population more effectively than the market. Socialists and those who agreed with their reasoning, such as Barbara Wootton, argued that a completely planned economy could resolve the unemployment problem without sacrificing efficiency. Others, such as President Roosevelt and the governor of Pennsylvania during that period, may not have had this confidence, but they believed that government had a role to play in slowing the adoption of new technology and in protecting and creating jobs when the market became too chaotic.

Yet what is the market doing when it sheds jobs? What is the cost of preventing the adoption of new technology or preventing the "creative destruction" of the market, as firms release workers or shutter their doors? Can the government effectively find new jobs for all laid-off workers, even in a completely planned economy, and would they be the right jobs?

Finally, socialists took the argument farther than many others when they predicted that paying the full value to labor and giving the worker control over production would lead to a new society and a new man. Scarcity could be eliminated by ridding the economy of parasitic capitalists, and labor could become "life's prime want." From socialism, in which labor is paid according to work performed, could emerge communism, in which distribution would be according to need alone.

THE SOVIET EXPERIENCE

> In the last analysis, productivity of labour is the most important, the principal thing for the victory of the new social system. Capitalism created a productivity of labour unknown under serfdom. Capitalism can be utterly vanquished, and will be utterly vanquished by socialism creating a new and much higher productivity of labour. — Lenin[25]
>
> Why can and should and necessarily will socialism conquer the capitalist system of economy? Because it can give...a higher productivity of labor. — Stalin[26]

Socialists believed that their system would produce a higher overall level of labor productivity because it would offer full employment and because work would become a joy when the workers were able to retain the full product of their labor. Full employment would be accomplished through planning of production.

Most people who are concerned about unemployment in a market society and support a government role to protect jobs would not advocate for a universal duty to work. Laws that require employers to keep employees are more popular than laws that require workers to remain at a given job. However, in the Soviet system, the right to work was one side of the coin; the duty to work the other.[27] In a planned economy, the needs of society must come first.

One might reasonably wonder how labor can be free if production is planned. In fact, this was an issue that Soviet planners had to consider. In a free market, it is demand for coal—the opportunity for profit—that drives entrepreneurs into the coal industry. If demand is high, the price rises, and profit-seeking firms expand output. As firms expand, they hire labor by offering a wage sufficient to induce workers to choose that profession. (In this way, workers are also profit-seekers.)

A planned economy is not driven by this automatic regulator. For planners to guarantee the production of a certain amount of coal, they must ensure that workers will produce it. Planners could do this in two ways. They could direct labor to the industries and firms where they are needed, or they could set wages in hopes of creating appropriate incentives. Using the latter mechanism, planners could not know for certain that enough workers would be enticed into the appropriate specializations. It would be difficult to set wages exactly right. Even more troubling, planners would need to differentiate wages to fill open positions, rather than according to the labor theory of value. Planners could not claim that workers were getting equal payment for equal work. Instead, workers would be paid according to the priority of production.

However, equal pay for equal work (or "to each according to his work") was the foundation of socialism, which was seen as a necessary step before communism would bring "to each according to his needs." For this reason, socialists knew that planners could not allocate labor using differentiated wages, so until the day that true communism arrived planners would need to direct labor allocation. In *The ABC of Communism*, which the party distributed to all schools and newspapers, Bukharin and Preobrazhensky wrote about the planning of the economy and the distribution of labor:

> [I]t is obvious that everything must be precisely calculated. *We must know in advance how much labour to assign to the various branches of industry*; what products are required and how much of each it is necessary to produce; how and where machines must be provided.[28]

Around the same time, the Party was trying to determine just how this would be accomplished. In 1919, Trotsky wrote an article for *Pravda* in which he pointed out that "a Socialist State demands a general plan for the utilization of all the resources of a country, including its human energy," and "industrial conscription is necessary for complete socialization." His proposal was one of military conscription and labor cadres. The proposal was printed in *Pravda* with a note from the editor inviting discussion. All the major party leaders wrote replies, and all agreed that something of the sort was necessary. A system of labor conscription was thereby agreed upon.[29]

This system was soon repealed in favor of the New Economic Policy. However, when NEP was rescinded the problem resurfaced. Planners needed to know that each enterprise and each ministry had sufficient and appropriate labor to perform its task. Yet when industrialization began under the first five-year plan, "Vesenkha [the planning commission] and the People's Commissariat of Labor," who were in charge of planning labor, "appeared to be caught off guard and at the mercy of market spontaneity."[30] This would not do if the plan was to be implemented. An article written for Vesenkha's journal declared that "it is self-evident that a planned economy cannot reconcile itself to the spontaneous ebb and flow of the labor force, because such spontaneity brings to naught the very principle of planning."[31]

Yet the job of planning the work for every single individual in the vast economy was simply overwhelming. The Commissariat of Labor warned that they should not "embrace the unembraceable"[32] task of trying to plan the allocation of labor completely.[33] A lack of skilled workers led managers to over-hire, and the labor exchanges that were set up to help allocate labor were unable to cope with the huge number of workers flooding through them. At a labor conference in 1930, it was admitted that "the construction worker gets a job by himself in spite of our every attempt at planned mobilization, and jeopardizes our giant projects of socialist construction."[34] Indeed, although factories soaked up all the labor they could, they did so because they were unable to obtain the skilled labor they required. This simply resulted in mass inefficiencies.[35] From 1928 to 1937, the total labor force was expanded by about 2.5 percent per year,[36] but productivity probably stagnated or fell.[37]

Following this failure, some freedom of labor was introduced, but it was restrained by a series of labor controls, including passports, drafts, and forced assignments, especially until 1955.[38] Yet workers and managers would often prefer to be tried for violating these laws than for underfulfilling the plan.[39] Workers learned that if planning and labor allocation lowered output considerably, the elimination of unemployment is of no use to the people. After the war, many letters were sent asking about the poor conditions of the workers who expected that things would improve once the war ended. One of them asked, "Why is it that unemployed people in the West live better than we do who are working?"[40]

After the war there were more and more demands to repeal the laws that "either directly or indirectly enslave our labor."[41] Finally, after 1955, the labor market was officially "free,"[42] but was still heavily restricted with controls on both workers and managers. Anti-parasite laws discouraged workers from taking a very long time off in between positions. Any willing worker had reasonable job opportunities according to the state, and refusal to accept one of these work opportunities was considered "parasitism" and was a criminal offense.[43] With limited exception, unemployment compensation was not available while Soviet citizens were out of work because they were expected to accept the available work the state offered.[44]

Official Soviet statistics list every year from 1930 forward as having zero unemployment. However, Western Sovietologists have found that a "natural rate" of unemployment persisted in the Soviet Union simply due to the nature of job searching and the time required for job matching.[45] Some have argued the Soviet rate did not differ greatly from the (non-recession) unemployment rate in market economies.[46] As one Western textbook on the Soviet economy explains, "it should come as no surprise that there is unemployment in the Soviet Union. In any dynamic economy, there must be unemployment. The economy could not function without unemployment unless it was totally static."[47]

The Soviet government attempted to keep the job turnover as low as possible, and this did make the economy more rigid, or "static," and it also resulted in widespread efficiency problems. In addition to the controls on workers, Soviet firms were forced to keep workers even when they were unneeded. Factories sometimes kept a staff of "seasonal workers" who were paid throughout the whole year. A joke in the Soviet Union explained that Soviet workers had unemployment insurance after all: They just called it a salary.

It was not easy to discharge labor.[48] A 1928 decree, confirmed in 1967, obligated managers to find new work for laid-off staff.[49] There was often no incentive to reduce labor usage because the full employment policy led planners to set targets for labor productivity, but not labor usage. At any time, a labor mobilization could take some of their labor,[50] and the excess workers might be useful if a change in plans were to occur. Hence, managers "hoarding" labor was a well-known problem.

It was also very difficult to hire new workers. Due to planner control over wage funds, "necessary tasks requiring the taking on of extra workers cannot be carried out except after a long and complex procedure for authorization of additional payments."[51] This added to the incentive to hoard labor because managers knew that in an emergency it would be impossible to hire new workers in time.

Exact and reliable labor productivity figures are difficult to obtain for any period in the Soviet Union. Labor productivity is calculated by dividing the value of output by the number of the workers, but valuing output in a socialist economy is nearly impossible. (See Chapter 6.) Those collecting statistics used this to their advantage to inflate productivity numbers.[52] However, it is generally agreed that Soviet labor productivity was probably as low as 50 or 55 percent of U.S. levels in industry, according to some sources "four to five times lower,"[53] and perhaps as low as 5 percent in agriculture.[54] Massive labor waste was evident. For example, labor hoarding led to many workers sharing a single machine, and in 1971, 60 percent of work in industry and construction was still performed by hand.[55] So much for the claims that socialism would make better use of labor-saving machinery.

Labor market controls made adjustments to improve efficiency difficult and directly contributed to the low productivity of labor. It also reduced planners' flexibility of resource allocation. When the supply of one good needed to be reduced, the ability to shutter a firm or reduce its size and release the workers was crucial. Planners had little ability to reduce large and inefficient factories or expand small ones. The economy was made more static, but this meant that any inefficiencies that crept in remained. Factories often found it impossible to respond to shifting demand or changes in technology in a timely manner.

Soviet authorities also faced the well known problem of "slacking," especially when workers faced little material incentive to work hard. Wages based upon the labor theory of value did not offer sufficient incentive to advance, and managers preferred to keep workers happy than to induce greater productivity. This was not a minor problem—for example, intra-shift downtime often amounted to 15-20 percent of total time spent on the job.

In comparing the two systems, some might not see this as a downside of socialism: if work is a necessary evil rather than a pleasure, then at least the low productivity of the economy is compensated by the more leisure-filled life of the workers. However, every bit of "slacking off" in one firm would slow down output in any other firms that depended upon it. Hence, "slacking off" not only led to lower output and therefore fewer goods for consumption—a lower standard of living—directly, it also posed an obstacle for those workers (and firms) trying to be productive. This must then further reduce final consumption.

The Soviet authorities recognized that productive resources were being wasted. At first, their response to low labor productivity was to introduce *subbotniki*, or "volunteer Saturdays," and a series of "socialist competition" campaigns, justified as the first steps toward the new proletarian man, who revered labor as "life's prime want."[36] Competitions, rewards, and propaganda encouraged hard work and norm-fulfillment in the factories, on the farms, and in the Gulag prison system. Punishment for "wreckers" and "saboteurs" discouraged laziness. Especially successful workers and prisoners, called Stakhanovites, after a man named Alexei Stakhanov who in 1935 had mined 102 tons of coal instead of the norm of 6.5, were rewarded handsomely. Free workers received bonuses and perquisites, along with accolades and medals.[57] Stakhanovite prisoners and prisoners receiving other commendation were granted better rations, better living quarters, privileges, such as the chance to send money home, and first access to books and newspapers in the prison library.[58] Politically conscious workers, including members of the Komsomol (the Communist youth group) or the Communist Party, would often create competitions and games to raise productivity. Party representatives were staffed at every major factory, and it was their duty to increase productivity through political awareness, socialist competition, and material incentives.[59]

These measures may have aided productivity. The combination of political and material incentives was retained throughout the Soviet period. However material incentives were relied on increasingly after Stalin's death. One problem with reliance on material incentives became apparent to planners.

> Here we have what would seem to be a vicious circle: the material incentive must be enhanced through raising wages, which entails higher productivity of social labor and greater output of consumer goods which in turn calls for greater material incentive.[60]

Because they were not depending upon greater efficiency or newer technology, but only incentives of workers, there was never enough money to pay the higher wages. This is reminiscent of the mistake that economists made during President Roosevelt's first term,[61] who argued for higher prices and wages as a path to prosperity. Higher wages and prices are the *result* of greater output, of prosperity, not its cause. Similarly, increasing wages will do little that leads toward higher productivity. Instead, higher productivity allows for higher wages. The Soviet system was caught in a vicious circle: they wanted to increase wages to boost productivity, but without higher productivity first, they could not afford to pay the higher wages.[62] What they needed was to find the root cause of their low productivity, and find some way to increase it.

Once it became clear that campaigns aimed at inducing *personal* worker productivity through moral or material incentives were not enough, planners finally considered reform of the system. One reform was known as Shchekino, after the factory that first used the method. Introduced in 1967, the reform program allowed firms to retain their full wage fund after reducing their workforce. In this way, the enterprise and the productive workers would benefit from changes that increased labor efficiency. This reform directly addressed the issue: rather than try to raise the material incentive by centrally directing an increase in wages (which creates a vicious circle, as no efficiency gain has created greater wealth to be distributed) it created the incentive to economize by allowing the funds saved through economies to be retained and shared.

Before the Shchekino reform, the Shchekino factory staff was three times the size recommended by foreign blueprints for the factory, due to the incentives for inefficient use of labor. The new program implemented at Shchekino froze the wage fund and permitted the factory to lay off workers and use extra wage funds for incentive bonuses at their own discretion. Out of the initial 7,500 workers, 1,000 were freed to work elsewhere during the first three years of the experiment, and output rose. The factory fulfilled its plan targets far better than average, and workers at the factory earned higher incomes due to the bonuses. Although there may have been initial apprehension, worker discipline and productivity as well as morale was greatly improved by the program. Workers became enthusiastic, hard working, and involved (there was a "sense of being the boss"), and labor turnover was dramatically reduced.

Despite the great initial success, the rules governing Shchekino were altered at least 16 times.[63] Planners were not happy with the factory letting workers go. They were unable to refrain from increasing plan targets to meet the higher levels of productivity ("planning from the achieved level"), and they reduced the "frozen" wage fund. Of course, this frustrated the factory's own goals and incentives.

The decentralized decision to reduce labor usage collided with the logic of the planned economic system. Planners arbitrarily changed the rules of the Shchekino experiment whenever they conflicted with the aims of the plan, contradicting the reform's purpose much of the time. Still, this reform attempt, which was introduced in select firms across the Soviet Union and lasted in some form over many years,[64] indicates that the planners recognized that lay-offs are critical to production efficiency. Reformers also directly addressed this issue in the lead-up to the 1965 reforms:

> We must devise an effective mechanism for combining technological progress with the most rational use of manpower resources. This calls for corresponding organization of the planning, accounting, allocating and training of manpower re-sources *released in some sections and channeled into other sections on a fully voluntary basis and with appropriate material incentives.* Attention should be drawn to this sphere because [after the reform] *the number of workers will be determined by the enterprises themselves.*[65]

After the reform, of course, the enterprise could not determine its own number of workers. This freedom was limited even at Shchekino. Soviet reformers learned the importance of releasing workers from positions in which they were not needed and allowing their voluntary movement into other sectors by way of material incentive. They also learned that leaving these decisions to the individual enterprise and the workers themselves is best. Yet a complete reform to a free and dynamic labor market would have required a free market overall. The Soviet firm was never allowed to determine its own number of workers.

Finally, although socialists had argued that capitalists kept workers at the barest subsistence level to force them to work, competition actually makes this impossible. If workers have value to employers, competition among the firms for labor will lift wages up from bare subsistence. The profit motive, which leads entrepreneurs to open firms or to expand production, leads them to bid up wages until they entice enough workers into the industry. However, the monopoly state-employer in the Soviet Union *could* pay only subsistence-level wages, and there is some evidence that the state did this. Constantin Krylov noted:

> All production is planned, and a certain amount of labor is required to accomplish it. The proportions of accumulation and consumption are planned, and these determine the material benefits that a worker may receive. Thus, the system and the leadership determine the inevitability of work and determine who should not have to work. Insufficient wages are the method used to force people to work.[66]

The monopoly employer, the state, could arguably do this. However, as we have seen, other methods were used to force people to work, such as anti-parasite laws. Wages, according to socialist theory, were supposed to be based on the labor theory of value. Under socialism, workers were to be paid according to work, while under communism they would be paid according to need. According to theory, workers were to receive the full value of their product. Lenin often referred to the experience of the "principles of the Paris Commune and of any proletarian rule, which demand the reduction of salaries to the standard of remuneration of the average worker."[67] However, this did not remain feasible for long. Because planners had difficulty allocating labor, wages ended up being used not just for material incentive, but also for allocative purposes.

Payments in factories during "war communism" were equal to all workers in a given enterprise, although they differed between firms and between industries. There was a considerable reduction in wage differentials from the pre-revolution period. Because rationed goods and free services made up the primary source of real income, equalization in real terms was even greater.[68] The 10th Congress of the Russian Communist Party in 1921 passed a resolution stating:

> The theory and practice as regards wages should be based upon as equal a distribution as possible of the standard articles of consumption. However, the Unions will make use of wages both in money and kind, as a means of improving discipline and production.[69]

These early, relatively flat wages of the "wage-scale system" had limited success.[70] Little by little, the socialist government was forced to reintroduce wage differentials.

Lenin regretted that necessity compelled the Russian government to pay high salaries to specialists. He said, "Such a measure is not merely a halt in a certain part and to a certain degree of the offensive against capitalism...but also a step backward by our Socialist Soviet State, which has from the very beginning proclaimed and carried on a policy of reducing high salaries to the standard of wages of the average worker."[71]

However, by the 1930s this goal had been abandoned. In 1931, Stalin gave a speech criticizing the "equalitarianism" of the left. He argued that high labor turnover was due to the lack of incentive to become skilled in a given industry:

> In a number of establishments the wage rates are established in such a manner that the difference almost disappears between qualified labor and unqualified labor, between heavy labor and light labor.... [T]he unqualified laborer is not interested in becoming a qualified laborer.... In order to destroy this [labor turnover] evil it is necessary to abolish equalitarianism and to destroy the old wage-scale system.[72]

Wage differentials continued during the 1930s. Skilled workers earned twice as much as unskilled workers. Yet recruiting workers when wages were still as equal as they were was difficult. At the enterprise level, managers often violated the rules to recruit new workers and obtain hard work from those they employed. For example, a survey published in *Pravda* in 1979 found that one-quarter of wage payments in the Ministry of Oil and Gas Construction violated legal requirements.[73] Recruitment to cities was difficult because wage differentials were not adequate to induce workers to the cities that were less desirable.[74]

Because planners found that they required freedom in the labor market and required wage differentials to recruit free labor to fill out the positions as needed, income inequality soon returned. Difficult positions that required long hours needed to be high paying and also tended to attract men. No amount of goodwill could change that, and discrimination was not the cause.[75] There were also a vast number of official, unofficial, and semi-official measures taken to introduce inequality (for material incentive reasons) and to reintroduce equality (to counter the inequality and offer benefits to those most disadvantaged). For example, special shops existed for the high-level party members that greatly increased their standard of living, but indirect taxation through higher prices reduced the money-wages of all but the lowest-earning workers.[76]

An analysis of social mobility in the USSR and USA in the 1930s found that mobility rates in the two countries were very similar.[77] Data from the 1960s showed that mobility was similar between the USSR and France, the U.S., and Japan.[78] Children of manual laborers were more likely to perform manual labor, children of intellectuals were more likely to obtain a higher education, and children of officials or white-collar workers became officials or white-collar workers. Despite the great efforts of these social reformers, children continued to take after their parents in occupation.

Socialists had thought that their system would produce a higher overall level of labor productivity because it would fully employ the people and because work would become a joy. Several major obstacles prevented achievement of this outcome. First, to employ all of the people while maintaining social ownership over production, planning of labor was deemed necessary. However, it proved nearly impossible to implement full planning of the workforce.

Second, the labor theory of value implied that all workers should earn the product of their labor, determined by the labor itself, not by demand in a free market. However, this implies near equality in all wages, and this prevented effective unplanned (market) labor allocation. Third, the socialist aim was to ensure full employment across the economy, protect the jobs of workers, and give workers power over their work situation. Yet these policies resulted in "unemployment on the job" and extremely inefficient factories which hoarded workers or retained unproductive workers based on politics, not on economic efficiency.

Far from surpassing the labor productivity of capitalism, socialism produced a fraction of the labor productivity of the capitalist system, and this contributed to the low living standards and difficult lives of Soviet workers. Finally, it also made the economy much more rigid and offered less opportunity and choice to the Soviet worker. Instead of benefiting the worker, these policies probably hurt the worker in the socialist society. Far from becoming "life's prime want," labor was (still) life's prime torment, but now it paid less.

Lessons

An important lesson for economists and policymakers is that all employment is not equal. Two countries with the same rate of unemployment may have entirely different levels of productive efficiency, and an economy with a higher level of unemployment is not necessarily making worse use of its resources. Policies that prevent the release of workers may reduce efficiency, even if the overall level of unemployment is kept low.

Economic models that treat all employment as equal suffer from a misleading simplification. If an economic model does not distinguish efficient employment from make-work, then the model may wrongly suggest any number of bad policies will be effective. Such flawed models largely explain why so many economists were misled by the official Soviet statistics and believed the Soviet economy was efficient. A recent paper on this subject explained the problem:

> [In the neoclassical model,] if all resources are "employed" the economy is efficient. This is not an unreasonable way to characterize a market economy with a good deal of competition but it isn't so clear that such a characterization extends beyond market economies. Indeed, in the late 1940s, Walter Eucken, the great German economist who survived the gestapo dungeons and whose intellectual heirs began the German economic miracle, pointed out that there will be no "unemployment" in a centrally administered economy. The phenomenon which goes by that name in a market economy will have another name in a planned economy. If the state runs the economy then everyone will have a job so there will be no "unemployment." The efficiency question remains: will these "employed" workers be doing anything useful?[79]

Models that do not make this distinction may lead to misguided efforts to contain unemployment through government programs. In the 1949 book *The Keynesian Revolution*, Lawrence R. Klein (who was awarded the Nobel Prize in Economics in 1980) described the thinking among economists and government policy advocates of the time. A Keynesian planning agency should be empowered to employ the American people when there was economic trouble, and then release them when the economy rebounded.

> We must have a planning agency always ready with a backlog of socially useful public works to fill any deflationary gap that may arise [financed by deficit spending]; similarly, we must have a price-control board always ready with direc-

tives and enforcement officers to wipe out any inflationary gap that may arise. . . . Government spending should be very flexible and subject to immediate release or curtailment, in just the precise amount which will maintain full employment, no more and no less. . . This is the road to the kind of full employment that we need.[80]

Although the idea may sound promising, Soviet planners learned the difficulty of simultaneously ensuring employment and promoting efficiency. A policy that "saves jobs" or offers public employment to the citizens may reduce unemployment, but it does not follow that this is more efficient than an economy without such a policy. The public tends not to appreciate the need for the economy to adjust, yet a short recession may be better than the alternative—government employment. Popular opinion may deride companies that make lay-offs, and companies are sometimes demonized for "downsizing." Yet what are the likely consequences of banning or even discouraging this practice? What can the Soviet experience tell us about the likely effects of policies that attempt to "save" jobs? Soviet central planners learned that restrictions on firing and attempts to save jobs through subsidizing losses led to "unemployment on the job" and low labor productivity. The only way planners found to significantly raise labor productivity was to allow firms to lay off all unproductive workers and keep the portion of revenues which had been used to pay them (such as in the Shchekino experiment). In other words, planners learned that their attempts to save jobs necessarily led to low labor productivity, and, despite allowing them to achieve "full employment," resulted in a net efficiency loss.

The $787 billion "stimulus package" passed in the United States is an example of a large state effort to save jobs. Projections of job creation produced for the White House were based on Keynesian economic models that assumed a "multiplier effect" of deficit spending; the published estimate offered the range 3-4 million jobs created by fall 2010.[81] The theory of the "multiplier" is that deficit spending boosts aggregate demand, and this demand prevents firms from closing, allowing workers to retain their jobs, further boosting demand and preventing a downward spiral. The official report provided for the administration estimated that with the stimulus package, unemployment would increase to no higher than 8.2 percent.

Unfortunately, the report was mistaken. By November 2009, the unemployment rate was 10 percent, and this figure may have understated the problem, as some job seekers left the job market unable to find work. As of February 1, 2010, unemployment remained at 10 percent. Although the economy was still shedding jobs, the primary cause of the high unemployment rate was a lack of new hiring.[82]

As of February 2010, much of the budgeted stimulus money had not been spent. One might ask, if government requires a year or longer to create these jobs, why would the private sector not have been able to do this? Would a downward spiraling economy have prevented private investors from creating jobs for an entire year? Arguably, no: the initial crash sent prices (for example in the housing market) sharply lower. Even with a risky environment for investment, drastic price reductions entice investors, and over a period this new investment will help a market to recover. Wary consumers may refrain from spending; but, although the Keynesian model depicts this as disastrous, this would help banks become solvent again, provide investment funds for recovery, and allow the interest rate to stabilize at a lower rate again. Economists do not disagree on this; it is only that some argue this process is too painful and extended.

Yet it is not clear that a year would not be long enough for this process to play out: for example, the 1920 stock market crash was as severe as the 1929 crash, but absent any government intervention the economy recovered in less than two years. The government provided no fiscal or monetary stimulus, yet the economy recovered quickly. "To be sure, the 1920–1921 depression was painful. The unemployment rate peaked at 11.7 percent in 1921. But it had dropped to 6.7 percent by the following year, and was down to 2.4 percent by 1923. After the depression the United States proceeded to enjoy the "Roaring Twenties," arguably the most prosperous decade in the country's history."[83] With no burden of debt following the contraction, taxes remained low and the economy soared.

Given massive government borrowing and spending, private firms may be in a worse position to aid recovery. Government borrowing and spending keeps prices up, crowding out private investment. Uncertainty about future tax increases to pay off the debt also hinders private investment. This explains the lack of new job creation in the private sector during 2009, and the relative shift from private-sector to public-sector employment (the lowest unemployment rates in the country in November 2009 were in still hurricane-devastated New Orleans and Washington, D.C., both at 6.1 percent[84]). A report based on a survey of small and independent businesses by the National Federation of Independent Businesses (NFIB) reveals that one primary reason for reduced hiring in 2009 was policy uncertainty and the fear of future tax increases.[85]

Government may channel the "stimulus" money into areas that the public believes to be worthwhile long-term investments: infrastructure, alternative energy, health care, and industries considered "core" to the economy, such as manufacturing. Spain recently invested heavily in alternative energy in part to create jobs. One flaw in the "green jobs" argument is that it often hinges on the idea that requiring more workers to produce the same number of kilowatt-hours of energy is by itself a boon to the economy. This argument is mistaken. Clearly, if the economy produces a low level of output, as occurred in the Soviet Union, then even though all workers may be employed, it is not a boon to the economy overall.

Hence, an alternative energy policy that reduces productivity in the energy sector is an economic cost, not an economic benefit. One study attempted to quantify the actual net job impact of the policy introduced in Spain—not only the jobs created by government, but also those that were lost in the private sector, and found that as many as 9 jobs may have been lost for every 4 created.[86]

Some might argue that Spain's investment in this technology is an upfront cost, but one that makes sense for the country to undertake, especially during an economic downturn. It could be seen as an investment for Spain to eventually become an energy exporter, instead of an importer—the same long-term kind of investment question that a CEO might face after a period of losses.

Yet is a country just like a firm? If it was, then it would make sense for any government to determine all of the investments in the country, just as any CEO decides the investments for his firm. In fact, the CEO decides the pay for the workers, what they produce, and at what price to sell it. Yet how can the government know if it should be an energy exporter or importer? Trade is beneficial for both sides due to comparative advantage and specialization. Spain can know that it should be an importer if it is costly to harness energy at home and cheaper to import. Trying to "create jobs" and "invest in Spain's future" by domestically investing in a technology when importing energy would be cheaper is counterproductive and nonsensical from an economic standpoint.[87]

There has been popular lament about the loss of manufacturing jobs in the United States over the past decade. Yet those who disparage this trend rarely see the full picture. As some jobs are lost, others are made possible. New technology makes some workers redundant, but it also increases the wealth that the industry produces, leading to lower costs and prices and a higher standard of living. As some industries contract, others are able to expand, and the shift of resources leads to production that is better able to fill the demands of the consumer.

In manufacturing, the recent shedding of jobs has been driven, at least in part, by substantial increases in productivity. Yet the response has been to try to "protect" the jobs by subsidizing major car manufacturers or through heavy-handed union negotiations. One Ohio newspaper recently reported:

> Using data from the federal government, state analysts figured that manufacturers here produced goods worth almost 11 percent more, in constant dollars, in 2005 than they did just four years earlier. That shows productivity is on the rise.
> The bad news, though, is that the number of Ohioans making things has dropped by the thousands almost every year for more than a decade because they were no longer needed.[88]

Although it was indeed bad news for the particular workers laid off, it was an integral part of a trend of technological improvements and increasing output, which was good for all Ohioans, all Americans, and all people generally. The misfortune of those laid-off workers could be addressed in better ways than trying to protect the jobs. Although no policy is costless, employment transition assistance would have only the cost of the tax imposed to fund it, while jobs protection could have far more serious ramifications.

In Ohio's free manufacturing market, as some jobs became extinct, others were created—jobs that could not as yet be mechanized. Very often these have been higher-skilled jobs working with new equipment or white-collar or service jobs, because machines cannot do these tasks. An economy that produces new technological innovations will tend to shed jobs, yet the jobs that replace them will tend to be jobs based on new innovations and advances.

The popular myth is that the United States "no longer makes anything" and is entirely a service economy. While the U.S. does have a large number of service jobs, including many in the fields of information technology and other high-skilled areas, it is not true that the U.S. produces no manufactured goods.

British Prime Minister Margaret Thatcher is remembered by some as the cruel figure that put workers in many industries out of their jobs by removing their employers' subsidies. However, she defended this choice for many of the reasons discussed here.

> Many of us, understandably, wish to avoid redundancy when major firms fail. In the short term, we argue, those made redundant will become unemployed. Consequently, the State will have to pay little more if it subsidises the firm to keep men at work than if it pays unemployment benefit. Because we all hate unemployment. Many of us approve of subsidies being given to firms in difficulties in order to keep men and women at work.
>
> As this is such an emotive question, we need more than usual to look closely at the issues....We live in a world where we can continue to raise our living standards only by moving steadily into the activities that will be profitable tomorrow, as other countries begin to engage in the activities on which the UK specialises today....
>
> The present Government's policy of resisting any redundancy when bad management, declining markets or advancing technology lead businesses to fail, merely guarantees that workers will not be available to fill tomorrow's jobs....We shall become one of the poorer countries in Europe, with little economic development. Our real incomes will rise slowly, if at all.
>
> And an unbearable percentage of those incomes will go in taxation to subsidise the employment of a growing percentage of the labour force in unprofitable firms, with out-of-date products or overmanning.[89]

Although it may have seemed cruel to allow these workers to lose their jobs, the policy of subsidizing unprofitable firms in order to save jobs could not continue indefinitely. The experience of the Soviet Union illustrates why this is unworkable. If government saves jobs and firms where they are not needed, the economy cannot adjust to shifts in demand and supply, and this rigidity causes stagnation and decay.

Upon arriving in market economies, Soviet exiles have reported gratitude about job placement and fear of unemployment.[90] Although the Soviet workers appreciated the job security, they may not have been cognizant of the trade-off they were making because they had not experienced the alternative. Not only did Soviet workers who were placed in their jobs miss out on the freedom to find jobs they might prefer, they also gave up the chance to create their own jobs through entrepreneurship. They lived in an economy that, by virtue of its static full employment state, had little innovation, technological advance, and economic growth.

Strong labor laws that fix wages and prevent layoffs are intended to protect workers, yet these workers are then not offered the highly technical positions that an innovative economy produces. The freedom to hire, fire, and set wages lays the groundwork for the productivity that drives growth, which allows for increasing standards of living. The growth of wages must come from productivity growth. It cannot be commanded.

Productivity and growth are the means for the people in society—the workers, but also the families and even the unemployed poor—to increase their individual prosperity. Advances in productivity—the ability to produce more goods with less work—have led to far higher living standards and more leisure time than in times past.[91]

A recent article compared China today to the industrial revolution, and credited Marxist thought for seeing that markets cause horrific factory conditions. The author quotes Engels on the Industrial Revolution in England and quotes a Chinese factory worker describing conditions today. He concluded, "Friedrich Engels, a child of the Industrial Revolution, speaks now with remarkable authority and insight to our own global age of exploitation and immiseration."[92]

Markets are taking hold in China and conditions are indeed bad. Yet if it is the fault of the market and capitalist exploitation, why do we not have those conditions in the developed world, where we have had markets for much longer?

A closer look at the factories with the worst conditions in China reveals that the state has a strong hand in making abuses possible and preventing competition from driving wages up. For example, according to an article in 1997, workers rush to the foreign companies to take jobs because the state factories often pay even less or are not hiring,[93] and factory jobs generally pay better than agricultural work. Foreign factories then offer jobs only on condition that the worker hand over his state-issued work-card or identification. The factories are then able to abuse the worker and refuse to let him resign, holding his state papers hostage.

These factories are using the state's power against the worker to prevent competition and to enslave the workforce. This is not inherent in a free market with protection of property rights. There is no market-based power that can prevent a worker from quitting and looking for a better job, just as there is no market power to prevent a consumer from looking for a better price.[94] This is why competition works in a free market, and why markets do not lead to falling wages (a "race to the bottom"), but have consistently led to higher and higher standards of living. This outcome depends on workers being free to look for better employment because this is the competition that drives up wages so that workers benefit from economic growth.

Although socialists argued that the "iron law of wages" dictated what workers were paid by capitalists—the bare minimum for their subsistence—there is clear evidence that this was not always the case. Just as supply and demand determine the price of any product, they determine the price of labor—wages. In 1893, economist Yves Guyot wrote of the iron law of wages that

> It is untrue both as a minimum and maximum. It is not true as a minimum: because if the employer has no need for manual labour, he will not trouble himself about the labourer's necessity of living; he will not employ him, and will not pay him. It is not true as a maximum; because the employer pays the labourer, not

according to the latter's convenience, but according to the use he can make of his work, according to the demands made upon him for the products he supplies.

In reality it is neither the employer nor the employed who regulates the price of labour; it is a third person, whom we are in the habit of forgetting, and who is known as the consumer. If the employer were to produce something which did not meet some want, or which, by its price, was outside the range of wants which could be satisfied, he would not be able to give wages either above or below the means of subsistence, to his labourers, for the very good reason, that he could not produce, and consequently would employ no one.

If an employer manufactures things that are in great demand, and which can only be made by a limited number of workmen, the workmen can command very high pay.

[Hence even the advance of technology and the introduction of machinery work for the worker, because they lead to greater output.] Machinery works for him. Whilst he watches it, it supplies a want which would have required the labour of twenty men. Instead of himself labouring, he simply directs it. The muscles which were formerly his instruments of labour, are now only the supports of his intellectual activity. [95]

Although union advocates believe that unions help workers, they sometimes may have the opposite effect. Economists recognize the unintended effects of a minimum wage that may actually hurt those that a minimum wage is intended to help.[96]

Those workers that would earn the least when negotiating directly with the employer, which are the supposed beneficiaries of the union wage agreement, will be the ones most likely to be left unhired or laid off when the firm is in trouble. Rather than being able to say, "I would rather earn $10 an hour than be unemployed," the worker has only the choice to earn $15 or to earn nothing. If he is not worth $15 to the employer, then he must go home with nothing.

Collective bargaining may hurt the business and individual workers equally because it creates an inflexible lump-sum choice for employers. Individual workers may be hurt if they must take a pay cut, because they were worth more to the employer but the higher wage of other workers has left less for them, or because they are not hired or are laid off because they are not worth the union wage to the firm. The enterprise may be hurt if it cannot choose to make new hires at a lower rate and is therefore forced to lay off workers or to shut down. In turn, what hurts the firm hurts the workers.

In addition to the disadvantages of collective bargaining, unions, if allowed to, may also hurt competition, and hence lower wages in the long run, by seeking protections and regulations that prevent entry by non-unionized firms and workers in order to ensure the high union wages are not competed away. This may help the unionized workers in the short-run, but will hurt all workers over the longer-term as productivity and the higher wages that come from it are curtailed. As one example, construction unions recently lobbied the United States Congress to change legislation that had exempted small start-up construction firms with fewer than 50 employees from a tax if they failed to provide health insurance to their employees. *The New York Times* reports that, "Their provision, added to the 2,074-page bill at the last minute, singles out the construction industry for special treatment, in a way that benefits union members and contractors who use union labor."[97]

The more that strict labor laws or union-negotiated rules are enforced upon a firm, the more danger that inflexibility may hurts both firm and worker. If the firm is banned from making layoffs, it must ultimately fail, possibly taking the retirement fund with it. No law can produce the productivity required to pay high wages, although subsidies and labor laws can redistribute existing wealth. Similarly, government cannot mandate innovation. Technological change, innovation, and growth do not come from government regulation. A regulation can force firms to adopt an existing technology or to improve wages or working conditions for current employees. However, this also may force the firm to cut other salaries, reduce new hires or make layoffs.

Labor laws and wage floors may be especially dangerous when flexibility and economic growth is most important, such as when struggling to recover from a recession, or when a country is under-developed. When the Berlin Wall fell and formerly socialist East Germany was merged into a new unified market economy, this lesson was ignored, and a few loud individuals who wanted to save their own jobs were allowed to slam the brakes on economic recovery and growth.

> The major problem was that a basic economic rule was stood on its head. If a new market economy is constructed from scratch, the endowments may be distributed arbitrarily, but one must not interfere with the free determination of prices and wages, because it fulfils a central steering function.
>
> ...As early as the spring of 1991, wage negotiations took place according to the West German collective bargaining law, although there were no private entrepreneurs at the time that could have fought the devaluation of their capital by wage increases. Before privatisation, there were proxy wage negotiations between West German competitors of East German firms sitting on both sides of the table. Their objective was to raise wages to the West German level as fast as possible in order to protect their own jobs. If foreign investors, who were in the starting blocks, were to come in to buy and restructure the East German state firms with their know-how and their products, they were to do so at West German wages.
>
> The investors preferred to stay away, the East German firms foundered, and in the end there were indeed no longer any assets left that could have been distributed. Sony, one of the most important investors of the first hour, meanwhile sold its imposing centre at the Potsdamer Platz, disappointed over the way things turned out.
>
> ...As a result of the proxy wage negotiations, East German wages rose much faster than East German productivity in those early years.... Due to the income transfers from the West, welfare incomes also rose much faster than productivity. They have largely arrived at West German levels and legal retirement pensions are even higher. Via the wage competition of the welfare state in the labour market, the welfare incomes cemented the wages above the level corresponding to productivity. It therefore did not help much when newly established East German firms gradually unshackled themselves from the collective wage agreements. Stagnation and mass unemployment were pre-programmed.[98]

Because of labor laws, the failing newly privatized firms were not a good buy for foreign investors. It would be too difficult to profit in such an environment. In fact, wages were rising faster than productivity, which is unsustainable. Only external subsidy could keep such an economy going, and although the propped up wages benefit those particular workers in the short run, only growth can benefit them in the long run. In the meantime, those left without a job were made far worse off.

The former-socialist economy was stifled by the wage law. Especially when an economy is in desperate need of growth, wages need to be flexible. United States President Herbert Hoover violated this principle after the stock market crash of 1929. He oversaw negotiations between unions and corporations to maintain high wages in the face of falling prices. Confusing cause and effect, he thought that this would help the economy recover. Instead, as in East Germany, it drove unemployment and precluded the flexibility that the economy required for recovery.[99]

Advances come from productivity enhancements, not from labor law. The labor theory of value has confused this truth by insisting that all value comes from labor power alone. Yet productivity is not due to labor alone, and for this reason firms must have the ability to lay off workers and to replace them where possible with more advanced (labor-saving) technologies. Some socialists understood this. In 1902, German socialist leader Karl Kautsky made this point:

> [T]hese figures...show that if the income of the capitalist was directed to the laborers wages would be doubled. But unfortunately things are not to be done so simply. When we expropriate capital we must at the same time take over its social functions. The most important of these is the accumulation of capital. Capitalists do not consume their entire income. A portion they lay aside for the extension of production. A proletarian regime would be obliged to do the same since it too must extend production....
>
> We shall see that there is none too much remaining over from the present income of the capitalist to be applied to the raising of wages even if we confiscate capital at one stroke. It will be one of the imperative tasks of the social revolution not simply to continue but to increase production. The victorious proletariat must extend production rapidly if it is to be able to satisfy the enormous demands that will be made upon the new regime.[100]

The West has developed past the level of China, and competition has driven wages up and improved conditions. Reinvesting profit allowed capital to grow, and greater capital meant greater productivity and higher wages. If labor alone created value (and kept all proceeds as the unions argued) then workers in any country and with any equipment would produce the same. Communist state factories in China, although not run by capitalists "exploiting" the workers, were arguably as bad for workers as the foreign-run and state-run factories of today denounced as being caused by the "exploitation and immiseration" of capitalism.[101]

Although socialists and others have often accused the capitalist multinational companies of exploiting workers in developing countries, operating sweatshops, and becoming rich at the expense of the poor, in fact this is how countries are able to develop at all. Humans are not inherently individually productive to the tune of tens of thousands of dollars a year. Only with capital and the development of technology can workers offer enough value to earn the wages reaped in the developed world. Until then, investment by those enticed by cheap labor can help to develop the skills and capital to grow the economy. For example, a recent article highlighted how the "exploitation" of poor Africans in Nigeria by the beer company Guinness helped some lucky Nigerian workers avoid the recession and send their children to better schools.[102]

Growth in any economy is not possible unless labor can be economized with labor-saving devices and other cost-reduction techniques and unless companies can lay off workers. When a company makes layoffs, it should be seen as an efficiency enhancement. Layoffs by a whole industry must be recognized as a shift in the economy, necessary, if disappointing. Both are a move toward greater efficiency and ultimately toward greater productivity and higher wages. Policies that "protect jobs" are costly to the economy and ultimately to the workers themselves. Transition assistance or unemployment insurance can help laid off workers without causing great harm to the economy, but intervention to prevent layoffs means reducing flexibility and thereby preventing growth.

In a sense, Marx was right that unemployment is necessary in a market economy. The "reserve army of unemployed" does help the market adjust. Yet these workers also represent individuals who would be excess workers if they were kept on. Any system that prevents their layoff, whether full-employment socialism or just a jobs-protecting market economy, must be less efficient. Firms must lay off excess workers or else they are simply paying workers—like the citizens in Wootton's example—to stand around on a street corner doing nothing.

It is also necessary to have a fair degree of inequality in a market economy. For firms to respond to changes in demand, they need not only the freedom to hire and fire, but also the freedom to offer whatever wage is necessary to attract the workers that they need into their industry. A dynamic labor market is a core part of a dynamic economy—allowing supply to respond to changes in demand,[103] resources to quickly move into new areas, and to allow firms to adopt new technologies. Firms must be able to bid up wages in competition with other firms—the very activity that leads to rising living standards among the workforce as productivity rises.

Yet as the Soviets learned, these are not simply problems of a market economy that go away with rational central planning. These problems of economics are inherent in economic activity, and their solutions are found in the flexibility and freedom of the market. The Soviet attempt to eliminate unemployment and inequality was unsuccessful on both counts, but even their later compromise policies, based on stringent labor laws and wage rules, caused significant problems for the economy and likely hurt the worker more than they helped him.

Market economies are the most dynamic of economies, which means that individuals have the most opportunity possible. Unless government (as in a serf or caste society) or social oppression (based on gender or race, for example) prevents it, the free agent of the market economy can ascend the income scale as she gains experience, or branch out on her own and start a business. Although Marx argued that capitalist economies are founded on fixed classes of workers and capitalists, in most modern market economies a large portion of the population plays both roles. Market economies have brought not only greater economic growth than feudal societies, but greater mobility and equality as well. Yet labor laws are capable of some of the same kinds of rigidity as the old laws and social biases.

In market economies, labor laws and policies that reduce inequality may also reduce the dynamism of the economy, leading to lower growth and reduced economic mobility. They may prevent individual workers from acquiring the best agreement that they can with an employer, and force lower-skilled workers out of the labor force altogether. These laws may also limit competition for labor, leading to lower wages for all workers. The steady increase in real wages in developed economies comes from the competition for workers and the freedom of firms to increase their productivity, not from labor laws. Although well-meaning, such laws may actually slow this steady growth.

Conclusion

Socialists derided the market economy for its "periodic crises" and problems of unemployment. They argued that rational planning of the economy would put an end to these economic ills because government could provide employment to all workers, and ensure a living wage for every worker. Today, many still look to government to "save" jobs or provide employment during economic slumps.

Socialists, and many economists, believed that the planned economy would be more efficient than a market economy because it could employ all citizens. Yet government cannot know how best to employ the workers because this is determined by market forces. Soviet planners soon realized that they could not determine how to employ all the workers in the jobs that best fit them. They had to reintroduce market forces in the labor market. Still, the Soviet government attempted to "save jobs" by restricting the ability of firms to lay off workers

If inefficient firms cannot lay off workers, they cannot become efficient. These workers remain as extraneous expenses where they are not needed. Even more importantly, efficient firms or firms in other industries that could expand to fill new demand or supply requirements cannot hire them. This rigidity prevented the Soviet economy from taking advantage of all of its productive resources. Western countries can learn from this that, as painful as they might be, layoffs are an important freedom that firms must be able to utilize.

"Bailouts" and subsidies, intended to protect jobs, can reduce this dynamic economic tool. Although policymakers argue that after a crash bailouts may prevent a domino effect, the period after a stock market crash may be a particularly important time for market flexibility—the firms that were only profitable during the preceding bubble must be able to contract so that the resources can be used where they offer greater value.

Wage controls and labor laws similarly prevent firms from freely adjusting their labor force to the economic needs of the country. Planners also learned that centrally setting wages, and setting them to reduce inequality, prevented the ability of the market to allocate labor to where it was needed. It also failed to increase the living standard of the workers—it did not achieve its objective. Inequality returned and mobility remained low. Labor policies in market economies that aim for equality or jobs protection may also reduce flexibility in the market, and prevent wage growth. The importance of labor market flexibility is often underestimated when analyzing the potential effects of labor policy. The Soviet experience is a useful case study, as it highlights the deficiency of standard models.

Endnotes

1. "Obama Warns of Turning a 'Crisis into a Catastrophe,'" CNN, February 4, 2009, at http://www.cnn.com/2009/POLITICS/02/04/stimulus (November 18, 2009).

2. *Ibid.*

3. *Ibid.*

4. Louise Radnofsky, "White House Reports Stimulus Saved One Million Jobs," *The Wall Street Journal*, September 11, 2009, at http://online.wsj.com/article/SB125261717671200941.html (November 18, 2009).

5. For example, see Rajshree Agarwal, Jay B. Barney, Nicolai J. Foss, and Peter G. Klein, "Heterogeneous Resources and the Financial Crisis: Implications of Strategic Management Theory," *Strategic Organization*, vol. 7, no. 4 (November 2009).

6. Brian M. Riedl, "White House Report Claims Stimulus Success-Despite 3.5 Million Job Losses," January 14, 2010, Heritage Foundation *WebMemo* No. 2755, at http://www.heritage.org/Research/Economy/wm2755.cfm (February 12, 2010).

7. Michael Grabell, "White House Changes Stimulus Jobs Count," January 11, 2010, at http://www.propublica.org/ion/stimulus/item/white-house-changes-stimulus-jobs-count-111 (February 12, 2010).

8. Paul Krugman, "The Jobs Imperative," *The New York Times*, November 29, 2009, at http://www.nytimes.com/2009/11/30/opinion/30krugman.html (December 7, 2009).

9. Barack Obama, "Remarks by the President on Job Creation and Economic Growth," The Brookings Institution, Washington, D.C., December 8, 2009, at http://www.whitehouse.gov/the-press-office/remarks-president-job-creation-and-economic-growth.

10. Karl Marx, *Capital*, Vol. 1, *The Progress of Production of Capital*, trans. Samuel Moore and Edward Aveling (Moscow: Progress Publishers, 1887), chap. 25, at http://marxists.org/archive/marx/works/1867-c1/index.htm (November 20, 2009).

11. *Ibid.*

12. Friedrich Engels, *Condition of the Working Class in England* (London: Penguin Books, 1987), p. 112.

13. Karl Kautsky, *The Capitalist Class*, trans. by Daniel De Leon (National Executive Committee Social Labor Party, 1911), chap. 3, at http://www.marxists.org/archive/kautsky/1911/cap-class/ch03.htm (November 18, 2009).

14. Marx, *Capital*, Vol. 1, chap. 1.

15. A letter that was part of a series of exchanges among George Bernard Shaw, Henry Hyndman, and Annie Besant, by Annie Besant, includes a good and fairly simple refutation of the labor theory of value by a socialist. Besant points out: "Marx speaks of 'value,' 'exchange value,' and 'use value' in the opening pages of the 'Capital.' He defines 'value' as a 'common substance' present in products of human labour, human labour being regarded 'in the abstract.'... We are then told that 'a use value or useful article' has 'value only because human labour in the abstract has been embodied or materialized in it'...; so that use value is value as before defined plus utility of the product. Having grasped this conception, the student of Marx is startled to learn, two pages later, that 'a thing

can be a use value, without having value,' as air, &c. (but why call this Use value, when value is absent?) and that 'lastly, nothing can have value without being an object of utility,' because 'if the thing is useless so is the labour contained in it; the labour does not count as labour, and therefore creates no value.' Now as we have already been told that the 'labour' which 'creates' 'value' is 'labour in the abstract,' its utility or non-utility cannot possibly come into consideration; we are bidden to 'put out of sight...the useful character of the various kinds of labour'...in defining value. Although I have no pretence to be a 'Socialist of note,' I make bold to say that this quagmire of contradictions and bad metaphysics is no safe foundation for modern Socialism." Annie Besant, in Bernard Shaw, Henry Hyndman, and Annie Besant, "Exchange of Letters on Value Theory in Marx," 1887, at http://www.marxists.org/subject/economy/authors/fabians/earlyenglishvalue/lettersonvalue.htm (November 18, 2009). There are many other refutations of the labor theory of value from both socialists and non-socialists; Eugen von Böhm-Bawerk's is easily readable. Eugen von Böhm-Bawerk, *Karl Marx and the Close of His System* (New York: Augustus M. Kelley, 1949), at http://mises.org/books/karlmarx.pdf (November 18, 2009).

16. "We are, therefore, forced to the conclusion that the change originates in the use-value, as such, of the commodity, i.e., in its consumption. In order to be able to extract value from the consumption of a commodity, our friend, Moneybags, must be so lucky as to find, within the sphere of circulation, in the market, a commodity, whose use-value possesses the peculiar property of being a source of value, whose actual consumption, therefore, is itself an embodiment of labour, and, consequently, a creation of value. The possessor of money does find on the market such a special commodity in capacity for labour or labour-power." Marx, *Capital*, vol. 1, chap. 1.

17. T. A. Jackson, "Wages and Wonderment," *The Communist*, May 21, 1921, at http://www.marxists.org/archive/jackson-ta/articles/1921/05/21.htm (November 18, 2009).

18. Karl Marx, "Critique of the Gotha Programme," 1875, at http://www.marxists.org/archive/marx/works/1875/gotha/ch01.htm (November 18, 2009).

19. The famous quote explains the relationship: "In a higher phase of communist society, after the enslaving subordination of the individual to the division of labor, and therewith also the antithesis between mental and physical labor, has vanished; after labor has become not only a means of life but life's prime want; after the productive forces have also increased with the all-around development of the individual, and all the springs of co-operative wealth flow more abundantly—only then can the narrow horizon of bourgeois right be crossed in its entirety and society inscribe on its banners: From each according to his ability, to each according to his needs!" Karl Marx, "Critique of the Gotha Programme."

20. Frederick Engels, "Socialism: Utopian and Scientific," part 3, at http://www.marxists.org/archive/marx/works/1880/soc-utop/index.htm (November 18, 2009).

21. Garet Garrett, *Salvos Against the New Deal* (Caldwell, IN: Caxton Press, 2002), p. 91.

22. Alexander Bogdanov, *Socially Organized Society: Socialist Society*, 10th ed., trans. by J. Fineberg (1919), chap. 10, at http://www.marxists.org/archive/bogdanov/1919/socialism.htm (November 20, 2009). See also in which he argues, "One is always justified in assuming that any scheme of economic reform, such as the introduction of new machinery, new raw materials, a new form of management of labour, or new systems of remuneration, will always be accepted by the owners if only these schemes can be shown to offer a commercial advantage. But in so far as we have to do here with the economy of society, that is not sufficient. Here, opposing interests are in conflict. What is advantageous for one is disadvantageous for another. The egoism of one class acts not only against the egoism of another, but also to the disadvantage of the whole community." Leon Trotsky, *Results and Prospects*, English trans. (Communist International, 1921), chap. 7, at http://www.marxists.org/archive/trotsky/1931/tpr/rp-index.htm (November 20, 2009).

23. Barbara Wootton, *Plan or No Plan* (New York: Farrar and Rinehart, 1935), p. 175.

24. *Ibid.*

25. Vladimir Ilyich Lenin, "A Great Beginning: Heroism of the Workers in the Rear 'Communist Subbotniks,'" in *Collected Works*, Vol. 29 (Moscow: Progress Publishers, 1919), pp. 408–434, at *http://www.marxists.org/archive/lenin/works/cw/index.htm#volume29* (November 18, 2009).

26. Joseph Stalin, quoted in Leon Trotsky, *The Revolution Betrayed*, trans. by Max Eastman (1936), at http://www.marxists.org/archive/trotsky/1936/revbet/index.htm (November 18, 2009).

27. While wealthy bourgeois societies had mass unemployment, before the revolution Russian workers and peasants were arguably more concerned with shortages, low wages, bad harvests, and war than with the inability to find work. "Peace, bread, and land" was the rallying cry of the Bolsheviks that won them popular support. Their program was to eliminate the capitalist "parasites" and usher in the era of the proletariat. Hence, the first Soviet Constitution included an article codifying a universal obligation to work. Only later was the universal right to work enunciated. The 1918 Constitution stated: "The Russian Socialist Federated Soviet Republic considers work the duty of every citizen of the Republic, and proclaims as its motto: 'He shall not eat who does not work.'" The 1936 Constitution guaranteed all Soviet citizens "the right to work...[and] the right to employment and payment for their work in accordance with its quantity and quality." The corresponding article in the 1977 Constitution was very similar, but included the freedom to choose one's work, tempered by the phrase "with due account for the needs of society." Constitution of the Russian Soviet Federated Socialist Republic, art. 2, para. 18 (1918); Constitution of the Union of Soviet Socialist Republics, art 12 (1936); and Constitution of the Union of Soviet Socialist Republics, art. 17 (1977).
28. Nikolai Bukharin and Evgenii Preobrazhensky, *The ABC of Communism* (New York: Penguin Books, 1969), chap. 3, at http://www.marxists.org/archive/bukharin/works/1920/abc/index.htm (November 19, 2009) (emphasis added).
29. Arthur Ransome, *The Crisis in Russia* (1920), at http://marxists.org/history/archive/ransome/works/crisis/ch08.htm (November 19, 2009).
30. Hiroaki Kuromiya, *Stalin's Industrial Revolution: Politics and Workers, 1928-1931* (Cambridge: Cambridge University Press, 1990), p. 200.
31. Cited in *ibid.*, pp. 200–201.
32. It is interesting to note that this phase became quite popular in the Soviet Union and was even mentioned in Kantorovich's Nobel speech: "In our time mathematics has penetrated into economics so solidly, widely and variously, and the chosen theme is connected with such a variety of facts and problems that it brings us to cite the words of Kozma Prutkov which are very popular in our country: 'One can not embrace the unembraceable.' The appropriateness of this wise sentence is not diminished by the fact that the great thinker is only a pen-name." Leonid Vitaliyevich Kantorovich, "Mathematics in Economics: Achievements, Difficulties, Perspectives."
33. Kuromiya, *Stalin's Industrial Revolution*, p. 221.
34. Cited in *ibid.*, p. 205.
35. "The massive addition of human resources to industry threatened to consume already scarce material resources and to make the accumulation of capital impossible without further squeezing national consumption." Kuromiya, *Stalin's Industrial Revolution*, p. 220.
36. Paul R. Gregory and Robert C. Stuart, *Soviet Economic Structure and Performance* (New York: Harpercollins College Division, 1990), p. 264.
37. Although the statistics are not reliable, there is general agreement that labor productivity fell during the first five-year plan, and that agricultural productivity plummeted. According to one source, "Only in 1940 did man-hour productivity exceed the 1913 level—and then, barely. A net gain of only one eighth is indicated for 1928–40. A serious decline is shown for the first plan period [1928–1933]. The 1940 level had not been reattained by 1947." —Irving H. Siegel, "Labor Productivity in the Soviet Union," *Journal of the American Statistical Association*, Vol. 48, No. 261 (March 1953), pp. 65–78. See also Anne D. Rassweiler, "Soviet Labor Policy in the First Five-Year Plan: The Dneprostroi Experience," *Slavic Review*, Vol. 42, No. 2 (Summer 1983), pp. 230–246. For discussion of the statistics, see Andre Gunder Frank, "General Productivity in Soviet Agriculture and Industry: The Ukraine, 1928–55," *Journal of Political Economy*, Vol. 66, No. 6 (December 1958), pp. 498–515. According to some sources, growth and productivity did rise during that period, although most growth was "extensive" and not "intensive," meaning that it came from bringing new labor and capital into use, not from improving technology or making more efficient use of existing technology. See, e.g., Robert C. Allen, "The Rise and Decline of the Soviet Economy," *Canadian Journal of Economics*, Vol. 34, No. 4 (November 2001), pp. 859–881, and William Easterly and Stanley Fischer, "The Soviet Economic Decline," *World Bank Economic Review*, Vol. 9, No. 3 (September 1995), pp. 341–371.

38. In 1932, a system of internal passports was introduced that tied workers to their places of residence. Passports were unable to resolve all employment allocation concerns, however, and in 1938, labor books were introduced which tracked worker's entire employment history and allowed planners to monitor movement and exert control where necessary. Labor contracts were also increased to five-year terms. In 1939, a decree declared that tardiness of 20 minutes or more constituted an unauthorized absence from work (wartime legislation was even harsher). Between 1940 and 1952, almost 11 million workers were convicted of absenteeism and lateness. In certain periods, such as between 1940 and 1955, there were policies of labor planning termed "labor drafts" or "labor mobilizations." All young men and women, once their schooling was complete, were subject to the labor draft except those subject to military service. The programs then trained the draftees and the Ministry of Labor Reserves assigned them to jobs where they had a mandatory minimum term of service of four years (or indefinitely, given a 1940 law fixing them to their place of employment). This terminology is certainly amusing, considering Marx's criticism of the need for a "reserve army of unemployed" under capitalism. These labor draft programs in fact resembled army training programs in many ways. Paul R. Gregory and Valery V. Lazarev, eds., *The Economics of Forced Labor: The Soviet Gulag* (Stanford, CA: Hoover Institution Press, 2003).
39. See Hiroaki Kuromiya, *Stalin's Industrial Revolution*, p. 211, and H. Hirsch, *Quantity Planning and Price Planning in the Soviet Union* (Philadelphia: University of Pennsylvania Press, 1961).
40. Gregory and Lazarev, *The Economics of Forced Labor*, p. 34.
41. *Ibid.*
42. It is important to note that if planners could not convince workers to do their bidding, they had another option: forced prison labor. The Gulag penal system constituted about 2 percent of the total labor force, but one in every five construction workers and most workers in several key mining sectors between 1940 and 1951. The Gulag system allowed planners to divert labor into unpopular and inhospitable areas. Because it was so difficult to find free workers for these areas, ministries and the Gulag administration fought over use of prison labor in remote areas. Gregory and Lazarev, *The Economics of Forced Labor*.
43. Even if the bourgeoisie as a class had been eliminated and the new proletarian man had emerged, there was good reason to keep duty-to-work laws on the books. If the state required workers for a certain industry, they would want to have the choice of all citizens. Furthermore, because social goods and protections were also encoded as rights, the duty to work must go hand in hand, otherwise those who receive but do not produce would be drains on the social resources. This is the meaning of "parasitism."
44. Paul Gregory and Irwin Collier, "Unemployment in the Soviet Union: Evidence from the Soviet Interview Project," *American Economic Review* (September 1988).
45. Job search and matching were "facilitated" by labor exchanges, which were also intended to help planners ensure that planned production was matched by available labor. Labor exchanges were introduced in the 1960s to perform the "matchmaking" function of bringing employer and employee together and to guide workers toward the industries most in need. Many highly skilled individuals also continued to be assigned to their positions, as in early days. Young students enrolled in the Young Pioneers and the Komsomols, the Party youth groups, were also used to complete construction projects and other kinds of labor tasks, many of them significant and similar to forced labor projects. For example, in the 1920s, the Komsomols were tasked with building a city (named Komsomolsk in their honor). In the 1930s, they worked on the Moscow subway system. In the 1950s, they plowed up virgin grass on the frontier in Asia, and in the 1960s they worked on 125 construction projects across the nation. P. Rutland, *The Myth of the Plan*, p. 151; O. S. Ioffe and P. B. Maggs, *The Soviet Economic System: A Legal Analysis*, Westview Special Studies on the Soviet Union and Eastern Europe (Boulder: CO: Westview Press, 1987), p. 165; and John N. Hazard, *The Soviet System of Government* (Chicago: University of Chicago Press, 1968), p. 38.
46. Gregory and Collier, "Unemployment in the Soviet Union."
47. *Ibid.*
48. Hazard, *The Soviet System of Government*, pp. 191 and 197; Rutland, *The Myth of the Plan*, p. 151; and Nove, *The Soviet Economic System* (London: Unwin Hyman, 1986), p. 224.

49. Henry Norr, "Shchekino: Another Look," *Soviet Studies*, Vol. 38, No. 2 (April 1986), pp. 141–169.

50. Nove, *The Soviet Economic System*, p. 224, and Gregory and Collier, "Unemployment in the Soviet Union."

51. Alec Nove, *Political Economy and Soviet Socialism* (London: Unwin Hyman , 1979), pp. 189–190.

52. Gross output of all products, including unfinished and unsalable products, was divided by just production workers, e.g., excluding those working in research and design. C. A. Krylov, *The Soviet Economy* (Lexington: Lexington Books, 1979), p. 143.

53. *Ibid.*

54. Rutland, *The Myth of the Plan*, p. 110 and note 20.

55. *Pravda*, December 6, 1971, quoted in Constantin A. Krylov, The Socialist Economy, p. 144.

56. Campaigns such as the "shock brigade," "socialist competition," or "socialist emulation"; criminal punishments for laziness, poor discipline, and lateness; and the "contract brigade system" attempted to induce higher productivity from the worker without addressing the allocation of labor. These were justified as the introduction of a socialist mindset, helping to bring about the experience of labor as "life's prime want."

57. Amy E. Randall, "Revolutionary Bolshevik Work: Stakhanovism in Retail Trade," *Russian Review*, Vol. 59, No. 3 (July 2000), pp. 425–441.

58. Gregory and Lazarev, *The Economics of Forced Labor*, p. 91. See also, Vladimir Shlapentokh, "The Stakhanovite Movement: Changing Perceptions over Fifty Years," *Journal of Contemporary History*, Vol. 23, No. 2, Bolshevism and the Socialist Left (April 1988), pp. 259–276.

59. J. Berliner, *Factory and Manager in the USSR*.

60. A. Volkov, "Profit and Personal Incentive," *Pravda*, November 14, 1965, p. 95, quoted in William B. Bland, *The Restoration of Capitalism in the Soviet Union*, 2nd ed. (1995).

61. For example, see Jim Powell, *FDR's Folly: How Roosevelt and His New Deal Prolonged the Great Depression* (New York: Crown Forum, 2003).

62. One is reminded that President Calvin Coolidge spoke about replacing the vicious circle with the charmed circle during the 1920s. "We have substituted for the vicious circle of increasing expenditures, increasing tax rates, and diminishing profits the charmed circle of diminishing expenditures, diminishing tax rates, and increasing profits." He believed that the way they had accomplished this was by replacing public spending with private spending. He argued that government had an "almost utter incapacity" to "deal directly with an industrial and commercial problem," and hence the path to prosperity was to reduce public provision of goods and services and government involvement in the economy. Taxes could then be reduced, allowing private industry to flourish. Hence, his charmed circle fed upon itself to allow for more and more tax reductions and greater output and prosperity. "Four times we have made a drastic revision of our internal revenue system, abolishing many taxes and substantially reducing almost all others. Each time the resulting stimulation to business has so increased taxable incomes and profits that a surplus has been produced. One third of the national debt has been paid, while much of the other two-thirds has been refunded at lower rates, and these savings of interest and constant economies have enabled us to repeat the satisfying process of more tax reductions. Under this sound and healthful encouragement the national income has increased nearly 50 per cent." Calvin Coolidge, speech at the White House, 1924, video at http://www.youtube.com/watch?v=5puwTrLRhmw (November 19, 2009); Calvin Coolidge, "Third Annual Message," December 8, 1925, at http://www.presidency.ucsb.edu/ws/index.php?pid=29566 (November 19, 2009); and Calvin Coolidge, "Sixth Annual Message," December 4, 1928, at http://www.presidency.ucsb.edu/ws/index.php?pid=29569 (November 19, 2009).

63. Norr, "Shchekino, pp. 141–169.

64. Norr relates how the planners weakened the experiment considerably due to their need to increase plan targets and restrict use of wage funds. By the late 1970s, it was all but dead. Then, suddenly interest reawakened in it. Norr argues that although the resumption of the experiment was serious, the statistics on how many firms participated are greatly exaggerated because many firms were only "partially" subject to the guidelines. Norr, "Shchekino."

65. *Ekonomicheskaya Gazeta*, No. 48 (December 1965), in *The Soviet Economic Reform: Main Features and Aims* (Moscow: Novosti Press Agency Publishing House, 1967) (emphasis added).

66. Krylov, *The Soviet Economy*.
67. Nikolai Lenin, *The Soviets at Work* (New York: Rand School of Social Science, 1918), p. 15.
68. Abram Bergson, *The Structure of Soviet Wages: A Study in Socialist Economics* (Cambridge, MA: Harvard University Press, 1944), p. 181.
69. Resolution, 10th Congress of the Russian Communist Party, 1921, quoted in Edgar Hardcastle, "Socialists Do Stand for Equality," *Socialist Standard*, August 1936, at http://marxists.org/archive/hardcastle/socialist_equality.htm (November 19, 2009).
70. Bergson, *The Structure of Soviet Wages*, p. 181.
71. Hardcastle, "Socialists Do Stand for Equality."
72. Bergson, *The Structure of Soviet Wages*, p. 178.
73. Rutland, *The Myth of the Plan*, pp. 151–152. See also Berliner, *Factory and Manager in the USSR*.
74. Ioffe and Maggs, *The Soviet Economic System*, p. 51.
75. It might be argued that Russia has a historical tendency toward sex discrimination and that this may be a cause, but such discrimination was harshly punishable, and wages were planned centrally. Hazard, *The Soviet System of Government*.
76. Data on Soviet gender inequality cited here can be found in Basile H. Kerblay, *Modern Soviet Society* (London: Methuen, 1983), especially pp. 127–129, 140. See also Gregory and Stuart, *Soviet Economic Structure and Performance*, pp. 273–274, and Samuel Hendel, ed., *The Soviet Crucible: Soviet Government in Theory and Practice* (New York: D. Van Nostrand Company, Inc., 1959), p. 412.
77. Hazard, *The Soviet System of Government*, p. 190.
78. Basile H. Kerblay, *Modern Soviet Society*, pp. 234–235. Most of these studies were of intergenerational mobility. There is an important distinction between income mobility and "social mobility," whether between generations or of a single individual or household. The United States is often accused of having low economic mobility, using statistics on "social mobility" that track changes in relative income of individuals over a long period. The countries which are said to have higher mobility tend to also have flatter income distributions, which means that the same increase in household income may produce a larger relative change, and therefore greater "social mobility." In absolute terms, income mobility is probably greater in the United States. See, for example, Gerald Auten and Geoffrey Gee, "Income Mobility in the United States: New Evidence from Income Tax Data," *National Tax Journal*, (June 2009), pp. 301-28
79. Levy and Peart, *Soviet Growth and American Experts*.
80. Lawrence R. Klein, *The Keynesian Revolution*, 1947, quoted in Richard M. Ebeling, *Monetary Central Planning and the State*, "Part 21: The Keynesian Revolution and the Early Critics of Keynes," 1998, at http://www.fff.org/freedom/0998b.asp.
81. Christina Romer and Jared Bernstein, "The Job Impact of the American Recovery and Reinvestment Plan," at http://otrans.3cdn.net/45593e8ecbd339d074_l3m6btlte.pdf.
82. James Sherk, "Reduced Investment and Job Creation to Blame for High Unemployment," Heritage Foundation *Backgrounder* No. 2349, December 9, 2009, at http://www.heritage.org/Research/Economy/bg2349.cfm.
83. Robert P. Murphy, "The Depression You've Never Heard Of: 1920-1921," *The Freeman*, Vol. 59, No. 10, December 2009, at http://www.thefreemanonline.org/featured/the-depression-youve-never-heard-of-1920-1921/.
84. "New Orleans ties with Washington, D.C., for lowest jobless rate in the country during November," *New Orleans Business News*, January 5, 2010, at http://www.nola.com/business/index.ssf/2010/01/new_orleans_ties_with_washingt.html.
85. "Owner optimism remains stuck at recession levels. The proximate cause is very weak consumer spending — better than a year ago, but that was pretty bad.... But the other major concern is the level of uncertainty being created by government, the usual source of uncertainty for the economy. The 'turbulence' created when Congress is in session is often debilitating, this year being one of the worst. Themes [include] 'tax more,' 'tax the rich even more,' 'VAT taxes,' higher energy costs due to Cap and Trade, mandates and taxes for health care, threats of 'Stimulus II,' incomprehensible deficits, and a huge pool of liquidity created by the Federal Reserve Bank that threatens price stability and higher interest rates. The list goes on and on. There is not much to look forward to, here, and good reason to 'keep your powder dry.' Uncertainly is the enemy of the

real economy as well as financial markets." "New Orleans ties with Washington, D.C., for lowest jobless rate in the country during November," *New Orleans Business News*, January 5, 2010, at http://www.nola.com/business/index.ssf/2010/01/new_orleans_ties_with_washingt.html.

86. Universidad Rey Juan Carlos, "Study of the Effect on Employment of Public Aid to Renewable Energy Sources," March 2009, at http://www.juandemariana.org/pdf/090327-employment-public-aid-renewable.pdf (December 7, 2009).

87. Of course, if importation is dangerous for reasons of foreign policy, this may change matters.

88. Kathie Kroll, "Amid Job Losses, Ohio Grows More Productive," Cleveland.com, April 11, 2009, at http://blog.cleveland.com/business/2009/04/amid_job_losses_ohio_grows_mor.html (November 19, 2009).

89. Margaret Thatcher, "Speech to National Union ("No Easy Options")," June 11, 1975, at http://www.margaretthatcher.org/speeches/displaydocument.asp?docid=102710. Details of Thatcher's economic policies can be found in Kent Matthews, Patrick Minford, Stephen Nickell, and Elhanan Helpman, "Mrs. Thatcher's Economic Policies 1979-1987," *Economic Policy*, Vol. 2, No. 5, The Conservative Revolution (October 1987), pp. 59–101.

90. This is why, although it took the average worker 1 hour and 20 minutes of work in 1919 to pay for a dozen eggs, a worker can now buy a dozen eggs with the income from only 5 minutes of work. Similarly, the Dallas Federal Reserve reports, "A pound of ground beef steadily declined from 30 minutes in 1919 to 23 minutes in 1950, 11 minutes in 1975 and 6 minutes in 1997. Paying for a dozen oranges required 1 hour 8 minutes of work in 1919. Now it takes less than 10 minutes, half what it did in 1950. The money price of a 3-pound fryer chicken rose from $1.23 in 1919 to $3.15 in 1997, but its cost in work time fell from 2 hours 37 minutes to just 14 minutes. The report shows that the same is true for housing, amenities, clothing, and vehicles. Hazard, *The Soviet System of Government*, p. 199.

91. Federal Reserve Bank of Dallas, "Time Well Spent," p. 4.

92. Tristram Hunt, "No Marx Without Engels," *History Today*, April 2009, at http://www.historytoday.com/MainArticle.aspx?m=33301&amid=30279138 (November 19, 2009).

93. Anita Chan and Robert A. Senser, "China's Troubled Workers," Foreign Affairs, Vol. 76, No. 2 (March/April 1997), pp. 104–117.

94. Some might argue that firms in a free market may indeed have "market power" to prevent a consumer from looking for a better price or from finding one. For example, it has been argued that a firm can tie the customer to a product (e.g., Microsoft's Windows operating system and its other software products) or by dominating the industry, locking in customers to its product (e.g., Microsoft Word). Another example cited is the firm that pushes out its rivals or locks the customer into a long-term contract to purchase only from it. However, in each of these situations the customer is not bound by law to remain with a single company (unless he has agreed for the period of a contract). Alternatives remain possible as long as the law does not mandate only one supplier.

95. Yves Guyot, *The Tyranny of Socialism* (London: Swan Sonnenschein and Co., 1894), Book II, chap. IV, at http://oll.libertyfund.org/index.php?option=com_staticxt&staticfile=show.php%3Ftitle=9 1&layout=html#chapter_21213.

96. Milton Friedman explained these unintended effects in an interview: --"[T]he minimum wage law is most properly described as a law saying employers must discriminate against people who have low skills. That's what the law says. The law says here's a man who would—has a skill which would justify a wage rate of $1.50, $2.00 an hour. You can't, you may not employ him. It's illegal. Because if you employ him you have to pay him $2.50. Well, what's the result? To employ him at $2.50 is to engage in charity. Now there's nothing wrong with charity. But most employers are not in a position where they can engage in that kind of charity. Thus the consequences of minimum wage rates have been almost wholly bad, to increase unemployment and to increase poverty. Moreover, the effects have been concentrated on the groups that the do-gooders would most like to help. The people who have been hurt most by minimum wage laws are the blacks." Milton Friedman, interview by Richard D. Heffner, "Living within our Means," WPIC Channel 11 (New York), December 7, 1975, at http://www.theopenmind.tv/searcharchive_episode_transcript.asp?id=494 (November 19, 2009).

97. Robert Pear, "In Health Bill for Everyone, Provisions for a Few," *The New York Times*, January 3, 2010, at http://www.nytimes.com/2010/01/04/health/policy/04health.html.1

98. Gerlinde Sinn and Hans-Werner Sinn, "Muffled Jumpstart," VOX, November 9, 2009, at http://www.voxeu.org/index.php?q=node/4177 (December 7, 2009).

99. Steven Horwitz, "Great Apprehensions, Prolonged Depression: Gauti Eggertsson on the 1930s," *Econ Journal Watch*, Vol. 6, No. 3 (September 2009), pp. 313–336, at http://www.aier.org/aier/publications/ejw_com_sep09_horwitz.pdf (December 7, 2009).

100. Karl Kautsky, *The Social Revolution* (Chicago: Charles H. Kerr & Company, 1916), pp. 135–137, at http://www.marxists.org/archive/kautsky/1902/socrev/pt2-1.htm.

101. There is a significant amount of evidence that the standard of living of workers and (even more so) peasants under Mao were far lower than before the revolution. For example, "food supply per head, even in the best years of the 1950s, had only just recovered to the 1933 level, and since then has been below it, in 1960–63 far below it." Colin Clark, "Economic Development in Communist China," *The Journal of Political Economy*, Vol. 84, No. 2 (April 1976), pp. 239–264. -- One Western observer who had lived in China prior to the revolution, travelled China just after Mao's death (in the late 1970s) and wrote that, to his surprise he found, "the prevalent lifestyle, in both cities and rural areas, had in fact declined in comparison with the past." -- However, although real wages were almost certainly lower prior to the introduction of the market, the actual working conditions in the factory may have to be described as "different" rather than better or worse. Just as in the Soviet Union, life was to be labor-centered. The report notes that the huge state factory the observer visited "had a hospital of 400 beds, kindergartens, five primary schools, three middle schools, recreation clubs, and so on. The workers lived, worked, and died all in the same place." Although on paper these conditions sound good, the hospital was unclean, had only the most primitive of equipment, and the primary surgeon was aged and deaf. Although the new foreign factories can leverage the power of the state to prevent workers from quitting, the old communist factories were like whole cities run by the state itself. —Franz Michael, "China Since Mao: A Travel Report," *Asian Affairs*, Vol. 5, No. 6 (July–August 1978), pp. 343–360.

102. Christian Purefoy, "Guinness' Success Highlights Opportunity in Nigeria, Africa," CNN, August 12, 2009, at http://www.cnn.com/2009/WORLD/africa/08/11/nigeria.success.guinness/index.html (November 19, 2009).

103. Economists recognize this use of wages, although most models are not capable of taking it into account. For a paper that discusses this role of wages, see A. L. Gitlow, "Wages and the Allocation of Employment," *Southern Economics Journal*, Vol. 21, No. 1 (July 1954), pp. 62–83.

CHAPTER 3. THE HOLISTIC TARGET: THE VALUE OF PROFIT AND LOSS FOR THE FIRM

INTRODUCTION

The profit motive often gets a bad name. Businessmen are seen as greedy and immoral for "putting profits above people" or "only thinking of the bottom line." The drive for profit is seen as distorting the ability of producers to serve the common good or even the good of the customer. In this view, when something is really important and moral, the profit motive should be restrained, and the service should be provided without regard to profit or profitability.

In 2009, U.S. Speaker of the House Nancy Pelosi called profit-seeking private health insurance providers "immoral villains."[1] President Barack Obama told the press, "If you take some of the profit motive out...you can get an even better deal."[2] He also isolated the profit motive as the culprit when asked about health care decisions. An NBC News reporter told the President that if the new health care reform bill passed, some were concerned that a governmental advisory committee would be making decisions about which treatments they could have. President Obama replied that under the current system, "The decisions, right now, are being made by insurance companies. People are having bad experiences because they know that recommendations are coming from people who have a profit motive."[3]

The profit motive is disparaged, but it is usually left unexamined. Does the profit motive drive businesses to overcharge for a shoddy product, or does it guide them to serve the customer well? Those that criticize the profit motive also do not explain or examine what would replace it if it were removed. Profit and loss have critical functions that altruism and good intentions cannot perform. Something must replace profit as a guiding force and an indicator of performance.

Profit and loss play an important role in guiding how a firm serves its customers. Profit guides producers toward the ends that best serve the consumer because it is the consumer that produces this profit. Similarly, loss is the revenge that the consumer takes upon those that do not serve his needs well. When profit and loss are taken out of the equation entirely, as with public provision of goods, the consumer is no longer in charge. Even if the public firm would like to serve the consumer, it needs the signals that profit and loss provide. The full implications of this became clear when profit and loss were removed entirely from regular production in the Soviet Union.

THE SOCIALIST ARGUMENT

> Upon surplus value live all the parasites who are bred by the capitalist system. — *The ABC of Communism*[4]

> As capitalist, he is only capital personified. His soul is the soul of capital. But capital has one single life impulse, the tendency to create value and surplus-value, to make its constant factor, the means of production, absorb the greatest possible amount of surplus-labour. Capital is dead labour, that, vampire-like, only lives by sucking living labour, and lives the more, the more labour it sucks. — Marx[5]

The economics of Marx were fundamentally different from the classical non-Marxist economists, such as Adam Smith and Carl Menger. Adam Smith wrote in *The Wealth of Nations* that the common good is served when the individual pursues his own private interest. He said, "It is not from the benevolence of the butcher, the brewer, or the baker that we expect our dinner, but from their regard to their own interest,"[6] a wonderful insight, if true. When men selfishly try to obtain wealth, they end up actually serving others. The pursuit of profit guides an entrepreneur to serve his customers; The reason for this, Smith explained, is that the baker bakes the bread in order to make profit, but he can only make profit if people want to buy the bread at the price he offers it. He can only sell it to these customers if he can produce it at a low enough cost that the price is a bargain for the customers. He only makes a profit to the extent that he reduces his costs below that which the customer is willing to pay. If the consumer can make bread more cheaply, he will not buy it from the baker; he will make it himself.

Marx did not see it this way. For Marx, profit was not earned by providing something to the customer that he could not produce at as low a cost himself—by providing value to the customer. Value, for Marx, came only from labor, and profit was taken at the expense of labor. Marx came to this conclusion because he took the subjective valuation of goods, which he called "use-value," out of his calculation. After omitting use-value, he was left with only exchange-value, which he based only on the labor involved in production. To Marx, the capitalist exploits the worker by taking some of this value in the form of profits. Therefore, the baker has not provided a service to the consumer by baking bread but has exploited the labor required to make the bread.

Workers should receive the full value of their product. (Of course, if the bakery is owned and employed by the same person, no exploitation is possible.)

For Marx, the purchase of consumer goods was not a voluntary trade of money for goods. It was an exploitation by the capitalist of labor and of the consumer. A greedy profit-seeking businessman monopolizes the market and uses his position to force low-quality products on consumers at a high price. They extract value from the defenseless worker and pay such low wages that the purchase prices of the goods leave the lower classes with nothing. In the *Manifesto of the Socialist League*, in 1885, William Morris and E. Belford Bax described the socialist view of how profit-seeking by firms hurts the consumer:

> The manufacturer produces to sell at a profit to the broker or factor, who in his turn makes a profit out of his dealings with the merchant, who again sells for a profit to the retailer, who must make his profit out of the general public, aided by various degrees of fraud and adulteration and the ignorance of the value and quality of goods to which this system has reduced the consumer.[7]

According to Morris and Bax, profit was taken at the expense of the consumer, and profit-seeking led firms to "adulterate" their products, and take advantage of the ignorance of the consumer. Socialism would replace this system driven by greed with one arranged by the people for the benefit of the whole society. It would put an end to this bitter struggle of "every man for himself."

> Socialism would inculcate as the goal of life something other than the *Bourgeois* gospel of success—acquisition for acquisition's sake. The selfish individualist *bourgeois* doctrine of life is for every man to aim at becoming a capitalist, large or small; and when he has attained to this, to buy his labour in the cheapest market (exploit the proletariat), and sell the resulting commodity in the dearest (i.e., overcharge the consumer).[8]

Overcharging the consumer and producing less than the socially efficient amount were two common accusations made by socialists against profit-seeking firms. There was also a general distrust of those seeking profits, and an assumption that if profit could be eliminated as a motive, firms would be more likely to serve the social interest. This belief was once widespread, even outside Marxist circles. At this time, those arguing this case sincerely reasoned that profit as a motive could, and perhaps should, be eliminated in firms across the whole economy. United States President Franklin Roosevelt's close advisor Rexford Tugwell wrote about the potential for planning in America. He argued that "market cornering and supply limitation" were among the favorite ways of business to make profit, and therefore it might be better if firms did not work for profit. Profits, he argued, "belong to a speculative age" and a new kind of enterprise could emerge that would not depend upon them:

> It would be untrue to maintain that profits do not supply one kind of motive for economic activity. Business, as we know it, is perhaps chiefly interested in them. This is to emphasize, however, the speculative rather than the disciplined aspects of production. *To say that this is one of the institutions which will have to be abandoned if planning is to become socially effective, is to make a sharp distinction among the effects to be expected from dependence upon alternative motives* [italics mine]. There is no doubt that the hope of great gains induces enterprise of a sort; and if these are disestablished, a certain kind of enterprise will disappear. The question is whether we cannot well

afford to dispense with it. It seems credible that we can. Industries now mature can be seen to operate without it; and new ones might be created and might grow from sheer workman-like proclivities and without the hope of speculative gains. [Italics mine.] [9]

This was an argument both about the individual enterprise running more efficiently without the profit motive, as well as an argument about the economy as a whole—which Tugwell argued would be served better to have less "speculation" and more "discipline" in production. (See Chapter 4.)

Many people still argue that firms produce shoddy products, overcharge, or force unnecessary products on an easily fooled public. Some even argue that advertising and aggressive marketing force products on the consumer that he does not desire at all. Nonprofits are respected because they produce *for the people*, without regard to profitability. Goods and services, such as health care, housing, child care, and education (but in most circumstances not food), are considered *so vital* that they should not be left in the hands of profit-seeking firms. Many argue that if private nonprofits cannot supply these necessities, the government ought to provide them so that profit is not placed ahead of the needs of the people.

The Soviet Experience

Soviet firms were allowed to produce "for the people" and not forced or driven to produce for profit motive. They could create high-quality products without concern over the higher cost. However, quality was lower, not higher. Soviet consumer goods were of notoriously low quality. Trotsky admitted in 1936:

> A unique law of Soviet industry may be formulated thus: commodities are as a general rule worse the nearer they stand to the mass consumer. In the textile industry, according to *Pravda*, "there is a shamefully large percentage of defective goods, poverty of selection, predominance of low grades." Complaints of the bad quality of articles of wide consumption appear periodically in the press: "clumsy ironware"; "ugly furniture, badly put together and carelessly finished"; "you can't find decent buttons"; "the system of social food supply works absolutely unsatisfactorily." And so on endlessly.[10]

In 1965, another Marxist told of the same phenomenon:

> Goods of shocking quality are turned out for the mass market. As an example *Izvestia* of 4th June criticised the nylon stockings produced in Russia. They were baggy and drab, came in odd sizes, were sold in unmatched pairs and a peculiar colour. Shoddy goods are piling up in the shops which are practically unsaleable to the tune of hundreds of millions of pounds.[11]

The reasons for this are clear. It was not because the workers simply did not care to produce high-quality consumer goods. Planners encountered problems of inefficiency from the beginning. Many of these problems stemmed from the shortage of inputs that factories faced. Managers also had to depend upon the planners to know what to make, and how. In addition, the hierarchical management structure meant that managers answered to their superiors, rather than to the customer. One problem with this arrangement was that there was no incentive to tell the truth. The following joke captures this problem well:

> The commissar went out to the farm, their state farm, and stopped one of the workers and asked him how things were, any complaints?
>
> The worker said, "Oh, no, sir. No, never heard anyone complain."
>
> "Well," he said, "how are the crops?"
>
> "Oh, the crops are wonderful."
>
> "What about the potato harvest?"
>
> "Oh, the potatoes.... Comrade," he said, "if we piled the potatoes up in one pile, they would reach the foot of God."
>
> And the commissar said, "This is the Soviet Union. There is no God."
>
> He said, "That's all right. There are no potatoes."[12]

This was a real problem. One reason for the lower efficiency of state farms, compared with private plots, was that workers and managers had a motivation to *convince* their superiors that they had produced, rather than a motivation to *actually* produce. Despite the fear of socialists that profit-seeking firms dupe their customers, firms in a market economy face competition, and the carrot of profit and the stick of loss keep them in line. Private firms must please their customers, or they will go out of business. Firms in the Soviet economy needed only to deceive their superiors into believing that they were doing their best, and their superiors had no reliable way of knowing whether it was true.

Joseph Berliner called this faking "simulation," and he named several ways that Soviet managers and workers did this. For example, managers would simulate cost cutting by cutting corners on quality. Managers would also simulate plan fulfillment by making a lot of the easiest products to produce at the expense of producing the more difficult ones, even though they were expected to make both. Workers would simulate working by standing near their equipment but not actually doing anything. As the old Soviet joke went, "We pretend to work; they pretend to pay us."

Firm managers would also inflate their costs and lobby their superiors for the easiest possible plan so that they could be sure they would achieve it, earn bonuses, and not be punished. Even more important, the plan for the following year would be based upon the current year, so that to limit future pain a manager had to obtain the lowest possible targets. Although the firm is the center of our focus, it was not only the firm that was given a plan to fulfill in the Soviet Union, and anyone given a plan faced the same incentives. Logan Robinson recounted his experience at Leningrad State University law school, where even students were given a plan:

> After one had made contact with the faculty, the next issue on the academic agenda was the Scientific Plan. Every person in the Soviet Union is supposed to have a plan. No organization is too small, no individual too insignificant, to be without a plan.... The Scientific Plan is the document that outlines one's research and scholarly objectives for the coming academic year. It also details what interviews the scholar would like to have, what study trips to other cities will be necessary, and to what archives or other Soviet institutions the scholar needs access. At the end of the year, there is another Soviet ritual called "plan fulfillment." Every organization from machine shops to lawyer's offices must go through this year-end accounting and report to higher authorities, detailing to what extent they have "fulfilled the plan." I too would be expected to prepare an *ochet*, or accounting, at the end of the school year. This can lead to endless inefficiencies, as rewards in all types of endeavor are based not so much on actual output as on plan fulfillment.

Article 152-1 of the Russian Criminal Code makes "padding" your plan an anti-state action punishable by up to three years in prison, but few Soviets I knew lost much sleep over this. They knew that they would never have to falsify their *ochet* if from the first their plan's target was easily reached. The lower the goals set, the higher the chances of fulfilling or slightly overfulfilling your plan. For a factory or individual to really work at full capacity is to court disaster. The next year's targets will be based on this past production and set even higher. The factory or individual will eventually fail to fulfill the plan and suffer for it. The wise Soviet citizen knows a thousand tricks to keep his quota low and his plan easily fulfilled.[13]

The plan for an individual firm was created, with some input from the firm and the economic ministry in charge of it, by the planning agencies based on the needs of society as a whole. Because the resources needed by some firms were made by other firms, and the economy was in this way interconnected, the individual enterprise could not have too much leeway in determining what it was to produce. The central planning board set output *targets* so that enterprises could meet the input needs of other firms and produce for consumers. Each target in turn must be expressed in terms of an *indicator*. For example, a factory might have output targets naming the amount of different types of nails that it must produce, and the indicator might be "tons." These targets are critical to any public-sector project, whether it is in a completely socialist economy or is just a public-sector firm in a market economy. Something must replace profit as a guiding force, and targets are used for this purpose. This is an important lesson from the socialist experiment.

The plan for firms in the Soviet Union was very detailed, directing the enterprise which inputs it should obtain and from where.[14] This was to ensure that the inputs of one firm would be fulfilled by outputs from other firms. Because it was set in advance, the firm's plan could become outdated, but the firms were expected to follow it even if conditions changed. This was true for all industries, including agriculture. For example, even if a potato harvest would be minimally productive in a given year, a farm could not choose to focus instead on the wheat harvest if the planning agency had directed it to produce potatoes.[15]

Firm managers were not only directed where to obtain inputs and what outputs to produce, they were also given guidance on how much and how to reduce costs, how much to pay in wages and material incentives, and on nearly every other detail of management. This was necessary because there was no external pressure to minimize costs; the firm's losses would be subsidized by the state. In a system of private property, when an individual owns a business his budget-constraint is "hard," meaning that when he runs out of money he will have to liquidate his resources; he will not be saved from competition or loss. In the Soviet Union, firm managers faced a "soft budget constraint."[16] Losses would never mean liquidation; at worst managers would face punishment, but often losses were unpunished, and if the plan was fulfilled, even rewarded.

In a market economy, firms can to some degree see what is profitable to produce, and what would be a foolish endeavor. If they do not see it before it causes them losses, they can at least learn from their mistakes. In the Soviet Union, firm managers had no other guidance on what to produce or how than that given by the state. Because the firm did not set its own price and customers could not freely take their business elsewhere, firms could not be guided by profit and loss and could not respond to the customer.

Instead, Soviet firms had to rely upon the plan to detail what to produce and how. A 1963 Soviet journal article described the 70,000 page long (91 volumes) plan for the Novo Lipetsk steel mill. The article explains, "Literally everything is anticipated in these blueprints, the emplacement of each nail, lamp or washstand. Only one aspect of the project is not considered at all: its economic effectiveness."[17]

The bonuses, or "premiums," that rewarded good work and plan fulfilment did encourage effort. However, they guided managers and workers to fulfil the targets that the planners chose, rather than to please the actual consumer. No set of targets or rules could capture all of the quality considerations that a customer might notice. Planners also had trouble controlling costs in Soviet firms using targets and premiums. Soviet economist Evgenii Liberman explained, "premiums are paid only on condition that the plan of cost of production is fulfilled," but "[t]he absence of a direct connection between the magnitude of the premium and the magnitude of the economy due to cost reduction, in our opinion, weakens the importance of the index of cost of production."[18]

Directly connecting the magnitude of cost and the magnitude of premium was not possible given the plethora of indicators. The planned profit or loss for the firm was also an indicator. The main purpose of the indicator was to aid in cost reduction, especially for new products, and to ensure that the products were being marketed and sold. Yet this use of "profit" as an indicator was very different from the use in market societies. It was only one among many indicators, and plan fulfillment was still paramount. Output targets were to be considered first, and premiums might still be earned even with underfulfillment of the profit and cost targets.[19] The profit and cost targets were also distorted by centrally set prices. (See Chapter 6.)

Because of the need to fulfill all of these targets, managers were left powerless to actually run the firm in the most efficient way that they could devise. Managers might see what their customers required, where to obtain inputs to produce those items, how many of each to produce, and of what quality, but mandated targets prevented them from adjusting production.

The selection of appropriate targets and indicators for the firms was critical. Originally planners used a gross output index based on 1926–1927 prices. However, managers diverted resources from finishing products toward amassing greater inventories of half-finished goods (to more easily increase gross output) and focused on those products with the highest 1926–1927 prices, despite the changes in technology and the new products that had been introduced since then.[20] The gross output target system was found faulty because the products that the planners most desired were not being prioritized. The primary indicator used after that, even though it caused many problems of its own, was "tons," though the output target in tons was supplemented with a variety of other targets.

A significant lesson from the Soviet experience is that no set of targets could guide the firm as well as profit and loss are able. Without the central role of the profit motive, planners were forced to use a hodgepodge of targets and regulations linked to various special premiums. Not everything could be included in the production plan, and anything that was left out could be exploited. If total output was set in tons, but not product quantity, the firm would produce fewer, larger products.[21] If quantity was set and one dimension of size was set, but not all dimensions, costs could be cut by making a narrower or flimsier product.[22] In summary, "a measure of effectiveness may incorrectly become a surrogate for the objective itself."[23] The absurdity of the response to targets became something of a running joke among critics of the Soviet system, and a famous cartoon in the Soviet journal *Krokodil* summed up the central issue: a factory manager stood proudly next to a gigantic nail, and the caption read 'The Month's Plan Fulfilled'.

All quality measurements cannot be contained in one set of criteria. The only measure that can take all the various aspects of preference, efficiency, and quality into account is a measure of total value: a monetary measure. Profit works as a holistic measure because it accounts for all aspects: quality, desirability of the particular product, the cost compared to other desirable products, and so forth. Profit allows the consumer to determine if a product is worthwhile. No set of targets and indicators can encompass all of those things. Planners added more and more targets, as if adding more and more sides to a polyhedron in the false hope of making it perfectly spherical.

> An influential group of conservatives among the Soviet planning executives and economists, while agreeing that the present system of planning does not work satisfactorily, attribute its failures to insufficient detail of information received and orders issued by the planners. They argue accordingly that the use of prices as the basis for decisions should be further restricted and replaced by ever more detailed calculations in physical terms. Decisions concerning the assortment and quality of the product which are still largely left to the managers should be taken away from them.[24]

Planners were trying to guide the firms with targets to produce exactly what the consumer wanted—yet perfect information and perfect ability to convey such information and motivate firms to use it would be required for this to be possible.

The plan, with its targets and premiums, attempted to meet consumer demand by providing a list of assorted goods for the enterprise to fill and doling out premiums according to how well the balance of goods was completed. The planners, of course, did not actually know consumer demand.[25] If the firms had been able to respond to its own customer's requests, instead of the plan targets, it would have been able to fulfill demand. Alec Nove summarizes the whole situation:

> Some critics consider that these problems arise primarily out of the lack of common interest between planners and managers.... Such considerations are im-

portant. This, however, misses the essential point, which is that in most instances *the center does not know* just what it is that needs doing, in disaggregated detail, while the management *cannot* know what it is that society needs unless the center informs it.... The attempt by management to obey plan-instructions, which gives rise to many distortions, is not evidence of lack of common interest; if anything it is the reverse. The trouble lies in the near impossibility of drafting microeconomic instructions in such a way that even the most well-meaning manager will not be misled. It is no use asserting that he should satisfy his customers by making the things they want. If he did that, he would be producing for his customers and not to the orders of his superiors; in other words, output would be determined by the market. It is precisely this type of reform that has been rejected, so far. Yet, paradoxically, the Soviet planners *do* want output to match user requirements. The whole contradiction of the reform measures to date is herein contained.[26]

Planners did not enact that kind of reform, because it would mean reforming the planned economy into a market economy. Profit drive would be used to allow firms to serve the customer in a decentralized manner, and in order to ensure efficiency, loss would have to be allowed to shut down firms that did not serve the customer. Yet this would mean allowing the market to function, not the plan. Hence, the Soviet government struggled with the fact that only profit could guide firms to produce what was needed, while the fundamental socialist antipathy to profit prevented use of this "target." Once again, this is true for one public firm as much as for an entire economy.

After the death of Stalin, and certainly by the reforms of the 1960s, economists writing for Soviet journals and even for *Pravda* admitted the necessity and advantages of using profit as an indicator: "Increase of profit under socialism is one of the means for the achievement of the aim of socialist production—to satisfy most fully the requirements of the people."[27] V. Trapeznikov wrote in *Pravda* in 1964, "A criterion that characterises to the greatest degree the operation of the enterprise...is profit."[28] Another Soviet economist argued in *Pravda*, "Profit serves as the most generalising criterion of the enterprise's entire activity."[29] "Profit generalises all aspects of operation," wrote the reform economist Evgenii Liberman in 1965.[30] At this time, Soviet economists and reformers also began to see that economic laws were universal and immutable. One wrote in *Pravda* in 1964:

> The problem which we now face in determining if profit should be the basic index in judging the work of an enterprise can be attributed in no small way to the lack of regard for the immutable law of economic construction during the Stalin era. This immutable law, regardless of the system under which it operates, is universal; an economy must produce more than is expended on production; and it is this principle, however unheeded it has been in the past, that theoretically provides the foundation for the acceptance of profits today in the Soviet Union.[31]

Soviet economists had argued in the past that, while the economy overall must be profitable, individual enterprises need not. However, by this time, many economists were beginning to see that this was an unworkable goal. Overall profitability of the economy was not possible without profit and loss accounting of the individual economic units.

Liberman explained the necessity of the congruence of the firm's goals and the economy's overall goals in the descriptions of his proposed 1965 reforms. "The 1965 economic reform embodies one of the primary principles of the socialist economy: what is of benefit to society must be of benefit to each enterprise."[32] However, his blueprint for reform was never enacted. The watered down 1965 reforms fell far short of these ideals.

LESSONS

Just as the socialists argued that, under capitalism, profit is the sole driver of business decisions, Adam Smith also argued that profit drove the producer. However, he argued that this was a good thing because it meant that the consumer would be served. He explained in *The Wealth of Nations* that the common good is served when the individual pursues his own private interest. In the market system, when men selfishly try to obtain wealth they end up serving others.

The baker bakes to make profit, but he can only make profit if people desire the bread, and if he can produce it for them at a low enough cost. The customers are made better off because they can purchase bread more cheaply than by baking it themselves. The baker is also better off. When both people are made better off by an exchange, these are called "gains from trade." Each person in the exchange values what they receive more than what they give up; this is why they trade.

Marx did not believe in gains from trade. His "labor theory of value" argued that two goods are exchanged because they are of *equal* value. This is how he deduced that the "objective value" must be the labor effort put into making the product. However, there are several reasons why both parties *can* gain from an exchange. One is that division of labor enables one person to make a product at a lower cost than another person can make it,[33] in which case the latter benefits from buying the product rather than making it himself. For example, most people find buying a loaf of bread easier (and less expensive) than baking bread themselves; the baker can do it cheaply because he can focus all his time and resources on baking, and purchase everything else from others in the market. Another reason is that each person may have a "comparative advantage" in certain types of work. One is a skilled baker, a second is a skilled carpenter, and a third is a skilled electrician. Rather than each person trying to do everything himself, he can gain more by concentrating his work in doing what he is better at (or has the resources to do) and then trading his surplus production for other needed and desired goods and services. Finally, people value things differently; the value they attach to the product is subjective.

Alec Nove explains how Soviet economists slowly came to realize the existence of subjective valuation and that their idea of "use-value" was not good enough. Use-value only admitted that the products must be of *some* use to the consumer and based the price only on the value of the labor involved in production. Nove explains:

> If two goods, both of some use, are unequally valued by the user, though they cost the same to produce, for every practical purpose in any type of economy their value is surely unequal. In fact, of course, this state of affairs could not subsist in a market economy [because prices would adjust based on demand]. To a Western economist this is the merest common sense. Yet it required long (and to some ex-

tent still inconclusive) argument to establish the point in the USSR and to draw conclusions from it applicable to pricing.[34]

Once subjective valuation is conceded, the idea that there is an objective amount of value—based on labor or anything else—must be dismissed. If this is the case, then profit cannot be reduced to exploitation. At the same time, it becomes clear that profit is only made when the exchange benefits both parties (because they subjectively value the things they are exchanging less than what they getting). From this perspective, profit cannot be seen as wholly bad.

Furthermore, Nove conjectures, "Probably in the end it will be found that demand reacts back on the degree of social necessity of the labor expended in meeting it."[35] By this he means that, just as the Soviet economists had to come to terms with the use of profit for helping to evaluate efficiency and the value of capital (both of which they translated into labor units), they would ultimately have to accept the importance of subjective valuation, and attempt to capture that in labor units as well. In other words, Soviet economists were beginning to accept consumer sovereignty.

However, the consumer cannot guide the firm if profit and loss are absent. Without profit to guide firms, public firms must be given instructions — whether they are firms in a planned economy or public firms in a market economy. In the United Kingdom targets (sometimes called "performance indicators") are frequently used in the public sector, and issues surrounding their use have entered public as well as academic discussion. For example, the use of targets to guide police has been criticized for distorting police priorities; the use of targets by NHS hospitals has been blamed for distorting the priorities of nurses and hospital administrators; and in response to complaints, local governments have recently been promised a reduction in targets. As in the Soviet Union, reforms have modified the number of targets and the indicators used, however issues with target use have remained.

The issue of target use in the public sector has also been discussed by the Organization for Economic Cooperation and Development (OECD). In the OECD publication, "Modernising Government: The Way Forward," some of the issues are identified: The problem of setting targets too low or too high, and the issue of how many targets to use. Too many targets, the OECD argues, may create information overload and make it difficult to select priorities; too few targets may create distortion effects. Distortion effects may include managers focusing on the most achievable targets, or even presenting misleading information.

Targets may also be used by government to guide firms in the private sector. For example, the government may set a cost-cutting target, or a floor or ceiling on the use of inputs or the amount of goods or services provided. In the UK, privatized water utilities were given targets for water leak reduction (perhaps because competition did not exist in the sector, given a "natural monopoly" by utilities over their local area). Just as in the Soviet Union, such targets have not proven as effective as the constraints of competition and loss: To get around the target, the water utilities reduced water pressure, thereby "simulating" the achieving of the target — providing a lower quality of product, but technically filling the target.

Just as with these "privatized" water utilities that were given targets by government, it is important to remember that when either profit or loss is removed from the equation, the results can be as bad or worse than when both are missing. This is probably the cause of many of the problems with the heavily regulated, but nominally private, health care system in the United States. Subsidized firms, and firms that can depend upon a government bailout, are often just as bad for the consumer as ones that face neither profit nor loss.

If firms in the health care industry can depend upon government to protect them from competition, subsidize demand, and control prices of inputs so that they never have to fear loss, they have a softened budget constraint. These firms tend to lobby for, not against, regulation as is often assumed. Economists call it "regulatory capture" when firms seek regulations because the regulations will give them an advantage over their competition. Without fear of loss, the need to serve the customer is dramatically reduced and the pressure to minimize costs is removed entirely. Because they need not fear loss, firms are also able to exploit the consumer through fraud and "adulteration" of products. Although the profit motive may still lead to some innovation of new products and other things beneficial for the consumer, loss is a necessary corollary to profit for true efficiency.

Firms that do not fear loss may blend in with truly private companies, and the profit motive may be blamed for the results. For example, Burton Folsom Jr., takes on the widespread impression of early big business in America as "exploiters" of the consumer in his book *The Myth of the Robber Barons*.[36] The author takes the reader on a tour of the steamship industry, railroads, iron, steel, and oil, and shows that the completely private companies—e.g., those run by Vanderbilt, James Hill, and Rockefeller—made huge technological advances and offered extremely low prices to the consumer. They made the American people significantly better off.

Although it is commonly believed that subsidies were required for the vast investment in railroad tracks, in fact private industry was already investing when Congress stepped in, and prices were falling. The "exploitation" of the consumer came from the subsidized firms, such as the Union Pacific and Northern Pacific railroads, which charged higher rates than James Hill's private railroad, while simultaneously costing the people money in taxes. The subsidized railroads were inefficient because they had soft budget constraints. They could depend on subsidies, so they did. The targets and regulations of the congressional charters distorted their actions: For example, they claimed subsidies for mileage and therefore laid long and inefficient tracks. When their costs increased and they had trouble competing, they returned to Washington to ask for more money and ran the names of private businessmen such as James Hill through the mud.

However, the private railroads were a huge boon for other businesses, and allowed the regular person to travel the country at will for the first time. It was the subsidized railroads that were built poorly and charged the consumer more. As Folsom points out, shoddy construction led to high fixed costs and lower chances for profit, so the subsidized railroads raised their rates. The rate hikes caused public outcry, especially when different lines charged different rates. The subsidized lines were charging more than James Hill's private Great Northern line, and public debate focused on this. The managers of the subsidized railroads did not want to innovate and compete with James Hill, and they did not want to lose public support and lose their funding. So, they acted as "political entrepreneurs" and went to Washington, instead of acting as market entrepreneurs like Hill.

Congress responded to their requests. They passed laws regulating price-setting in the industry, and they created the Interstate Commerce Commission. Rather than end the subsidies to Union and Northern Pacific and allow private companies to compete with James Hill for the considerable potential profit, the government's Interstate Commerce Commission prosecuted him for "rate discrimination." Meanwhile, socialists and others accused him of being a "robber baron" and called for nationalization of the railroads.[37]

John D. Rockefeller is often accused of having been a "robber baron." Some argue that he colluded with Vanderbilt when Vanderbilt's railroad gave discounts to Standard Oil for delivery. However, as Folsom reminds readers, Vanderbilt offered the same discount to anyone else who could provide the railroad with that same amount of business. It was simply a volume discount. Nobody else could offer the same volume of business because no one else was as *efficient*. Rockefeller was able to capitalize on his success, but his success was a *result* of his efficiency. Only by continuing to improve his operations was he able to build on this success and maintain his dominant position.

Folsom points out that before Rockefeller's Standard Oil, most oil producers wasted more oil than they sold, and rivers ran with wasted (dangerous and polluting) oil. Rockefeller's innovation was to refine the oil and create hundreds of products from it, wasting almost none of it. His efficiencies and the discount from Vanderbilt allowed Rockefeller to cut the price of kerosene from 58 to 26 cents per gallon by 1870 and to keep cutting it each year after that. While "before 1870 only the rich could afford whale oil and candles," "[b]y the 1870s, with the drop in the price of kerosene, middle and working class people all over the nation could afford the one cent an hour that it cost to light their homes at night," allowing many Americans for the first time to work and read at night.

Recently a local London newspaper ran a story on John Bloom, a businessman who was also seen by many in a negative light for chasing profits. Yet, like those called "robber barons," in pursuit of profits he served the people. The story begins,

> For a large part of the 1960s, John Bloom was cast as little better than a crook—
> an East End wiseboy businessman who got rich quick, then crashed spectacularly.

But history has shown Bloom in a rather more sympathetic light—as a man who broke open the price fixing, cartels and complacency of British business. For good or bad, Bloom ushered in the era of consumer goods affordable for working people. And John Bloom is the main reason why, today, there is a washing machine in almost every British home.[38]

I am not sure why, for this author, it might be "bad" to have ushered in affordable washing machines (perhaps they corrupt the soul), but it was in seeking profits that John Bloom succeeded in doing this. All throughout his career, Bloom chased profits. He introduced innovations to undercut his competitors and reinvested the proceeds to expand. He served in the Royal Air Force and it was there that he undertook his first business venture. His fellow airmen took buses back to London for the weekend. A friend of Bloom's ran a fleet of buses, and together they undercut the local bus company. Instead of accepting this friendly competition, the incumbent bus company tried to sue, but the judge could see no crime. "It's no sin to make a profit," he said, and John Bloom made this his motto; he wrote a book many years later, using it as the title.

In between, he did just as Rockefeller and the other "robber barons" did. He chased profits by cutting costs and undercutting the prices of his competitors. In so doing he ushered in an age of abundance in his industry. His first innovation allowed him to chop the price of washing machines in half. But that was only the start. He went into heating systems and brought comfort to millions of homes. A 1961 *Time* magazine article tells readers, "In a land where only 3% of the houses are centrally heated, Bloom's Rolls Razor Ltd. has begun to sell thermostatically controlled heating units at prices that would warm even a Scotsman's heart. For a three-bedroom house, the Bloom heater (which electrically heats light oil) costs about $400, one third as much as competing coal or oil systems."[39]

Perhaps because seeking profit is seen as morally questionable, or simply because incumbent firms do not like the extra work of competing, these private entrepreneurs who have brought such prosperity are made out as villains and crooks. Meanwhile those in charge of subsidized or nationalized firms that offer little to the people, and nothing to technological advancement, are accepted as performing a public service.

Firms in the public sector are occasionally found to be so inefficient that they are privatized. However, "privatization," the way that it is often carried out, may not lead to the efficiencies of Rockefeller or John Bloom. When publicly supplied goods are privatized, it often amounts to simply purchasing the goods through private contractors, who still can depend on the generosity of the government—which has a soft budget constraint. If a contractor faces no real competition and can depend on the government contract, it may have "socialized losses," but "privatized profits." Essentially, the firm has none of the discipline of the fear of loss and the hard budget constraint, but can retain any profits that accrue.

This kind of "privatization" tends to give the market a bad name. Private companies fail the consumer, and the profit motive is blamed, when in fact it is the distortion of the government subsidy that causes the failure.

The government often fails as a consumer in these situations. Rather than threatening to abandon the company as a customer and thereby providing that market pressure, the government caves in to the wishes of the companies (and perhaps their campaign contributions). A recent *Washington Post* article described how the U.S. government has been giving in to the demands of Internet companies rather than forcing them to compete with each other for government contracts. The article quoted Cindy Cohn, legal director for the Electronic Frontier Foundation, a privacy group: "It appears that these companies are forcing the government to lower the privacy protections that the government had promised the American people," rather than government "requiring companies to raise the level of privacy protection if they want government contracts."[40]

Conclusion

Profit is the only measure that can direct the firms to produce what the customer wants and to do it well. In equal measure, loss directs the firm away from inefficiency by providing an incentive to reduce costs. The soft budget constraint on socialist firms entirely removes these constraints. Targets have as little ability to keep costs down as they do to fulfill consumer demand in the place of profit.

Rather than demonize the profit motive, as a society we should appreciate the holistic, well-rounded motivator that it actually is. Loss forces out undesirable products and curbs wasteful spending, and profit is a guide to better serve consumers. This lesson is important for policymakers and the public when contemplating policies that eliminate the profit motive, and economists also need to remember it when building models and analyzing markets. One fundamental distinction between public provision and private provision of any good or service is that the private firm will have the profit and loss system to guide it in serving customers, while the public firm will be guided only by targets and orders from above. Any model of nationalizing or privatizing health care or education, for example, should be informed by this lesson.

Endnotes

1. Glenn Thrush, "Nancy Pelosi: Insurers Are 'Immoral' Villains," Politico, July 31, 2009, at http://www.politico.com/news/stories/0709/25651.html (November 20, 2009).
2. Barack Obama, news conference, The White House, July 22, 2009, at http://www.whitehouse.gov/the_press_office/News-Conference-by-the-President-July-22-2009 (November 20, 2009).
3. Ernest Istook, "What Obama Doesn't Know Can Hurt the Rest of Us," *Human Events*, July 27, 2009, at http://www.humanevents.com/article.php?id=32863 (November 20, 2009).
4. Bukharin and Preobrazhensky, *The ABC of Communism*, chap. 1.
5. Karl Marx, *Capital*, Vol. 1, *The Progress of Production of Capital*, trans. Samuel Moore and Edward Aveling (Moscow: Progress Publishers, 1887), chap. 10, at http://marxists.org/archive/marx/works/1867-c1/index.htm (November 20, 2009).

6. Adam Smith, *The Wealth of Nations* (London: Penguin Books, reprinted 1999), p. 119.

7. William Morris and E. Belfort Bax, "The Manifesto of the Socialist League," 2nd ed., 1885, at http://www.marxists.org/archive/morris/works/1885/manifst2.htm (November 20, 2009).

8. E. Belfort Bax, "Modern Socialism," *Modern Thought*, Vol. 1, No. 8 (August 1879), pp. 150–153, at http://www.marxists.org/archive/bax/1879/08/socialism.htm (November 20, 2009).

9. Rexford G. Tugwell, "The Principle of Planning and the Institution of Laissez Faire," *The American Economic Review*, Supplement, Papers and Proceedings of the Forty-fourth Annual Meeting of the American Economic Association, Vol. 22, No. 1 (March 1932), pp. 75–92 (p. 81).

10. Leon Trotsky, *The Revolution Betrayed*, trans. Max Eastman (1937), at http://www.marxists.org/archive/trotsky/1936/revbet/ch01.htm (November 20, 2009).

11. Ted Grant, "Crisis in Russia," *Militant*, No. 9 (September 1965) and No. 10 (October 1965), at http://www.marxists.org/archive/grant/1965/09/russia.htm (November 20, 2009).

12. Ronald Reagan, "Remarks at a White House Reception for the National Association of Elementary School Principals and the National Association of Secondary School Principals," July 29, 1983, at http://www.reagan.utexas.edu/archives/speeches/1983/72983c.htm (November 20, 2009) (edited slightly for clarity).

13. Robinson, *An American in Leningrad*, pp. 31–32.

14. "Not only the bulk of investment, but also most material inputs are subject to control. A large proportion of materials and components required by enterprises may only be obtained against an allocation certificate (naryad), which commonly specifies not only the quantity but also the supplying enterprise, with whom the director must enter into a contract." Nove, *The Soviet Economy*, p. 37.

15. "Too many compulsory indicators are imposed from above...particularly frequent is the prescription of areas to be sown. The agronomist cannot decide what to sow, exact orders are imposed on him, and he is ordered to strictly carry them out.... Thus our farm was forbidden to reduce the area under potatoes." *Pravda*, 1981, quoted in Nove (1986), p. 123.

16. Eric Maskin, Gérard Roland, and János Kornai, "Understanding the Soft Budget Constraint," *Journal of Economic Literature*, Vol. 41, No. 4 (Dec., 2003), pp. 1095–1136. Also see J. Kornai, *Contradictions and Dilemmas: Studies on the Socialist Economy and Society* (Cambridge, MA: MIT Press, 1986).

17. T. Khatchaturov, *Voprosi Ekonomiki*, 1963, No. 11, p. 31, cited in Leon Smolinski, "What Next in Soviet Planning?" *Foreign Affairs*, Vol. 42, No. 4 (July 1964), pp. 602–613.

18. Liberman, "Profit Planning in Industry," 1950, quoted in Berliner, *Factory and Manager in the USSR*, p. 41.

19. Berliner, *Factory and Manager in the USSR*, pp. 72–73.

20. *Ibid.*, pp. 35–36.

21. Hence, Soviet sheet metal was notoriously heavy because the indicator used was "tons." This also led to the cartoon in *Krokodil* of one huge nail. Nove, *The Soviet Economic System*, p. 88.

22. This was a problem for glass and cloth, for example. *Ibid.*, p. 88.

23. "Report of the Committee on Non-Financial Measures of Effectiveness," *Accounting Review*, Vol. 46 supplement, (1971), pp. 165–211.

24. Smolinski, "What Next in Soviet Planning?" pp. 602–613 (p. 608).

25. For this reason, the targets for all the goods were intended to be high in order to motivate managers. The exact assortment of products had to be left to the enterprise as a decentralized decision because planners could not possibly know the local conditions and inputs that the firm could find in time, even though they tied the firms to a supplier. Thus, even if planners had known consumer demand, the enterprise would rarely fulfill the plan's targets to fill that demand.

26. Nove, *The Soviet Economic System* (original emphasis).

27. L. Gatovsky, "The Role of Profit in a Socialist Economy," *Kommunist*, No. 18, 1962, in Myron E. Sharpe, ed., *Planning, Profit and Incentives in the USSR*, Vol. 1, *The Liberman Discussion; A New Phase in Soviet Economic Thought* (White Plains, NY: International Arts & Science Press, 1966), p. 92, quoted in William B. Bland, *The Restoration of Capitalism in the Soviet Union* (1980), at http://www.oneparty.co.uk/html/book/ussrmenu.html (November 20, 2009).

28. V. Trapeznikov, "For Flexible Economic Management of Enterprises," *Pravda*, August 17, 1964, in

Sharpe, *Planning, Profit and Incentives in the USSR*, Vol. 1, p. 196.

29. L. Leontiev, "The Plan and Methods of Economic Management," *Pravda*, September 7, 1964, in Sharpe, *Planning, Profit and Incentives in the USSR*, Vol. 1, p. 209.

30. E. G. Liberman, "Are We Flirting with Capitalism? Profits and 'Profits,'" *Soviet Life* (July 1965), in Sharpe, *Planning, Profit and Incentives in the USSR*, Vol. 1, p. 309.

31. L. Leontiev, *Pravda*, July 10, 1964, in Jere L. Felker, *Soviet Economic Controversies: The Emerging Marketing Concept and Changes in Planning, 1960–1965* (Cambridge, MA: MIT Press, 1966), pp. 77–78, quoted in William B. Bland, *The Restoration of Capitalism in the Soviet Union*.

32. E. G. Liberman, "Plan, Direct Ties and Profitability," *Pravda*, November 21, 1965, in *The Soviet Economic Reform: Main Features and Aims* (Moscow: 1967), p. 50.

33. Marx argued that with social ownership of the means of production, division of labor would no longer be necessary. Many socialist firms in fact produced their own inputs because the supply system was undependable, however, this was not an efficient development.

34. Nove, *The Soviet Economic System*, p. 353.

35. *Ibid.*

36. Burton Folsom Jr., *The Myth of the Robber Barons* (Herndon, VA: Young America's Foundation, 1987).

37. See "'Socialize Now—Railroads First!' That Is the *Appeal*'s Plan of Action," *Appeal to Reason*, February 10, 1917, p. 1, at http://marxists.org/history/usa/parties/spusa/1917/0210-appeal-socializenow.pdf (November 20, 2009). Of course, Amtrak is run by the US government. It was created in 1971, but the history of railroads before that is an interesting case study. Railroads were subject to price controls and then briefly nationalized during World War I. For some time after that they had booming business again as private companies, laying vast amounts of new rail. Then a series of taxes and regulations were imposed on them to raise local revenue. During the same period, huge subsidies financed the national highway system. The combination destroyed the viability of the railroad industry, and it literally crumbled: Miles of track were abandoned and deteriorated. Finally, by the 1970s a case could be made again that only government could afford to run the railroads.

38. John Rennie, "Washing Machine Whizz Who Always Had an Eye for Profit," *East End Life*, November 23, 2009, at http://www.towerhamlets.gov.uk/news/east_end_life/23_november/washing_machine_whizz_who_alw.aspx (December 7, 2009).

39. "Business Abroad: Bloom at the Top," *Time*, October 13, 1961, at http://aolsvc.timeforkids.kol.aol.com/time/magazine/article/0,9171,939283,00.html (December 7, 2009).

40. Spencer S. Hsu and Cecilia Kang, "U.S. Web-Tracking Plan Stirs Privacy Fears," *The Washington Post*, August 11, 2009, at http://www.washingtonpost.com/wp-dyn/content/article/2009/08/10/AR2009081002743_pf.html (November 20, 2009).

CHAPTER 4. THE RAT RACE: THE VALUE OF PROFIT AND LOSS FOR THE ECONOMY

INTRODUCTION

According to socialists, "putting profits ahead of people" not only corrupted the individual firm or capitalist, it also corrupted the whole economy. Socialists argued that profit was "surplus value" that capitalists stole from workers, and that the profit motive meant that many socially important goods and services were not being produced. The drive for profit, they argued, leads to the production of luxury goods for the rich, but not the basic necessities that the poor require. In a socialist system, firms could produce these "socially necessary" goods, and their loss could be subsidized by the extra revenue from firms producing luxury goods at a higher price. In this way, socialism would more efficiently provide the people with what they need and not benefit some at the expense of others.

The same reasoning underlies arguments for government provision of goods and services that the poor may not be able to afford but which are generally considered to be of great value. In addition, there are arguments for government to play a role in providing "public goods," goods or services that can be enjoyed commonly and for which it is difficult to exclude non-paying consumers, such as police and national defense. Some argue that government has a role in providing these services as well as any service in which a private company would obtain a "natural monopoly" due to the nature of the market. These might include highways, postal and phone service, and air traffic control. The lesson of the Soviet experience sheds light on the role of profit in the market, and this offers a new lens through which to consider these arguments.

The Socialist Argument

> [T]he statement that the unplanned economy gives us what
> we want often amounts to little more than saying that it makes
> us want what we are given. — Barbara Wootton[1]

Socialists made the case that social goods, which are important to the prosperity of the regular person, will be increasingly under-provided by the market system because they cannot generate profit for a company, even though they are in demand by the people. Instead, capitalists tend to bully consumers into buying low-quality goods, and try to make them dependent, because this drives up the capitalist's profit. *The ABC of Communism* explains it in this way:

> The question now arises, for what reason does the capitalist class hire workers? Everyone knows that the reason is by no means because the factory owners wish to feed the hungry workers, but because they wish to extract profit from them. For the sake of profit, the factory owner builds his factory; for the sake of profit, he engages workers; for the sake of profit, he is always nosing out where higher prices are paid. Profit is the motive of all his calculations. Herein, moreover, we discern a very interesting characteristic of capitalist society. For society does not itself produce the things which are necessary and useful to it; instead of this, the capitalist class compels the workers to produce those things for which more will be paid, those things from which the capitalists derive the largest profit. Whiskey, for example, is a very harmful substance, and alcoholic liquors in general ought to be produced only for technical purposes and for their use in medicine. But throughout the world the capitalists produce alcohol with all their might. Why? Because to ply the people with drink is extremely profitable.[2]

The writers Bukharin and Preobrazhensky implicitly assume that they know better than customers that whiskey should not be made. One may argue that it would not be profitable if the customer did not desire it, but socialists reply that the producer—the capitalist—has power over the consumer, and induces them to buy the products he wants them to buy. The Soviet publication *Problems of Economics* frequently included arguments on how the pursuit of profit misdirects production. One article explained that in the capitalist economy:

> [The goal] is the creation and enlargement of surplus value, the sweating out of profits. To attain this goal, enormous productive powers are destroyed. In contrast herewith, the goal of Socialist production consists of assuring maximum satisfaction of man's material and cultural needs.[3]

A socialist society could provide an answer for this. Central planning of production would mean that the people could direct investment and could choose to provide social goods rather than merely profitable ones. The people could bring their investments to the local council and obtain money to try them out—a far more humane and reasonable way to choose what to invest in than that of the crude capitalist system. Not only could the people stop producing profitable but destructive goods, and replace them with socially beneficial ones, socially-directed production would also be more efficient. The people could choose the best things to produce, and produce them efficiently for the consumer, rather than for a base profit motive. Marxist Karl Kautsky described the advantages of centralized investment and production in 1902. He argued that big "trusts," or cartels, were more efficient than small business due to economies of scale and because one owner could take control of all of them and put the less efficient ones out of business. He argued that socialists could take lessons from these large capitalist trusts on how to allocate investment better and make adjustments more quickly than through profit and loss in the market. "The whiskey trust," he argued, "obtained eighty large distilleries and, at once put out of operation sixty-eight out of the eighty. It is only operating twelve distilleries but in these twelve it produces even more than hitherto in the eighty."[4] He then made the case that a socialist government could do even better:

> The culling out of the inefficient by way of free competition is a very slow process. The trusts can only displace the less productive industries through the fact that they have destroyed private property in them by uniting all under one head. The method which the trusts can only apply to a relatively small sphere of production may be extended by a proletarian regime to the whole sphere of social production, since it will have totally abolished capitalistic private property.[5]

The state could control all the enterprises under one management and close the inefficient ones immediately. This rational direction would be much simpler and faster than the ad hoc process of competition and profit seeking. Economies of scale could be exploited in all industries, and no inefficient firms would continue to barely survive until they ran into great losses, as happens in a capitalist system. Rather than let the chaos of the market slowly chip away at inefficiencies, socialists could take the reins and immediately improve the situation.

Karl Kautsky also tied this argument to the Marxist concept of the "reserve army of unemployed." According to this theory, capitalists benefit if a greater percentage of the workforce is unemployed, because this will suppress wages. Kautsky explained that worker control would mean that this "reserve army" could be eliminated. Those that need to be laid off by one firm could be relocated. The socialist government could simply move the workers to other factories. Production would also be higher because the nationalized trusts would not keep output low in order to prop up prices:

> [Under capitalism] laborers who are rendered superfluous by reduction of surplus industries it simply discharges. It utilizes them mainly as a means of pressing down the wages of the laborers who are at work and in increasing their dependence.
>
> Very naturally a victorious laboring class would proceed differently. It would transfer the laborers rendered superfluous by the closing of industries to other industries where their activity would continue.... The trusts fight against all decline in prices. They would much rather limit production than extend it.
>
> ...A proletarian regime, however, would act for the purpose of extending production, for it does not desire to raise profits but rather wages.[6]

Socialists argued that profit and loss in the market was a slow, inefficient, and non-egalitarian method of producing goods and allocating resources. Socialists could improve upon it in several ways: They could produce without regard to the base standard of profit, which favors the wealthy. They could immediately shut down inefficient factories, rather than waiting for the slow process of loss-making to run its course. They could relocate laid-off workers, so they would not face unemployment or drag down wages. Finally, they could produce at appropriate levels, rather than those simply used to keep prices and profits high.

The arguments seem sound, but the socialists based all of this on intention and did not fully consider the problems of implementing their plans. Economist Barbara Wootton explicitly argued that if socialists intended to allocate investment and distribute resources more equitably, then one must assume that they will achieve these results better than the market system, which is not driven by this intention and in which there is inequality in bargaining:

> I do not think that it can be denied that if the planners honestly desire to act in the interests of the people at large, and so to order economic production and distribution that the available resources of the country may give the maximum satisfaction to the people who have to work them...then they are likely, humanly speaking, to get nearer to it than is a society in which decisions are made by contracts between parties of whom one is often under much greater necessity of coming to immediate terms than is the other.[7]

Profit and loss were seen as hindering the optimal allocation of resources in the economy. Barbara Wootton argued that, although planners might not be immune from corrupting influences, "they are at least exempt from the temptation, which is the despair of capitalism, to frame plans according to which the industry which with they are personally concerned will deliver as little product as possible in exchange for as much money, that is for as large a slice of the product of other industries, as possible."[8] In other words, the profit motive was likely to lead to cartels and monopolies, not to the level of production best fitted to satisfy the consumer.

Just as with the arguments regarding the affect of profit on the behavior of the individual capitalist and firm, the arguments regarding profit as a guide in the economy were shared outside Marxist circles. Rex Tugwell argued that, far from helping to produce at efficient levels in the various industries, profit prevented rational production:

> Most of us ought not to have been quite so free in our predictions that the institutions of Soviet Russia would break down from a failure of [profit] motive. Yet some of us have gone on saying that even in the face of evidence. Not more than a month ago a past president of this association assured me again, as he had done before, that here was the source of weakness which must finally ruin all the Russian plans. There are numerous difficulties there, plenty of chances for failure; but the failure of non-commercial motives cannot honestly be said, at this late date, to be one of them. Nor is this a source of necessary alarm—any more than the technical difficulties need be—concerning any planned economy we may devise. *It ought rather to be a source of wonder that a society could operate at all when profits are allowed to be earned and disposed of as we do it. The hope of making them induces dangerous adventures, more speculative than productive; and the uses to which they are put are a constant menace to general security.* These conclusions only become clearer as time goes on, yet no movement to limit them or to control their uses has made headway among us. If there had been a more widespread suspicion of this sort over some period of time *there would be more reason to expect success for proposals looking toward a profitless regime. The universal confidence in profits, still unshaken in the Western World, is quite likely to hinder measurably the advance of planning.* [Italics mine.] [9]

Socialists were not afraid of eliminating the profit motive: they believed it was a destructive force upon society, and its elimination would be a great advantage in the new society.

THE SOVIET EXPERIENCE

Among the first decrees of the Soviet government were the elimination of capitalist profit and the nationalization of large industry. During the early "war communism" period, profit was eliminated entirely, and "profiteers" were executed:

> The Council of People's Commissars directs the All Russia Food Council and the Commissariat for Food to send out more and numerically larger armed detachments as well as commissars to take the most revolutionary measures to expedite shipments, collect and store grain, etc., as well as to wage a ruthless struggle against profiteers, even to the extent of calling on the local Soviets to shoot convicted profiteers and saboteurs on the spot.[10]

Of course, these excessive measures did not help to expedite shipments or increase grain deliveries. Grain production fell to 50 percent of prewar levels, by some estimates much lower.[11] Of course, these measures were taken under conditions of war and revolution, and were not the ideal socialist program.

The socialist ideal was to direct investment centrally and to aim it at social ends rather than according to profitability. This was intended to produce exciting new innovation. Workers could suggest projects that they would not have enough capital to undertake in the old capitalist system. Inventors from all over the Soviet Union came to Lenin with their ideas.

However, evaluating the profitability and advisability of these projects now rested with the state. In a market system, an inventor must convince a private investor to risk his own money. If it is a poor project, the private money is lost, and the project dies. With Lenin's policy, the inventor had to convince the Party to invest. If the Party could not be convinced, the inventor had nowhere else to go; if the Party was convinced then the project would have the complete backing of the state, even if it might not be optimal. Sometimes political, not economic, factors drove investment choices; but even when decisions were not political, they were often not purely economic either, because planners had difficulty determining the costs and benefits of investment choices, as will be discussed further in this chapter and Chapter 6.

(When the state made agreements with foreign parties, cost-benefit analysis certainly played a role. For example, although the grandson of Karl Marx made a bid for the project of electrifying Russia in 1921, the project was given to a higher bidder.[12]) Choices were difficult to make purely based on cost-effectiveness, but they were also not supposed to be made on that basis.

> Under Socialism economic development is never allowed to be hampered by a lack of finance. If there are physical resources available and if the production is socially desirable, it goes without saying that the means of financing will be provided. The economic plan has a counterpart of the credit plan which is worked out by the central bank in co-operation with other banks.[13]

Yet how can the state know if something is socially desirable? What if a socially desirable good can be produced in multiple ways? How will the state know whether production is cost-effective if it provides all the inputs to the firm free of charge? Although socialists viewed the whole society as benefiting from the ability to allow some firms to produce without concern for profitability, the individual firm facing a soft budget constraint has altered incentives, and the society that allocates investments without knowledge of profitability also suffers. The state is left with no way of determining whether something is a cost-effective investment. In some cases, the state may not even realize that it cannot accurately judge this. The economist Barbara Wootton, who was sympathetic to the Soviet experiment, told a story about her experience with the soft budget constraint there in the 1930s. She learned of a Soviet school for rescued children, in which the children worked for four hours and had lessons for four hours each day:

> When I was in [the USSR] I visited one day a large home for rescued street children situated a few miles outside Kharkov.... [It was a] well-designed and reasonably well-furnished building in which were housed some 300 or more children.... The authorities of this home told me with pride that, though the actual building had been given them by the State Political Police...the institution was otherwise "entirely self-supporting."... [I]t certainly seemed remarkable that a four hours' working day, on the part of what was practically apprentice labour, would suffice to maintain such a large and relatively comfortable institution.[14]

The idea that this state-run school was entirely self-supporting was a pride to the school and may have left Wootton with a positive impression of the possibilities of public investment. However, she did some further digging:

> Further enquiry elicited (1) that the gear made by the children was not produced anywhere else in the Union...[and] (2) that the products were sold exclusively to certain State trusts engaged in electrical engineering....
>
> These facts put the statement that the home was self-supporting in a new light. Obviously this term had no real meaning, since the planning authorities could both give the home a monopoly of production in its own particular line and at the same time see that the industrial enterprises which required this product were supplied with funds to buy as much as they wanted, notwithstanding the high price.[15]

Regardless of how the entries are written in the accounting books, when the state is the buyer and the supplier, the firm cannot say with certainty that it is "self-funding" or profitable. Not only would any price the planners set be paid, but it would be impossible to know what the right price should be. The actual *willingness to pay* for these products would be unknown. In other words, the state would have a hard time determining how much the people *want* the products that the subsidized firm is making. In this case, perhaps it would not matter if there was no demand because the school may have been funded as a social service either way, but it was treated as a self-sustaining firm, while the true cost of the school to the state was unknown.

When the need to compete and offer a low price is removed and the customer is subsidized, the ability to determine whether a firm is profitable vanishes. When the consumer is subsidized in his purchase, the firm will be "profitable" no matter what. This occurred in every industry in the Soviet Union, even in something as simple as the sale of potatoes. Comparing the sales of potatoes in a market economy with sales in a socialist economy, Barbara Wootton explained:

> Suppose...that I live in an unplanned price economy like ours by growing pota-toes and taking them to market. In this case, the production of potatoes comes to an end when nobody can be found willing to pay a price for an additional pound of potatoes which either I or any of my fellow growers (if there are any) considers sufficient compensation for the trouble and expense of producing that pound.... [This] is the normal regulative machinery of the price economy.
>
> ...[In a socialist economy like the USSR, I] sell my potatoes to a food trust or to a publicly owned cooperative wholesale agency. These organizations again, pay me a price and the same balance is apparently achieved as in the preceding case. I find the price sufficient inducement to grow the potatoes.... [However] In this case...since the food trust is a publicly owned institution, the price which it offers need not in any way reflect what the proletariat, in whose eventual interest the potatoes are brought to market, considers these potatoes worth. The trust may be highly subsidised, in which case it is offering me a price greater than those who consume them personally consider justified; or it may itself be subsidising some other entirely different branch of production.[16]

Therefore, the normal mechanism by which the farmer stops producing when the people no longer desire any more is gone. Instead, if the planners cannot calculate precisely the amount that the people desire, the farmer may produce too many or too few. Of course, the same is true of any subsidized industry, including health care or housing. The government may hope that it is helping the people by subsidizing more of a good than the people could otherwise afford, but it loses the signal that tells it whether the people actually want it and in what quantities. Because people make trade-offs in their own purchasing, the amount of each good that they buy reflects their preferences. When government takes on this role, it cannot aggregate the pref-erences of all the consumers and accurately reflect them through the subsidies.

Planners allowed each year for planned losses[17] in accordance with the tenet that socially necessary but unprofitable production was a responsibility of the socialist state. Yet without profit guidance and with a soft budget constraint, it was impos-sible to know if production was efficient or whether the services were demanded in proportion to production.

During the 1965 reform discussions, Soviet economists argued the merits of prof-it, not just as a guide for firms internally and as a better cost-minimization target, but also for allocation across the economy. Although this was rejected under Stalin, planners and economists came to realize the use of profit for this purpose. Stalin ex-plained of the planned economy under his control:

> Totally incorrect...is the assertion that under our present economic system... the law of value regulates the "proportions" of labour distributed among the vari-ous branches of production. If this were true, it would be incomprehensible why our light industries, which are most profitable, are not being developed to their utmost, and why preference is given to our heavy industries, which are often less profitable, and sometimes altogether unprofitable.
>
> If this were true, it would be incomprehensible why a number of our heavy in-dustry plants which are still unprofitable...are not closed down, and why new light industry plants, which would certainly be profitable,...are not opened.

If this were true, it would be incomprehensible why workers are not transferred from plants that are less profitable, but very necessary to our national economy, to plants which are more profitable — in accordance with the law of value, which supposedly regulates the 'proportions' of labour distributed among the branches of production.[18]

Stalin understood that profit directs investment in a market economy, and he rejected its use. He concluded that "there can be no doubt that under our present socialist conditions of production, the law of value cannot be a 'regulator of proportions' of labour distributed among the various branches of production" because "[t]he aim of socialist production is not profit, but man and his needs."[19] However, serious distortions and "contradictions" emerged from the elimination of profitability as an economic regulator, leading later reformers to reconsider this commitment.

For example, during the Stalin period, Machine Tractor Stations (MTS) were used to supply collective farms, and payments were made in kind with the farms paying for their tractors with produce, rather than with money, and costs were disregarded. However, this led to a system of allocation that was entirely irrational. Alec Nove described the problems that occurred:

> [T]he whole system of payments in kind, and indeed of MTS work, had no economic *rationale*. Thus, for instance, the payments in kind not only had no connection with the costs of the given MTS, but in a sense were inversely related to cost.... There was also no way of assessing the profitability of this or that machine or type of tractor, and no attempt was in fact made to do so. Machinery was centrally allocated to the MTS, despite numerous complaints that it was often unsuitable to the requirements of the given area.[20]

"The captain of the land of the Soviets leads us from victory to victory." Cartoon from *Izvestija*, August 5, 1933. Artist: Boris Efimov.

Allocating without the guide of profit meant that farms were stuck with unusable machinery. This same consequence was seen in every sector of the economy. At the time of the 1965 reforms, the problem of production unsuitable for the customer had "recently assumed extraordinary proportions." For example, "unsaleable stocks of textiles, clothing and shoes" were increasing "on the average four times as fast as sales."[21] Because profit did not determine what goods would be made, there was no way to know whether they were desired by the consumer at all, let alone how much they were desired, or whether they were desired more than alternative uses of those resources.

Stocks of raw materials were also building up. The Soviet Union had "produced 206 million tons of crude oil, but the total annual capacity of Soviet oil refineries reached only 50% (!) of this level of production."[22] For this reason and others, a huge number of investment projects were "frozen" unfinished for years, and sometimes finally abandoned.[23] Other investment projects were completed but turned out to be inefficient. According to a 1964 article in *Pravda*, in 10 of 39 firms analyzed, investment had resulted in lower, rather than higher, productivity.[24]

The lack of profit guidance meant that planners could not judge the cost effectiveness of projects and could not know whether production was worthwhile. The disproportions between supply and demand meant that there were stocks of unsold goods, when supply exceeded demand. It also meant that there were extreme shortages of goods that people wanted, because supply fell short of demand in these areas.

János Kornai has studied the phenomenon of shortage in socialist economies extensively. In his book *The Socialist System* Kornai cites some statistics regarding shortage in several socialist economies including the Soviet Union. Shortages occurred both for consumers and for firms. For producers this included "shortages of machines, equipment, and construction capacity for investment schemes," while consumers faced shortage in a vast array of both necessities and luxury goods. For example, the average wait for housing in the 1980s in the Soviet Union was 10–15 years. Kornai then comments that, "Statistical proof of the statement's truth is not needed, however, by those living in a socialist country. They experience the countless frustrations of thwarted purchasing intentions, queuing, forced substitution, searches for goods, and postponement of purchases in their daily lives as consumers and producers."[25]

In the 1970s, the American visitor Logan Robinson found striking consumer shortages. "There are fewer stores in Soviet cities than in Western cities of equivalent size, and as a result they are always thronged. The profit motive which would cause an entrepreneur observing customers lined up to get into one store to open another one across the street, does not play a role in the Soviet economy. As a result you can't get toothpaste on just any corner. You must know of a store that would carry it, and there is always the possibility that toothpaste, or any other item you might seek, would be entirely sold out citywide and remain so for months."[26]

Planners recognized that these disproportions between supply and demand could be solved by introducing profit into the economy as an "automatic regulator" of production. The 1965 reforms attempted to resolve these disproportions. Soviet reform economists described the many uses of profit that they were discovering. Profit could offer incentives, and loss could force firms to keep costs lower; and profit could also tie the incentives of the firm to the needs and desires of society.

> To exert effective economic influence on economic activity, it is essential to choose a criterion that characterises to the greatest degree the operation of the enterprise and meets the interests of both the national economy and the personnel of the enterprise.... It is profit that constitutes such a criterion.[27]

Reform economists concluded that, for the new reforms to ensure greater efficiency and resolve the problems facing the Soviet economy, profit would have to guide production and aid in allocation of resources. "Production will be subordinated to changes in profits," in the new system, read one article.[28]

Hence, in addition to recognizing the role of profit as a holistic target for the individual enterprise, reformers also saw the role of profit in guiding the economy to produce the goods most demanded and to reduce resource-use on goods no longer considered as worthwhile. Some have described the Liberman–Trapeznikov reforms as split along these lines: Liberman highlighted the role of profit for the individual firm, and Trapeznikov highlighted its use as an economic regulator for the economy. For example, an article for *International Socialist Review* explained that,

> Liberman and Trapeznikov would eliminate this waste and disorder by making one factor, profit (which constitutes a kind of synthesis or common denominator of all economic relations closely or remotely involved in the considered production), the measure of planning performance. For Trapeznikov, however, the question is not so much that of a single index, but rather one in which the system of "indexes" is replaced with a system of economic levers; by means of such a set of economic levers, the Soviet authorities will be able to count on inducing the managers of enterprises to act for the common good through their own private interest. The scope of the Liberman-Trapeznikov reforms (as well as those introduced in other European workers states) boils down to this: to replace planning based on administrative directives by planning founded on the use of economic levers.[29]

Hence, for Liberman profit represented the "holistic target," while for Trapeznikov profit was the best economic lever to induce firms to produce for the common good. When seen across the whole economy, this would mean that the goods demanded, and only those, would be produced. In other words, Trapeznikov recognized that profit-seeking by firms did not induce them to produce only for the rich, and fail to produce socially necessary goods. Instead, as Adam Smith said, seeking their own interest, they inadvertently served the common good by producing that which was demanded most by society.

Soviet economists could see that the problems of planning could be resolved if profit could be used again in its role as an economic regulator. They only had to justify its use and find a way to insert it into the socialist system.

> A way out of the apparent contradictions has been suggested in our press in the form of a kind of automatic "self-regulator."... The role of such an automatic self-regulator, it is claimed, can be performed by profitability.... In the profitability

controversy some economists have based their objections to making it a regulator of social production on the contention that profit is a capitalist category. Such objections, of course, are untenable.[30]

Loss was also recognized as important during this period. Karl Kautsky had argued that a planned economy would be more efficient in part because a single owner would replace the profit and loss of the competition process, and be able to close inefficient firms more quickly, and then transfer labor to where it is needed. However, planners found that they did not know which firms were least efficient, nor which firms excess labor should be transferred to, without profit and loss indicators—and without markets and hard budget constraints these signals were not reliable. In addition, the socialist argument had also indicated that some firms should be allowed to take a loss, hence loss and inefficiency were not to be considered the same. Yet planners found no other way to determine which firms were most efficient and necessary to the economy.

Facing gluts of labor in obviously inefficient places, but recognizing their own ignorance of the optimal distribution, planners began to consider reforms that could reintroduce the market solution to this problem. The primary experiment with reintroducing a market response to loss was the Shchekino reform discussed in Chapter 2. As discussed, this reform allowed the managers of the Soviet enterprise to release workers that were unable to produce as much as they cost to the enterprise—still determined by the wages that planners set. Because they had soft budget constraints, the firms had been keeping excess workers for emergencies. According to Kautsky's vision, the planners should have seen which firms were efficient, which ones had too large or too small a workforce, and transfer the workers between them, shutting inefficient firms. Yet planners had no way of knowing which firms were efficient or how many workers they required.

One of the primary roles that loss plays in the economy is to pull resources from where they are not needed, and release them for use where they are needed. The Shchekino reform was an attempt to do this with at least the human resource of labor. Unlike Karl Kautsky's vision, in which the central planner owning all the firms shuts the inefficient ones and transfers labor to the remaining top performers, the Shchekino reform was a return to the market solution whereby the individual firm determines whether the workers are worth their wage or whether they contribute to losses. This experiment started in 1967 and was another outgrowth of the Liberman–Trapeznikov reform plan.

However, effective regulation by profit and loss would not be possible while planners determined prices centrally. As one Western economic textbook states, "While theoretically appealing, the meaning of profit guidance is often unclear in a system where prices bear little or no relation to relative scarcities." Although the Shchekino reform was an improvement for the factories that were guided by it, if wages were set centrally then profit and loss by each factory may not guide workers to where they would be most productive—if allowed to pay more or less a different firm might make better use of the resource. Similarly, seeking profit should help firms to produce goods in demand and stop producing unsalable products, but it would not do an especially good job of this if planners continued to set the prices of the final products as well as the prices of the inputs required for making them. Once again, planners would need to know what is efficient, and where resources should be allocated, without the guidance of profit and loss—in order to set the prices so that profit and loss could be used. The only way out of this dilemma would be to allow the market to set prices.

Planners also could not achieve their goals if they allowed profit and loss to guide production.[31] They could base the plan on profit, or proxies for profit, but then it is no longer clear what the advantage of socialism would be. As Barbara Wootton explained in 1935:

> It is evident, however, that it would not be worthwhile to undergo the arduous labour of socialising industry, and setting up a workable planning authority, merely in order that this authority might employ a single conscious will as the means of bringing about results identical with those previously achieved by the aggregate of millions of uncoordinated decisions.[32]

The fact that planners were moving more and more in this direction—although ultimately unwilling to go all the way—is an admission that profit was determined to be necessary for guiding production efficiently. Similarly, the struggle with cost targets and the need to punish—and even close—unprofitable enterprises indicates that they were learning the necessity of loss for redirecting resources into the areas in which they are most needed.

Lessons

Profit and loss play two major roles in the economy: They guide each firm to produce for the consumer at the lowest cost possible, and they guide production across the economy toward things most desired in the most efficient way. These are the micro- and macroeconomic effects of the same role. An article on the United Kingdom's regulation of profit in the pharmaceutical industry explained how limiting profit affected both the firm and the industry:

> In competitive markets, firms increase their profits by cutting costs and by investing in capital only when the expected increase in revenue exceeds the expected increase in costs. The [profit regulation], however, distorts firms' incentives to make such efficient decisions...since firms that cut costs are not allowed to keep the savings...Those distortions are well understood and lead to further intervention by the [Department of Health] as a corrective measure.... In addition to distorting decisions by each firm, rate-of-return regulation distorts the decisions of investors by confusing the signals given by capital markets. In competitive financial markets, investors choose to invest in different firms by examining their returns and the degree of risk.... Under rate-of-return regulation, however, assets no longer provide these signals. Firms cannot make themselves more attractive to investors by increasing their returns; similarly, returns do not reflect the risks of investing in a firm. As a result, the [regulation] may support investment in less efficient pharmaceutical companies and prevent efficient pharmaceutical companies from growing. The scheme may also distort incentives to invest in the pharmaceutical industry, as opposed to other sectors, by masking the riskiness of the sector. The cumulative effect of capital market distortions can wreck an industry.[33]

Socialists believed that profit was driving production into frivolous areas, such as luxury goods, while ignoring the necessities required by the poor. They argued that rationalization of investment would vastly improve the equity and efficiency of investment and production choices. Although many of their arguments sounded reasonable, they failed to account for the roles of profit and loss in an economy, the results of which are often taken for granted. Although few today argue that the government should plan all investment, many arguments still stem from the same kind of reasoning.

In the example from *The ABC of Communism*, the capitalist produced whiskey, instead of socially necessary goods like medicine or housing, because of profit. Yet manufacturing and selling whiskey is profitable because customers value the product. The factory owner does not hire workers out of benevolence. He hires them for the sake of profit, and he produces for the sake of profit. Indeed, as socialists argued, profit is the motive of all his calculations, but this does not mean that society does not produce the things that are necessary and useful to it. Some people may resent the fact that whiskey is desired, but that is why it is produced. This is what is meant by the "consumer sovereignty" that exists in markets, and its importance was something that the socialists of the Soviet Union learned.

The more people who find a product useful or necessary, the more demand there will be for it and the more potential for profit. Initial purchasing power is not equally distributed; hence, some can "vote with their dollars" many more times than others. This led socialists to imagine that producers would disproportionately make things that the wealthy desire. Yet poor people outnumber the rich. In the example above, whiskey is produced due to broad demand, not demand by a few wealthy consumers.

The basic necessities for the poor that socialists were concerned would not be produced are also demanded by a broad population and thus are produced for profit. It is also important to remember that different entrepreneurs seek different markets. Some will seek profit by producing luxury goods for the rich, while others will seek profit by producing cheap items for the poor. This decentralized chasing of profit manages to fill more demand for more consumers, including many "niche" markets, than any central planner ever could.

In the Soviet economy, many products that were not valued were produced—yet the products were counted in aggregates like total output. This illustrates one problem with such aggregates, for example, when used to compare output between countries, or to determine whether government can successfully "stimulate investment" or "stimulate the economy" through public investment. Alexander Solzhenitsyn described four kinds of products produced in the Soviet Union that contributed to a misrepresentation of total output in the Soviet economy: "(1) nonexisting goods [existing only on paper], (2) overvalued goods, (3) valueless goods, and (4) social bads."[34] Because the consumer did not exert pressure upon enterprises to produce what they desired, and firms could not chase profits in order to fulfill this demand, many such goods were produced (or documented) and counted toward total output. If nothing else was available, these goods might be purchased.

Aggregate totals of production, if used for statistical or empirical work, rest on the assumption that the value of the goods being totaled is accurate, or that all the goods are valued. This is a lesson that Western economists recognized when, after decades of discussion of the high rate of Soviet growth, the Iron Curtain opened and the quality and assortment of Soviet production was laid bare for all to see. The lesson is clear: aggregates are meaningless if the products are not valued. Soviet output reported in rubles was meaningless because the products were summed using prices that the planners set, not prices that reflected demand or scarcity. One might as well add up a column of random numbers. Even reports of pure, unpriced output—tons of steel or miles of railroad track—may be misleading because the output may not be valued by consumers.

However, the market's ability to respond "perfectly" to consumer preferences may also have some limitations. Some of these limitations have led to calls for government intervention or government production either in certain industries or (as in the case of socialism) across an entire national economy. These limitations are critical for economists and policymakers to understand. It is also critical to determine whether government can resolve the difficulty and, if so, how best to resolve the difficulty.

One limitation is that the poor may not only "vote less" with their dollars, they may actually be unable to purchase things that morality or group consensus would wish them to purchase. For example, income support for the poor to purchase health insurance in the form of a voucher program is in essence a subsidy. However, it subsidizes purchase through the consumer rather than directly subsidizing the producer. This makes health care cheaper relative to other goods, and enables those that could not (or would not) otherwise purchase health care to do so. However, it drives demand up and arguably distorts the allocation of resources by driving more resources into the health care sector.

But is this "distortion" a problem if the goal is to make health care more affordable? One must consider the purpose—the ends—of a given policy, and then determine whether the means achieve these ends. If a policy's goal is to help the poor purchase health care that they previously could not afford, then this must be how the policy is valued. Many programs to help the poor purchase something are criticized on the grounds that the poor could purchase it without aid and that the program is dimply diverting resources toward something that these individuals did not want. If consumer sovereignty is strictly assumed, then this would be the natural conclusion. The market supplies whatever the consumer demands, and if the consumer was not purchasing it, then he must not have wanted it.

However, what if these poor consumers did not purchase it because they *could not*, rather than because they *did not* desire the good? As a thought experiment, there is the extreme case that those people that would not buy (as much or any) health care absent the vouchers of this program would not do so because they had to spend every penny on food, shelter, and other necessities for survival. It is not so much that these individuals were not *willing* to buy health care products and services (as in "willingness to pay" and "demonstrated preferences"), but that they were not *able* because purchasing health care at that time would mean sacrificing food or shelter to the point that they would die. This distinction is what separates choice from necessity. If a gun is pointed at a person's head (or if government threatens the person with the death penalty), then the person does not really have a choice. If the choice is between something and dying, we do not consider it a choice.

The problem is that when someone buys something, there is no way to distinguish whether the buyer is buying as much as he is *willing* to buy (demonstrating his preference) or just as much as he is *able* (which would not reveal his complete preference set). By assuming that the preferences of the consumer are "revealed" or "demonstrated" in the market, it is easy to show that the market is working well. The market sorts those who really want or need a service from those who do not by letting the price rise enough to exclude the latter population. If the people really want something, they will demand it, and the market will supply it. All sorts of difficult questions can be answered by this simple assumption. However, it omits the fact that some people are not *able* to buy what they want. Someone who cannot work at all would still have preferences.

On the other hand, those who advocate public provision, regulation, or other ways to ensure that those *unable* to purchase something can purchase it often make the reverse error: They omit willingness from their analysis. For example, they say that making health care equally accessible to all means that health care is available regardless of *ability* to pay. What they omit is that it is also accessible regardless of *willingness* to pay. In other words, it is made equally available to all, regardless of whether a person desires it just a little bit or it is matter of life or death. Yet making it accessible to those individuals who have little willingness to pay will tend to drive up demand excessively, potentially creating severe shortages and leading to the need for rationing, or creating a bubble. Demand information is also lost in this case because the price can no longer sort consumers by their willingness to pay.

Both sides have made a mistake. Both willingness and ability to pay need to be considered. Hence, a targeted voucher scheme that enhances the *ability* to purchase the good is different from a policy that broadly makes the good cheaper or free. In the latter case, those who have the ability, but not as much *willingness* at the market price to purchase the good, also purchase more. If a society values the ability of all individuals to purchase a certain good, the voucher scheme may offer a potential way to do this without driving up demand across the board.

There may also be some goods that are unlikely to produce a profit, but are still arguably important social goods. For example, some "non-excludable" goods are difficult to exclude individuals from using, except by banning them from the area. In some cases non-excludable goods are "non-rivalrous," meaning that use by one person does not diminish their use by others. These properties make it difficult to charge customers and make a profit selling the product. Economists call these "public goods." Police and national defense are perhaps the best examples of public goods, although many other goods are said to have similar properties. For example, if national defense were a private opt-in system, any one individual may choose not to purchase it, but he would still be protected if others in the area bought into it, and his "use" of it would not affect the others' use of it very much, if at all. If it is not possible to make a profit in the private sector by providing goods like these, because selectively charging those that use the service would be difficult, then the advantages of profit would not apply in these areas. Many economists argue that this is one obvious arena for government provision.

The scope of public goods is sometimes expanded to include goods that have "positive externalities," meaning that, while they may benefit the individual consumer of the good, they also positively affect others who do not pay for this benefit. These are bundled with public goods because the profit that the producer can reap is lower than the "social benefit," leading to underproduction of these goods. Education is cited as an example because society is said to benefit by the education of each individual. Infectious disease control is perhaps an even more clear-cut example. Conversely, a good may have "negative externalities," such as pollution of air or water. If private companies earn too large a profit because the company or the consumer is not required to pay for the costs that are born by others in the area, the price is artificially low, which leads to overconsumption of these goods.

However, negative externalities are actually a problem of a lack of property rights. If individuals had a property right over the air they breathe, then the company polluting would need to pay for the privilege to pollute, and this would cut into the profits or increase the price to the consumer. When nobody owns these rights, all those who could gain from using these resources—air, water, public land—are likely to over-use them and treat them poorly. This is the "tragedy of the commons."[35] If government's primary purpose is to protect individual rights, there might be a way to negotiate rights over these more ephemeral pieces of property.

Government provision is also suggested for goods with positive externalities. Sometimes there is a social desire to have more of something than individuals in the society choose to purchase. Yet this does not always mean that government must step in to subsidize it. A social networking site such as Facebook is of no value to one person unless others are using it; this is a classic problem of "public goods" with positive externalities. Yet, because it is owned privately, the profit-drive led the creators to find a way to surmount this obstacle. There may be other ways in which a society, through the market or through other kinds of social cooperation, can come together to resolve the paradox of the individual reluctance to buy, but a social preference for, goods with positive externalities.

Government provision also may not overcome the problem of "externalities." Although many advocates of government intervention and even socialism argue that it is profit-seeking that leads to problems like pollution, it may be a lack of property rights that creates such problems and government may not always solve them.

> In the Soviet Union there was a vast body of environmental law and regulation that purportedly protected the public interest, but these constraints have had no perceivable benefit. The Soviet Union, like all socialist countries, suffered from a massive "tragedy of the commons."...Water pollution is catastrophic. Effluent from a chemical plant killed almost all the fish in the Oka River in 1965, and similar fish kills have occurred in the Volga, Ob, Yenesei, Ural, and Northern Dvina rivers. Most Russian factories discharge their waste without cleaning it at all. Mines, oil wells, and ships freely dump waste and ballast into any available body of water, since it is all one big (and tragic) "commons."[36]

Pollution was a worse problem in the Soviet Union than in the West possibly for two reasons. First, innovative technologies helped the West to reduce pollution and these technologies were not invented by socialist firms (for reasons discussed in Chapter 1). Second, the institution of common ownership meant that far more resources were able to be exploited in the way that forests, water, and air can be exploited in most market economies: the tragedy of the commons. The theory that government can intervene in a tragedy of the commons situation relies on the assumption that government knows how to do so. In the Soviet Union all resources were publicly owned; this meant that the state had a massive task before it to guard all the commons.

One problem that emerged was that planners could not know whether pollution was necessary for production of a certain good. In a market economy, if polluters must pay for the privilege to pollute then competition and profit and loss will ensure that firms strive to pollute as little as possible. If they are not required to pay, pollution will be a problem. The market cannot do its job of disincentivizing costly activity if the activity is commonly owned and made free. In the planned economy, the planners could price this activity centrally, or could simply allow the production or disallow it, and set pollution targets. Either way, the problems of centrally set prices (discussed in Chapter 6) or the problems of targets (discussed in Chapter 3) make this difficult.

If property rights are enforced, the market arguably can resolve problems like pollution of air and water. These resources were actually once protected by property rights in America and England. In an article in a pro-market magazine, Thomas Dilorenzo argued that pollution is not caused by market failures, but rather from the weak property rights of the current legal system:

> The heart of the problem lies with the failure of our legal institutions, not the free enterprise system. Specifically, American laws were weakened more than a century ago by Progressive Era courts that believed economic progress was in the public interest and should therefore supersede individual rights.
>
> The English common law tradition of the protection of private property rights—including the right to be free from pollution—was slowly overturned. In other words, many environmental problems are not caused by "market failure" but by government's failure to enforce property rights. It is a travesty of justice when downstream residents, for example, cannot hold an upstream polluter responsible for damaging their properties. The common law tradition must be revived if we are

to enjoy a healthy market economy and a cleaner environment. Potential polluters must know in advance that they will be held responsible for their actions.[37]

Enhancement of the institutions that allow for profit and loss may provide a better solution than government provision: Negative externalities can be reduced by enhancing property rights protection, as well as through innovation and growth. Competition and the availability of profit may also help private entrepreneurial solutions emerge to overcome the collective choice problem where there are positive externalities.

In addition to provision of public goods, many have argued that government could be used to direct investment toward social goods or to boost investment spending during economic downturns. Today in many countries increases in government spending and investment are used to stimulate growth. At one time many economists argued that investment should be guided or planned by the state, because only the state had the power to direct investment economy-wide, and the centralized vantage point would allow rational long-term choices. These economists argued that savings and investment are the causal factors for economic growth, hence rational central direction of investment would allow for greater economic growth. Economists studying the Soviet Union argued that because the Soviet government had complete control over investment it could achieve any level of economic growth that it desired.

For example, economist and Sovietologist Abram Bergson recounted the following during a discussion on the 1965 Soviet reforms: "A decisive factor in Soviet rapid growth has been the authoritarian control of the rate of investment. Given this, it was widely assumed that, if there were retarding factors in the growth of the Russian economy...by exercise of this authoritarian control of the share of output going to capital, the government could offset the retarding factors and more or less assure whatever growth was sought." However, by the time of the discussion, Bergson explained, the accepted wisdom had changed: Control over the quantity of investment was not enough, and much of the investment in the Soviet Union yielded little return.[38]

Similarly, in the 1930s John Maynard Keynes argued that government could direct investment and in so doing stabilize the business cycle. In the 1950s, economist Robert Solow argued that investment—public or private—was the primary driver of economic growth. More recently, economists have questioned whether the government can invest without "crowding out" private sector investment.[39] Even if the money the government spends is not immediately taken from the private sector through taxation, the resources used by government cannot be used by private businesses, and the inputs used are bid up in price. If the government crowds out an equal amount of private investment, and government investment is less efficient than private investment, then the result would be less economic growth.[40] The validity of the Keynes and Solow models depends upon the efficiency of government investment.

Some of the same problems of centralized investment may occur when government merely encourages investment. For example, government subsidies of ethanol production in the U.S. and elsewhere, passed for the purpose of guiding investment toward "greener" fuels, contributed to a spike in world food prices. The higher prices led to an increase in world poverty and even a reduction in UN food aid.[41] It was later discovered that the "clean" ethanol technology was inefficient and probably not even better for the environment.[42]

There is good reason to believe that without government subsidies this spike in prices due to heavy ethanol use would not have occurred, and the crisis could have been averted. If demand for green energy was high, without subsidies the provision of green technologies would have been more diversified and some errors would likely have been corrected sooner. For example (in a story reminiscent of one told by Simon Liberman about Lenin's investment policy[43]), one additional cost of using corn-based ethanol, which makes it inefficient and increases its environmental footprint, was discovered rather late. In calculating the costs of fueling a car with ethanol, a certain familiar detail was omitted: The corn used for ethanol must be transported by truck over long distances. This is more expensive (and creates more pollution) than transporting oil, which is largely moved by pipeline, but this cost was not initially included in analysis of cost-effectiveness.

Private producers, without subsidies, could have made the same mistake. However, without subsidies driving investment into only one technology, entrepreneurs seeking profit would tend to diversify, trying many alternatives, and each producer would compare the alternatives for profitability. Technologies that incur extra costs must fail in a competitive environment. However, with subsidies, producing ethanol was profitable for firms even with the extra costs. Firms could save money by not bothering with careful comparisons to alternative—unsubsidized—choices.[44] When private entrepreneurs test technologies simultaneously, more technologies are introduced, and failures occur more quickly, with less invested in each one. In this way, the market helps to determine the most efficient choice and may be less wasteful than a "rational" single choice by the state. There is also evidence of public energy projects in market economies becoming "frozen," similar to many Soviet investment projects:

> In 2001, the Government Accountability Office found that many federally subsidized clean coal projects had "experienced delays, cost overruns, bankruptcies, and performance problems." Of 13 projects the GAO examined, 8 had serious delays or financial problems, 6 were behind schedule by up to seven years, and 2 went bankrupt. Some projects have had successes, but a project in Alaska illustrates the more typical result of federal subsidization. The Healy Clean Coal Plant gobbled up $117 million of federal taxpayer money, but the project never worked as planned, it cost too much to operate, and it was finally closed down as a failure.[45]

Some may argue that without subsidies there would be *no* investment in alternative energies, but this is not obviously true. Over 75 percent of the world's oil is owned by governments,[46] which have the power to eliminate rivals. In countries where oil is privately owned, the companies are generally subsidized[47] and protected from competition. Oil is not only limited, it may not be very efficient. If entrepreneurs could produce an alternative that is less costly, they should be able to earn a large profit. However, currently, the nationalization or protection of oil companies and the subsidization of oil exploration and refining, along with numerous regulations and restrictions on alternative energy sources (e.g., nuclear) makes it very difficult for a profit-seeking entrepreneur to enter the market.

High oil prices put pressure on consumers and increase profits for energy suppliers. This creates incentives for entrepreneurs to offer lower-priced alternatives and reap some of the profit. If the government was not impeding the market process, sufficient incentive should exist for firms and new entrepreneurs to invest in alternatives.

Instead of allowing this process to occur on its own, the U.S. government and the European Union chose a favorite alternative energy and used subsidies to direct investment into it. On the presidential campaign trail, Barack Obama admitted he supported ethanol in part because Illinois, his home state, was a major corn producer. He also supported tariffs to reduce U.S. imports of sugarcane-based ethanol, which is estimated to be about eight times more efficient than corn-based ethanol.[48] These were clearly decisions based on politics, not economics.

Rather than choose a particular alternative energy, the government could try to step out of the way as much as possible and see whether a profit opportunity is available for private firms and new entrepreneurs to produce the alternatives. Yet what if there is not? Socialists had argued that government must provide goods that the market would underprovide because they are not profitable. Perhaps in addition to the potential problem of necessities for the poor and certain public goods, there may be underprovision of infrastructure in rural areas and in significant other areas of the economy. Economist James K. Galbraith (son of the famous John Kenneth Galbraith) argues that a major role of government should be provision of certain goods. He even goes so far as to give credit to the "soft budget constraint," a feature of socialist production that is rarely endorsed:

> I have never accepted that the United States fits the mold of a "free market economy." If we ever did, that model collapsed in the Great Depression. What was built in its place was a remarkable mix of public and private. There was, of course, plenty of room for enterprise. But it came in a framework, of a government that was, at its best, competently concerned with research, infrastructure, national security, the workplace and the environment, that provided Social Security and a large share of education, health care and housing. Part of the accidental genius of the system was that the public-private mix in those three areas, especially, created "soft budget constraints" that caused *higher education, the medical sector and the mortgage market* to grow very large—far larger than they ever could have, under either the free market taken alone or under socialism.[49]

He goes on to advocate that government "get back in the game" of planning. Yet although Galbraith admires the fact that the soft budget constraint allows sectors to grow larger than they would in a free market, how can he know whether they *should* be provided in larger amounts? The recent housing bubble and crash in the United States (and elsewhere) indicate that the soft budget constraint and subsidization designed to encourage home ownership may have been misguided. Although government wanted to increase the size of the mortgage market, it might have been a mistake to do so.[50]

Some economists also argue that there is too much spending on higher education[51] in the United States and too much spending on health care.[52]

It is impossible to know how big these sectors should be when they are not subject to profit and loss consideration. The soft budget constraints of these public-sector firms, just as under full socialism, mean that they are not constrained by their own budgets or fear of bankruptcy. Just as with the potato market that Barbara Wootton described, the consumers and firms are subsidized, and it is no longer clear how much of the product the consumer wants. The consumer no longer makes the choice to increase (or reduce) the size of the industry. Those decisions are made politically.

However, these political decisions are not generally made by the voters, as socialists imagined in their democratic vision. The millions of voters may or may not desire an increase, but interest groups will always want an increase. Because interest groups have a large stake in the outcome (there are "concentrated benefits") and can band together easily and cheaply, their voice is generally the loudest. The cost is spread out over the entire taxpaying population ("dispersed costs"), so that for each particular program that aids an interest group, it is rarely worth the bother for a single voter to oppose it.[53]

Politicians respond to interest groups to gain their endorsement and their campaign funds. As economist Don Boudreaux explained in the case of the housing bubble, "Ever-increasing home ownership is not the American dream. It is the dream of the [United States] National Association of Home Builders."[54] One might add that it was also the dream of the bureaucrats in the U.S. government programs and offices that benefited from additional funds, for example Fannie Mae and Freddie Mac, the U.S. government-sponsored enterprises (GSEs) charged with realizing this dream. It may also be the dream of the private firms that would benefit from subsidization, and the dream of those politicians that may be offered perks and funds by private firms that benefit from their policies.[55]

Of course, it may also be popular with the voters, but popularity does not necessarily correspond to economic efficiency or even viability. Credits, low-interest loans, and other policies that encouraged home-ownership in the United States were extremely popular. Interest groups representing minority groups lobbied for new low-interest government loans, and looser low-income lending standards. The first of these programs had been introduced prior to the Great Depression, but decades later, "as homeownership grew, political pressure to allow riskier loans increased, too... Under pressure to keep meeting housing demand, the government began loosening its mortgage-lending standards—cutting the size of required down payments, approving loans with higher ratios of payments to income, and extending the terms of mortgages."[56]

Starting with Herbert Hoover's Own Your Own Home campaign in the 1920s, expanding vastly with the Depression-era Federal Housing Administration (FHA) insuring mortgages, and Fannie Mae and Freddie Mac purchasing those government-insured mortgages, and then increasingly through tax credits and policies for low-income first-time home buyers, the U.S. government tirelessly worked toward higher home-ownership rates. Whether or not this was popular and compassionate, it may have been misguided.

Not surprisingly, the banks that made the most loans under new guidelines and subsidy-incentive schemes were the first to fail when the housing bubble popped.[57] When interest rates rose and housing prices fell, many of these low-income loans went into default. Some economists have argued that the combined effect of low-interest-rate policy, subsidies and tax breaks for mortgages, and the policies pressuring banks to lend to low-income groups helped to create the risky "toxic loan" environment that made the bursting of the bubble so much more dangerous.[58] These GSEs were also the creators of many of the complex securitization financial instruments indicated as one cause of the financial collapse.[59]

After the housing bubble popped, United States President Barack Obama introduced a program to help low-income buyers stay in their homes. However, *The New York Times* reported on January 1. 2010, that the program was widely perceived to be a failure:

> The Obama administration's $75 billion program to protect homeowners from foreclosure has been widely pronounced a disappointment, and some economists and real estate experts now contend it has done more harm than good.
>
> Since President Obama announced the program in February, it has lowered mortgage payments on a trial basis for hundreds of thousands of people but has largely failed to provide permanent relief. Critics increasingly argue that the program, Making Home Affordable, has raised false hopes among people who simply cannot afford their homes.
>
> As a result, desperate homeowners have sent payments to banks in often-futile efforts to keep their homes, which some see as wasting dollars they could have saved in preparation for moving to cheaper rental residences. Some borrowers have seen their credit tarnished while falsely assuming that loan modifications involved no negative reports to credit agencies.
>
> *Some experts argue the program has impeded economic recovery by delaying a wrenching yet cleansing process* through which borrowers give up unaffordable homes and banks fully reckon with their disastrous bets on real estate, enabling money to flow more freely through the financial system." The choice we appear to be making is trying to modify our way out of this, which has the effect of lengthening the crisis," said Kevin Katari, managing member of Watershed Asset Management, a San Francisco-based hedge fund. "We have simply slowed the foreclosure pipeline, with people staying in houses they are ultimately not going to be able to afford anyway."[60]

Despite the evidence that these policies helped to inflate the housing bubble and make it more toxic, they have continued and may be expanded. On Christmas Eve 2009, the House passed a bill lifting the $400 billion cap on potential losses for Fannie Mae and Freddie Mac as well as the limits on what the two could borrow, ensuring that the companies have perfectly soft budget constraints. [61] There have also been new low-income mortgage subsidy schemes. One section of the Waxman–Markey cap-and-trade bill[62] includes a program that offers a subsidy to low-income households currently living in manufactured homes built before 1976 toward a mortgage on new "energy efficient" manufactured homes. The old homes may then be destroyed or "recycled."

Subsidizing energy efficiency may sound good, however it is not easy for government to tell whether a subsidized industry is cost-effective. Thus, the state might simultaneously create a bubble, or inject additional risk into a market, and also invest in an inefficient technology. As seen in the Soviet children's school, a soft budget constraint makes the estimation of profitability impossible. Recently, subsidies given by the Spanish government to develop solar power created an unsustainable bubble:

> Lured by the promise of vast new subsidies, energy companies erected the silvery silicone panels in record numbers. As a result, government subsidies to the sector jumped from $321 million in 2007 to $1.6 billion in 2008.
>
> When the government moved to curb excess production and scale back subsidies late last year, the solar bubble burst, sending panel prices dropping and sparking the loss of thousands of jobs, at least temporarily.[63]

The Spanish government chose a technology and subsidized it. The subsidies made an otherwise unprofitable business strategy pay off. When the subsidies were removed, the firms collapsed. This indicates that it was not just a matter of needing initial investment funds to try a new technology. The solar panels remained unprofitable because they were still not cost-effective, despite the public investment.[64] A subsidy-driven unsustainable bubble can also wreak havoc on the rest of the economy. Just as with the housing bubble and financial crash in the United States, the risk injected into the market in Spain may have had far-reaching consequences:

> [S]ome power distributors in Spain have converted their government guarantees for higher-than-market energy prices into complex financial instruments, then sold them off to the highest bidders in a manner similar to the repackaging of subprime mortgages in the United States. If the government doesn't make good on those guarantees, critics fear, the securities could suddenly devalue, soaking the investors who hold them.[65]

Because profit and loss accounting is not available to determine the appropriate size of the sector, or the economic efficiency of the investments, subsidy-driven bubbles can be dangerous and expensive. Subsidies may have created or worsened the bubble and the crash in the United States, but some have argued that the bailouts were necessary to prevent a complete meltdown of the economy. Although the bursting of the housing and financial bubbles scared a lot of people, many economists have questioned this nightmare scenario. Nobel Prize winner Joseph Stiglitz, who is usually considered a left-leaning economist, argued recently that it is not true that there would have been a cascade of failures without the bailouts. He argued:

> We've really extended the safety net beyond too big to fail, and my view is that there's been no convincing argument that any of this was ever needed. It was based on the notion of fear—that if you didn't do it, the whole financial set of markets would fail.[66]

Nobel prize-winner Edward Prescott, who is generally considered a right-leaning economist, also blames fear driven by government, and argued that "[with] benign neglect the economy would have come roaring back quite quickly."[67] A few economists have pointed to the crash of 1920–1921 as an example of the potential success of this "benign neglect" strategy. Although the crash itself was as severe as the 1929 stock market crash in the United States, the recession which followed was relatively mild.[68]

It is not the case that, without government stepping in, the banks would necessarily have crumbled and all the money would have been lost. The assets would not have vanished. Private investors, for example, could have bought these failing firms for a cheap price. Warren Buffet was interested in buying Wells Fargo but was not allowed to do so. This would have acted like a "bailout," but would have cost taxpayers nothing and left the bank in private hands and with a hard budget constraint. As one commenter argued, "To not let a well capitalized company like Berkshire Hathaway acquire a bank when banks are clearly struggling to raise more capital makes no sense. Since Buffet claims he would "love" to buy the entire bank I suggest he should be allowed to do so."[69]

Regulators claimed that this would be "uncompetitive," but that government ownership of the bank's assets would somehow not be. While the American government theorized and speculated about what the "right" and "fair" price would be to pay for these banks, Warren Buffet simply said that it should be the market price, and if a wise investor bought the banks for the market price, he should come out ahead.[70] He also bid on or invested in several other failing companies during the collapse, including General Electric and Goldman Sachs.[71] The idea that these companies had nowhere to turn other than government cannot withstand close scrutiny.

General Motors and Chrysler were bailed out by the U.S. government, but the idea that the whole industry and regional economies would have been devastated without this government help is clearly unwarranted. In the absence of a bailout, these companies might have gone into bankruptcy. However, another auto company would likely have taken their place, buying the old capital and putting it to better use, avoiding the practices that got GM and Chrysler into trouble. Although it was not bailed out or nationalized, Ford Motor Company earned a profit in 2009.[72] Whatever companies emerged in the aftermath of the automakers' bankruptcy would necessarily be profitable ones, not ones that could only survive with help from the taxpayer.

Conclusion

Socialists argued that profit was the wrong basis on which to allocate resources in an economy. The problem with this reasoning is that profit and loss are critical for creating the price signals in the economy to indicate when something is desired and how much of it is desired. By controlling the levels of profit and loss of suppliers and by shifting funds from one firm to another, socialist planners lost sight of the requirements of the people. They did not know whether the production they invested in was desired. They also could not determine whether the firms and projects that they chose were cost effective.

Profit and loss are the signals that help entrepreneurs recognize whether something is desired or not, and these signals provide incentives for individuals to provide the most highly desired goods. The signals put out of business those firms that are inefficient or produce unwanted goods, and they shift investment funds from inefficient firms to those firms engaged in more productive activity. Although frequently denounced, profit and loss play critical roles, which need to be considered whenever policies are suggested that exclude their use.

The many advantages of the profit motive and the competitive pressures that face profit seekers with hard budget constraints are absent with public provision. Because of their absence, the net advantage of "socially necessary production" in many cases is not obvious. Profit and loss play a critical role in overall allocation of resources, technological improvement, and economic growth. Profit drives entrepreneurship, and loss weeds out inefficient and unwanted ventures. Socialization of profit removes any incentive to branch out into new product areas, effectively fill consumer demand, or take economically sensible risks. Socialization of loss keeps undesired investment projects growing, drives investment in technologies and industries even when it is inefficient or creates a bubble, and keeps "zombie" enterprises afloat.

These considerations weaken the arguments for government direction of investment or support for socially desired, but unprofitable, investment projects. The case is stronger for strictly defined public goods and other areas where it may be more difficult to make sufficient profit to ensure broad provision or where consumer sovereignty is weakened by the inability of poor individuals to purchase the good in question along with other necessities. Yet even in these areas, government may be wise to abstain from policies that prevent new competition from entering the market or make earning a profit in the market even more difficult.

ENDNOTES

1. Barbara Wootton, *Plan or No Plan* (New York: Farrar & Rinehart, Inc, 1935).
2. Bukharin and Preobrazhensky, *The ABC of Communism*.
3. Hirsch, *Quantity Planning and Price Planning in the Soviet Union*, p. 74.
4. Karl Kautsky, *The Social Revolution*, trans. by A.M. and May Wood Simmons, vol. 2, *On the Day After the Social Revolution* (Charles Kerr & Co., 1903), at http://www.marxists.org/archive/kautsky/1902/socrev/index.htm (November 24, 2009).
5. *Ibid.*
6. *Ibid.*
7. Wootton, *Plan or No Plan*, p. 172.
8. *Ibid.*, p. 217.
9. Rexford G. Tugwell, "The Principle of Planning and the Institution of Laissez Faire," *The American Economic Review*, Vol. 22, No. 1, Supplement, Papers and Proceedings of the Forty-fourth Annual Meeting of the American Economic Association (March 1932), pp. 75–92 (p. 81–82), and Rexford G. Tugwell, *Planning and the Profit Motive, in Socialist Planning and a Socialist Program* (Falcon Press, 1932), pp. 40–41.
10. V. I. Lenin, "Measures for Improving the Food Situation," January 14, 1918, at http://marxists.org/archive/lenin/works/1918/jan/14a.htm (November 20, 2009).
11. R. W. Davies, ed., *From Tsarism to the New Economic Policy* (Ithaca, NY: Cornell University Press, 1991), and Rutland, *The Myth of the Plan*.
12. The story is recounted in Simon Liberman, *Building Lenin's Russia*, pp. 146–147.
13. J. Wilczinski, *The Economics of Socialism* (London: Allen & Unwin, 1977), p. 146.

14. Wootton, *Plan or No Plan*.
15. *Ibid.*
16. *Ibid.*
17. Alec Nove, *The Soviet Economy: An Introduction* (New York: Praeger, 1966), p. 136.
18. Stalin, *Economic Problems of Socialism in the U.S.S.R.*, pp. 27–28.
19. *Ibid.*, pp. 28–29.
20. Nove, *The Soviet Economy*, pp. 53–54 (original emphasis).
21. Ernest Germain, "Soviet Management Reform," *International Socialist Review*, Vol. 26, No. 3 (Summer 1965), pp. 77–82, at http://www.marxists.org/archive/mandel/1965/03/sovreform.htm (November 20, 2009).
22. *Ibid.*
23. *Ibid.*
24. *Ibid.*
25. Janos Kornai, *The Socialist System*, p. 233–234. Kornai adds that shortages may exist in capitalist countries too-tellingly, his examples are the health care and education sectors, along with some urban housing. These are the sectors in these countries most dominated by state provision.
26. Robinson, *An American in Leningrad*, p. 121.
27. V. Trapeznikov, "Socialist Economic Management and Production Planning," in *Kommunist*, No. 5, 1964, in Sharpe, *Problems of Economics*, Vol. 1, *The Liberman Discussion: A New Phase in Soviet Economic Thought*, p. 196, quoted in William B. Bland, *The Restoration of Capitalism in the Soviet Union* (1980), at http://www.oneparty.co.uk/html/book/ussrmenu.html (November 20, 2009).
28. G. Kosiachenko: "Important Conditions for Improvement of Planning," *Voprosy ekonomiki*, No. 11 (1962), in Sharpe, *Problems of Economics*, Vol. 1, p. 158.
29. Germain, "Soviet Management Reform."
30. B. Sukharevsky: "On Improving the Forms and Methods of Material Incentives," *Voprosy ekonomiki*, No. 11 (1962), in Sharpe, *Problems of Economics*, Vol. 1, pp. 116–118.
31. Soviet reformers argued that they could use profit within the planned economy. Unless profit was just one of many targets (which is in fact all that was adopted out of the reform discussions) it would not be compatible with planning. Planning requires specific output targets, otherwise the planners could not be sure that the parts of the plan are reconcilable (e.g., that there are enough inputs to produce the desired outputs). In arguing that profit-guidance was compatible with planning, Liberman attempted to dress it in socialist clothing. He argued that it was subordinate in a socialist economy. In one article he made the interesting distinction that, "Under capitalism, profit is the basic aim, whereas satisfaction of the needs of the public is the means of attaining that aim and is secondary. Under socialism, on the contrary, the aim is to satisfy the needs of the public, and profit is the means toward that end." This may be reminiscent of the Soviet joke that "Under capitalism man exploits man, whereas under socialism it is the reverse." However, there is a serious distinction between profit under a system of private ownership and profit under collective ownership. Without private property, there is no market; without a market there are no market prices, and without market prices profit is meaningless. (We will return to this in Chapter 6). Liberman adds that "This is not a verbal distinction but the crux of the matter, since in our conditions profit does not work counter to social needs but helps to satisfy them," however just two sentences before he had conceded that the means to attain profit in a capitalist economy is to serve the needs of the people. His distinction is merely about intentions—whereas a much greater distinction consists in whether there is a way (such as market prices) to determine demand and cost.
32. Wootton, *Plan or No Plan*.
33. Richard T. Rapp, "'Civilized' Pharmaceutical Price Regulations: Can The U.S. Have It Too?" *Regulation Magazine*, vol. 17, No. 2 (Spring 1994), at http://www.cato.org/pubs/regulation/regv17n2/v17n2-7.pdf.
34. Rosefielde, "The First 'Great Leap Forward' Reconsidered," p. 569.
35. The term "tragedy of the commons" comes from a 1968 article which describes how rational individuals will over-use a common resource because their own over-use will not hurt them perceptibly, even though when all over-use the resource each individual will be hurt by

the destruction of the resource. Garrett Hardin, *Science*, December 13, 1968, at http://www.garretthardinsociety.org/articles/art_tragedy_of_the_commons.html

36. Thomas J. DiLorenzo, "Why Socialism Causes Pollution," *The Freeman*, Vol. 42, No. 3 (March 1992), at http://www.thefreemanonline.org/columns/why-socialism-causes-pollution (December 7, 2009).

37. *Ibid.* The idea that progressive courts might put economic growth ahead of individual rights might strike some as surprising. However, it should be noted that this has occurred recently as well in the United States—the 5–4 *Kelo v. New London* U.S. Supreme Court decision that put "economic development" above the property rights of the homeowner passed with a majority of judges generally deemed to be "liberal" or "progressive" in the American sense.

38. Abram Bergson, Alexander Erlich, Herbert S. Levine, G. Warren Nutter, Stanislaw Wellisz, and Henry L. Roberts, "Soviet Economic Performance and Reform: Some Problems of Analysis and Prognosis (A Round-Table Discussion)," *Slavic Review*, Vol. 25, No. 2 (June 1966), p. 243.

39. For example, see Alberto Alesina, Silvia Ardagna, Roberto Perotti, and Fabio Schiantarelli, "Fiscal Policy, Profits, and Investment," *American Economic Review*, Vol. 92, No. 3 (June 2002), pp. 571–589.

40. One of the responses to this argument is that government investment should be used when these resources are "idle," such as during a recession. However, the resources may only be idle for a short time while private entrepreneurs let prices fall and make plans to take advantage of the cheaper opportunities for investment. If government steps in, these plans may never see the light of day. Even if the resources are "idle" at the moment that government invests, this does not mean that no crowding-out occurs. This is similar to the case made in Chapter 2 that even if workers are unemployed when hired by government, this does not mean that government cannot wastefully employ them. Poor investment of idle resources is also discussed in Chapter 7.

41. For example, see Lester R. Brown, "Why Ethanol Production Will Drive World Food Prices Even Higher in 2008," Environment News Service, January 25, 2008, at http://www.ens-newswire.com/ens/jan2008/2008-01-25-insbro.asp (November 20, 2009); "Why the Era of Cheap Food Is Over," *Christian Science Monitor*, December 31, 2007, at http://www.csmonitor.com/2007/1231/p13s01-wogi.html (November 20, 2009); and Lester R. Brown, "Supermarkets and Service Stations Now Competing for Grain," Earth Policy Institute, July 13, 2006, at http://www.earth-policy.org/Updates/2006/Update55.htm (November 20, 2009).

42. For example, see John Roach, "Ethanol Not So Green After All?" *National Geographic News*, July 11, 2006, at http://news.nationalgeographic.com/news/2006/07/060711-ethanol-gas.html (November 20, 2009), and Alan Bjerga, "Ethanol Demand in U.S. Adds to Food, Fertilizer Costs," Bloomberg, updated February 28, 2008, at http://www.bloomberg.com/apps/news?pid=newsarchive&sid=aUIPybKj4IGs (November 20, 2009).

43. Liberman recounts a story about an investment in extracting fuel from Pine Cones, a project which failed because the distance to transport the pine cones required more fuel than they produced. Simon Liberman, *Building Lenin's Russia* (Chicago: University of Chicago Press, 2007), pp. 27–28.

44. Subsidies that shift investment from a more efficient to a less efficient technology (because the subsidy covers more than the difference in cost to the firm) in this way are similar to the "subsidy" of a low interest rate driven by monetary policy, which will be discussed in Chapter 7.

45. Jerry Taylor and Peter Van Doren, "Energy Intervention Today," Cato Institute, February 2009, at http://www.downsizinggovernment.org/energy/intervention (December 7, 2009).

46. Tim Padgett, "Chavez's Not-So-Radical Oil Move," *Time*, May 1, 2007, at http://www.time.com/time/world/article/0,8599,1616644,00.html (December 7, 2009).

47. Keith Bradsher, "Fuel Subsidies Overseas Take a Toll on U.S.," *The New York Times*, July 28, 2008, at http://www.nytimes.com/2008/07/28/business/worldbusiness/28subsidy.html (December 7, 2009).

48. For example, see Alec MacGillis, "Obama's Evolving Ethanol Rhetoric," *The Washington Post*, June 23, 2008, at http://blog.washingtonpost.com/44/2008/06/23/obamas_evolving_ethanol_rhetor.html (November 20, 2009), and Larry Rohter, "Obama Camp Closely Linked with Ethanol," *The New York Times*, June 23, 2008, at http://www.nytimes.com/2008/06/23/us/politics/23ethanol.html (November 20, 2009).

49. James K. Galbraith, "What Is the Predator State?" TPMCafe, August 11, 2008, at http://tpmcafe.talkingpointsmemo.com/2008/08/11/what_is_the_predator_state (November 20, 2009)

(emphasis added). The last admission—socialism could not support larger sectors—is probably a recent phenomenon due to the collapse of communism and the recognition that it produced lower output overall. Earlier socialists always argued that they could create whatever size sector that they wanted.

50. For an excellent and readable explanation of how the policies aimed at home-ownership in the United States may have contributed to the housing bubble and crash, see Steven Horwitz and Peter Boettke, "The House That Uncle Sam Built: The Untold Story of the Great Recession of 2008," Foundation for Economic Education, at http://fee.org/wp-content/uploads/2009/12/HouseUncleSamBuiltBooklet.pdf.

51. For example, George Leef, "Are Government 'Investments' in Higher Education Worthwhile?" Library of Economics and Liberty, December 1, 2008, at http://www.econlib.org/library/Columns/y2008/Leefeducation.html (December 7, 2009). Some have also argued that it may be a regressive form of redistribution: Armen Alchian, "The Economic and Social Impact of Free Tuition," *New Individualist Review* (Winter 1968), at http://oll.libertyfund.org/?option=com_staticxt&staticfile=show.php%3Ftitle=2136&chapter=195494&layout=html&Itemid=27 (December 7, 2009).

52. For example, see Arnold Kling, "Crisis of Abundance: Rethinking How We Pay for Health Care," Cato Institute, April 26, 2006.

53. For a simple overview of how this works, see John Stossel, "Influence-Peddling," ABC News, March 5, 2008, at http://abcnews.go.com/2020/Stossel/story?id=4392850 (December 7, 2009).

54. Russ Roberts, "Good Tax Policy," Cafe Hayek, December 19, 2008, at http://cafehayek.typepad.com/hayek/2008/12/good-tax-policy.html (November 20, 2009).

55. Countrywide Financial gave thousands of dollars in savings in low-interest loans to the politicians that could vote to increase the funding of Fannie Mae and Freddie Mac. Fannie Mae was the number one purchaser of Countrywide loans, and Countrywide was bailed out by these same politicians. When Fannie Mae and Freddie Mac were under public scrutiny, they fought back by raising millions of dollars for members of the relevant oversight committees and opening up "partnership offices" that funneled money into various housing projects in districts of key members of Congress. Daniel Golden, "Countrywide's Many 'Friends,'" Portfolio.com, June 12, 2008, at http://www.portfolio.com/news-markets/top-5/2008/06/12/Countrywide-Loan-Scandal (December 7, 2009); Glenn R. Simpson and James R. Hagerty, "Countrywide Friends Got Good Loans," *The Wall Street Journal*, June 7, 2008, at http://online.wsj.com/article/SB121279970984353933.html (December 7, 2009); and David S. Hilzenrath, "Fannie, Freddie Deflected Risk Warnings," *The Washington Post*, July 14, 2008, at http://www.washingtonpost.com/wp-dyn/content/article/2008/07/13/AR2008071301462.html (December 7, 2009).

56. Steven Malanga, "Obsessive Housing Disorder," *City Journal* (Spring 2009), at http://www.city-journal.org/2009/19_2_homeownership.html (November 20, 2009).

57. *Ibid.*

58. For example, see Arnold Kling, "Not What They Had in Mind: A History of Policies That Produced the Financial Crisis of 2008," George Mason University, September 15, 2009, and Bruce Yandle, "Lost Trust: The Real Cause of the Financial Meltdown," The Independent Institute, February 2010, at http://www.independent.org/pdf/tir/tir_14_03_02_yandle.pdf.

59. In 1997, an article by the Cato Institute explained that "the mortgage GSEs pioneered a financial vehicle called securitization that allows them to bundle mortgages into securities that are sold to investors. The securities are backed by the payment stream of the underlying mortgages. Through securitization, the GSEs have the option of avoiding interest-rate risk and credit risk by passing them on to the holders of the securities. However, the credit risk is generally retained by the GSEs by offering a guarantee to the securities holder against the mortgages going into default, a contract for which the GSEs receive a fee. The entire process becomes a cycle that feeds on itself." Vern McKinley, "The Mounting Case for Privatizing Fannie Mae and Freddie Mac," Cato Institute *Policy Analysis* No. 293, at http://www.cato.org/pub_display.php?pub_id=1152 (December 7, 2009).

60. Peter S. Goodman, "U.S. Loan Effort Is Seen as Adding to Housing Woes," *The New York Times*, January 1, 2010, at http://www.nytimes.com/2010/01/02/business/economy/02modify.html?hp.

61. "The Biggest Losers: Behind the Christmas Eve taxpayer massacre at Fannie and Freddie," *The Wall Street Journal*,   January 4, 2010, at http://online.wsj.com/article/SB100014240527487041528045746283509800043082.html.

62. H.R. 2454 § 203, 111th Congress, 1st Sess.

63. Anthony Faiola, "Spain's Answer to Unemployment: Go Greener," *The Washington Post*, September 24, 2009, at http://www.washingtonpost.com/wp-dyn/content/article/2009/09/23/AR2009092302152.html (November 20, 2009).

64. This inefficiency directly affects workers and consumers. For example, although the policy was intended to create "green jobs," in fact far more jobs were destroyed than were created As already mentioned in Chapter 2, it is estimated that 2.2 jobs were destroyed in the private sector for every one created by the policy. Gabriel Calzada Alvarez, "Study of the Effects on Employment of Public Aid to Renewable Energy Resources," Universidad Rey Juan Carlos, March 2009, at http://www.juandemariana.org/pdf/090327-employment-public-aid-renewable.pdf   (February 13, 2010).

65. Faiola, "Spain's Answer to Unemployment: Go Greener."

66. Joseph Stiglitz, quoted in "The Stiglitz View," *The Economist*, September 27, 2009, at http://www.economist.com/blogs/freeexchange/2009/09/the_stiglitz_view (November 28, 2009).

67. Edward Prescott, quoted in Brad DeLong, "Do Chicago Economics Nobel-Prize Winners Live in the Consensus Reality?" J. Bradford Delong's Grasping Reality with All Eight Tentacles (blog), September 27, 2009, at http://delong.typepad.com/sdj/2009/09/do-chicago-economics-nobel-prize-winners-live-in-the-consensus-reality.html (November 28, 2009).

68. Robert P. Murphy, "The Depression You've Never Heard Of: 1920-1921," *Freeman*, Vol. 59, No. 10 (December 2009), at http://www.thefreemanonline.org/featured/the-depression-youve-never-heard-of-1920-1921 (December 7, 2009).

69. Mike Shedlock, "Let Warren Buffett Buy Wells Fargo," Market Oracle, May 4, 2009, at http://www.marketoracle.co.uk/Article10433.html (November 20, 2009).

70. Henry Blodget, "Warren Buffett Reveals Bailout's Dirty Little Secret," Business Insider, at http://www.businessinsider.com/2008/9/warren-buffett-reveals-bailout-s-dirty-little-secret (November 20, 2009).

71. "Warren Buffett Boosts Confidents amid the Financial Crisis," 100 Mortgages, October 2, 2008, at http://www.100mortgages.org/20081002/warren-buffett-boosts-confidents-amid-the-financial-crisis (November 20, 2009).

72. Associated Press, "Ford earns $2.7 billion in 2009," Jan 28, 2010, at http://apnews.myway.com/article/20100128/D9DGO8O80.html.

CHAPTER 5. MIDDLEMEN, TRADE, AND THE MARKET SYSTEM

INTRODUCTION

Socialists argued that capitalism was inefficient because it engenders enormous wastes of duplication, marketing, and middlemen. The middleman is thought to steal profit by raising the price for the consumer without adding anything. The chaos of the profit system may drive men to buy and sell products in the role of middleman, but this is wasteful to the economy, and costly to the consumer.

When wholesalers offer products directly to the customer, the products are cheaper because the "middleman was eliminated." Socialists took this concept to its ultimate conclusion. In a planned economy, production and distribution could be streamlined, and all the profits made by middlemen along the way could be cut out, benefiting the consumer enormously. Today, these arguments are still used to support the idea that socialized health care can be more efficient than privately provided health care by eliminating profit-taking middlemen. Yet, if profit guides the entrepreneur to serve his customers, what is the actual role of these middlemen in the market economy? Can the state really cut costs by eliminating them?

THE SOCIALIST ARGUMENT

Classical economists extolled the benefits of specialization, comparative advantage, and trade. If a firm is able to a make profit, like Adam Smith's baker, then it must be providing some socially desired product or service. Even though there are "economies of scale" for large firms, having many smaller firms performing different services or producing different components may be more efficient because of the gains from specialization and comparative advantage.

Socialists did not see the market as efficiently delegating tasks. Instead, they saw it as chaotic, with the lure of profit driving men into wasteful and exploitative ventures. Socialists argued that "middlemen" are a wasteful byproduct of the chaos of the capitalist order. In a planned society, it would be unnecessary to have rungs of the production process in which greedy companies and capitalists shave off excess profits in the guise of added value and in the process engage in wasteful advertising and marketing. These intermediaries were doing work that could be streamlined by a single planner. There is no need, they argued, for some middleman to skim the cream off along the way. Friedrich Engels provided this example:

> Let us take, for example, a bale of cotton produced in North America. The bale passes from the hands of the planter into those of the agent on some station or other on the Mississippi and travels down the river to New Orleans. Here it is sold—for a second time, for the agent has already bought it from the planter—sold, it might well be, to the speculator, who sells it once again, to the exporter. The bale now travels to Liverpool where, once again, a greedy speculator stretches out his hands towards it and grabs it. This man then trades it to a commission agent who, let us assume, is a buyer for a German house. So the bale travels to Rotterdam, up the Rhine, through another dozen hands of forwarding agents, being unloaded and loaded a dozen times, and only then does it arrive in the hands, not of the consumer, but of the manufacturer, who first makes it into an article of consumption, and who perhaps sells his yarn to a weaver, who disposes of what he has woven to the textile printer, who then does business with the wholesaler, who then deals with the retailer, who finally sells the commodity to the consumer. And all these millions of intermediary swindlers, speculators, agents, exporters, commission agents, forwarding agents, wholesalers and retailers, who actually contribute nothing to the commodity itself—they all want to live and make a profit—and they do make it too, on the average, otherwise they could not subsist. Gentlemen, is there no simpler, cheaper way of bringing a bale of cotton from America to Germany and of getting the product manufactured from it into the hands of the real consumer than this complicated business of ten times selling and a hundred times loading, unloading and transporting it from one warehouse to another? Is this not a striking example of the manifold waste of labour power brought about by the divergence of interests? Such a complicated way of transport is out of the question in a rationally organised society.[1]

Socialists believed that they could improve upon this chaotic and long journey that a product takes in a market economy. A planner would have a bird's eye view, and be able to rationally organize the supply chain, streamlining production and cutting out the middlemen. One producer—the benevolent state—would take one piece of "profit," which could then be wisely invested, rather than having many profit-seeking firms in a messy struggle for a piece of the pie.

John Stuart Mill quotes his contemporary Victor Considérant, a student of the socialist François Fourier, who similarly argued that not only one middleman, but often many, make off with the value that rightly belongs to the consumer:

> [F]or products do not pass only once through the greedy clutches of commerce; there are some which pass and repass twenty or thirty times before reaching the consumer. In the first place, the raw material passes through the grasp of commerce before reaching the manufacturer who first works it up; then it returns to be sent out again to be worked up in second form; and so on until it receives its final shape. Then it passes into the hands of merchants, who sell it to the wholesale

> dealers, and these to the great retail dealers of towns, and these again to the little dealers and to the country shops; and each time that it changes hands, it leaves something behind it.[2]

According to this argument, the profit that each of these companies extracts when they do their piece of the production is lost to the consumer. A streamlined process would avoid this and therefore allow for a lower price of final goods. In addition, the streamlined process would save enormously in terms of simplicity and coordination. It would also avoid the wastes of the intermediary firms' advertising, packaging, and overhead, and the haggling and quality-reducing practices of vicious competition. One overarching rational representative of the people could better organize the whole process and could bypass the various interests that exploit the process to extract gains for themselves:

> It is evident that the interest of the trader is opposed to that of the consumer and of the producer. Has he not bought cheap and undervalued as much as possible in all his dealings with the producer, the very same article which, vaunting its excellence, he sells to you dear as he can? Thus the interest of the commercial body, collectively and individually, is contrary to that of the producer and of the consumer—that is to say, to the interest of the whole body of society.[3]

In this view, the middleman extracts the maximum value from the customer and the producer. These middlemen are basically "parasites" who rob society with their unproductive activity, their waste, and their ruthless drive for profit, whereas in a socialist society they could do productive and peaceable work, under the guidance of a benevolent planner who sets up a rational system that streamlines and coordinates the process.

THE SOVIET EXPERIENCE

Middlemen as such were to be eliminated with the introduction of socialism. The 1919 Communist Party program explained that "In the sphere of distribution the task of the Soviet government at the present time is persistently to continue to replace trade by planned, organized distribution of products on a national scale."[4] In 1919 the Executive Committee of the Communist International described what Russia had achieved so far:

> Everything which the industries produce goes now not to enrich a small parasitical section of the community but the whole community. In each town and district, there are local councils of Public Economy linked up with the supreme body. This system of public management does away with a whole host of middlemen who, in capitalist countries, make huge profits at the expense of the consumers.[5]

As mentioned in Chapter 4, in the early period, drastic measures were taken to suppress "speculation," which included all kinds of trade, especially that of the middleman. This was the hectic period of war communism. Russia had just fought a world war, underwent a revolution, and was still fighting a civil war. Although Lenin and the other Bolshevik leaders planned to outlaw private ownership for the long-term, the policies enacted and the hardships endured during this period were in part due to this "emergency situation."

In some ways this period resembled the chaos that follows a natural disaster, in which martial law and the outlawing of "speculation" and "price gauging" are often deemed necessary due to severe shortages of necessities. After the policies of war communism were instituted, some ex-merchants were still trying to buy and trade—to use market relations instead of planned distribution. On January, 1918, Lenin announced:

> All these data show that the workers of Petrograd are monstrously inactive. The Petrograd workers and soldiers must understand that they have no one to look to but themselves. *The facts of abuse are glaring, the speculation, monstrous*; but what have the mass of soldiers and workers done about it?... We can't expect to get anywhere unless we resort to terrorism: *speculators must be shot on the spot*. Moreover, bandits must be dealt with just as resolutely: they must be shot on the spot.
>
> The rich section of the population must be left without bread for three days because they have stocks of other foodstuffs and can afford to pay the speculators the higher price.[6]

These measures were put in place. A resolution was passed calling for "A plenary meeting of the Petrograd Soviet...to take revolutionary measures to fight speculators and overcome the famine." The draft resolution read in part:

> (4) Speculators who are caught and fully exposed as such shall be shot by the groups on the spot. The same penalty shall be meted out to members of the groups who are exposed as dishonest.[7]

Of course, eliminating the middleman in this way—literally—did not lead to a more efficient economy. Instead, shortage and famine were widespread, and a black market emerged and persisted even as those supplying on this free market were arrested and shot. "To the surprise of Bolshevik theoreticians, the more the nationalized sector expanded, the larger loomed what one Bolshevik economist called its 'irremovable shadow,' the free sector."[8]

The state stores, which depended upon centralized distribution, faced chronic shortage; but the private market was booming. Men and women risking execution to peddle goods literally saved millions from starvation: in the winter of 1919–1920, 66–80 percent of the food consumed in Russian cities was furnished by the free market. This was in part because peasants would not raise crops for the meager prices the state was willing to pay (when it would pay them at all) and partly because the state distribution system was unable to deliver goods to where they were most needed. Middlemen and other private traders were needed to deliver these goods. "The government found itself in the absurd situation in which the strict enforcement of its prohibitions on private trade would have caused the entire urban population to starve to death."[9]

Lenin concluded that they had rushed the transition to socialism and would need to step back, reintroduce markets, and then proceed with more careful planning. The New Economic Policy of the 1920s reintroduced "speculation" by legalizing many forms of private ownership and trade. This policy was only intended to be temporary. The state would soon organize production rationally and make the middleman, or speculator, unnecessary. In 1928 the private trader was once again banned. Yet middlemen had served a purpose; it was not as easy to do away with them as social-ists had hoped. Trotsky described the problem in *The Revolution Betrayed*:

> Present market relations differ from relations under the NEP (1921–28) in that they are supposed to develop directly without the middleman and the pri-vate trader between the state co-operative and collective farm organizations and the individual citizen. However, this is true only in principle.... Not only the indi-vidual peasants, but also the collectives, and especially individual members of the collectives, are much inclined to resort to the middleman.... From time to time, it unexpectedly transpires that the trade in meat, butter or eggs throughout a large district, has been cornered by "speculators." Even the most necessary articles of daily use, like salt, matches, flour, kerosene, although existing in the state store-houses in sufficient quantity, are lacking for weeks and months at a time in the bureaucratized rural co-operatives. It is clear that the peasants will get the goods they need by other roads....
>
> "The basis of speculation in our land is destroyed," announced Stalin in the autumn of 1935, "and if we have speculators none the less, it can be explained by only one fact: lack of class vigilance and a liberal attitude toward the speculators in various links of the Soviet apparatus." An ideally pure culture of bureaucratic thinking! The economic basis of speculation is destroyed? But then there is no need of any vigilance whatever. If the state could, for example, guarantee the population a sufficient quantity of modest headdresses, there would be no necessity of arrest-ing those unfortunate street traders.[10]

During the Stalin period, the state severely cracked down on "speculation" and merchants and middlemen acting in any way privately. Rational central direction determined supply, cutting out all profit-making middlemen. The plan determined what each firm made and where it was to obtain inputs. Inputs of enterprises were strictly controlled: An allocation certificate was required for many of the materials and components required by firms, and firms were usually tied to a single supplier.[11]

The use of allocation certificates to arrange supply led to frequent supply break-downs. Alec Nove recounted one example of the many complaints about supply printed in the Soviet newspapers: "For instance, one reads of a building site in Kuiby-chev held up through failure to deliver machinery, which in turn is held up by failures to deliver components to the machinery manufacturers in Saratov, which failure is then traced up the line until it is discovered that the Cherepovets steelworks had been expected to deliver steel from a workshop which had not yet been completed."[12]

Suppliers were so often unreliable that many larger enterprises would manufac-ture their own inputs. The largest firms would often supply for themselves everything from housing and meals for their workers to core materials and components required for production in the factory. Firms boasted of being able to produce everything "from a screw to a battleship."[13] In this way, specialization of labor was greatly reduced. The benefits of specialization, comparative advantage, and trade were lost.

The absence of middlemen could be very costly. Alec Nove points to this with regard to agricultural "traders" who could act as a middleman between the farmer and the farmer markets:

> The absence of professional traders (whose activities are illegal in the USSR), and the inadequacies of cooperative commission trade, daily compel hundreds of

thousands of peasants to take their onions, cheese, beef, potatoes, etc., to often distant markets at great expense in time.[14]

These traders were reintroduced in a limited capacity once this expense was discovered. Commission traders were introduced in 1953 to allow the *kolkhoz* (collective farm) farmer to remain at the farm, and to supply more produce to the cities. An additional benefit was that these middlemen acted as further competition on the usual *kolkhoz* farm markets.[15] However, restrictions on trade and on private activity as a "trader" remained, and still led to bizarre inefficient choices. These inefficient choices were then blamed on "speculation" and profit.

> It is obvious that many of the journeys made by kolkhoz members make no kind of sense in economic terms, and are only justified by the erratic behavior of prices and the great variations to be noted from place to place. For example, *Pravda*, 14th January 1962, criticizes a kolkhoz in Alma-Ata whose members went as far afield as Omsk and Chelyabinsk to sell fruit, vegetables and wines in the markets there: the kolkhoz chairman, wrote one of his members to the newspaper, knows only one word: profit. One hears of instances where it pays a kolkhoz worker to take a train to go and sell a sack of apples, or even a plane for a sack of oranges or lemons (which fetch extremely high prices in the towns) all the way from Georgia to Moscow or other large towns.[16]

This was in part because the planned distribution of produce and fresh foods was extremely lacking. Most areas did not see fresh fruit except for a few months in the summer, and frequently goods such as cheese were no longer fresh by the time they arrived on the shelves of the state stores.[17] There were difficulties in the economy well beyond the distribution of farm produce. A far greater difficulty was the problem of supplying the enterprise with the necessary inputs to fulfill the plan. This was one of the supposed great advantages of planning—that the middleman could be cut out and a rational supply chain from the raw materials all the way down to the consumer could be coordinated and streamlined, saving vast sums in previous waste and extracted profits. However, this supply chain was riddled with problems.

Soviet firm managers rated supply problems as their most pressing concern, and high level ministry officials spent two thirds as much time on supply problems as on production.[18] Most firms faced a shortage of at least some of their inputs. To enhance their self-sufficiency, in addition to producing their own inputs, many firms would "hoard" the inputs they could obtain, adding to the generalized shortage in the economy. Firms would also break the law in various ways to obtain their inputs. Black markets emerged to fulfill needs not only of the consumer, but also of the socialist firm. Firms would also barter with other firms, trading excess inputs that they hoarded for inputs in short supply—essentially replacing the planned distribution system with an ad-hoc market.

Factory managers frequently admitted that if they did not break the law regularly, they had no chance of fulfilling planned output.[19] This input trading was so important that a brand of middleman called *tolkachi* grew up and was tacitly accepted by planners[20] because they played such a critical role in allocating resources:

> Plan fulfillment is every manager's prime concern, if only because this is the only way his or her career can advance. Hence, various extra-plan strategies are

used to cut through bureaucratic bottle-necks or to procure supplies, transport, repair, extra labor, and spare parts. This shadow economy involves misreporting to the authorities and bribing or making connections with other managers in what are known as family circles. Most factories retain a fixer (in Russian, tolkach), who functions as middleman, broker, and network entrepreneur.[21]

A *Pravda* article read, "It is only possible to get rid of the *tolkach* if supplies are properly planned, and for this one must take into account the real possibilities of supplying enterprises,"[22] which was to say that the plan alone could not supply the firms. Due to the incessant shortages of so many of the inputs that each enterprise required, Soviet managers had to use middlemen to negotiate with the suppliers, essentially to push their way to the front of the line. In a market economy, middlemen would bid up the price if the "line" was long (if there was a lot of demand), and this would also induce new supply. In the Soviet economy prices were centrally set, so bribes and other sorts of substitutes were used; and of course this could not induce new supply because production was planned and profit outlawed.

The supplying firm had its own plan, which it usually could not fulfill completely (because targets were set high) and which would take time over the course of the year. The plan might include several different products in a variety of shapes and sizes or other specifications. A successful *tolkach* middleman could convince the supplying enterprise to make the products that *he* needed first and put *his* firm's purchase ahead of others. This might be done by bribe or political intimidation, but it was very often done with negotiation and barter.

To maximize one's chances of successful negotiation, the use of "personal influence," or *blat*, was critical. *Blat* may be based on family relationships, or friendship, but "great care is often taken in cultivating the friendship by means of little gifts."[23] Long term reputations were built on this basis, a kind of replacement for the market signals of advertising and branding.

Joseph Berliner described *blat* as "the use of personal influence for obtaining certain favors to which a firm or individual is not legally or formally entitled." For firms, he explains, this means for example, "obtaining materials contrary to the intention of the plan, or persuading ministry officials to relieve one's own firm of a difficult production task and assign it to another firm with less influence," while for consumers it means "obtaining consumer goods without having to queue up, or securing an apartment to which one is not strictly entitled by his occupation." The *tolkachi* were specialists at using *blat*.[24]

Berliner describes how "armies" of *tolkachi* would swarm around the larger factories that supplied intermediate goods to other socialist enterprises. They would spend months in nearby hotels, without concern for cost, and often spend huge amounts of money bribing the manager of the factory to obtain the goods, even if the goods were themselves very cheap.[25]

The time spent soliciting the goods was considerable and this was wasteful for the economy. Yet this practice made sense at the firm level, given that the firms were funded by government and obtaining a supply of shortage goods was more critical to the manager than any particular expense. Even if the expense was not planned, running over costs was less of a problem than running short of supplies. *Tolkachi* middlemen did aid the process of supply by helping to direct goods to the firms that needed them most, but they lacked the efficiencies of profit-seeking middlemen.

Middlemen in market economies compete to provide to retailers, for example, the cheapest and best products that they can obtain from suppliers, but the *tolkachi* acted more like bureaucrats than competitive businessmen because they bid up the price of the goods they obtained unrestrained by their own budget constraint. They faced no pressure from below. Whereas in a market system, the consumer exerts pressure on the middleman to efficiently and cheaply provide his service, the *tolkachi* faced no such pressure.

Still, the *tolkachi* kept the Soviet system running. They emerged because they could solve a problem. There was a lack of coordination among firms and supplies because of faults in the plan. An intermediary between firms could aid horizontal distribution—trading of outputs for inputs, of excess supplies for ones in shortage. Just as the middleman in a market economy is born when an entrepreneur sees a need that she can fill, and inspired by profit chases after it, in the Soviet economy the *tolkachi* emerged to fill a need.

Just as private traders had emerged during war communism, and great violence was required to suppress the market they created, the ad-hoc markets that emerged within the planned economy were a result of natural and spontaneous interaction between individuals seeking ways to resolve their own problems. Only strict prohibition combined with harsh punishment could prevent the emergence of markets and middlemen where they were needed; and they were needed throughout the Soviet period because planned production and distribution was an unworkable ideal. As one Sovietologist put it,

> The official economic system of the Soviet Union is to a great extent a highly artificial machine, whose operation can only be ensured by a complex edifice of legal commands and prohibitions. A great variety of economic activities in which people will more or less spontaneously engage will have to be forbidden in order to prevent the collapse of an economy which is in principle owned and operated by the state. If individual citizens are not prevented from owning means of production, taking part in the production process themselves, participating in the distribution of production (trading), providing services, etc., the state will lose control of the corresponding sectors of economic life. Consequently, a fair part of the Criminal Code is taken up by detailed prohibitions of all kinds of private economic activities. In fact, the ideal of a totally state controlled economy is so difficult to realize that the Soviet regime has long ago been forced to make concessions to the requirements of reality. [26]

Socialists never succeeded in completely stamping out the middleman, but they did manage to persecute him and reduce the value of his services by eliminating competitive pressures.

Wherever possible, the middleman was replaced by a "rational" supply chain and centralized distribution; however, just as under "war communism," the role played by the middleman, or speculator, was not adequately filled by the socialist supply and distribution system. Where the middleman was eliminated, not only shortages, but a tight web of bureaucracy grew in his place. Centrally organized production required an intricate supply plan. The firm was a part of this plan, and permission was required if any part of it was to change:

> As a general rule, Soviet enterprises are not allowed to sell producer goods to each other except by previous authorization and in amounts prescribed by higher authorities.... The prohibitive amount of paperwork involved may be gathered from the well-publicized experience of the Moscow automobile plant named after Likhachev. The documentation required for it to obtain its annual supply of ball bearings from the adjacent GPZ factory weighs over 400 pounds and is handled by 14 agencies. After this laborious process is completed, the Likhachev factory will obtain the permit to buy the ball bearings it needs. But will it now get the ball bearings? This is by no means certain. In fact, its supplier, the GPZ factory, received as many as 4,000 complaints about the non-delivery or delayed delivery of ball bearings during the first six months of 1963. Persistent shortages of ball bearings have been reported throughout the country, and in some cases led to work stoppages of entire factories. The fault was attributed to errors and miscalculations in the supply plans.[27]

The bureaucracy that replaced the middleman, and direct exchange, was considerable. Four hundred pounds of paperwork was necessary because the plan required information at every level—ascending and descending the hierarchy. Because orders came from above to organize supply, information had to be passed along every link, rather than allowing each link in the chain to gather and utilize information independently.

Yet the plan information was often wrong. Errors and miscalculations interrupted supply, and misguided projects were undertaken even while local knowledge was sufficient to avoid them. This created a fundamentally different kind of system. Leon Smolinski described it this way:

> A centrally planned economy is usually looked upon as a more or less efficient machine for the production and distribution of goods. A cybernetician would view it somewhat differently: as a machine which, more or less efficiently, generates, processes and distributes information. The two functions are intimately related. Channels of information and flows of commodities are, in fact, interrelated parts of a highly complex network. To produce a car load of, say, ball bearings, it takes not only so much steel, machinery, manpower and time; it also takes an information input in the form of data concerning the availability of resources and the demand for the product. These data are gathered, processed and forwarded to the decision-makers who issue orders to producers and receive reports which may give rise to new, modified decisions. All these activities can obviously be handled in a variety of ways. The flow of information may take place within the confines of a small privately owned shop or, at the other extreme, it may involve thousands of messages passing among hundreds of agencies. Whatever the nature of the information system involved, a cybernetician would begin his analysis with such questions as: How much information is needed per unit of output (say, per carload of ball bearings), and what is its cost? Who receives the data and in what detail? Who processes them and by what means? Who makes the decisions? How is their exe-

cution controlled? To provide satisfactory answers to these questions in the Soviet case and to follow our carload of ball bearings through all the recesses of the information system, nothing short of a treatise on the organization and functioning of the Soviet economy would do. Significantly enough, such a treatise would also go a long way toward answering the question how Russia is ruled. Information flows point toward centers of power. "Knowledge is power," asserted Francis Bacon.[28]

Marx arguably described this in a critique he wrote of Hegel's philosophy. "The bureaucracy is a circle from which no one can escape. Its hierarchy is a hierarchy of knowledge,"[29] he said. To plan an economy, the Soviet planners learned, one needs a great deal of knowledge—and the knowledge needed is always changing. Moment to moment, the needs, the requirements of every person and every action change; every relationship is changing through time.

The plan made it difficult to handle change—to pass information along the supply chain: what to make, where to obtain materials, in order to guide firms through production. The plan must contain every piece of information necessary first to know, and then to create, every product that the consumer wants. Then the consumer changes his mind. For the firm to respond to this change, information about the change in demand must reach planners and then the new plans must filter back down to the firm.

The flexibility of a market economy comes through the ability of firms to make contracts with those around them, rather than having to wait for permission from a central planner to trickle down through the bureaucracy. The middleman is simply the actor who sees a need to be filled by a firm—the firm needs a supplier—and comes to fill that need, in order to earn profit. This profit can feed the middleman's family—can send her kids to school. It is an incentive that guides the middleman not just to serve her customer, who requires an input, but also the supplier who wants to sell it. As competitive pressures keep the middleman in line, she acts like an arbitrator for the market, brokering the deal that best serves both parties.

LESSONS

Socialists had argued that rational production and distribution could replace the "chaos" of the market system of profit-chasing and the "waste" of profit-extraction by various middlemen. However, this argument was based on a misunderstanding of the role of the middleman in market exchange. In an economy without prohibitions on private trading, trade naturally occurs between individuals who can see an advantage in it—it "emerges." Similarly, middlemen emerge in the process of producing, distributing, and delivering goods as individuals specialize in different parts of the process.

By attempting to plan a more rational system of production and distribution and outlawing private trading and transactions, socialists repressed this natural, spontaneous process, but were unable to improve upon it. The single rational mind centrally coordinating the process could not find a better, cheaper way of accomplishing what the market and its various middlemen and specialists had previously achieved.

Even, perhaps especially, during a tumultuous time such as the "war communism" period, "speculation" by private traders helps to ensure the production of important goods, and their distribution to those in need. Recently, economist Steve Horwitz argued that something similar occurred after the disastrous hurricane that hit New Orleans. "The untold story of Katrina involves the way in which Wal-Mart in particular responded with speed and effectiveness, often in spite of government relief workers' attempts to stymie it, and in the process saved numerous lives and prevented looting and chaos that otherwise would have occurred."[30]

Although many worry that "speculation" during times of disaster will result in the suffering of the poor, as greedy speculators exploit their situation, private merchants both during war communism and after Hurricane Katrina brought relief to those in need, as they moved faster than government and produced and distributed more of what was needed:

> In the three weeks following the storm's landfall, Wal-Mart shipped almost twenty-five hundred truckloads of merchandise to the affected areas and had drivers and trucks in place to ship relief supplies to community members and organizations wishing to help. Home Depot provided more than eight hundred truckloads of supplies to the hard-hit areas and used buses to transport one thousand employees to the region from other areas. Besides what Wal-Mart sold as a result of quickly reopening its stores, the company also provided a large amount of free merchandise, including prescription drugs, to those in the worst-hit areas. Several truckloads of free items went to New Orleans evacuees staying at the Astrodome and at the Brown Convention Center in Houston. Most important, Wal-Mart got this assistance to the devastated areas almost immediately after the storm had passed rather than in the days—in some cases weeks—that it took government agencies to provide relief to residents.[31]

The middleman, as the experience of the Soviet Union highlights, also plays an important role in production and distribution. There are unique advantages to private, decentralized coordination that express themselves through the middleman. On the surface, it may look as if the profit earned by a middleman is waste and that prices are unnecessarily high due to this profit. Yet a middleman plays a critical role, and the waste and loss are much greater if he is stopped from playing this role.

Socialists assumed that a rational streamlined distribution system could replace the "wastes" of a plethora of profit-taking middlemen. An example may help to illustrate the problems with this theory. One example of a simple "middleman" who would be eliminated by a planned economy is the gumball machine dealer. Many small restaurants and stores have gumball machines for children and local customers to buy gum while they wait. These could be delivered directly from the factory that makes them, but usually there is a middleman that buys from the factory and then sells them to the shops. These middlemen represent precisely the kind of wasteful trader that Considérant accused of extracting profit at the expense of the consumer.

Surely, these traders cannot perform a service that justifies the profit they make? Yet consider what would occur under a socialist distribution. The state would determine the number of gumballs to produce and the size and number of machines to dispense them. The state would locate the factories and instruct the factories to deliver the machines to the shops that are cited in the plan. Yet how would they determine how many gumballs are desired at each location?

The role of the middleman is important here. In the market system, the middleman seeks out the shop owner as an appropriate customer. The dealer researches the area and the product and tries to sell the shop owner the machine by providing the shop owner with information about potential profit. The shop owner then must decide whether he will in actuality earn the profit that the dealer suggests. He can make a deal with this middleman according to how much he expects to sell, and the middleman can help him gather the information necessary to strike this deal. The two can work together to increase sales, because sales will benefit both of them.

The middleman seeks out markets and works out new ways for his customers to dispense the product because this is how he earns profit. His role is to take the product and ensure that it reaches every nook and cranny of the economy where it is desired. He ensures that it reaches every customer that demands it. But he cannot force the shop owners to take the machine if they cannot sell the product. The shop owners do not want to lose money. They will not buy the machine if their own customers have no teeth or no taste for sugar. Thus, the middleman plays an important role in helping the product reach just the customers who most demand it.

The state distribution system cannot do this. The state can only allocate the machines to those set out in the plan, but the planners have none of the middleman's advantages. They do not know demand, except based on past statistics and questionnaires. They have no local, on-the-ground knowledge about the different shops. They have no profit motive to take on the specialized role of seeking out the best neighborhoods to sell the product. The private middleman is also in a unique position to respond to changes in demand by the customers of different shops. They can take these demands to different suppliers and find the cheapest priced alternatives or new supply. They have the incentive and ability to research the customers and the suppliers and to efficiently connect the two, streamlining the distribution process.

If you have ever asked yourself how the food on your dinner table got from the farms and fields where it was grown to the grocery store where you bought it, you might have wondered if it was the most efficient way. The socialist argument was that hiring all of the middlemen—those who bought it wholesale, took some profit, and passed it along—is a huge waste. Further waste, they argued, results from allowing transport companies to profit from moving it from place to place and from middlemen at the retail level, and so on. Engels' tale of the bale of cotton emphasized the long and wasteful route that products take in modern profit-driven economies.

Today, there is a movement for "locally grown produce" which makes a similar case. Although the argument centers less around the profit extracted along the way, this movement argues that the packaging and transport is excessively wasteful. Yet the socialist experience may help us to see that this argument is questionable.

The delivery routes that have emerged in the market system were not the result of a sneaky middleman trying to extract the greatest profit at the expense of the consumer—competition would prevent that. Instead, the middleman is only able to acquire profit if he can offer the most efficient delivery route. The author and "skeptic" Brian Dunning recently wrote a blog article that exposed the mistake made by this local produce movement. He tells the story of Henry's, a produce retailer founded on the principle of selling only locally grown food. To reduce waste and conserve energy, the model of stores like Wal-Mart that truck their produce miles out of the way was to be replaced with a simple system of farmers delivering their produce directly to the closest local store. However, this turned out to be a mistake:

> In their early days, they did indeed follow a true farmers' market model. Farmers would either deliver their product directly to the store, or they would send a truck out to each farmer. As they added store locations, they continued practicing direct delivery between farmer and store. Adding a store in a new town meant finding a new local farmer for each type of produce in that town. Usually this was impossible: Customers don't live in the same places where farms are found. Farms are usually located between towns. So Henry's ended up sending a number of trucks from different stores to the same farm. Soon, Henry's found that the model of minimal driving distance between each farm and each store resulted in a rat's nest of redundant driving routes crisscrossing everywhere. What was intended to be efficient, local, and friendly, turned out to be not just inefficient, but grossly inefficient. Henry's was burning huge amounts of diesel that they didn't need to burn.
>
> You can guess what happened. They began combining routes. This meant fewer, larger trucks, and less diesel burned. They experimented with a distribution center to serve some of their closely clustered stores. The distribution center added a certain amount of time and labor to the process, but it (a) still accomplished same-day morning delivery from farm to store, and (b) cut down on mileage tremendously. Henry's added larger distribution centers, and realized even better efficiency. Today their model of distributing locally grown produce, on the same day it comes from the farm, is hardly distinguishable from the models of Wal-Mart or any other large retailer.[32]

The reason Henry's ended up with the Wal-Mart model is because Wal-Mart also valued efficiency. Whether or not it cared about environmental friendliness, Wal-Mart certainly wanted to save on gas. The distribution-center model emerged from a process of profit-driven cost cutting. If you look at the path traveled by any one given box of produce, it is indeed longer than it used to be, but overall it is much more efficient. It achieves what the movement wanted to achieve better than their own vision.

In this example, the distribution center was not a separate contracting company—it was part of Henry's. However, this is a role often played by a middleman. The attempt by Henry's to eliminate this step and connect farms directly to the store is reminiscent of the socialist solution which eliminated the middleman between the cooperatives and the consumer, and between the farmer and the farmers' markets (which would "daily compel hundreds of thousands of peasants to take their onions, cheese, beef, potatoes, etc., to often distant markets at great expense in time"). In both cases, the middleman was more efficient, and whatever profit he took was well deserved.

Whether it is provided by the supermarket or by a contracting company, in a market economy the distribution center tends to emerge if it is more efficient, as Henry's learned. A bit of consideration about Wal-Mart's own desire to conserve fuel, and hence make a larger profit, might have suggested this to the management at Henry's.

Similarly, arguments that the middleman extracts profit at the expense of the consumer take into consideration only part of the picture. Considérant argued that the middleman buys as cheaply and sells as expensively as he can (and so steals from the consumer and puts suppliers out of work). Yet, Considérant focused solely on the actions of the middleman without seeing the pressures exerted on the middleman himself that constrain his profit taking. The middleman does buy as cheaply as he can, and this forces the suppliers to compete and offer better products. The middleman may also try to sell for as high a price as he can get, but just as he tries to buy cheaply from his suppliers his customers buy as cheaply as they can, so he is forced to compete on price as well. Each level keeps the one above it in check.

That is, unless one or more of these levels is supported by subsidies or is publicly funded. The middlemen in the Soviet Union did not need to compete to offer their services more efficiently because their salary was not a concern to the firms employing them. Soviet middlemen did not pressure the suppliers to keep costs down because the cost of supplies was automatically covered by the state. In a market economy, the firms hiring middlemen would ensure that those middlemen not only performed their function well, but that their costs and the costs of the suppliers were minimized. Hence, in the market, the middleman is a specialized dealer that integrates production or distribution. With competitive pressure, local knowledge, and a profit motive, he has a strong incentive and ability to perform his unique function well. A centralized production and distribution system that is "rationalized" to omit the middleman actually suffers from his absence.

Just as the *tolkachi* emerged to facilitate distribution within the vast "single factory" of the socialist system, middlemen emerge in all areas of the market economy to bring goods from the factories where they are produced to the factories and stores where they are needed. This is no different than the emergence of trade in any other area of the economy. Just as produce markets and black markets sprung up in the Soviet economy, and *tolkachi* emerged to fulfill the needs of state enterprises, trade will always emerge where it is advantageous because it is simply a voluntary exchange between two individuals with needs. The only way it does not occur is if it is suppressed by some authority. When it is suppressed, it must be replaced by another supply system—and the way to ensure supply without free exchange is through a plan and a hierarchical bureaucracy to enforce it.[33]

Middlemen are necessary, whether something is provided publicly or privately, so they will eventually emerge unless brutally repressed. The difference is that, when the system is private, middlemen compete with each other. Competition among middlemen tends to drive the price down, as each provider of these services reduces his costs to win business. The potential for profit also spurs new innovation in this intermediate industry, and the profit is reinvested when there is a chance to expand a useful service or invest in a new technology.

Therefore, middlemen are useful. In fact, as discussed in Chapter 1, they are efficient *even if* they spend a large amount of money on advertising, brand naming, and marketing services. Yet, it is often argued that public-sector provision of services like health care is efficient because it can save on these costs by eliminating the middleman. Given what Soviet planners learned, it is not clear that public provision of health care could cut the middleman out and reduce costs.

For example, it has been argued that use of private health care providers in the United States is more expensive than a public health care system would be. This is purportedly because the private health management organizations (HMOs) cost more, in part because they take a cut (as profit), acting as a middleman. These are perhaps some of the most hated middlemen in the market economy. Yet is this profit a pure waste that "cutting out the middleman" could eliminate and in so doing make the customer better off?

Careful analysis by the Congressional Budget Office[34] revealed that, although the amount spent on these private providers by the state-run Medicare program was more than the amount the state spent when providing the service publicly, the consumer also received greater benefits. The additional value to the consumer actually exceeded the additional cost, meaning that these private providers were more efficient, not less efficient, than the public ones. This explains why so many consumers switched from public provision to private provision when given the chance. Yet these facts are hidden beneath the headline that "costs are higher under private plans, due to additional payments to HMOs."

Some also argue that the fragmented provision of services by so many different medical providers causes inefficiencies that increase administrative costs. It is argued that this could be streamlined and that economies of scale would result if all of these disparate providers were placed under one umbrella. One article, which claimed that a single-payer plan would save massively on administrative costs, argued that "functions essential to private insurance but absent in public programs—e.g., underwriting, marketing, and corporate services—account for about two thirds of private insurers' overhead."[35]

However, as we have seen, "middlemen" provide a service: This is why they emerge in a market system and why they survive and profit. To evaluate whether costs would be lower with a single provider system, it is necessary to ask: What will replace the HMOs and other middlemen? Will there still be competition among different kinds of provision? Will a state-controlled production and distribution line really be more efficient than a private one? Or will the middleman be replaced with the bureaucrat?

The supply line that replaces the middleman may become a vast bureaucracy. It may also require advertising, marketing, and other services. (See Chapter 1.) The services that it tries to cut out by streamlining distribution may actually be useful, especially in conditions of market competition. There also may be services discovered by competing firms, acting as middlemen, in the market—services which a government bureaucracy may not realize are important. In their private, specialized role, market middlemen may discover services that they can offer clients. Although they may play an important role in the profit-seeking of private firms, they may be seen as wasteful. Yet, because profit-seeking is the way that firms efficiently serve customers, the waste may be at least partly an illusion.

For example, underwriting is a service provided by HMO middlemen that is highly disparaged and which many would like to see eliminated by public provision. Underwriting is a service that measures risk of potential clients, and determines the premium that needs to be charged to insure that risk. A public program may charge all clients equally (or fund the program through taxation). However, without a service such as underwriting, a public program would not know the expected cost of each of the insured in the program, and could not effectively perform cost-benefit analysis of various levels of insurance provision. Although risk is pooled by public provision of insurance to the entire population, it may still be beneficial to estimate the risk of individual policyholders, and determine what level of care they are likely to require.

There are also costs to equity: if premiums are not charged based on risk, there are problems of "moral hazard." In the private insurance market, the "fragmentation and multiplicity" of private "middlemen" performing these services allow for competition and innovation in technologies to reduce this waste. Although there are benefits to offering health insurance without charging premiums based on risk, there is a cost. Reducing this cost, or at least estimating it, may be important for making quality health care affordable for the society as a whole.

A recent paper that studied public and private medical coverage costs argues that "private insurers compete by devising ways to control moral hazard more cost-effectively" and "in a competitive environment, insurers incur costs to control moral hazard only as long as this yields at least equivalent savings from control of overuse."[36] Although society may choose to incur the cost of offering health insurance with no premium, or with an equal premium regardless of risk, it should be recognized that there is a cost. Although often regarded as a cause of waste, middlemen HMOs do reduce this cost in private markets. Competition between HMOs also leads to a variety of different products which can compete to fill different needs at different costs:

> Control of moral hazard through price- and information-based strategies requires time and effort of patients and providers—filling in forms and proving that services were medically justified, appropriately priced, and covered by the terms of the insurance contract. But insurers cannot ignore these costs and treat the time of providers and patients as a free resource. On the contrary, competition forces insurers to internalize costs that they impose on patients and providers; these costs influence the prices patients are willing to pay and the terms on which providers are willing to participate. Thus, the diversity of insurance plans that emerge in competitive insurance markets reflects the diversity of patients' preferences between premiums, copayments, paperwork, and restrictions on freedom of choice;

and the willingness of providers to trade off among higher reimbursement, freedom of practice style, and administrative expense.[37]

The paper argues that while the costs of the overhead to enforce the private solution are easily documented, the public-provision costs of overuse, including waiting periods and reduced medical options, tend not to be counted as costs.

HMOs are also accused of earning profit by denying claims. As Considérant argued, the middleman supposedly buys as cheap as he can and sells as dearly—the HMO is accused of paying hospitals as little as possible, while charging customers exorbitant rates.

Yet as with all other middlemen, this would only be possible if the customer exerted no pressure on the middleman. Although competition is stifled by protections, subsidies, and barrier-creating regulations in the health care industry, it has not been eliminated completely. Furthermore, government is also capable of denying claims. The 2008 National Health Insurer Report Card[38] published by the American Medical Association reported that, out of all providers, the firm with the highest percentage of claims denied (6.85%) was the public health provider Medicare.

Middlemen emerge in the evolving market because they can offer a service that is valued by those that hire them or buy from them, not because greed has led to wasteful duplication and profit gained at the expense of the consumer. "Eliminating the middleman" through public provision, whether in the health care sector, organic farming, or in gumball machine delivery, is probably not a way to improve efficiency or reduce costs.

CONCLUSION

Despite their bad name, middlemen are a critical part of a dynamic economy. They serve valuable roles, including efficiently joining parts of the supply chain, promoting competition, and enhancing the responsiveness of firms to consumer demand. Furthermore, they are invaluable to an economy—even a socialist one. Even though they were suppressed, middlemen reemerged in the socialist economy. Yet middlemen play a more valuable role in an environment in which they can make profit, reinvest it, and compete with other private firms. The new socialist middlemen were less efficient than the middlemen in market economies.

Hence, even if government is able to significantly reduce the use of middlemen when providing services such as health care, those that remain may be less efficient if they are regulated heavily by the state. This lesson is important to keep in mind when evaluating whether public provision can reduce costs in areas such as health care.

ENDNOTES

1. Frederick Engels, speech, February 8, 1845, in "Speeches in Elberfeld," in *Marx/Engels Collected Works*, Vol. 4 (Moscow: Progress Publishers, 1975), at http://marxists.org/archive/marx/works/1845/02/15.htm (November 25, 2009).
2. Victor Considérant, quoted in John Stuart Mill, *Chapters on Socialism*, in *Principles of Political*

Economy with Chapters on Socialism (Oxford: Oxford University Press, 2008), p. 395.

3. *Ibid.*, p. 392.

4. Political Program of the CPSU, March 22, 1919, at the Eighth Congress of the Russian Communist Party, *International Socialist Review*, Vol. 22, No. 4 (Fall 1961), pp. 115-124, at http://www.marxists.org/history/ussr/government/1919/03/22.htm.

5. Executive Committee of the Communist International, "Capitalist England—Socialist Russia," 1919, at http://www.marxists.org/history/international/comintern/sections/britain/capitalist-britain.htm (November 25, 2009).

6. V. I. Lenin, "Meeting of Presidium of the Petrograd Soviet with Delegates from Food Supply Organisations," January 14, 1918, at http://www.marxists.org/archive/lenin/works/1918/jan/14.htm (June 12, 2009) (emphasis added).

7. *Ibid.*

8. Richard Pipes, *The Russian Revolution*, p. 700.

9. *Ibid.*, p. 701–702.

10. Trotsky, *The Revolution Betrayed*, chap. 6.

11. Nove, *The Soviet Economy*, p. 37.

12. *Ibid.*, p. 210.

13. Rutland, *The Myth of the Plan*, p. 130.

14. Nove, *The Soviet Economic System*, p. 276.

15. M. Goldman, "Retailing in the Soviet Union," *Journal of Marketing*, Vol. 24, No. 4 (April 1960), pp. 9–15.

16. Philippe J. Bernard, *Planning in the Soviet Union* (Pergamon Press, 1966), p. 25.

17. Logan Robinson recounted his experience with cheese in the Soviet Union in the 1970s: "The worst problem was in the distribution system; by the time the cheeses got to the store they were a little like the Politburo—old, tired, and dried out. The same cheeses, fresh from the certificate-ruble stores, were quite good." The certificate-ruble stores were only for high Party members, diplomats and foreign students. Robinson, *An American in Leningrad*, p. 180.

18. Paul Gregory, *Restructuring the Soviet Economic Bureaucracy* (Cambridge: Cambridge University Press, 1990), p. 94.

19. See e.g., Nove, *The Soviet Economy*, p. 38.

20. Nove, *The Soviet Economic System*, pp. 38 and 209–210, and Aron Katsenelinboigen and Herbert S. Levine, "Some Observations on the Plan-Market Relationship in Centrally Planned Economies," *Annals of the American Academy of Political and Social Science*, Vol. 434, Social Theory and Public Policy (November 1977), pp. 186–198.

21. Steven L. Sampson, "The Second Economy of the Soviet Union and Eastern Europe," *Annals of the American Academy of Political and Social Science*, Vol. 493 (September 1987), p. 128.

22. Nove, *The Soviet Economic System*, p. 95.

23. Berliner, *Factory and Manager in the USSR*, p. 191.

24. *Ibid.*, p. 182

25. *Ibid.*, pp. 210–214

26. F. J. M. Feldbrugge, "Government and Shadow Economy in the Soviet Union," *Soviet Studies*, Vol. 36, No. 4 (October 1984), p. 529.

27. Smolinski, "What Next in Soviet Planning?" pp. 605–606.

28. *Ibid.*, pp. 602–603.

29. Karl Marx, *Critique of Hegel's Philosophy of Right* (1843).

30. Steven Horwitz, "Wal-Mart to the Rescue: Private Enterprise's Response to Hurricane Katrina," *The Independent Review*, Vol. 13, No. 4 (Spring 2009), pp. 511–528 (p. 512), at http://www.independent.org/pdf/tir/tir_13_04_3_horwitz.pdf.

31. *Ibid.*, p. 514 (citations removed). Horwitz also has argued that the institutions of the market economy guided these firms to "do the right thing," another instance of "putting social responsibility ahead of profits in order to make more profits." See, Steven Horwitz, "Doing the Right Things: The Private Sector Response to Hurricane Katrina as a Case Study in the Bourgeois Virtues," Working Paper, Mercatus Center at George Mason University, 2009, at http://mercatus.org/sites/default/files/publication/WP0933_Hurricane%20Katrina%20and%20

the%20Bourgeois%20Virtues.pdf.

32. Brian Dunning, "The Fallacy of Locally Grown Produce," Skepticblog, May 28 2009, at http://skepticblog.org/2009/05/28/the-fallacy-of-locally-grown-produce (November 25, 2009).

33. On the question of whether a plan requires hierarchy, see Chapter 9.

34. Congressional Budget Office, "Medicare Advantage: Private Health Plans in Medicare," *Economic and Budget Issue Brief*, June 28, 2007, at http://www.cbo.gov/ftpdocs/82xx/doc8268/06-28-Medicare_Advantage.pdf (November 25, 2009).

35. Public Citizen, "USA Wastes More on Health Care Bureaucracy Than It Would Cost to Provide Health Care to All of the Uninsured," *Medical News Today*, May 28, 2004, at http://www.medicalnewstoday.com/articles/8800.php (November 25, 2009).

36. "Hidden Overhead Costs: Is Canada's System Really Less Expensive?" *Health Affairs*, Vol. 11, No. 1 (Spring 1992), p. 26, at http://content.healthaffairs.org/cgi/reprint/11/1/21.pdf (November 25, 2009). Do they only control overuse, or do they control costs only by denying those most in need of coverage? Although their reputation is formed around the latter assumption, this would not earn the HMO the most profit. Maximum profit would be made not by denying coverage completely (turning away customers) but by charging a higher rate, based on the results of underwriting. Federal regulations in the United States limit the amount that providers can tailor coverage to the customer, and the rates which can be charged. If HMOs had greater flexibility they might offer coverage at a high rate, and then a voucher program could help high-risk individuals pay the higher premiums.

37. *Ibid.*

38. American Medical Association, "2008 National Health Insurer Report Card," 2008, at http://www.ama-assn.org/ama1/pub/upload/mm/368/reportcard.pdf (December 7, 2009).

CHAPTER 6. THE HIGH PRICE OF PRICE CONTROL

INTRODUCTION

Price controls have been used since ancient times.[1] It is common to hear people say that a price is "too high" or "too low" and that a "fair price" should replace it. For example, if greed has driven firms to set prices "unreasonably" high, then government should restrain them with a price ceiling. On the other hand, if the market has driven prices too low, firms may suffer and lay off workers; also some greedy firms may set prices at a "predatory" level to drive out competition. Hence government should also step in on occasion with price floors.

Socialists believed that government could set all prices in the economy and use prices as levers to direct the economy until the point that money and prices would be no longer necessary. (Some argued that they would not even be necessary in the short term.) In the socialist vision, prices should not be determined by market forces. The "law of value," a law of the market, should not determine allocation. Instead, planners would make rational choices about production to serve the common good, and set prices based on social equity.

THE SOCIALIST ARGUMENT

> Only a false consciousness, caught in the net of commodity fetishism, puzzles itself with market and price problems. — Paul Mattick [2]

Socialists believed that market prices were just a phenomenon of the capitalist system, and would not be necessary under socialism. Instead, socialist society would be organized on the basis of a plan, which would replace allocation by market forces and market prices.

In the capitalist economy, the poor faced prices that were unfairly high for necessities, leaving them at bare subsistence. With planning, the people would decide what price is fair for each good in the economy. In the short term prices could be controlled for fairness and used for accounting. In the long run, even this use would fade away. The planners would set, use, and manipulate prices as the planners desired and would dispense with them when they no longer served any purpose. Economist Barbara Wootton wrote:

> Under an unplanned economy, movements of price, and the responses of individuals to these, are themselves the forces which direct the country's industry here or there, open up this enterprise and close that down. Under the planned system these movements are merely the tools by which industry may be directed into the channels along which the plans intend it should go.[3]

Planners could adjust the prices to control the use of resources. Power over prices would mean control over the direction of the economy. What better evidence that planners could direct the economy at their will than that they could continue to use and manipulate prices in a socialist economy? Wootton summed up this vision, saying that "[a] planning authority, with full control over all prices and wages, can raise the price of this and lower the price of that so as to keep *any* plan going."[4]

Because Marx did not write extensively about planning, many people assume that he did not advocate such a method. However, in several passages he discusses rational control and planning, and he alluded to it elsewhere. He discussed the "anarchy of production" that he saw as plaguing capitalism, and he described the way in which rational control by the whole of society would bring abundance and usher in a new age. Yet, what is "rational control by the whole of society" but a description of some form of planning?

Friedrich Engels, Marx's close friend and financial backer, spoke about it more directly and often. The works in which he explicitly described the rational planning of the future socialist society were endorsed (and sometimes co-written) by Marx.[5] In 1847, in the important popular work *Principles of Communism*, Engels explained that under socialism,

> Society will take all forces of production and means of commerce, as well as the exchange and distribution of products, out of the hands of private capitalists and will manage them in accordance with a plan based on the availability of resources and the needs of the whole society.[6]

It was the "anarchy" of the market that Marx and Engels wanted to suppress—they wanted to control the chaotic, spontaneous economic and social order and arrange production and civil society according to a rational plan. In his well-known 1871 book *The Civil War in France*, Marx argued that this must result in communism. He asked, "If united co-operative societies are to regulate national production upon a common plan, thus taking it under their own control, and putting an end to the constant anarchy and periodical convulsions which are the fatality of capitalist production—what else, gentlemen, would it be but communism, 'possible' communism?"[7]

Marx felt strongly that rational direction was not only possible, but paramount. The modern age was an age of reason, and modern man must bring society from the chaos of nature into the enlightened world of reason. Man could and must take the reins and steer society into the future. In the famous work *Socialism: Utopian and Scientific*, Engels wrote:

> Active social forces work exactly like natural forces: blindly, forcibly, destructively, so long as we do not understand, and reckon with, them. But, when once we understand them, when once we grasp their action, their direction, their effects, it depends only upon ourselves to subject them more and more to our own will, and, by means of them, to reach our own ends. And this holds quite especially of the mighty productive forces of today.
>
> ...With this recognition, at last, of the real nature of the productive forces of today, the social anarchy of production gives place to a social regulation of production upon a definite plan, according to the needs of the community and of each individual.[8]

At the helm, rational man could organize all of society, direct production, determine the quantities and values of each resource, and direct the orchestra of life. Ultimately, this would mean the orchestra, beautifully coordinated, could then live on without a conductor. The state would wither away, and the people would continue to rationally produce for their needs.

Socialists did not question whether this was possible; it was only a matter of will. The chaos of the market economy may produce and depend on market-based prices, but the socialist economy would not. Instead, man would dominate and become master over the price. Man could use and manipulate prices or abolish them altogether. This is the freedom that socialism would bring: Man would finally control his nature and his world.

Once in power, the Soviet authorities maintained this goal, and proudly spoke of planning the economy as a superior method, which would achieve their aim of true communism. In 1920, Bukharin and Preobrazhensky wrote that "Without a general plan, without a general directive system, and without careful calculation and bookkeeping, there can be no organization. But in the communist social order, there is such a plan."[9] Gregory T. Grinko, vice chairman of the planning commission (Gosplan) and one of the authors of the first five-year plan, wrote in *The Five-Year Plan of The Soviet Union: A Political Interpretation*: "Planned economy is as inherent to the socialist system as hopeless anarchy in production and merciless competition, whether among individual capitalists or among capitalist groups and states, are to capitalist society."[10]

THE SOVIET EXPERIENCE

> [N]ow that we have crushed the exploiters, we must learn to run the country. — Lenin, 1921[11]
>
> What we have with Trotsky and his comrades in the Great October Revolution is the spectacle of a few literary-philosophical intellectuals seizing power in a great country with the aim of overturning the whole economic system—but without the slightest idea of how an economic system works. — Ralph Raico[12]

Although planning in the Soviet Union is often cited as beginning in the late 1920s, with the first five-year plan and collectivization, Lenin actually attempted the first

Soviet plan much earlier. He set up a committee on electrification known as GOEL-RO in 1921, and it produced a 10-year plan for the Soviet economy. Lenin described it as a rough draft but a real "scientific" plan:

> The plan ranges over about ten years and gives an indication of the number of workers and capacities.... Of course, it is only a rough draft, with possible errors, and a "rough approximation," but it is a real scientific plan. We have precise calculations by experts for every major item, and every industry. To give a small example, we have their calculations for the output of leather foot wear at two pairs a head (300 million pairs), etc. As a result, we have a material and a financial (gold rubles) balance sheet for electrification.[13]

The first taste of the problems of economic calculation surfaced during this period. It was the first attempt at a pure socialist economy, and the outcome resembled the predictions by anti-socialist economists. The economist Ludwig von Mises described what he thought would occur:

> A socialist management of production would simply not know whether or not what it plans and executes is the most appropriate means to attain the ends sought. *It will operate in the dark*, as it were. It will squander factors of production both material and human (labour). Chaos and poverty will unavoidably result.[14]

Evidence suggests that Mises was correct. Barbara Wootton, an economist sympathetic to the socialist experiment, used similar phrasing to describe the difficulties faced by planners during war communism; difficulties that were caused by economic planning, not by civil war:

> Whereas, under the price mechanism, the rising price of products which were urgently demanded, and of which there was a great shortage, would have provided an immediate index of the need for those products, and an inducement to producers to expand and hurry on their production programmes, the Supreme Economic Council had to *make guesses in the dark* as to the relative urgency of different needs, and to carry those guesses into practical effect through the machinery of committee minute and administrative decree. They had to give preference to one industry or factory, and to decide the point at which each preference should cease, on principles of their own and without any accurate quantitative index to guide them.[15]

The market provides natural mechanisms that help to allocate resources. Without them the socialist planners had no way to compare various uses of scarce resources or to determine what was and was not efficient, or even necessary. For this reason, in 1924, Trotsky defended a return to profit and loss accounting, the economic independence of enterprises, and market relations, because: "With the liquidation of the market and of the credit system each factory resembled a telephone whose wires had been cut."[16]

Trotsky understood the reason for this and argued that "[w]hether a particular railway is beneficial to the economy can be ascertained only through the medium of the market" until the time when they had mastered socialist planning. Except for faith in the ultimate triumph of socialism, it is not clear why Trotsky saw this as a temporary problem while transitioning to socialism and not as a permanent necessity. Using the railroads as an example, he explained the problem of central planning:

> [B]y following an abstract technico-socialist plan, we ran the risk of completely losing all control over what was necessary and what was not, over what was profitable and what was not in the case of each individual railway and the

network as a whole. Which line should be expanded and which one should be contracted? What rolling stock and what personnel should a given line have? How much freight could the state transport for its own needs and what share of the carrying capacity should be allotted for the needs of other organizations and private individuals? All these questions—at the given historical stage—cannot be resolved except by fixing rates for transportation, by correct bookkeeping, and exact commercial calculation. *Only by maintaining a profit and loss balance between the various sections of the railway network, coupled with the same sort of balance among other branches of economy*, will we be able to elaborate methods of socialist calculation and the methods for a new economic plan.... For a certain and rather long period of time, the workers' state shall have to utilize capitalist methods, that is, methods of the market, in operating the railway network.[17]

Hence, retreating from the rush to socialism, Lenin and Trotsky allowed private ownership and limited exchange within free markets. However, the state continued to own much of the capital goods industries and large factories, and it continued to set many of the prices in the economy. This "commanding heights" planning was also plagued by price distortion.

As a market emerged in the early 1920s, with the introduction of the New Economic Policy, inflationary pressures triggered by the policies of "war communism" led to a problematic divide between agricultural products produced by the peasants, and industrial products, such as tractors, that they required. In response to this, Soviet leader Nikolai Bukharin introduced a plan of "rationalization of the economy," which was to close the "scissors," the name for the extreme difference between the high prices of industrial goods required by these farmers and the low prices of the agricultural goods that they harvested and sold.[18]

"Rationalization" took the form of a set of price controls. NEP allowed for private ownership and trade, but there were price controls on many goods. The effect would be difficult to label "rational." When price controls on wholesale goods, including industrial farm machinery, led to shortage, the retail prices rose. However, instead of recognizing that the high price was a result of the shortage caused by the policy, the Soviet government blamed it on "speculation" in the industrial goods market.

In response to the escalating retail prices, the Soviet government took over the industrial goods market, setting both wholesale and retail prices for industrial goods. However, although the "terms of trade" for farmers was improved by letter of law, this led to an incredible shortage of industrial goods in the countryside — because industrial goods prices were fixed so low. Although speculation may have been the proximate cause, the market forces that drove the price up were based on a real factor: there was a shortage due to the price ceiling.

Seeing that the peasants were not able to purchase the equipment they needed, and wanting to keep good terms with the peasants, industrial prices were further reduced, leading to even greater shortage. Many Soviet leaders felt that the only way to resolve this problem without eliminating the price controls would be for the state to take over production of industrial goods completely. If the government was the producer, it could increase output and prevent shortage. This was the argument of the "left," which finally became state policy under Stalin.[19]

The relative prices between agriculture and manufacturing was only one market that the Soviet government had to keep in balance, another was between private and public farming. The Soviet government could not effectively control the price of agricultural goods. Private grain prices rose, but state and collective farm prices were fixed, leading them to take out loans. This then resulted in further inflationary policy, and yet higher private grain prices. There was also a problem with the relative prices of food crops and industrial crops:

> The authorities were confronted with a delicate balance. If they relatively increased grain prices, as they did in the summer of 1925, peasants tended to switch resources away from industrial crops essential for industrial development. If they reduced grain prices too far, as they did a year or so later, the peasants withheld grain and reduced their grain sowings.[20]

Historians Davies, Harrison, and Wheatcroft described the difficulty in predicting the behavioral response to relative price differences. Regarding the prices that the Soviet government should have set for agricultural goods, they argue that "we are unable even 70 years later to agree even the general direction prices should have moved."[21] This is because low prices may lead peasants to sell less of the produce (and keep more for their own consumption), or may lead them to sell more, out of necessity.

A central authority can never be sure how the price he sets will affect behavior because it cannot know the subjective valuations of the individuals concerned. It cannot know their "elasticities" (how much an increase or decrease in price will affect their demand or supply) with regard to the product in question or their trade-off between "income" and "substitution" effects (for example, whether they will produce more when the price is lower because they care more about earning *income*, or produce less or produce a *substitute* because they care more that the price is so low). If both of these are factors, the behavioral response to price changes cannot easily be predicted, as the Soviet government learned.

Price setting by authorities for various agricultural outputs and industrial outputs was complicated and was a major cause of the collapse of NEP. Common wisdom among Communist Party members was that these problems would be solved by a push for more complete planning of the economy.[22] With complete planning, there would be no problems of shortage due to low prices, because planners could determine output as well as price.

After the end of NEP, planning took hold of the economy. From that point on, most everything in the economy was part of the national economic plan. With the exception of very limited private plots in agriculture and heavily restricted private food markets, a few service professions, such as household repair and artisan work in which an individual could hire out his own labor, and the black market, every resource in the economy was commonly owned and part of the national economic plan.

The main tool used by planners to calculate output needs across industries was the "material balance" table and (the similar method) input-output tables. Planners attempted to organize production mainly in terms of physical output, although they more and more supplemented the calculations with value-based tables, which used planned prices, called "monetary balance" tables.[23] The "material balance" or input-output table allowed planners to set the quantity of final consumption products desired and then determine the quantity of the various inputs needed to produce them. Because the quantity-based tables were only concerned with quantities of goods, they did not require prices. They were a form of "in-kind planning."

However, these tables contained two critical flaws. First, they depended upon planners knowing what should be produced in the first place. But how could planners know demand without markets and market prices? To estimate consumer demand, planners used surveys and statistical data about consumption, which they projected forward and corrected based on new information. For producer demand, they relied on data to create technical "norms" of production. However "scientific" these techniques might be, the information could easily become outdated.

Second, they relied on the planners knowing exactly which resources firms should use to produce the final products, but the choice of the best inputs — the most economically efficient — had to be made without prices, because the tables were in physical units. Market prices would provide the information necessary to determine the lowest cost inputs for a given kind of production. Without prices, planners could only guess at whether the techniques and combinations of inputs that they chose for production at a given factory were the most efficient.

Hence, the tables actually depended on the planners knowing things that they could not know given the fact that such tables, and not free markers, were being used to organize the economy. The logic of the tables depended knowledge given by market prices, but the reason they were using the tables was in order to replace the market. At best, the "material balance" method could only help to ensure that the plan was consistent. It could not ensure that it optimally used resources. As Alec Nove put it, "One cannot see from an input-output table that there ought to be a shift from coal to natural gas, or from metals to plastics."[24]

A planner must know all the possible combinations of resources and be able to judge them against each other in order to choose cost-efficient methods of production. In a market economy, each producer uses the prices that emerge from the market to help make cost calculations. The planner does not have market prices, but must still make comparisons if he wants to be efficient. David Ramsay Steele described the problems he saw with the socialist Otto Neurath's arguments for in-kind planning in this way:

> Neurath foresees a single supreme body directing the economy...He is most emphatic that this democratically-chosen body will have no use for general units of any kind, not even labor-hours, just as commanders on the battlefield do not employ 'war units'...all productive projects are to be evaluated "through direct observation," solely according to their "economic desirability." The headquarters will

draft several plans, on different assumptions, the plans will be compared, and the most desirable outcome selected. Neurath's examples include a choice between a. a power dam and agricultural improvements and b. a canal and a steel mill. He seems unaware that for the whole economy there would be billions of combinations of millions of projects, not to mention an infinity of different precisely defined ways in which each project could be executed. He also seems to assume that the headquarters will be able to pick among combinations of feasible projects which use available resources to the full. But either this requires an exhaustive inventory of all available resources and a perfect knowledge of all their potential uses, all centralized in one office, or it requires projects to be compared for cost as well as desirability, which necessitates the very units Neurath hopes to dispense with.[25]

The technique of comparing plans based on the consistency of inputs and outputs cannot be used to choose the most cost-effective techniques or the most preferable mixture of final output. The only capability it offers is the creation of a consistent plan. Consistency, while certainly not enough to deliver an end to scarcity, would have been a good start. Planners in the Soviet Union actually based the new plan, each five-year period, on figures set "from the achieved level" of each enterprise. This was assumed to be a fairly simple way to create a plan that offered a good chance of providing enterprises with realistic targets that would be both consistent and, hopefully, efficient. However, a lot changes over the course of five years. The achieved level of a plan created five years ago, if it had in fact ever been achieved, might by that time be neither consistent with the plans of other firms nor efficient. Changes in demand, new demands, and changes in costs and available resources would be left out because they were never revealed through changes in price.

In each plan period, more information was lost. This information included not only the necessary supply and demand for the whole economy, but also the requirements and capabilities of each enterprise. Planners may initially have had some idea of what factories could produce and what efficient production would look like, but over time this information became outdated. The problems inherent in in-kind plan control were described by Hans Hirsch:

> The point from which the need for money accounting arises in the Soviet planning system is the need for control of plan fulfillment....[T]he economic control measures are intended to ensure that the lower producing economic units, the "enterprises," fulfill their production tasks quantitatively and qualitatively but that on the other hand they remain within the limits of the prescribed use of various input items per unit of product. It is immediately apparent that such control is inconceivable in material units.... If at all, it could be carried out only by an apparatus so extensive that it could recapitulate every single economic movement within an enterprise.... Furthermore, *such a material control would produce a mixture of surplus and shortage items, but would give no picture of the total performance of the enterprise.* This is because discrepancies in performance are unavoidable and their causes are partly beyond the responsibility of the enterprise, lying in the realm of delivered and intermediate products.[26]

The problem is that the planners must know which inputs and how many of them would be efficient for a firm to use in order to create a plan and judge the firm's performance against it. They also must know why the enterprise used more or less of the inputs than expected, including whether it was the fault of the enterprise or the fault of its suppliers. Yet they must know all of this without the aid of market prices. *In other words, the planners must already be omniscient for them to determine the efficiency of plan fulfillment.*

Yet, without this information the next plan period would necessarily start from a less efficient place than the prior period. The economist Oskar Lange argued in the 1940s that surplus and shortage could be used by planners, in an economy with a free labor market and a free market for consumers, to determine prices for the capital goods market.[27] However, the experience of the Soviet Union illustrates several reasons why this would not work.

One reason, as indicated by Hans Hirsch, is that the cause of the shortage may not be clear: Is the item in short supply, indicating that supply has fallen short of demand and should be increased in the plan, or was an input or technology necessary to make that item in shortage? Or perhaps the transport required to deliver inputs was lacking? Planners would not know if a given surplus was real, or if it was an inventory stored up due to a coordination problem. The output statistics available to planners for their material balance tables were unable to help them distinguish the true reason for shortages and surplus.

In addition, consumers will not choose to starve while waiting for planners to remedy a shortage—they will purchase a substitute instead. A sort of cynical Soviet joke captured this phenomenon of the socialist economy:

> A naïve young Russian passes by a store whose sign says, "Vegetables, Fruit." As it is winter and he has not had fruit for some time, the young man joins the queue. But when he asks the clerk for fruit she tells him they never have any. Feeling foolish, the young man asks the store manager why it is that a fruit store sells no fruit. The manager tells him to wait and watch the queue a few minutes and he will understand. After observing numerous customers asking for potatoes or cabbage, the young man says to the store manager that he still doesn't understand why the fruit store carries no fruit. "Have you heard anyone ask for fruit?" the store manager asks. "Obviously, there's no demand."[28]

The Soviet consumer was forced to purchase whatever the shops carried, if he wanted anything at all—the shops of course could not respond to changing demand themselves, nor could an entrepreneur offer alternatives to dissatisfied customers. Consumers could not walk away empty-handed when there was no fruit because they still needed to eat dinner, so they were forced to buy potatoes instead. By doing so, the consumer deprived the state of that "in-kind" information that surplus and shortage offer.

This kind of "distortion" of information, caused by substitution and other dynamic and interactive elements of the economy, is an important feature of prices in a market economy. Prices do not exist in isolation. Instead, the relative levels of prices shift as the supply and demand of each item shifts, spurring producers and consumers to alter their behavior. In this way, market prices help to adjust production and prevent shortage. In a planned system, the substitutions made by consumers are not captured by prices, but they do distort the "in-kind" signals of shortage and surplus. Planners are left with no reliable information with which to adjust the plan. By 1932, Trotsky understood the problem more deeply. In his sometimes eloquent phrasing, he described what would be necessary for planners to actually produce an efficient plan for the economy:

> If a universal mind existed, of the kind that projected itself into the scientific fancy of Laplace—a mind that could register simultaneously all the processes of nature and society, that could measure the dynamics of the union, that could forecast the results of their interconnections—such a mind, of course, could a priori draw up a faultless and exhaustive economic plan, beginning with the number of acres of wheat down to the last button for a vest. The bureaucracy often imagines that just such a mind is at its disposal; that is why it so easily frees itself from the control of the market and of Soviet democracy. But, in reality, the bureaucracy errs frightfully in its estimate of its spiritual resources.[29]

If planners could know every detail of every enterprise, the options it faces, the capabilities and tradeoffs, and the ways that each of these decisions would affect every other enterprise, then planning in physical units would be possible. Price setting would also be possible. In truth, anything might be possible if government was omniscient and omnipotent, but it is not.

Planners slowly became aware that planning the economy in physical units was chaotic and perhaps impossible. Although output targets remained, planners began to use prices for calculations more, creating "monetary balances" to supplement material ones. However, prices were set centrally, so they could not surmount the obstacles facing planners. The problem was that planners were both setting prices and depending upon those prices for plan calculations—but how could planners know how to set these prices? In a market economy it is the free interaction of buyers (expressing demand) and sellers (revealing supply) that sets prices. This ensures that the price carries this crucial information, and is therefore useful for calculating cost and locating profit opportunities. If planners set the prices centrally, how can they be sure that the prices reflect the true demand and scarcities in the economy?

Socialists did not foresee this problem because their theories relied on the labor theory of value. If the true value of a product can be expressed in terms of socially necessary labor, then planners could calculate prices based on labor time required, and the problem would be solved. Soviet economists soon ran into trouble with this approach, however. It was obvious that labor was being wasted, and that the products being produced were not always those most in demand. If prices were based on the labor hours required at that moment to produce goods, this would not help reveal to planners whether this was the best way to produce the good, or whether the demand for the good justified that number of hours. Furthermore, it took a different number of hours at different factories, with different equipment and different inputs, and the prices of all of these components had to be centrally set.

Even many economists who were skeptical of Marxian labor theory did not sufficiently recognize this problem. Economist Barbara Wootton described how she saw prices being useful for Soviet planning. After warning that the experiment with a moneyless economy in the Soviet Union during war communism taught us that this was not feasible, she continued, "The first function, therefore, of the price mechanism under a planned economy will probably be to serve as a means of expressing the content of the plans, and therewith also as a means of checking the measure of their fulfillment."[30] Wootton argued that, although "the method of calculating these costs and prices...is necessarily somewhat arbitrary," it would "make it possible to judge whether the planners have accomplished what they set out to do."[31]

As an example, Wootton argued that even if a rate of interest set at 4 percent was set arbitrarily, if a firm using that interest rate only accrues a profit of 2 percent, it will then be clear that the firm did not fulfill "the intention of the plan." However, what Wootton does not address here is the problem that it is not a single price—just this 4 percent rate of interest—which the planners are setting. The planners are setting, quite arbitrarily, both the interest rate and the price of the inputs that the firm must purchase with its loan, and the price of the final product the firm is producing, along with prices of the other products at the shop which the consumer must decide between, and all the other prices in the economy.

Hence, that the firm was able only to produce a 2 percent profit and not a 4 percent profit may or may not mean that the "intention of the plan" was fulfilled at that firm; it will be hard to say unless the planner can know with perfect certainty that all the prices in the economy had been set accurately to reflect true supply and demand conditions.

Nor can a shortage or surplus tell the planner which prices were set inaccurately (as Oskar Lange had argued) if each price in the economy is capable of affecting the behavior of economic actors. Forced substitution again masks this signal. For example, when one input is in abundance, even though it is of lower quality it may be used in place of one that is running low. In such a case, both the surplus of the under-desired good, and the shortage of the one in demand would be made smaller because of the "forced substitution." In a vast complex economy there may be many such substitutions within the long planning period.

However, the problem went far beyond this in the Soviet Union. Planners in the Soviet Union did base their plan on calculations which relied on the prices they set. However, firms were allocated inputs; they did not freely purchase them in a market. Hence demand for these inputs was solely based upon the plan for the period, not upon the price setting itself. This meant that planners could not rely on responses by firms to price, and so a surplus or shortage of the good could not tell planners if they had set the price incorrectly according to the firms' cost calculations. The only goods for which there was any price response was for consumer goods. However, even there planners faced the problem of forced substitution, as citizens bought dresses when they wanted skirts, and potatoes when they wanted fruit.

Still, planners wanted to set accurate prices and use them to design an efficient plan. Soviet economists created theories of optimal planning and efficient price setting, and advised the planning bureau. Based on their recommendations, planners used "norms" of production and consumption in their calculations. For the estimation of the effect of technological progress on output in an industry, surveys of technological development were compiled, and coefficients of technological innovation were created from them to apply to the given industry:

> For example, when calculating the 1970 input–output table for the Soviet Union as a whole more than 200 industrial research and project institutes were asked to estimate future developments in their industries....Experience showed that the big problem in projecting the technical coefficients for the Baltic republics was not in estimating technical progress in the production of goods already in production but in estimating changes in the structure of production, i.e., the "birth" of new products and the "death" of old ones.

> When projecting technology the compilers of the Estonian tables considered, for some industries, various coefficient vectors, embodying various methods of production. For the construction industry linear programming was used to choose the optimal plan.[32]

Yet these norms were hardly better than guesses. For production, planners could only rely on existing technology and achieved levels of productivity; and planners had to rely on empirical data on consumption, and surveys, to gauge demand. Even if demand was captured by the data or survey initially, which was unlikely given forced substitution and other issues, it might then change before planners had a chance to write up, let alone implement, the national economic plan.

It may help to look at an example. In the Soviet planned economy, the output of each resource was determined at the start of the planning period. It was intended to be an accurate estimate of the output needed for the entire period. Ideally, it would not change. For example, the output of leather products was determined at the beginning of the plan period, with the amount of leather destined for footwear also earmarked in the plan. How was the demand for leather footwear determined? Surveys and calculations based on "norms," or "reasonable assumptions," were used:

> Rational consumption norms are extensively used when projecting personal consumption. In one variant of the Estonia calculations norms of consumption of food products, suggested by the Laboratory for the study and planning of nutrition of the Academy of Sciences of the U.S.S.R., and consumption norms of non-food products recommended by the Scientific Research Institute of trade and social nutrition, corrected for Estonian conditions, were used.

> One variant of personal consumption for Estonia for 1970 was based on income elasticity calculations. The population was divided into two groups, rural and urban, and the data of a family budget survey was used to calculate linear consumption functions for all the consumer goods specified in the input–output table for these two groups. The base year used in these calculations may have been unrepresentative. To overcome this problem, in the Estonian calculations a control year—1963—was used to check the representativeness of the base year—1961.[33]

Once the amount of the good—in this example, leather for shoes—is calculated, the amount is fixed for the plan period. Assuming that it is correct and that the income elasticities and other estimates of subjective valuation are reasonably accurate, what happens if something changes? For example, what happens if the winter is unexpectedly harsh and a large number of families that normally would not have purchased coats and boots and winter hats must do so? These families may have less need for cloth shoes, and more need for leather boots and woolen hats.

In a market economy, the price of resources adjusts continually, and output then adjusts in response to price changes. If there is less need for cloth shoes, they will sit on the shelves unsold and will be marked down. If stores start selling out their boots, they will raise the price of the boots. This is a way of rationing to those most in need, as expressed by their willingness to pay the higher price. This is not perfect, of course, because some families will have an easier time than others paying the higher price. However, this is not the only thing that the price changes achieve.

Along with the higher price, the stores also demand more from their suppliers, the factories making the boots. They have a special incentive to do so, as they can earn more profit from the boots at the new price. As the factories run low on leather, they can charge a higher price, and they demand more from the tanneries, and the tanneries from the farms. At the higher price, factories earn profits that they can invest in expansion of boot-making, buying machines, and enticing new workers with a high wage. At each stage of this process the higher price urges the supplier to expand production if he is able, and high profits induce entrepreneurial spirits to enter the market. In this way, production responds to the higher demand.

Similarly, as the cloth shoes sell at a lower price, or sit on the shelves unsold, the stores buy fewer from the wholesale supplier, which spends less at the shoe factory, which in turn buys less cloth from the fabric factories, and the factories demand less cotton. In this way, production is shifted from making cloth shoes toward making leather boots. Meanwhile, the funds spent on cloth can be spent on leather, as leather supplies expand in response to its higher price.

Although the price of the boots spikes for a short period, new supply soon comes on the market and the price falls again. This mechanism explains why shortages are rare in the free market, even when there is an unexpected spike in demand. In a planned economy, none of this is allowed to occur. Prices are fixed for the entire plan period. The amount of leather has already been set by the planners. The number of factories making cloth shoes, and the amount of their inputs has also been set. Even if planners would like to be responsive to changes in demand, they have no reliable way of knowing how to alter supply because prices do not provide the information, and substitutions mask in-kind signals. During the harsh winter, there will be excess cloth shoes and a shortage of boots, or families will be forced to wear cloth shoes even though the shoes do not keep their feet warm.

This is not the only difference. In the market economy, the price of cloth fell due to the lower demand for cloth shoes. With this fall in price, it may have become profitable for an entrepreneur to make something new with the cheap cloth. The high price of leather that encouraged new supply, including new entrants by entrepreneurs, may also lead to innovation. Price changes represent new opportunities. But this is only possible when people are free to respond to them in their own innovative ways and only if they have use of these price signals. This was not possible in the Soviet economy. Prices did not affect use of resources because resources were allocated by the plan. This was intentional, of course. Alec Nove summarizes this:

> [T]he center decides what is to be done and how to do it, and prices and profitability do not play an active role at any level in the allocation of resources. Nor do they affect the incomes of either workers or management; thus if the price of coal was below cost, or above it, it made no difference to anyone concerned with mining, whose incomes were determined by wage and salary scales.... Nor do changes in the price of coal affect the use of coal by industrial enterprises, since coal is allocated to them administratively and they are not free to change to some other fuel.[34]

This meant that if leather became scarce and cloth was abundant, no shifts in supply would occur based on the price. Of course, the price would not change due to scarcity unless the planners altered it themselves, anyway. Nove also argued that it was probably a *good* thing that firms did not respond to price change on their own in the Soviet economy, because of these problems with pricing:

> The Soviet economy remains in essence a 'command economy', because, despite all *de facto* operational autonomy, its functioning is based on instructions, and frequently the behaviour of men on the spot in their area of autonomy consists in manoeuvring to obtain the biggest advantage within the rules and instructions promulgated by the authorities. *This is why a price system which would create an intolerable muddle if enterprises were free to react to the profit motive has not prevented the economy from functioning* [emphasis added].

In market economies, prices convey the information to expand or contract supply, and to enter or exit the market. In the Soviet economy, firms did not have this price information because the price was fixed for the whole plan period. Even if there were someone who could act in the role of entrepreneur and expand supply, such as a Minister of Leather, he would also not have this price information.

This lack of information also plagued innovation and change at the central level. The plan, in order to remain at least as correct as the prior plan period, took account of the level of achievement in the prior plan period. It was informed by statistics about the results of the previous plan. Yet planners could not discern the true relative performance of an enterprise because their prices were centrally set. Despite truckloads full of information on every firm in the economy, planners did not know which firms were efficient, or how to make them more efficient, because they did not have the supply and demand information carried in market prices. In the end, this information was the most important:

> At the same time that central planners are "drowning in an ocean of data," they nevertheless suffer from a shortage of information. The knowledge which they ultimately distill from that ocean is largely of the wrong kind; it is useless or inadequate for making those crucial choices which, in the Soviet economy, they alone can make. It enables them to determine the emplacement of each nail in a new steel mill. But should the steel mill have been built in the first place? "Knowledge is power," but only to the extent that it renders the decision-maker aware of the various alternative courses of action open to him and of their probable implications.[35]

The only way to know if the steel mill should have been built in the first place is to know whether and how much it was demanded, and what the cost would be to build it—how the cost, the alternative use of the resources, compares to this demand. A private investor in a market economy would research demand based on what consumers were freely buying at other prices, and would be able to calculate costs given the prices of the inputs. Planners could not do either of these because there was no market for alternative uses of resources—there were no prices with which to calculate. Despite massive amounts of collected data, the Soviet authorities lacked this information.

Each year this caused distortions and waste in the economy. In a market economy, overproduction by a firm would force the firm to lower the product price, and provide a signal and an incentive to reduce production. Planning and centrally set prices meant that the Soviet economy had no similar mechanism for self-correction. Hence, Sovietologist Constantin Krylov wrote that "this planned price-setting procedure is the basic cause of general disproportions in the national economy." The Institute of Economics of the Academy of Science agreed with this, proclaiming that "the main political and economic problems of the Soviet state revolve around the question of prices."[36]

Soviet prices were supposed to be used for "accounting purposes," in other words, to help planners as they designed the plan. For example, planners could set a price for steel, and then use this price as they determined costs of all the methods of constructing buildings and railroads. However, as economist Morris Bernstein put it, "[s]uch accounting prices clearly do not offer sound guidance to the planning authorities in the choice among alternatives regarding production and investment, since they do not accurately measure the marginal costs of alternative inputs or the marginal values of alternative outputs."[37]

Using prices that did not reflect marginal costs of inputs, or values of outputs, led to vast disproportions across the economy. This is key: prices are all relative and inter-related. Any one price that does not reflect true valuation and marginal cost will affect the other prices in the economy—whether it does so through planners' monetary balance table or through the market. Each inaccurate price entered into the balance caused ripple effects, triggering waves of distortion across the planner's calculations and then across the national economy. This meant that planner's calculations were not just slightly wrong, because they were based on statistics from a few years ago and a few prices should have changed, they were significantly wrong.

For example, if the price of coal is too low this will figure in to the price of all the goods which rely on coal during production. For example, the cost of producing steel may be underestimated, and hence its price set too low as well. All the products which rely on steel will in turn be affected, including construction and transport. Once this occurs with multiple prices in the economy, the cumulative effects become serious. Planners often did not know true costs, and chose prices arbitrarily, or based them on world prices. Many industries operated with planned losses for this reason.[38]

Socialists argued for the value of operating loss-making firms, yet the use of prices that did not reflect costs, combined with subsidies for those firms, created a cascading effect that prevented consumer prices from carrying any information about the real costs of the products in question. Although planners could use the profits from one firm or industry to subsidize another, they could not depend upon prices in their cost calculation to know which firms were efficient and which products were valued in the society. Soviet reform economists stressed that prices must reflect the "socially necessary labor value" of the product, but they did not explain how to determine this value. In fact, there was no way to determine these prices without a market. Stalin indicated just how badly they suffered from the price-setting problem in 1951:

> Here is one of many examples. Some time ago it was decided to adjust the prices of cotton and grain in the interest of cotton growing, to establish more accurate prices for grain sold to the cotton growers, and to raise the prices of cotton delivered to the state. Our business executives and planners submitted a proposal on this score which could not but astound the members of the Central Committee, since it suggested fixing the price of a ton of grain at practically the same level as a ton of cotton, and, moreover, the price of a ton of grain was taken as equivalent to that of a ton of baked bread. In reply to the remarks of members of the Central Committee that the price of a ton of bread must be higher than that of a ton of grain, because of the additional expense of milling and baking, and that cotton was generally much dearer than grain, as was also borne out by their prices in the world market, the authors of the proposal could find nothing coherent to say.[39]

The problem was often even worse than Stalin presented it. One cannot know for most products in the economy what Stalin seemed to know about cotton and bread in this passage. The state often cannot know whether prices are right or wrong, or too low or too high. Even for cotton, Stalin confirmed with world (market) prices, not any signal internal to the Soviet economy. How could a planner know whether the price of leather or dyed polyester cloth was at the right level?

In a market economy, prices aid supplying firms not only in determining profitability (and hence demand relative to costs), they also help to guide the firms to produce the product in the most efficient way. In the Soviet economy, the plan had to serve both these roles. Once the planners determined what they wanted firms to produce, they then needed to convey that information to firms. Centrally set prices did not help planners in this effort either. The Soviet economist Novozhilov explained:

> [If] prices do not inform producers of *what* needs to be produced, nor of what *quality*, nor the socially necessary limits on costs of production, [then] the missing information will have to be provided by plan-instructions.... If the information contained in prices often contradicts the plan-instructions, then the instructions must be strengthened by threats. But as the experience of centuries shows, fear is a less effective stimulus than economic or moral interest.[40]

Even the attempt to use the profit signal for this purpose (See Chapter 3.) is distorted to the point of uselessness by inaccurate prices. For example, a garment factory reportedly[41] driven by the desire to fill its "planned profit" target altered its assortment of production from the planned assortment. The firm could earn greater profit from wool dresses than children's suits, so it increased their relative output. An article in *Pravda* explained, "As a result of this the output plan of wool dresses was greatly overfulfilled despite the absence of a large demand for them, while the output of children's items lagged behind the plan, although there was a large demand for these goods."[42]

Because the prices of the dresses and suits were not determined by market forces, the drive to fill the profit target did not induce the enterprise to produce products that were actually demanded. Pursuing profit when prices are set in the market would not cause these distortions because falling demand would lead to a falling price. Many reformers suggested during the discussions preceding the 1965 reforms that profit should be used as an indicator of efficiency, but recognized that the then-current price system would make this unworkable.[43]

The determination of accurate prices and their relationship to the use of a profit indicator became a hot topic among Soviet reform economists. However, their logic was often confusing and circular because they had no basis on which to form initial prices. One reformer explained that profit should be related to the value of productive assets, which he in turn explained requires that, in the process of price formation, profit be distributed within each sector proportionately to the ratio of profit to the value of the assets. This head-spinning "logic" could not resolve how to make the initial economic calculation that would start the process of price or profit determination.[44]

In a market system, supply, demand, and market competition set the price initially and continue to adjust it to new conditions. The basis for prices in the Soviet economy underwent several reforms and over time shifted more and more toward this market-based approach, in tandem with the movement toward using profit as an indicator. Although production costs had been the basis for prices, the problems with this approach soon became clear: instead of reducing costs in order to fill profit targets, firms would report high production costs in order to be given high prices.[45]

If an enterprise is asked its cost of production and the price for the product is set to reimburse this cost and ensure a small profit, the enterprise will have no great incentive to reduce that cost by using its existing assets more efficiently. If it reduces production costs, the price may be lowered. If the enterprise becomes more wasteful, the planners may raise the price of the product to compensate for the additional costs reported. Hence, even the incentive of keeping extra profit is voided if the price of the product is based on the "cost" that the firm reports to the planners.

Reform economists argued that basing the price on *existing known assets* instead of on *reported production costs* would ensure that managers made better use of existing assets if they could retain the additional profit in their incentive funds.[46] With assets as the foundation, the *use* of the assets would have to be efficient for the firm to earn profit, whereas basing price on cost had allowed the firm to be inefficient and make up for it with a higher price. In a market system, competition plays this role, but it takes it a step further. Not only does competition force the firms to make efficient use of *existing assets* to make a profit, but it also applies pressure for firms that have *less productive assets* to *invest* and for the rest to *improve* even the best existing technology.

The reforms to the price system made by Soviet economists and planners did not resolve the problems. As the Soviet economist Novozhilov reminded us, prices in the

Soviet Union did not tell an enterprise (or a planner) "what it should produce, what the quality should be, or what the limit of socially necessary expenditures in production is."[47] Prices were essentially useless to firms, and were if anything a cause of confusion for planners, and even defenders of the system recognized this. One sympathetic economist speaking of socialist countries in 1977, including the Soviet Union, described the problem like this:

> [S]o far *no rational and workable pricing system has been devised.* Prices do not fully reflect factor costs, as rent and interest are not necessarily fully accounted for in them, and furthermore different criteria for price-setting are used for different categories of products. As a result, prices do not, and cannot, perform a rational allocative function. The irrationality of prices in this sense in fact makes the whole system of economic decision-making largely arbitrary—as Tindenberg puts it, "optimization of what?"[48]

The confusion created by the lack of market prices extends much farther than is sometimes recognized. People living in a market economy are so used to depending on price signals that their absence is difficult to comprehend. For example, in 1961, economist Naum Jasny tracked the inefficiencies of Soviet pricing from 1928 to 1960.[49] He estimated that total inefficiencies caused by pricing problems were massive: "One can but hope that the immense extent of the losses caused by irrationality and inefficiency emerges clearly from our analysis. The reader should bear in mind that the source for covering the losses is also immense. It is the underpayment of labour; a hundred million persons are toiling for rewards which, in the most modest reckoning, are a quarter or a third less than what they should be."[50]

Jasny made specific estimates about waste in different sectors of the Soviet economy. He estimated real costs in the sectors and concluded that, in about half of the years, most producer goods were sold below cost, often far below cost, even though cost was calculated without interest. He then compared several producer goods—gas, coal, and petroleum—and concluded that an inefficient mix of those goods was supplied.

In his paper, he provides calculations and examples as evidence of inefficiencies. A petroleum plant received coal from 2,000 kilometers away rather than using its own petroleum product, at a net loss of 27 million rubles per year according to Jasny's calculations. Yet, how can Jasny make this calculation if he has no access to the true market price of the coal and petroleum? He cannot know the price that would coordinate supply and demand, because there was no market in the Soviet Union from which such a price might emerge. Although the petroleum plant in question was likely wasteful, Jasny could not calculate the inefficiencies of the planners' choices any better than the planners could.

Jasny's calculations of relative efficiency were based on the cost of wages and the production costs for each energy source. Yet these costs were themselves affected by the price setting of the planners. Production costs,[51] as he admitted, did not account for interest payments or rent. They also included use of technologies and products made in other factories. The prices of those products not only may have excluded the cost of interest payments and rent, but *they might not have reflected cost at all.*

Just as the prices he criticized likely did not reflect cost, the prices of the inputs on which he was basing this judgment likely did not reflect costs. Furthermore, the prices clearly did not reflect relative demand for use of the scarce inputs by other industries. For these reasons, a comparison of input costs using planned prices may tell us nothing about whether the enterprises were efficient with respect to energy sources. While Jasny thought he had determined the level of inefficiency caused by Soviet pricing, he barely scratched the surface of the problem. This is just one example of the "largely arbitrary" nature of Soviet pricing.

Finally, it is important to note that Soviet planners depended upon black market prices, in addition to foreign prices, in their own price setting. Black markets could help planners to see the whether their prices were too low, because they emerged due to the prices that planners set. If prices were very low, long lines would form for the good, bribery would help ration the good to those willing (and able) to pay the bribe, and some customers would purchase a large amount and sell it on the black markets. Black market prices rose because of real shortage, but they also reflected the risk of punishment for engaging in illegal trade and the work involved in purchasing and reselling the good. Black market prices were shaped by the planned economy that produced the product and which offered the substitute and complement goods. Soviet society was also influenced by the black market. Black markets and bribery figure in many memoirs and other accounts of the Soviet Union.

Lessons

Without market prices, planners were unable to produce what they wanted to produce efficiently, and they could not know what the people needed. Planners were left not knowing what to produce or how to produce it. In market economies, if the state provides goods and services or tries to set the prices of goods in the market it may face the same problem. For example, the health insurance industry in the United States is partly public, and the industry is affected by centrally set prices. One recent article, inspired by the arguments made by Ludwig von Mises about calculation in socialist economies, argued that the United States government faces the same calculation problem determining health care costs:

> Simply put, Medicare, Medicaid, workers compensation, HMOs and even private health-insurance firms that follow Medicare rates, rely on cost reports submitted by providers. This cost data is then pushed through mathematical models and additional data generated by government, such as inflation and regional-labor-cost modifiers, to unilaterally (or in agreement with lobbyists and industry groups) determine what the prices for services should be.
>
> But it is theoretically and practically impossible for a bureaucrat—no matter how accurate the cost data, how well intentioned and how sophisticated his computer program—to come up with the correct and just price. The just price of a health service can only be determined by the voluntary exchange of a patient with his hospital, physician, and pharmacist. The relationship between the patient and

his private provider has been corrupted by the intrusion of government and its intermediaries (HMOs, for example) to such an extent that we can no longer speak of a relationship that can produce meaningful pricing information.[52]

Although this may sound like an extreme statement, the lesson that Soviet planners learned was that no matter what sophisticated techniques they employed in estimating costs and estimating demand, and using them to calculate the value of the resources and products in the economy, they lacked the basic information they needed to determine whether production was worthwhile: they lacked the information to set prices, because only prices from the market could supply them with it.

This same problem may face governments in market economies when they attempt to set too many prices in a single industry, and arguably even when they try to set a single price. The article above makes the case that even if the prices available for determining costs are accurate, and even if prices for substitute goods are accurate, the single price that the government is attempting to set can only be set accurately by the forces of supply and demand in that market.

An important distinction should be made here. There are several ways that the government can help the disadvantaged in society obtain health care or health insurance. For example, income support may increase demand in the given market, but it would not require the government to estimate the supply and demand for a given product. If the goal is to ensure that every citizen is able to purchase health insurance, this might be better achieved by supplementing the incomes of the poor than by attempting to estimate the price that would allow all individuals to afford health insurance and then imposing this price on the market.

In the Soviet Union, planners attempted to set all prices. In colonial America, and throughout the history of the United States, especially during war, attempts have been made not so much to *set* (come up with a price and impose it), but to *control* (prevent existing prices from changing), all prices in the economy in order to moderate inflation.[53] These attempts were consistently counterproductive in several serious ways. For example, one colonial newspaper reported the ways in which a price-fixing law had backfired:

> [The law] was made to cheapen the articles of life, but it has in fact raised their prices, by introducing an artificial and in some articles a real scarcity. It was made to unite us in good agreement respecting prices; but hath produced animosity, and ill will between town and country, and between buyers and sellers in general. It was made to bring us up to some equitable standard of honesty...but hath produced a sharping set of mushroom peddlers, who adulterate their commodities, and take every advantage to evade the...act, by quibbles and lies. It was done to give credit to our currency...but it tends to introduce bartering and make a currency of almost everything but money.[54]

This did not come as a complete shock to the Congress. Such schemes had been attempted and had failed before. Benjamin Rush argued in the Continental Congress against price controls and cited Hume, who described the attempt by Parliament to fix food prices during the famine of 1315 as a "monument to human folly," leading to much more starvation than should otherwise have occurred.[55]

This horrific outcome could have been predicted. Price fixing disrupts the allocation of resources when the price of just a single product is controlled, as much as when, as in the Soviet Union, many prices are set centrally. Economist Ludwig von Mises described the problem created by a "price ceiling," such as a rent control, food price ceiling, or price cap on pharmaceuticals:

> [The market's] primary function is the direction of production. It directs the employment of the factors of production into those channels in which they satisfy the most urgent needs of the consumers. If the government's price ceiling refers only to one consumers' good or to a limited amount of consumers' goods...[t]here emerges a tendency to shift production activities from the production of the goods affected by the maximum prices into the production of other goods. This outcome is, however, manifestly contrary to the intentions of the government. In resorting to price ceilings the authority wanted to make the commodities concerned more easily accessible to the consumers [not less].[56]

Therefore, price controls tend to be counterproductive. In the short run, some poor may be better off, but others may be worse off because they cannot obtain the product, which has been made cheap but is now in shortage. In the long run, everyone may be worse off because new supply and innovation have been thwarted by the controlled price. Instead of making food, medicine, or housing more easily available to the poor, the government may just succeed in diverting resources away from that industry.

This can also be seen in the outcome of the gasoline price controls in the 1970s in the United States. Two things occurred when price controls were put into place. The first thing that occurred was that gasoline rationing went from being based on price to a first-come-first-served basis. Usually in a market economy, things are rationed on the basis of price. This means that those people who want something, can afford it, and are willing to pay the price for it are the ones who get it. The price rises if more people demand it or demand more of it, and the price drops if fewer people demand it or demand less of it. In this way, the price is always the factor that rations the good.

If the government keeps the price artificially low, then the demand will be high, because price is no longer helping to reduce demand. More people will demand more of it. Something else must become the rationing factor. In general, it is "time." People are served on a first-come-first-served basis, and lines form. This may be inefficient because people will lose work time or leisure time to wait in line. In some cases, they will need to wait days or weeks (or years, as in the Soviet Union) on a waiting list. The government may also control how much of the good each customer may purchase. However, some may see this as a better way to ration certain goods because it seems more fair when everyone waits his turn and takes only what he needs, rather than only the wealthy obtaining that good.

Yet replacing price rationing has a second effect. When prices were kept low for gasoline, not only did long lines form at the gas station, but profits were reduced due to the lower price. The lower profits meant that suppliers had no incentive to increase supply, and some may have been encouraged to reduce output or been forced to close down. One of the critical features of the price system is that the price signals suppliers when to expand or contract in a given industry. This is how the price system helps to allocate resources.

When demand exceeds supply the price rises. This signals to producers to increase supply so they can obtain more profits. Once supply has increased, the price falls again through competition and demand saturation. The price ceiling on gas meant that supply of gasoline *never expanded*. A larger supply would have allowed the price to naturally fall because demand would have become saturated. The artificially low price meant that this would never occur. As long as long lines remained preferable to high prices, the price control could remain, *but the problem would never be solved*. The price would need to rise again before supply would increase. British Prime Minister Margaret Thatcher described the waste that price controls may engender at the time of the spiking oil prices of the 1970s:

> The increase in the price of petrol since the end of 1973 shows that it now takes more British exports to buy a gallon of oil than it did. By causing us to economise in our use of petrol, that price increase has resulted in a smaller amount of foreign currency leaving Britain to buy oil than would otherwise have been the case. By responding to the price increase and buying less petrol, we have helped Britain. *Subsidising prices on a large scale, whether food or of the products of nationalised industries, conceals from us the true cost of the resources being used to obtain those products.* It enables us to be more wasteful of them than we otherwise would. When food or electricity prices rise rapidly, as they have done recently, there are good reasons for ensuring that the relatively poor can buy much the same amounts of food or fuel as before: but subsidising food and fuel [with price controls] does more than that. It means that some will waste these things because they appear cheaper than they really are. *By taking the easy option, and keeping down prices instead of altering incomes, waste is encouraged.*[57]

Thatcher was arguing that the government could provide income support to those who cannot afford these goods, instead of altering the price. The side effects of price-controls could be avoided and those in need would still be helped.

Price controls tend to create other distortions in addition to the shortage and waste, as Soviet planners learned. These distortions are not easy to contain without removing the price control. President Nixon discovered this during the gasoline shortages of the 1970s, as an article by the Cato Institute explains:

> In the United States, the effects of a tighter world oil market were aggravated by President Richard Nixon's price controls, which gave special attention to oil because oil prices were rising rapidly. The Nixon price controls, which began in August 1971, were complex and they went through a series of phases over time. The controls interacted with changing market conditions to create shortages of different products at different periods during the 1970s. For example, heating oil shortages arose during late-1972, but most other oil products were less affected at that particular time.
>
> Then in 1973, severe shortages of gasoline developed at independent retailers. Oil price controls collided with the rising cost of imports, forcing oil companies to cut back on imports. Those cuts in turn particularly hurt independent refiners and retailers, who obtained a large share of their supplies from the major importers.... [In response,] Congress passed the Emergency Petroleum Allocation Act in 1973, which...created a two-tier system of price controls on domestic oil. The price of "old" domestic oil was frozen, but "new" domestic oil was decontrolled.

The EPAA created many distortions, as one example will illustrate. Expensive imported oil was not subject to price controls and it determined the marginal cost, and thus price, of gasoline sold in the United States. But since many refiners had access to domestic old oil that was subject to price controls, they made larger profits than refiners dependent on new domestic oil. In response to this situation, the Federal Energy Administration created complex new rules in 1974 to spread around the refiner benefits of price-controlled old oil. Those rules, in turn, created incentives for refiners to further increase oil imports.

The EPAA helped to create the very shortages that it was supposed to ameliorate. By attempting to insulate the US market from world oil prices, EPAA actually created incentives to hoard just at those times when inventories should have been released on the market—during the disruptions of 1973 and 1979. In sum, a range of new government interventions in the 1970s exacerbated the conditions that they were supposed to resolve.[58]

In many ways, this experience is reminiscent of the price struggles during the New Economic Policy that led to the "scissors." In response to shortage the government has only a few options: ration the goods in question, subsidize production, or remove the price control.[59] During wartime, rationing has tended to be the preferred choice,[60] and generally the controls are removed when the war ends. During peacetime, governments have often used a mixture of rationing and subsidies to boost production of price-controlled goods. However, subsidies create a soft budget constraint. Hence new problems are introduced. (See Chapter 4.) This can potentially spiral out of control.

A 1977 report by the United States Federal Reserve Bank of St. Louis[61] outlines many of the same problems encountered in the Soviet Union. The report explains that the Agricultural Adjustment Act, passed in the 1930s under Franklin D. Roosevelt, supported farm prices based on production costs including labor. First, there were problems with determining the "appropriate" price:

> Those who advocate a Government guaranteed farm commodity price support program based on costs of production are first faced with the problem of determining a cost of production measure that has meaning for any specific farm or commodity. There are a number of different concepts of costs: total, average, marginal, fixed, variable, short-run, long-run, and various combinations.[62]

The determination of the cost of production for this kind of program runs into the same problems as in the Soviet Union. First, there is a basic calculation problem: What should constitute the true costs of any given firm (or in this case, farm)? Which inputs are necessary? If farms differ, which farm's costs should form the basis of the "norm" to be used for *all* farms?

Second, there is the problem that Soviet planners faced that firms (or in this case, farms) will be motivated to report elevated costs and allow waste, knowing that prices will be set based on the costs that they report. Finally, differently sized farms had very different costs (The report reminded readers that, "[i]n 1976 there were about 2.8 million farms in the United States, each having a different cost structure."), and costs tend to fluctuate, so that any "norm" might advantage some farms at the expense of others; aside from questions of equity, this would degrade the efficiency properties of profit and loss. Additional problems came after choosing the price:

Artificially high prices resulting from these programs led to major surplus accumulation, which in turn created demands for new legislation to control production, enhance food consumption, and provide for surplus disposal through export (subsidy) schemes.[63]

Setting the price artificially high led to too much production and too little consumption. In fact, any price set higher than the market price—not just for agriculture, but for any good—must necessarily cause these problems. The article explains why this is true for farm prices:

Any level of price supports which is above market levels for a commodity will tend to increase output and raise marginal costs of production.

Hence, the price supports themselves, if effective in raising prices, stimulate the production of "surplus" commodities, and result in higher food costs, reduced farm commodity exports, and higher taxes to cover the higher Government outlays.[64]

Many problems of price controls are now fairly well known,[65] although the policies are still in use in agriculture, housing, and the medical sector. In each of these areas, the problems caused go beyond the simple creation of a surplus or shortage. In agriculture, the demands for increased subsidies and controls on imports and exports have ballooned into a national farm bill that costs American taxpayers many billions directly and many more indirectly through higher prices on products subject to tariffs, without producing obvious benefits. Reforms were proposed in 1996 that would have ended farm subsidies and controls, but political pressure from interest groups forced through a bill with greater subsidies than ever before.[66]

According to the United States Congressional Budget Office, the 2007 farm bill is expected to directly cost about $307 billion between 2008 and 2012.[67] One report suggested farm bills have cost American consumers and taxpayers more than $1.7 trillion over the past 20 years.[68] Yet this calculation was only of the direct costs. As planners learned in the Soviet Union, when prices are set centrally, true costs are not known, demand is not known, and other industries and prices are affected. These can have far worse effects than just directly costing the taxpayer and consumer billions of dollars.

Price ceilings also tend to lead to degradation in the quality of the good. During World War I, grain prices were fixed, and many of these problems surfaced. Shortages predictably emerged for every controlled item, and rationing was instituted. Costs were padded in order to obtain higher fixed prices, and quality fell:

In addition to shortages, there is also some evidence of evasion. Some millers padded their cost reports with improper items, including new construction, increased salaries, and so on, in order to qualify for higher margins.... There was also a bit of chiseling, to use the contemporary term, with inferior grain being sold at the price of the best grade.[69]

These familiar problems could be a real concern if an industry has prices fixed for an extended period. Setting prices for fairness and equity may result in shortage, lower quality and reduced innovation. If investors know that making a profit will be difficult then they will not bother to take the risk, and producers will tend to do the minimum.

This is an especially dangerous problem in an industry such as health care, in which innovation can save lives and investment is measured in billions of dollars. A recent *Nature* article cited price controls as the main reason for lower health care innovation in Europe than in the United States:

> The advantage of the US is almost wholly down to its lack of price controls, says [Kenneth Kaitin, Director of the Tufts Center for the Study of Drug Development]. "Investors tend to invest in places where there is less control over prices, and it is always better to do your clinical trials in the countries where you plan to market," he says.
>
> The shift of R&D [Research and Development] out of Europe to the US is now "a pretty robust trend," adds Kaitin. "There is no indication that it will flop back unless the US switches to a different regulatory or pricing policy."[70]

In fact, the United States may adopt a more European model for its health care sector, in which case innovation may fall off in the United States as well. President Obama is proposing "giving the federal government new power to block excessive rate increases by health insurance companies." This price control on insurance companies may be popular with Americans at present, due to "outrage over recent premium increases of up to 39 percent announced by Anthem Blue Cross of California," according to the New York Times.[71] However, the Wall Street Journal reported that "these steep premium increases are the direct result of California's state insurance regulations."[72] Price controls on the premium charged for expensive state-mandated "conversion policies" have forced Anthem Blue Cross to raise premiums on its other customers. President Obama would simply be extending the price controls over all policies offered.

A recent paper from the Montreal Economic Institute makes a case against Canadian price controls on pharmaceuticals. The paper argues, "Artificially low price levels for patented drugs and the resulting distortions in the price structure hinder the introduction of new drugs."[73] Canadian authorities also face the familiar problem of how to estimate cost, and choose a price to fix for products. They recognize that other prices in the market will be affected. The report explains:

> [T]o estimate the price of a new drug, the [price review board] relies on the prices of drugs in the same therapeutic category, whether patented or generic. However, R&D spending on patented drugs took place 10 or even 15 years earlier (when costs were much lower), while R&D costs for generic drugs are almost nil because they are copies of brand-name drugs whose patents have expired.
>
> It is obvious these price-fixing conditions are broadly unfavourable to new drugs whose R&D costs are incomparably higher. A policy of price controls thus eliminates any incentives for pharmaceutical firms to lower the prices of drugs *already* on the market, since the [review board] uses them for comparative purposes.[74]

As with any time that prices are set centrally, the authorities are left unable to determine the true costs of manufacturing, the suppliers have incentives to inflate their costs, and their behavior is distorted by the change in relative profitability. The report also makes the case that "[p]rice controls cause a direct reduction in volume" and lead "inevitably to slower pharmaceutical innovation" in the health care industry.

The report concludes, "Canada seems to be on the same track as Europe, where there has been a notable drop in pharmaceutical R&D."[75]

Just as with any other product or service, when medical care is price-controlled rationing also will also tend to become necessary. Yet, on what basis should medical care be rationed? The British National Institute for Health and Clinical Excellence (NICE) created a standard that health expenditures should in general cost less than £22,000 per six months of life saved.[76] Because of this, some medicines and procedure for cancer patients, the elderly, and the chronically ill that are standard in the US are not offered to British patients.[77] In the United States, it is the patient who must make the difficult choice of whether a treatment is worth the cost—and whether he can afford it. Although many see this is a flaw in the American system, one of the areas in which the UK trails behind the US and much of Europe is cancer treatment, especially the treatment of elderly cancer patients.[78] Of course, the US system could be improved, but the best way to improve access to medicines for the poor may involve supplementing incomes rather than controlling prices.

This may not be the direction the US system is headed. White House health advisor Ezekiel Emanuel (brother of White House Chief of Staff Rahm Emanuel) wrote an article advocating the allocation of health care resources based upon the maximization of collective life years. He admitted that his system "discriminates against older people," but, he argued, "[u]nlike allocation by sex or race, allocation by age is not invidious discrimination; every person lives through different life stages rather than being a single age. Even if 25-year-olds receive priority over 65-year-olds, everyone who is 65 years now was previously 25 years."[79] In an earlier article, Emanuel had argued that health services should not be guaranteed to "individuals who are irreversibly prevented from being or becoming participating citizens." He argued that, "An obvious example is not guaranteeing health services to patients with dementia."[80]

Perhaps there is a way to ration medical care that is more socially desirable than through prices in the market. However, it may be difficult to determine a just set of rules to ration another way. The low prices and subsidies in the industry will also tend to fuel demand and create shortage, balloon costs, and reduce quality and innovation. In contrast, income support for those in need would probably not cause these distortions, and it would allow the market to ration the goods and services.

Finally, there is the lesson that planners learned about the interconnectedness of prices. There are so many lessons within this one lesson—it is the essence of a dynamic economy. How will the economy be affected by a policy that centrally controls prices in one or more industries for long periods? Some of the effects might occur in industries not directly targeted. One outcome might be a bubble. Another might be an unseen thwarting of innovation, or an unnecessary ballooning of costs. One important implication is with regard to monetary policy because the price signal that affects the largest portion of the economy is the price signal of money itself. This will be addressed in Chapter 7.

CONCLUSION

Soviet planners learned that they did not have the information to set prices in such a way as to allow them to be useful. Because price did not reflect costs or relative demand for different goods, the Soviet government was unable to determine what goods should be produced in what amounts and many disproportions developed across the economy.

Western governments have encountered similar problems when using price controls during wartime, however, prices are often still controlled through other policies under different names. The Soviet experience sheds light on the mechanism by which central price setting can wreak havoc in an economy. Price controls, whether on one price or many, cause distortions in the information needed for the economy to respond appropriately to change. Prices naturally emerge from the interactions that take place in the economy as suppliers offer a good and consumers demand it. As signals, prices play a critical role in allocating the scarce resources of the economy. Controlled centrally, they cannot play this role.

Economic models also must account for the downstream consequences of centralized price setting, and of policies that restrain or control prices. The effects of a policy aimed at modifying one price may be felt in many other sectors of the economy. Because prices carry information, and are interrelated, the economic ramifications of such a policy must be modeled dynamically.

ENDNOTES

1. Hugh Rockoff cites the ancient Babylonian code of Hammurabi, 1790 B.C., and the Edict of the Emperor Diocletian in A.D. 301. Hugh Rockoff, *Drastic Measures*.
2. Paul Mattick, "The Inevitability of Communism," 1936, at http://www.marxists.org/archive/mattick-paul/1936/inevitability.htm (November 28, 2009).
3. Barbara Wootton, *Plan or No Plan*, pp. 202–203.
4. *Ibid.*, p. 202.
5. *Principles of Communism*, cited below, was written by Engels, but it represented what both Marx and Engels offered to the Communist League (of which they were lead members) as preparation for the program. *The Communist Manifesto*" was based upon "Principles of Communism" and is credited to both Marx and Engels. "Socialism: Utopian and Scientific, also cited below, was based on the first three chapters of Engels's Anti-Duehring. In the preface of the latter Engels writes: "[I]nasmuch as the mode of outlook expounded in this book was founded and developed in far greater measure by Marx, and only to an insignificant degree by myself, it was self-understood between us that this exposition of mine should not be issued without his knowledge. I read the whole manuscript to him before it was printed, and the tenth chapter of the part on economics ("From Kritische Geschichte") was written by Marx."
6. Frederick Engels, "The Principles of Communism," in *Karl Marx and Frederick Engels: Selected Works*, Vol. 1 (Moscow: Progress Publishers, 1969), pp. 81–97, at http://marxists.org/archive/marx/works/1847/11/prin-com.htm (November 28, 2009).
7. Karl Marx, *The Civil War in France* (1871), chap. 5, at http://www.marxists.org/archive/marx/works/1871/civil-war-france/index.htm (December 2, 2009).
8. Frederick Engels, "Socialism: Utopian and Scientific," *Karl Marx and Frederick Engels: Selected Works*, vol. 3, (Moscow: Progress Publishers, 1970), pp. 95–151, at http://marxists.org/archive/marx/

works/1880/soc-utop/ch03.htm (November 28, 2009).

9. Bukharin and Preobrazhensky, *The ABC of Communism*, chap. 3.

10. Gregory T. Grinko and Grigorii Fedorovich Grinko, *The Five-Year Plan of the Soviet Union: A Political Interpretation* (London: Martin Lawrence Limited, [1930?]), p. 12.

11. V. I. Lenin, "Integrated Economic Plan," *Collected Works*, Vol. 32 (Moscow: Progress Publishers, 1965), at http://marxists.org/archive/lenin/works/1921/feb/21.htm (November 28, 2009).

12. Raico, "Trotsky," p. 40, quoted in Sheldon L. Richman, "War Communism to NEP: The Road from Serfdom," *Journal of Libertarian Studies*, Vol. 5, No. 1 (Winter 1981), p. 92, at http://mises.org/journals/jls/5_1/5_1_5.pdf (November 28, 2009) (emphasis omitted).

13. Lenin, "Integrated Economic Plan."

14. Ludwig von Mises, *Planned Chaos* (1947), at http://mises.org/web/2714 (November 28, 2009) (emphasis added).

15. Barbara Wootton, *Plan or No Plan*, p. 58 (emphasis added).

16. Leon Trotsky, "The New Economic Policy of Soviet Russia and the Perspectives of the World Revolution," November 14, 1922, in *The First Five Years of the Communist International*, Vol. 2 (London: New Park, 1974), at http://www.marxists.org/archive/trotsky/1924/ffyci-2/index.htm (December 2, 2009).

17. *Ibid.*

18. Stephen Cohen, *Bukharin and the Bolshevik Revolution: A Political Biography 1888-1938* (Oxford: Oxford University Press, 1980), p. 247.

19. This crisis is well examined in Simon Johnson and Peter Temin, "The Macroeconomics of NEP," *Economic History Review*, Vol. 46, No. 4 (November 1993), pp. 750–767.

20. R. W. Davies, Mark Harrison, and S. G. Wheatcroft, *The Economic Transformation of the Soviet Union, 1913–1945*, (Cambridge: Cambridge University Press, 1994).

21. *Ibid.*, p. 10.

22. "The Bolsheviks had come to power believing in the doctrinal sanctity and economic superiority of large-scale, collective agricultural production." Cohen, *Bukharin and the Bolshevik Revolution*, p. 194.

23. Nove, *The Soviet Economic System*, pp. 215–218.

24. *Ibid.*, p. 218.

25. David Ramsay Steele, *From Marx To Mises* (Chicago: Open Court, 1992), p.125.

26. Hirsch, *Quantity Planning and Price Planning in the Soviet Union*, p. 50 (emphasis added).

27. Lange and Taylor, *On the Economic Theory of Socialism*.

28. Joke recounted in Robinson, *An American in Leningrad*, p. 181.

29. Leon Trotsky, "The Soviet Economy in Danger," (New York: Pamphlet Pioneer Publishers, 1933), uncopyrighted, originally published in *The Militant* during the months of November and December, at http://www.marxists.org/archive/trotsky/1932/10/sovecon.htm.

30. Barbara Wootton, *Plan or No Plan*, p. 325.

31. *Ibid.*

32. Michael J. Ellman, "The Use of Input-Output in Regional Economic Planning: The Soviet Experience," *Economic Journal*, Vol. 78, No. 312 (December 1968), pp. 857–858.

33. *Ibid.*, p. 858.

34. Nove, *The Soviet Economic System*, p. 174.

35. Smolinski, "What Next in Soviet Planning?" pp. 602–613 (p. 607).

36. Krylov, *The Soviet Economy*, pp. 35–36.

37. Morris Bornstein, "The Soviet Price System," *The American Economic Review*, Vol. 52, No. 1 (March 1962), pp. 64–103.

38. There are many sources that confirm this. There are discussions in Alec Nove, *The Soviet Economic System* and Constantin A. Krylov, *The Soviet Economy*.

39. Stalin, *Economic Problems of the USSR*, chap. 3, at http://www.marxists.org/reference/archive/stalin/works/1951/economic-problems/index.htm (November 28, 2009). This chapter is very interesting because it illustrates the Marxist understanding of "the law of value," the emergent prices from market exchange.

40. Novozhilov, quoted in Nove, *The Soviet Economic System*, p.354 (original emphasis).

41. Berliner, *Factory and Manager in the USSR*, p. 124.
42. *Ibid.*
43. E.g., O. Nekrasov, *Voprosy Ekonomiki*, No. 11 (1965); Y. Liberman, *Pravda*, November 21, 1965; and V. Sitnin, *Ekonomicheskaya Gazeta*, No. 1 (1966), in *Soviet Economic Reform* (Moscow: Novosti Press, 1967).
44. Y. Liberman, *Pravda*, November 21, 1965, and V. Sitnin, *Ekonomicheskaya Gazeta*, No. 1 (1966), in *Soviet Economic Reform*. I would remind the true believer, who might suggest that the initial calculation could be made from pre-revolution market prices, that demand and supply conditions change, so that this "initial" calculation will have to be repeated periodically.
45. See the discussion in *Soviet Economic Reform*.
46. *Ibid.*
47. N. N. Novozhilov, also quoted in Krylov, *The Soviet Economy*, p 35.
48. Wilczinski, *The Economics of Socialism*, p. 212 (original emphasis).
49. Naum Jasny, "A Note on Rationality and Efficiency in the Soviet Economy I," *Soviet Studies*, Vol. 12, No. 4 (April 1961), pp. 353–375, and Naum Jasny, "A Note on Rationality and Efficiency in the Soviet Economy II," *Soviet Studies*, Vol. 13, No. 1 (July 1961), pp. 35–68.
50. Jasny, "A Note on Rationality and Efficiency in the Soviet Economy II," p. 62.
51. As far as production costs, wages perhaps ought to be the most reliable. Yet without completely free labor able to move among jobs or to become entrepreneurs and without free and competitive wage rates, the economy-wide opportunity costs of hiring differently skilled workers is unknown. Hence, even this input cost is unreliable.
52. Gabriel E. Vidal, "Why Obamacare Can't Work: The Calculation Argument," *Mises Daily*, July 17, 2009, at http://mises.org/story/3543.
53. For several such cases, see Rockoff, *Drastic Measures*.
54. *Ibid.*, p. 31.
55. *Ibid.*, p. 29.
56. Mises, *Human Action*, chap. 30. See also Michael J. Ellman, "The Use of Input-Output in Regional Economic Planning: The Soviet Experience," *Economic Journal*, Vol. 78, No. 312 (December 1968), pp. 855–867.
57. Margaret Thatcher, "Speech to National Union ('No Easy Options')."
58. Peter Van Doren, "A Brief History of Energy Regulations," Cato Institute, February 2009, at http://www.downsizinggovernment.org/energy/regulations (December 7, 2009).
59. Nationalization simply gives government more power to institute rationing and subsidy—it does not change the fact that if the price is fixed below the market level one or the other will be necessary. Nationalization may also exacerbate the problem by leading more prices away from their market level.
60. Rockoff, *Drastic Measures*. Price controls have often been used during wartime not only to ensure that the population can survive, but very often also to keep prices low for government purchases to supply the army. It would not make sense to use such controls if the government would then have to subsidize the firms. Instead, the citizens are asked to sacrifice for their country until the war is won. Inflationary monetary policy (discussed in Chapter 7) and price controls are policies that can be passed much more quickly and easily than a tax increase, and can often serve the same purpose.
61. Clifton B. Luttrell, "Farm Price Supports at Cost of Production," Federal Reserve Bank of St. Louis, December 1977, at http://research.stlouisfed.org/publications/review/77/12/Production_Dec1977.pdf (November 28, 2009).
62. *Ibid.*, p. 3.
63. *Ibid.*, p. 5.
64. *Ibid.*, p. 7.
65. Hugh Rockoff documented the need for rationing in nearly every instance of price controls (that were ceilings on how high a price could go) that he studied in the United States, especially if the price was set below demand or demand was rising. He studied policies of price control from colonial times through the Vietnam War. From the World War I period, he concludes: "The lesson to be learned from both the sugar and the wheat controls is that with prices fixed, the

government must substitute some form of rationing or other means of reducing demand for the price system." Rockoff, *Drastic Measures*, p. 57.

66. Chris Edwards and Tad DeHaven, "Farm Subsidies at Record Levels as Congress Considers New Farm Bill," Cato Institute *Briefing Paper* No. 70, October 18, 2001, at http://www.cato.org/pubs/briefs/bp-070es.html (December 2, 2009).

67. Peter R. Orszag, Director, Congressional Budget Office, letter to Senator Tom Harkin, May 13, 2008, at http://www.cbo.gov/doc.cfm?index=9230 (December 2, 2009).

68. Sallie James and Daniel Griswold, "Freeing the Farm: A Farm Bill for All Americans," Cato Institute *Trade Policy Analysis* No. 34, April 16, 2007, at http://www.freetrade.org/node/609 (December 2, 2009).

69. Rockoff, *Drastic Measures*, p. 56.

70. Peter Mitchell, "Price Controls Seen as Key to Europe's Drug Innovation Lag," *Nature Reviews Drug Discovery*, Vol. 6, No. 4 (April 2007), pp. 257–258, at http://www.nature.com/nrd/journal/v6/n4/full/nrd2293.html (December 2, 2009).

71. David M. Herszenhorn and Robert Pear, "Obama to Urge Oversight of Insurers' Rate Increases," *The New York Times*, February 21, 2010, at http://www.nytimes.com/2010/02/22/health/policy/22health.html.

72. "The WellPoint Mugging: The brawl over rate increases is a preview of ObamaCare," *The Wall Street Journal*, February 18, 2010, at http://online.wsj.com/article/SB10001424052748704804204575069833643345608.html.

73. Montreal Economic Institute, "Drug Price Controls and Pharmaceutical Innovation," April 2004, p. 1, at http://www.iedm.org/uploaded/pdf/pharma_en.pdf (December 2, 2009).

74. *Ibid.*, p. 2 (original emphasis).

75. *Ibid.*, p. 3.

76. NICE guidelines for 2007 read, "Where one intervention appears to be more effective than another, the [NICE Guideline Development Group] will have to determine whether the increase in cost associated with the increase in effectiveness represents reasonable 'value for money'. There is no empirical basis for assigning a particular value (or values) to the cut-off between cost effectiveness and cost ineffectiveness. The consensus among NICE's economic advisers is that NICE should, generally, accept as cost effective those interventions with an incremental cost-effectiveness ratio of less than £20,000 per [Quality-adjusted life year] and that there should be increasingly strong reasons for accepting as cost effective interventions with an incremental cost-effectiveness ratio of over £30,000 per QALY." National Institute for Health and Clinical Excellence, *2007 Guidelines Manual*, April 2007, at http://www.nice.org.uk/niceMedia/pdf/GuidelinesManualChapter8.pdf. -- The guidelines for 2009, the most recent as of this writing, retained this basic formula. National Institute for Health and Clinical Excellence, *2009 Guidelines Manual*, April 2007, at http://www.nice.org.uk/media/68D/29/The_guidelines_manual_2009_-_Chapter_7_Assessing_cost_effectiveness.pdf.

77. See, for example, "British health agency wrestles with cost of cancer drugs," *USA Today*, April 8, 2009, http://www.usatoday.com/news/health/2009-04-08-britain-cancer-costs_N.htm. However, the extent of this problem may be exaggerated. For another perspective on this, see Roxanne Nelson, "Access to Expensive Cancer Drugs Limited in Both the US and UK," *Medscape Medical News*, January 14, 2010, at http://www.medscape.com/viewarticle/715110.

78. See Sarah Bosely, "Up to 15,000 older cancer patients die prematurely each year, says study," *The Guardian*, June 25, 2009, at http://www.guardian.co.uk/science/2009/jun/25/cancer-treatment-premature-deaths.

79. Govind Persad, Alan Wertheimer, and Ezekiel J Emanuel, "Principles for allocation of scarce medical interventions," *The Lancet*, Vol. 373 (January 2009), p. 429.

80. Ezekiel J. Emanuel, "Where Civic Republicanism and Deliberative Democracy Meet," The Hastings Center Report, Vol. 26, No. 6, In Search of the Good Society: The Work of Daniel Callahan (November–December 1996), pp. 12–14 (p. 13). In contrast, some might argue (as I argued in Chapter 4) that individuals unable to afford medical care because they cannot work should be the primary beneficiaries of income support or vouchers to aid purchase.

Chapter 7. The Root of All Prosperity: Money and the Danger of Centralized Monetary Policy

Introduction

"Money is the root of all evil" is a common adage. It is said that if not for the pernicious role of money in society, fellow men could get along, and both greed and the violence of desperation would subside. Socialists were not alone in wishing for a future society in which money would first lose its importance and then be eradicated entirely. It is an old Utopian dream. The Bible is one source of this idea saying, "For the love of money is the root of all kinds of evil,"[1] but Marx gave it a "scientific" foundation.

Socialists understood the central role of banking in the economy. It was the Bolshevik plan first to control all banks and centralize lending into a single central bank, then to direct investment using the power of this central bank, and finally to eliminate money in the economy and close the bank. Banks would therefore be a key tool for directing the economy; and in turn, central direction of the economy would allow the socialist government to put an end to the use of money.

Some of the potential problems of bad central banking policy are well known today. Germany suffered hyperinflation in the 1920s. Since then, Hungary after World War II, Yugoslavia in the early 1990s, and most recently Zimbabwe experienced severe hyperinflation. Central banking policy is also blamed for some of the severity of the Great Depression, and many blame it for causing the Great Depression. The inflation of the 1970s in the United States is blamed on inflationary banking policy. Today, industrialized nations no longer imagine that printing money can solve a recession—at least we claim to know this. We have a "nuanced" position, which is a compromise between the awareness of inevitable inflation and the temptation of short-term stimulant effects.

But this nuanced position only considers the magnitude of the obvious aggregated effects of the policy—the rise (or fall) in average price level. It overlooks the *process* by which the price level rises (or falls), so it does not capture any other distortions that the policy may cause. However, Marx and Lenin considered the process. They knew well that control over the banks meant control over this process. They understood the power of printing money and lending it from a central position. What they did not understand is that the power of this centralized control does not imply the power to use it effectively or efficiently.

The Socialist Argument

The vision of money as a great evil that must be abolished permeated many divergent socialist and anarchist (or anarcho-communist) strands of thought.[2] "Wage-slavery" and money-wages were tightly linked. Moses Hess, a contemporary and friend of Marx and Engels, argued:

> So we all have to peddle our life-activity in order to buy in exchange the life-activity of other men — and what is the sum total of all our faculties and of all our forces, which we throw on the market and which we must turn into money, but our own whole life? It is not our body, which we only touch from the outside, but its real force that constitutes our life. When we sell this force of ours we ourselves sell our very life. Money is the mark of slavery; is it not therefore but human value expressed in figures? But men who can be paid, men who buy and sell each other, are they anything but slaves? How can we begin to escape from this traffic in men as long as we live in isolation and as long as each person has to work for himself on his own account in order to gain the means of existence?[3]

Ultimately, the only way to abolish this society of slavery would be to abolish money. Marx argued that money was a result of the private property and exchange (commodity production, in his words) of the market economy.[4] Under social ownership, money would cease to be necessary. In *The Principles of Communism*, Engels called for "Centralization of money and credit in the hands of the state through a national bank with state capital, and the suppression of all private banks and bankers." He argued that "when all capital, all production, all exchange have been brought together in the hands of the nation, private property will disappear of its own accord, money will become superfluous, and production will so expand and man so change that society will be able to slough off whatever of its old economic habits may remain."[5]

More succinctly, Marxist Sylvia Pankhurst said, "Full and complete Socialism entails the total abolition of money, buying and selling, and the wages system."[6] Until then, power over money would offer power over the economy. If socialists could take control of it, it could be used to advance social goals and work toward a socialist society. Socialists interested in reform of capitalism aimed to increase government's power over money for use toward progressive ends and to reduce corporate influence on the use of monetary policy and bank policy. Radical socialists called for nationalization of the banks and complete control of the money supply and lending as a tool for economic planning and a first step toward the elimination of money.[7]

Reform socialists and other progressives favored expansionary monetary policy when used for redistribution and economic stimulus, but also argued for its use in directing investment. The elimination of the gold standard empowered government with levers to control the economy. Garet Garrett, a journalist specializing in economic policy during the 1930s, explained this power in an article describing a 1933 law that outlawed payments made with gold.

The law reads: "That every provision contained in or made with respect to any obligation which purports to give the obligee a right to require payment in gold, or a particular kind of coin or currency, or in an amount of money of the United States measured thereby, is declared to be against public policy; and no such provision shall be contained in or made with respect to any obligation hereinafter incurred." Garrett explained:

> It follows, literally, that it is now unlawful in this country for a borrower, be it the Government, a corporation or a private person, to promise that the value of what is to be paid back shall equal the value of what was borrowed. The ostensible reason for this amazing prohibition is that the Government shall be free by fiat to fix the dollar at any value it may deem expedient; that it shall have the power to say of a 50-cent dollar, a 25-cent dollar or a 5-cent dollar, as it has already said of a 60-cent dollar, "This is the standard dollar and full legal tender in settlement of all obligations." It follows again, literally, that no one knows today what the value of the dollar will be tomorrow, or a month hence, or a year from now. The Government itself does not know. And that is now the state of the currency.[8]

This was a radical change; government could now determine that contracts made for payment of a certain sum would now be worth another sum, as set by the state at its own whim. Garrett saw the dangers contained in such a policy. After this law, how can any lender know the value of the loans he makes?

A lender may imagine that he knows the value of his loans. He may think he knows the level of inflation or can accurately predict it. But inflation is not only difficult to predict, it is impossible to accurately measure.[9] This is because the value of money does not affect all products and loans equally and in unison, but instead spreads its influence slowly through the economy. Prices rise at different rates, and the broad measure of inflation—the average price rise across the whole economy—cannot distinguish between those prices that have risen due to scarcity, government regulation, changes in demand, or other factors, and those that have risen due to the devaluation of money. Furthermore, some prices are held low by government mandate, and taxes and subsidies affect many other prices.

In practice, inflation is measured by tracking only a few prices in the economy in question. Hence, even if a loan is made with an interest rate that rises with inflation, the lender still cannot be sure of the actual value of the earned interest. The opaque nature of money and inflation makes monetary policy more powerful for the state. Marxist writer William Ward, writing in the 1940s, explained the power of this deceptive tool:

> The people know from personal experience what the high cost of necessities means in terms of reduced standards of living. But all the agencies of capitalism

work in unison in order to prevent them from grasping the connection between the high cost of living and the financial policies of the government. When new money is issued without any corresponding backing, the gold value of all the money in circulation is decreased. This means that each unit of the currency, each dollar, can buy less goods. But since the dollar *appears* to remain what it was, people have the illusion that the value of the dollar is the same while the value of the commodities has risen. They do not say: We have been deprived of half our income by this monetary manipulation. They say: The cost of living has gone up.[10]

Socialists argued that the burden of inflation was on the worker, not the capitalist or the state. Capitalists and the state worked together and took on debt, and the debt would then be reduced as money lost its value. Workers essentially paid part of this debt through an increased cost of living, as prices rose. The prices of necessities would go up, hurting the worker and peasant, but the capitalist passed on the price increases to the consumer, so he did not feel the burden. In the hands of socialists, of course, this tool could be used for good—to help instead of hurt the worker.

Capitalists could also trade and speculate, and make money off of inflation, especially if they obtained inside information from those in power. Monetary policy is a powerful tool for government. As Garrett explained, it gives government the ability to devalue money at will, and it also gives the government the ability to take from one group and give to another, often without the losers even noticing. Speaking about the progressives—many of whom had socialist sympathy—and their desire to use the power of inflation to advance social goals, Garrett asks:

> Who wanted inflation and why? All distressed debtors, naturally, because it would cheapen the money with which debts are paid…. But there were others who saw only and clearly the power of inflation as a social instrument, and how, once control of it was set in the popular hand, it could be employed to redistribute the nation's wealth and income…. [T]he political power to regulate money and credit might be employed, not simply to give and take, not simply to ruin creditors for the happiness of debtors, but to control the distribution of the nation's wealth and income symphonically, for the purposes of the new order. These [progressives] wrote the laws of inflation and took care to put plenty of power in it.[11]

Although Marxists criticized the use of inflation by capitalist governments, they were not averse to using it themselves if it were used for progressive purposes. Marx recognized the power of the control of banks and credit—control that could be used for good or ill. He also saw the relationship of credit and banking to production and the "crises" of capitalism. He observed that central control over interest rates and the value of loans could bankrupt lenders and cause credit crunches and panics:

> By means of the banking system the distribution of capital as a special business, a social function, is taken out of the hands of the private capitalists and usurers. But at the same time, banking and credit thus become the most potent means of driving capitalist production beyond its own limits, and one of the most effective vehicles of crises and swindle.[12]

Monetary policy could cause these "crises" if the currency was inflated. Marx explained that this is done by extending production beyond what is required by the consumer. Marxist writer Ted Grant explains Marx's insight as follows:

> [B]y means of credit policies...[c]apitalists produce more than is required by the market. This is due, on the one hand, to the fact that the producers of capital goods have credit extended to them and, on the other, that through hire purchase, mortgages and other means the consumers, too, actually purchase beyond the limits of their levels of income. When the serious representatives of the social system realise that this process has gone too far and threatens its very foundations, they are compelled by economic necessity to call a halt.[13]

The expansion of the money supply facilitates production and consumption that cannot be sustained, and when it ends there is a "crisis." This analysis is very similar to the analysis made by the anti-socialist economists (for example, Ludwig von Mises) of the Austrian School.[14] However, while Austrian economists saw this as a reason to avoid centralized control over banks, Marx argued that control over the banks would be critical for the transition to socialism. Finally, he argued, credit would cease to exist under communism:

> Finally, there is no doubt that the credit system will serve as a powerful lever during the transition from the capitalist mode of production to the mode of production of associated labour.... As soon as the means of production cease being transformed into capital (which also includes the abolition of private property in land), credit as such no longer has any meaning.[15]

Lenin also understood that monetary power could effect large swings and crises and that business could be controlled through the banks. The control of investment and production through a monopoly of investment funds and close monitoring of all purchases could only be made possible by nationalizing the banks. In 1917, Lenin argued:

> Only by nationalising the banks *can* the state *put itself in a position* to know where and how, whence and when, millions and billions of rubles flow. And only control over the banks, over the centre, over the pivot and chief mechanism of capitalist circulation, would make it possible to organise real and not fictitious control over all economic life, over the production and distribution of staple goods, and organise that "regulation of economic life" which otherwise is inevitably doomed to remain a ministerial phrase designed to fool the common people.[16]

This control is most powerful when the state can use it to fund industry, but by controlling the money supply, central banks can take on this role in part. Under true socialism, this power over the money supply could be used to direct all investment toward the ends of the planners. Of course, the state's executive committee must control the central bank to do this. As Trotsky explained:

> In order to create a unified system of investments and credits, along a rational plan corresponding to the interests of the entire people, it is necessary to merge all the banks into a single national institution. Only the expropriation of the private banks and the concentration of the entire credit system in the hands of the state will provide the latter with the necessary actual, i.e., material resources—and not merely paper and bureaucratic resources—for economic planning.[17]

The central banking system would be in complete control of money circulation and lending. Nationalization of the banks and use of them for central planning would allow the socialist government to eliminate "unearned income," in the form of interest and capital gains, and to control loans, wages and investment.

The abolition of unearned income was a key goal of socialists. The "speculator" was seen as a parasite, and the investment and lending function that he played would be played by a benevolent state, so that the "exploitation" would end. Although clearly someone or some process must govern the investment in an economy—so that borrowing and investment are possible—socialists argued that private investors and lenders making profit from doing this were simply exploiting the people. They played no useful role, and hence their profit was "unearned income."

Socialists were not alone in this belief. Rex Tugwell, part of President Roosevelt's "brain trust," asked "who thinks of the securities he buys or sells as having anything to do with an economic function?" Tugwell argued that speculators seeking profit "have a considerable effect on the distribution of capital amongst the various enterprises" but that the result "seems clearly enough inefficient so that other methods might easily be better."[18] The leading German Marxist Karl Kautsky explained that socialists were not interested in just redistributing labor income along egalitarian lines, but in abolishing unearned income to end the exploitation of workers by the capitalists. He said:

> What is decisive for Socialism is not the fixing of a special formula of just dis-tribution, but the abolition of the exploitation of labour, or the abolition of un-earned incomes. The abolition of rent, interest, and profit. This is only possible through the abolition of private property in the means of production.[19]

Hence, the end of interest payments was a core feature of theory, and control over the banks was a key to implement the socialist program. This would be a significant step in ending exploitation and implementing planning. Only then, after the economy was planned and the people took control over production, could the need for money dissolve away and bring true communism.

The Soviet Experience

One of the first steps that Lenin took after gaining power was the nationalization of the banks. In Year One of the Russian Revolution, Victor Serge recounts:

> The economic program of the Bolsheviks called for workers' control of industry and the nationalization of the banks. The decree on workers' control was passed on November 14. It legalized the introduction of workers into the control of busi-ness, made the decisions of the control commissions binding, and abolished trade secrets... By exercising control, the working class would learn to direct. By the nationalization of the banking establishments and credit institutions, the working class would recover through the state a part of the profits levied on their work by capital, and thus their exploitation would be diminished.[20]

Nationalization would take time; however, the Soviet government could make use of its control over the banks right away. In the early days of the Soviet Republic the belief in sound money was widespread, but the new government was not shy in taking advantage of its new power. One memoir of the very early years recounts the new government's bank policy:

> I took in my hands bars of gold worth ten thousand dollars each. I saw also high piles of English fivepound notes and smaller piles of American paper money.
> "You have made all this gold in one year from paper?" I asked President Schein-mann in wonder.
> "Not at all," he answered quickly. "But from the resources of a great nation."

"How did you do it?" I asked. He was quite willing to explain, for his job does not depend on secrecy but on public service.

"We loaned money, for instance, to the Timber Trust. We gave them paper roubles, which they used to pay all their bills in Russia. They exported timber to England. They paid us in English pounds. They paid us not only the loan with interest, but part of their profits. Sometimes as much as half of all they made! The fur industry also has been very profitable, making as much as 200 and 300 per cent. in export trade. On all of these profits the State Bank demanded its share, for making the first loan."

I gasped at this. "No wonder the State Industries call you a robber," I said, "when you make terms like that."

President Scheinmann smiled. "It is a question of public policy. The next Congress of Soviets may decide on a different method. At present we are building up a gold reserve for Russia."[21]

The Soviet central bank did not restrict itself to lending; it also engaged in currency speculation:

Even out of the fall of the rouble, the State Bank made money. There is a private semi-legal exchange where men speculate in the sale of dollars and pounds and roubles. Here also the State Bank had its agents, sometimes known, sometimes unknown. No tricks of high finance were alien to it. With its superior knowledge it could unload dollars or pounds to force down the price, and buy in again till it increased its reserve. It could not prevent the rouble from falling, for roubles were being printed for State needs, uncovered by gold. But the State Bank knew beforehand when the money was to be issued; it knew what transactions were under way in the big industries. It speculated with its knowledge on the Black Exchange; the little private traders who gambled there sometimes lost and sometimes won; the State Bank always won.[22]

This is similar to casino owners who know more than the gamblers and thus always win in the end. Economist John Maynard Keynes similarly described stock market speculators, "When the capital development of a country becomes a by-product of the activities of a casino, the job is likely to be ill-done."[23] Yet speculation among traders that all have a stake in the outcome and stand on equal footing is different from casino gambling, in which the house has a permanent advantage.

During this early period, the Soviet government also worked toward the future moneyless society of the socialist vision. The 1919 Communist Party program read in part:

The Communist Party of the Soviet Union, having set itself the aim of consistently completing the work started by the Soviet government, brings to the forefront the following principles:

(1) The monopolization of the whole banking system by the Soviet state.

(2) A radical change and simplification of banking operations by transforming the banking apparatus into an apparatus for uniform registration and general accounting in the Soviet republic, in proportion as planned national economy is organized; this will lead to the *abolition of the bank and to its transformation into the central bookkeeping department of communist society.*

....Basing its policy on the nationalization of the banks, the Communist Party of the Soviet Union strives to carry out a number of measures which will widen the sphere of non-cash transactions, *measures preparatory to the abolition of money*: the compulsory depositing of money in the people's bank, the introduction of budget books, the replacement of money by checks, short term notes entitling the possessor to receive products, etc.[24]

This period, the war communism period, or "military communism" in Trotsky's terminology, was an attempt to introduce a planned economy and to move toward direct distribution and the abolition of money. Significant steps were taken in this direction, but they led to chaos and impoverishment. Trotsky describes the period in *The Revolution Betrayed*:

> The Soviet government hoped and strove to develop these methods of regimentation directly into a system of planned economy in distribution as well as production. In other words, from "military communism" it hoped gradually, but without destroying the system, to arrive at genuine communism. The program of the Bolshevik party adopted in March 1919 said:
>
>> "In the sphere of distribution the present task of the Soviet Government is unwaveringly to continue on a planned, organized and state-wide scale to replace trade by the distribution of products."
>
> Reality, however, came into increasing conflict with the program of "military communism." Production continually declined, and not only because of the quenching of the stimulus of personal interest among the producers. The city demanded grain and raw materials from the rural districts, giving nothing in exchange except varicolored pieces of paper, named, according to ancient memory, money.... The collapse of the productive forces surpassed anything of the kind that history had ever seen. The country, and the government with it, were at the very edge of the abyss.[25]

Money had lost its value, and hence its role in helping to coordinate production, exchange, and distribution. Yet even when Trotsky wrote this in 1932, he maintained faith in a future moneyless economy and advocated taking steps in that direction: "In a communist society, the state and money will disappear. Their gradual dying away ought consequently to begin under socialism."[26]

The currency fell apart for several reasons. In part, it was done on purpose. The goal of moving to a moneyless economy led the Soviet government to ignore the effect that its policies were having on the currency. Incredible inflation was followed by a "money shortage"[27] in many areas, which may have been the result of the destruction of banks as well the price policies enacted by the new government. Direct distribution and barter replaced money exchange in many areas—both where this was the intention of the new government and where there was simply a lack of currency.

The government, with the goal of abolishing money, instituted rationing and a number of free goods and services. Return to barter due in part to lack of sufficient currency was hailed as a step toward socialism. Among those who cheered the collapse of the money economy was Grigory Zinoviev, a member of the Party Central Committee.

"We are approaching," Zinoviev declared, "the complete abolition of money. We are making the wages of labour a payment in kind; we are introducing free trams; we already posses free education, free dinners, even if of a poor quality, free housing and free lighting."[28] A decree on April 30, 1920, established that wages were to be paid in kind. In the same year, Lenin wrote to the Commission for Abolishing Cash Taxes, "There is no doubt about switching from money to the exchange of products without money,"[29] but it could not occur just yet. First, it was necessary to end direct appropriation of the peasants' surplus and temporarily move to a tax in kind. A declaration on February, 3, 1921, stated the intention to "abolish all money payments of taxes."[30]

But the economy was falling apart. What Zinoviev saw as a positive step on the road to socialism was actually the collapse of modern trade, and the return to a crude system of barter. The Soviet government came to realize this. At the Congress of the Soviet of National Industry in 1918, the People's Commissary of Finance said that "finance should not exist in a socialistic community, and I must therefore apologise for speaking on the subject." In 1922, the official in the same post said "Now we see that it is not so."[31]

During those few years, the complete chaos and poverty of the barter economy had convinced these officials that money was necessary. Direct distribution and rationing could not provide for the economy. Despite harsh laws against private trading, the majority of the food that entered the cities came through the black market.[32] Lenin soon realized that a "temporary retreat" to the use of markets was necessary, but the more the Soviet government was forced to reintroduce markets, the more the necessity of money became clear.

In 1921, in the first months after trade in agricultural products was declared free, the opinion prevailed that it was possible even with uncontrolled trade to manage without money and to carry on trade in the form of so-called "direct-barter." However,

> These survivals of the illusions of "direct-barter" were abandoned some months later, when the utter failure of all attempts to organize an exchange between town and country without the medium of money became evident. At the end of 1921 the Soviet Government not only considered it necessary to re-establish the monetary system, but had definitely expressed the opinion that it must try to build up a circulation of money on a gold basis.[33]

This was not the first time that socialists had expressed a belief in "sound money," or commodity-backed currency. Although many socialists saw the value in using inflationary monetary policy for redistribution and direction of the economy, others pointed to dangers of using monetary policy in conjunction with other kinds of economic direction. They argued that a variable unit of exchange would confuse the planners' valuation, making planning more difficult. Trotsky explained in 1934 how planning was only possible with a stable monetary supply:

> It is impossible to regulate wages, prices and quality of goods without a firm monetary system. An unstable ruble in a Soviet system is like having variable molds in a conveyor-belt factory. It won't work.
>
> Only when socialism succeeds in substituting administrative control for money will it be possible to abandon a stable gold currency. Then money will become ordinary paper slips, like trolley or theater tickets. As socialism advances, these slips will also disappear, and control over individual consumption—whether by money or administration—will no longer be necessary when there is more than enough of everything for everybody!
>
> ...As a matter of fact, during the first few years a planned economy needs sound money even more than did old-fashioned capitalism. The professor who regulates the monetary unit with the aim of regulating the whole business system is like the man who tried to lift both his feet off the ground at the same time.[34]

Lenin's temporary retreat, the New Economic Policy, put the moneyless economy on hold, but the intention to one day abolish money never disappeared. In 1932 the Commissar of Finance described the policies as preparation for when money would be "handed over to the museums."[35] Although many Soviet economists lost faith in the goal (One Polish economist said in 1968 that given recent developments, "Perhaps not all paths leading to Communism must deviate from money."[36]), the official Party line remained that when socialism underwent its transformation into communism, the state and money would both wither away.

Planners also used in-kind benefits in addition to money bonuses throughout the Soviet period to introduce the inequality which they found to be important to the economy (as discussed in Chapter 2). Sometimes workers earning lower wages found themselves better off than those with higher nominal wages, because the former had privileges such as the right to buy cheap meals in factory restaurants, while the rents charged for living space were on a sliding scale according to income.[37] Part of the reason for this choice may be the doctrine that a privilege, while still a privilege, is less devastating to the ideal of equality if it is received in-kind, rather than in cash. This is, after all, what the superiority of the moneyless economy depends upon.

However, if anything, it seems to be the reverse. Some of the more elite privileges granted to top Party members, such as limousines, parties with caviar and champagne which only the top Party members could attend, and "foreign dignitary" and "hard currency" shops, probably separated this class from the masses more than income differentials alone ever could. In fact, things are often coveted simply for their rarity—so that if they are given as a privilege in place of money, they may stir envy even more than cash would. Logan Robinson tells the story of the rare Bulgarian toothpaste he acquired in Leningrad. One shop clerk was hiding away the rare tubes for her friends, while another had ensured that Logan could obtain one, probably because he was foreign. But it turned out to be awful—no better than the Soviet toothpaste.

> Why then, I asked, if the Soviet toothpaste was awful at eleven kopeks, and the Bulgarian toothpaste was awful at thirty-two, was this clerk going to the trouble to hide away the imported stuff for her friends? Well, Slava pointed out, there is after all a certain status in brushing your teeth with hard-to-come-by Bulgarian toothpaste![38]

After the repeal of NEP, allocation of resources was based on a plan, but planners used money to track accounting costs, and as a flexible way to guide firms, in conjunction with allocation certificates. They used money as a tool for aiding allocation according to the plan. Evgeny Preobrazhensky, coauthor with Nikolai Bukharin of *The ABC of Communism*, predicted how nationalization of the banking system would aid planners in his 1921 book, *From NEP to Socialism: A Glance into the Future of Russia and Europe*. Writing as if it had already occurred, he said:

> As regards new enterprises, it was almost impossible to establish these without the Bank's participation.... Consequently, the Bank not only ensured itself exceptional profits but also obtained influence on the management of enterprises. At the same time...[it] enabled the state to implement its economic plan, encouraging

the establishment only of such enterprises as were expedient from the standpoint of this plan.[39]

This is, in fact, how the state bank worked under planning. Not only could the state bank determine which firms would be allowed to open and could keep an eye on the management of the firm, but it could precisely determine how the firms could spend their money. This allowed the bank to act as the right hand of the planners, ensuring that only planned exchanges were made.

Although money was used, purchases by enterprises generally required allocation certificates, so that, as the saying went, money became only "pieces of paper, which, with enough other documentation, allow you to purchase something." The enterprise's budget was also divided into "funds" to be used for individually specified purposes, such as wages, investment, or maintenance. In fact, "all but the pettiest of petty cash must be kept at the state bank, and the bank is under an obligation to disallow payments which are improper (e.g., for an unauthorised purchase, or at the wrong price)."[40]

Investment was not only tightly regulated, but it was also allocated to firms without interest charges. Marx had argued against all forms of "unearned" income including interest. However without interest, it was impossible to determine the best way to allocate investment funds. Not charging interest made borrowing highly attractive, and left planners with no way to determine which investments were worthwhile.

Alec Nove provided a simple example: "To put the matter crudely, if building operations are suspended for two years, the extra cost [that planners calculate] is limited to keeping a night-watchman plus perhaps deterioration of the half-completed building."[41] In such a case, the opportunity cost of not using the building for two years would be ignored: this is a huge waste. A capital charge would prevent this waste, because the building would have to be used for something productive enough to pay the charge. In the 1960s, these problems led to the introduction of capital charges, which were then ideologically "justified":

> Until the early 1960s, a large proportion of the enterprises' investment needs in the European [Communist bloc] countries was met by interest-free non-repayable grants from the state budget. But this practice only encouraged enterprises to place extravagant demands for larger and larger allocations, leading to an alarmingly increasing capital-output ratio and tremendous waste.... However this wasteful practice has been almost completely discontinued since the mid-1960s by the introduction of annual capital charges. It is now recognized that interest is ideologically justified because capital is nothing else but materialized labour, and as such it should be rationally distributed, because it represents a means of economizing live labour.[42]

Soviet economists had realized by the 1960s that "rational allocation" of capital requires charging of interest. By this time there was debate about the use of profitability as an indicator. Reform economists argued that a firm should keep costs below revenue if the investments were to prove worthwhile. However, planners were invested—ideologically and practically—in subsidizing firms that were unprofitable. Still, planners realized that they would still need to keep track of interest costs. Even if unprofitable firms were subsidized, it would still be important to know the relative costs of investments in order to determine the best use of resources. As with profitability more generally, the planners may want to know the status of the firms' budget, but still subsidize losses.

However, planners soon learned that the soft budget constraint—the subsidizing of loss-making firms—affected how the firm responded to their queries about investment needs. Firms had no need to keep their costs low and hence lied to planners about their true needs. Soviet reform economist L. Gatovsky described the problem in his proposal for the 1965 reforms. He explained that, in designing new construction plans,

> [Design firms] become interested in an artificial lowering of the estimated cost of construction, which exists only on paper, and in effect, bear no material responsibility for the actual high outlays which are really incorporated in the design though in a concealed way.[43]

The true costs of the investment are unknown when there is a soft budget constraint.[44] If interest is used only for accounting purposes and firms can run a loss, firms can disregard the length of time that the investment will ultimately take. Soviet firms would bid and overbid for more and more projects, especially as unfinished products often counted toward production targets, and the projects would end up costing much more than was planned and take longer than alternative projects may have taken.

Shortages resulted from excess demand for resources, and many projects were left unfinished.[45] Often, technology advanced between when the projects were started and when they were completed.[46] Along the way, some projects were abandoned entirely, and others probably should have been abandoned. An article in the *International Socialist Review* on the 1965 reforms commented:

> There are cases where these delays in completing investment projects reach the proportions of a real scandal. Thus, the chemical combine of Gurjec has been under construction for ten (!) years. Seven large wood and cellulose combines in Siberia have been under construction for thirteen (!) years; machinery imported from Great Britain in 1952 was never used and has by now become obsolete and gone to rust, etc., etc.[47]

The 1965 reforms aimed to curb the practice of over-investing and abandoning investment projects by charging for capital and holding the enterprises accountable. The importance of the capital charge was not limited to helping the planners determine the most worthy projects. Soviet economists discovered several interrelated functions of the charge on capital. First, the capital charge made some projects uneconomical, saving the state from investing in projects that were not worthwhile given the investment costs. Second, revenue from the capital charge allowed planners to reduce the prices of the products produced, and some revenue used for production could come from the resource use (the interest charge), not from consumption (the products sold). This helped to ensure efficiency in production because more efficient production would be re-funded.[48]

In short, the interest charge helped prices better reflect true costs and helped to stimulate better use of resources. As Alec Nove pointed out, "A capital charge...has both macro- and micro-economic effects, and reminds one that the distinction between these categories is often blurred in practice."[49] Soviet planners learned that investment is best allocated when costs reflect the time taken in production and prices of the final products reflect this cost, otherwise the demand for the products may not be in line with the ability to supply them.

Planners also learned that each price in the economy affects the prices facing other firms, and every investment uses resources that could be used elsewhere. Because of the interrelated nature of pricing and investment, every poorly priced resource or product and every poorly chosen investment affected the ability of planners to price the other items in the plan. (See Chapter 6.) Planners ultimately came to realize that charging interest was important in order to invest in the most worthwhile projects and to have any chance of pricing planned production effectively.

This was a significant step toward understanding rational allocation by the market's economic mechanism. It also indicated the birth of awareness of non-labor-based value. It was an early recognition by socialists that "capitalists" provided value by lending their capital out and had a *justification* for charging interest. Perhaps it is not exactly right to call it "unearned income." If the profit earned by the capitalist from charging interest is reinvested, then this would have the same benefit that planners discovered: When revenue from investment (rather than only from consumption) is used for additional investment, it reinforces efficient use of capital.

Although planners and Soviet economists came to realize the need for interest charges, they still kept interest rates incredibly low and even negative in practice.[50] When real (inflation-adjusted) interest rates were negative, as they often were in the Soviet Union and other socialist countries, there was a great incentive to incur as much debt as possible. The debt would offer a small subsidy from the state.

Although many socialists believed in sound money, without a banking system isolated from political influence they were unable to maintain a sound currency in practice. They also could not effectively control the economy through the monetary system. In a planned economy, the demand for resources as inputs and the supply of those resources are both centrally controlled. If the two are balanced and the supply of consumer goods is able to fill increasing and changing demand, then prices can remain steady, and there should be no inflation.[51] However, the planners were never able to accomplish this feat. Inflation was hidden in such various forms as "shortages, queues, grey or black markets, high prices in the legal free markets, unspent or unspendable cash balances in the hands of enterprises or individuals" and "disguised price increases."[52]

One of the ways that firm managers regularly disguised a price increase was by introducing a "new" product that was essentially the same as the old product and obtaining permission to sell it at a higher price. The price of the old product would be fixed for the plan period, but a new product could essentially skirt this price control, and a recommended higher price would be enforced until such a time as the product could be evaluated and given an official price. These prices increases would not be reported as inflation because the product with the higher price was "new."

Interestingly, American businesses used nearly this exact method to evade price controls that were enacted during World War II to prevent inflation. The policy froze the prices of all products that a firm sold at the start of the war, but the rules that determined the price of a new product were more complex and hence had wiggle room. This led many entrepreneurs to change their product lineup.[53]

Socialists had hoped to use the levers of the banking system to apportion invest-ment rationally and stabilize the economy. Instead, they found no way to rationally choose investment projects because their interference in the process *displaced the forces that create the signals necessary for rational allocation*. They could also not stabilize the economy because their method only hid the instability they were creating, but could not actually control it. They did not eliminate inflation. Instead their price con-trols just led to the same evasions seen in market economies when prices are fixed centrally. Finally, they were never able to eliminate money. Their first attempt was disastrous, and over time they learned that the use of money could aid both in their attempts at planning and as they moved toward more market-oriented pricing.

LESSONS

Socialists essentially argued that money is "the root of all evil." To do away with money once and for all would be freeing, allowing true equality. It would allow ev-eryone to live free of necessity and without having to buy and sell his soul and person. The need for money and the disparities in amounts of money are chains upon society. Therefore, eradicating money would allow for true freedom and compassion.

However, this argument conflates the existence of money with the phenomenon of scarcity. The free feeling of not worrying about money comes from abundance or having one's needs met,[54] not from the lack of use of money. If neither money nor goods existed, there would be no feeling of freedom, but there would be starvation. With limited goods and no money, there is just confusion over how to distribute the limited goods. A lack of money is only workable in situations of absolute abundance. There would be no need for it because absolute abundance would eliminate the need for trade. But these are unattainable, Utopian circumstances.

The argument for a moneyless society also assumed that without money there would not be any disparity in wealth, but this is not true either. The existence of scar-city would still mean that some could own more resources than others. Money is sim-ply a means of exchange. It is what we each trade to each other to enable us to trade with a third person for what we truly desire. Scarcity, and the way that society copes with it, were the true objects of distaste. Yet scarcity cannot be eliminated by elimi-nating money or by collectively managing production, or by any other means known to man. Sadly, as Alec Nove bluntly put it, "Soviet economists have long shown a dislike for the concept of scarcity."[55]

Money emerges naturally out of barter. If you want a coat, and I want a roast pig, we can trade if you have the pig and I have a suitable coat. However, if we do not both have exactly what the other wants, we may need to trade with several other people before we are all satisfied. As societies everywhere and always run into this problem, money—some kind of means of exchange—must always emerge. The economist Rudolf Hilferding, a Marxist that Lenin frequently cited, wrote about this, even describing how it could emerge without the help of the state:

> Money thus originates spontaneously in the exchange process and requires no other precondition.... Neither the state nor the legal system determines arbitrarily what the nature or medium of money shall be....
>
> In the absence of state intervention an agreement with respect to a specific money can also be worked out by private persons—for example, by the merchants of a city.[56]

There is nothing more natural to an economy than the emergence of a medium of exchange. Yet socialists wanted to abolish money and essentially return to barter by creating a direct-distribution economy. It is no wonder that they succeeded in wiping out all economic activity with war communism, because indeed they had wiped out the most basic tool of the economy: the means of exchange. They did essentially succeed in their task, returning the economy to barter.

Any call for an end to money is a destructive call for a return to a primitive barter economy. Money is the most primary tool of a functioning economic system—one that will emerge from the basic social interactions between people because it is a function of exchange. As Hilferding pointed out, money will emerge even in the absence of the state's minting and coinage. There are many historical cases of this.[57] The state tends to take over this function, but it is not clear that it does so for the sake of society, rather than for the sake of its own treasury. Once the state holds this function, it can leverage this power to inflate its own budget and reduce its debts at the expense of the purchasing power of the public.

The government may then go so far as to use the power of the central bank to direct investment in the economy. A 1999 Congressional Research Service report discussed the use of interest rates and bank lending to direct investment in Asia. In many ways the attempt to do so through the central bank, and the results, are reminiscent of the Soviet experience:

> The financial difficulties in Asia stemmed primarily from the questionable borrowing and lending practices of banks and finance companies in the troubled Asian economies. Companies in Asia tend to rely more on bank borrowing to raise capital than on issuing bonds or stock. Governments also have preferred developing financial systems with banks as key players. This is the Japanese model for channeling savings and other funds into production rather than consumption. With bank lending, the government is able to exert much more control over who has access to loans when funds are scarce. As part of their industrial policy, governments have directed funds toward favored industries at low rates of interest while consumers have had to pay higher rates (or could not obtain loans) for pur-

chasing products that the government has considered to be undesirable (such as foreign cars). A weakness of this system is that the business culture in Asia relies heavily on personal relationships. The businesses which are well-connected (both with banks and with the government bureaucracy) tend to have the best access to financing. This leads to excess lending to the companies that are well-connected and who may have bought influence with government officials.[58]

This reliance on personal relationships is much like *blat* (see Chapter 5), or like the political direction of investment (see Chapter 4) that were features of the Soviet system. An even more common use of central bank control is inflationary monetary policy. In 2006, a US law banning the melting down of pennies and nickels was introduced.[59] This was necessary because these coins have greater inherent value as metals than as currency. This control of coinage has existed in most societies over the course of history, but combined with inflationary monetary policy it has tended to empower and enrich the state at the expense of the majority of the people. Adam Smith spoke of it and cited cases of governments using the "juggling trick" of inflationary policy to reduce their own debt:

> When it becomes necessary for a state to declare itself bankrupt, in the same manner as when it becomes necessary for an individual to do so, a fair, open, and avowed bankruptcy is always the measure which is both least dishonourable to the debtor and least hurtful to the creditor. The honour of a state is surely very poorly provided for when, in order to cover the disgrace of a real bankruptcy, it has recourse to a juggling trick of this kind, so easily seen through, and at the same time so extremely pernicious.
>
> Almost all states, however, ancient as well as modern, when reduced to this necessity have, upon some occasions, played this very juggling trick.[60]

Centralized control over money can cause more damage than just raising the price level (with inflation) and redistributing from savers to borrowers (by lowering the interest rate). Keynesian economic theory, developed during the Great Depression, argued that deficit spending and inflationary monetary policy could bring about full employment without crowding out private growth, at least when used during a recessionary period. However, these policies can lead to "stagflation," the phenomenon of simultaneous inflation and stagnation in the economy.

This phenomenon was a shock to many economists when it surfaced in the 1970s, because they had believed that inflation stimulated the economy, and unemployment and inflation could be traded-off. Keynesian models were based on aggregates of economic activity—aggregate demand, savings, investment and government spending. These aggregates, and their interaction in the simple Keynesian economic models, did not distinguish between efficient investments and investments driven by low interest rates that might turn out to be inefficient. Although "stagflation" was introduced as a concept in the 1970s, the Great Depression itself may have been a prolonged downturn in part because deficit spending and monetary interventions altered the allocation of resources, making recovery difficult.

As Soviet planners learned, interest is necessary for efficient use of the economy's resources because of the need to economize these resources in time and space. The same machinery cannot be used for every potential project. There is a scarcity of time, space, labor, raw materials, capital, and other goods. Because of this, interest must be charged to test whether a project is still worthwhile even though it must use certain resources. Yet state control over the money supply will affect the interest rate and therefore affect the choice of projects undertaken in the economy.

For example, if project A costs $1 million and project B costs $950,000, without any interest payment project B will be chosen. But if the equipment necessary for project B costs an additional $75,000 in interest (calculated for the number of years of use) then project A will be chosen. If the two projects produce the same output, this is a more efficient use of resources because the interest rate is a real cost. The interest rate is determined by the competing demands on that capital equipment. A third project that demands capital, but is still economically viable after interest is taken into account, has competed to set that interest rate. In this way, the interest charge represents not only the time needed to complete project A or B, but also the relative value of those projects compared with all other existing and potential projects in the economy.

Eliminating the interest rate in the Soviet Union meant that the projects undertaken took no account of the amount of resources necessary—and planners did not know which ones were worthwhile and which were wasteful. It also meant that the costs and prices set for the goods created by these projects did not reflect the true costs of the investment. This meant that the disregard for investment costs was passed throughout the economy in the form of incorrect prices, affecting other cost calculations and yet other prices.

In the market economy, policies that affect interest rates, including inflationary monetary policy, may also cause inefficiencies in investment and therefore in the allocation of resources. Lowering the interest rate through monetary policy, government in effect induces "forced savings" by driving more money into long-term investment projects (which will pay off later) at the expense of present consumption. Inflation reduces consumption because prices are higher, while low interest rates encourage business to borrow and invest in long-term projects that are cheaper because of the low rate.

However, because consumers did not actually save more to drive the interest rate down, when the government ends the policy (to prevent hyperinflation) the rate must ultimately rise again, because there are not enough investment funds to go around. This means some of the projects will have to be abandoned. Projects that require borrowing for especially long periods (that rely on delaying consumption the longest) will be most likely to fail, because they were the ones receiving the greatest subsidy from the government-set interest rate.

Centrally controlled interest rates may also fuel bubbles. In fact, these policies may drive the business cycles we experience, *just as socialists argued*. When inflationary policy is used to try to spur the economy out of recession, it may drive investment into areas that it would not otherwise go. This is because, like projects A and B described above, one might be cheaper with a zero or low interest rate, but too expensive if the interest rate is high. When the interest rate inevitably rises again, these projects will be seen as wasteful, and have to be abandoned—causing the crash that we tend to see after a bubble.

Just as government employment, as we saw in Chapter 2, may be inefficient *even if workers were unemployed when initially hired by the state*, investments triggered by inflationary policy being used to "stimulate" the economy during a downturn may be inefficient. Idle resources brought online by interest rates that are low *only because the government has inflated the currency* may be channeled into areas where they do not fill true demand or fill it inefficiently. The artificially low interest rate hides the fact that the investment is not worthwhile.

These "malinvestments" may then cause further problems in the economy.[61] Because capital investments are at the top of the supply chain of the economy, mistakes in new investments can affect the entire economy, and quickly fixing these mistakes can be difficult. As discussed in Chapter 6, Soviet planners learned how the prices of raw materials, inputs, and capital trickle through the whole economy, affecting the pricing of many other firms and the allocation of resources. Planners saw that the low price given to coal and iron led to inefficient pricing in a large number of industries that relied on coal, iron, and steel.

A recent economic paper made the case that economic models should account for the many different kinds of capital goods used for production because generically spurring investment may sound good, but what happens if the wrong investment is promoted? The authors argue that "in a world of heterogeneous capital resources, spending on some assets but not others alters the pattern of resource allocation, and, in a path-dependent process, the overall performance of the economy in the future."[62] In other words, the stimulation of investments in potentially inefficient projects and areas of the economy may have downstream and lasting effects. "Even idle resources can be misallocated," the authors argue, "if invested in activities that do not produce the goods and services the economy needs."[63]

Economists often simplify this problem away, looking only at the aggregates: the total amount of consumer spending, the total amount of investment in the economy, and the total income. Once the picture is aggregated and simplified, the economist can easily suggest that what government should do is "spur investment" or "spur consumption" because the potential pitfalls of the approach will never show up in the model. This then leads to, or justifies, policies that spur investment with low interest rates.

Yet how could the model predict the results of this policy if it assumes away the differences for which the interest rate is purposed? Interest is a charge levied for the time that capital equipment is to be used (or money is to be borrowed). Yet, these models simplify investment to such a degree that the length of time different investments will take is ignored. Economist Kenneth Boulding described the danger of these simplifications in 1946:

> [I]t is a question of acute importance for economics as to why the macroeconomics predictions of the mathematical economists have been on the whole less successful than the hunches of the mathematically unwashed. The answer seems to be that when we write, for instance, "let *i*, Y, and *I* stand, respectively, for the interest rate, income, and investment," we stand committed to the assumption that the internal structures of these aggregates or averages are not important for the problem in hand. In fact, of course, they may be very important, and no amount of subsequent mathematical analysis of the variables can overcome the fatal defect of their heterogeneity.[64]

In other words, modeling investment as an aggregate (represented by the letter I) when analyzing a policy that affects interest rates may not be defensible.[65] It may yield results entirely inconsistent with the actual results of such a policy. For example, projects that require long-term use of expensive capital equipment may be made cheaper by the policy, while other projects that do not are unaffected. Hence the relative cost of the former is reduced, and more such projects are undertaken. This may affect the viability of the economy, especially after interest rates rise again.

An economist's predictions are only as good as the assumptions that he makes. Many economists have rejected this common sense notion, arguing that if a model can make accurate predictions,[66] the assumptions do not matter. However, the real economy is too complex for this to be a workable solution. Many macroeconomic models appeared to produce accurate predictions for many years, but then began to fail. Sometimes the earlier predictions do not hold upon closer scrutiny.

The Soviet experience with central banking offers an important lesson because any centralized monetary policy will affect the interest rate. If the interest rate is not zero, but is still lower than the rate that free supply and demand for investment would produce (the "natural rate"), then investment will be undertaken that would not have been otherwise. The true cost of the use of resources over the investment period will not be taken into account. This undervaluation will then affect other cost calculations and prices throughout the economy. The 2007–2008 housing crisis and the subsequent financial collapse and recession may be an example of this—30-year mortgages include a lot of interest. Economists from across the spectrum have argued this.[67] The reason is simple: mortgages are affected more by changes in interest rates than most anything else. Economist Lawrence H. White explained it this way.

> Because real estate is an especially long-lived asset, and thus has an especially large part of its value depend on the discounting of far-distant future cash flows, its market value rises relative to those of other assets with a fall in the interest rate used for discounting. The dramatic fall in interest rates made 2001 real estate prices seem like bargains.[68]

However, this was not the only effect of lowering interest rates. Monetary policy also helped to fuel greater use of risky types of mortgages. The Federal Reserve directly controls only the short-term interest rate, although this rate tends to affect other rates. Lowering the short-term rate also caused a distortion because some mortgages are more closely connected to the short-term rate than others:

The dramatic lowering of short-term interest rates not only fueled growth in the dollar volume of mortgage lending, but had unintended consequences for the type of mortgages written. By pushing very short-term interest rates down so dramatically between 2001 and 2004, the Fed lowered short-term rates relative to 30-year rates. Adjustable-rate mortgages (ARMs), typically based on a one-year interest rate, became increasingly cheap relative to 30-year fixed-rate mortgages.... Not surprisingly, increasing numbers of new mortgage borrowers were drawn away from mortgages with 30-year fixed rates into one-year ARMs. The share of new mortgages with adjustable rates, only one-fifth in 2001, had more than doubled by 2004. An adjustable-rate mortgage shifts the risk of a rise in interest rates from the lender to the borrower. Many borrowers who took out ARMs implicitly (and imprudently) relied on the Fed to keep short-term rates low for as long as they kept the mortgage. As is well known, they have faced problems as their monthly payments have reset upward. The shift toward ARMs compounded the mortgage-quality problems arising from other sources such as regulatory mandates.[69]

This also sheds light on how the financial markets—lenders and investors—help to allocate resources efficiently by seeking profit and responding to supply and demand information through price signals. They also help to allocate resources more evenly across time by responding to interest rates. Both firms as investors and capitalists as speculators help to do this, and monetary policy creates confusion and distortion in all these areas.

Profit-driven firms' demand for investment funds drives the level of the interest rate. When new investment funds are in little demand—overall in the case of a slump or in certain industries when demand for something drops—the interest rate falls. When demand is very high for investment, the interest rate rises, rationing the investment funds to only the most worthy projects. In this way, the private activities of consumers, firms, and investors create a price signal that helps to allocate resources efficiently. The signal attracts new investment (in the case of a falling interest rate) or weeds out unneeded projects (when the rate rises).

Similarly, speculators bid on expected price changes in different industries, which helps to plan for efficient future use. Speculators are often accused of "creating volatility" or "profiteering" at the expense of the public,[70] but in truth speculation reduces volatility by helping to predict future needs and by bringing prices in line with those needs. Profit is not made at the expense of the public, but is made by fulfilling the very important role of allocating resources more evenly across time.

Periodically, the U.S. Congress rounds up speculators from Wall Street and questions them about their supposed misdeeds. One recent article presents evidence suggesting that such congressional accusations are misguided:

Before the US Commodity Futures Trading Commission starts scrutinizing the role that speculators may have played in driving up fuel and food prices, investigators may want to take a look at price swings in a commodity not in today's news: onions.

The bulbous root is the only commodity for which futures trading is banned. Back in 1958, onion growers convinced themselves that futures traders (and not the new farms sprouting up in Wisconsin) were responsible for falling onion prices, so they lobbied an up-and-coming Michigan Congressman named Gerald Ford to push through a law banning all futures trading in onions. The law still stands.

> And yet even with no traders to blame, the volatility in onion prices makes the swings in oil and corn look tame, reinforcing academics' belief that futures trading diminishes extreme price swings.[71]

The reason for this is simple: The traders have a vested interest in obtaining knowledge about future conditions of supply and demand, and they have the trade specialization and time to do so thoroughly. This information and incentive allows them to push the price in the direction it must go a little bit at a time through their trades, and as the price moves suppliers can respond to the movement.[72] Without speculation, the market is left in confusion as to the future supply until the last moment. Thus, when the supply or demand change finally becomes obvious to traders, the price of the commodity will shoot up or fall suddenly.

However, centralized monetary policy may affect the ability of speculators to accurately predict the future direction of prices. Artificially low interest rates and inflation confuse the speculator's valuation of the industry and individual investments. Although financial speculators have been blamed for their role in creating an unsustainable financial and credit bubble, they may have played a positive role if not driven by inflationary policy into investments that would cease to be profitable after interest rates and prices eventually returned to Earth.

Speculators and investors failed to predict the 2007–2008 housing and financial collapse in part because their view was fogged by the inflationary (and other) policies that spurred the bubble. Many of them lost their fortunes during the crash. It seems reasonable to suspect that the prices on ultimately unprofitable mortgages would not have risen so dramatically if investors were able to predict their ultimate crash, but inflation and artificially low interest rates made this much more difficult.

Conclusion

Although socialists sentimentally wished for an end to money—as many people sometimes do—money itself is not the villain. Scarcity is the culprit for the ills perceived, and scarcity makes money (and the market influences on it that produce prices and interest charges) necessary for the allocation of those scarce resources. Because scarcity cannot be wished away, money is not only necessary, but critical. It must be left free, or all of the important market signals that facilitate efficient investment and allocation will be compromised.

Centralized monetary policy, especially policy that inflates the currency or tends to direct investment by affecting interest rates, drives inefficient investments and therefore has long-term consequences. Driving down interest rates may also affect certain industries more than others, creating bubbles and crashes. Those industries in which costs are affected most by interest rates will tend to be the most distorted during an artificial boom caused by inflationary monetary policy. These bubbles must eventually burst, and when they do all of the miscalculations will be revealed.

Socialists were wrong to think that their own control over this tool would cause fewer "crises" than its use by the "capitalist" governments. They were unable to eliminate money or use it to control the economy. Attempting to control prices did not prevent inflation, it only hid it. First eliminating and then controlling interest rates both led to an inability to make rational investment choices. Although they had aimed to take control of the money supply and use this power for the good, socialists learned that anyone attempting to centrally control the money supply will tend to cause the same types of malinvestment and crises as had occurred under capitalism.

ENDNOTES

1. Timothy 6:10.
2. Probably the most complete eradication of money by a socialist regime was under Pol Pot in Cambodia. It was a markedly unsuccessful experiment, and even Pol Pot admitted it was a mistake. In 1979, he told ABC News that it was the one thing he regretted. Anthony C. LoBaido, "Face to Face with Pol Pot's Evil," WorldNetDaily.com, April 18, 2001, at http://www.wnd.com/news/article.asp?ARTICLE_ID=22460 (December 2, 2009).
3. Moses Hess, "Speech on Communism," February 5, 1845, at http://www.marxists.org/archive/hess/1845/elberfeld-speech.htm (December 2, 2009).
4. For example, see Karl Marx, "The Chapter on Money," in *Grundrisse der Kritik der Politischen Ökonomie*, trans. Martin Nicolaus (New York: Penguin, 1973), at http://www.marxists.org/archive/marx/works/1857/grundrisse/index.htm (December 2, 2009).
5. Frederick Engels, "The Principles of Communism," in *Selected Works*, vol. 1 (Moscow: Progress Publishers, 1969), pp. 81–97, at http://www.marxists.org/archive/marx/works/1847/11/prin-com.htm (December 2, 2009).
6. E. Sylvia Pankhurst, "Future Society," August 2, 1923, at http://www.marxists.org/archive/pankhurst-sylvia/1923/future-society.htm (December 2, 2009).
7. This was not limited to the Russian Bolshevik program. Communist parties in many countries included the abolition of money in their programs. For example, the communist party of Ireland included in its program: "(4) Closing of banks and abolition of money." E. Sylvia Pankhurst, "Communism Versus Reforms," 1922, at http://www.marxists.org/archive/pankhurst-sylvia/1922/ireland.htm (December 2, 2009).
8. Garet Garrett, *Salvos Against the New Deal* (Caldwell, IN: Caxton Press, 2002 [1934]), p. 105.
9. See A. Alchian and B. Klein, "On a Correct Measure of Inflation," *Journal of Money, Credit and Banking*, 1973, pp. 173–191, for some of the problems of inflation indices known in the early 1970s. In 1996, the Boskin Commission, a panel of experts led by Stanford economist Michael Boskin, put forward reasons why the Consumer Price Index (CPI) had been overstating the rate of inflation in the American economy. It was so persuasive that no one contested it. They determined that for two decades the real rate of inflation had been 1.3 percent per annum below the official figure. This had major implications for Social Security pensions (indexed to the CPI) as well as the perception of real wage increases. Linking Social Security to the lower CPI saved $1 trillion over one decade. In 1996, the conventional wisdom that American families experienced a decline of 9 percent in real hourly earnings from 1975 to 1996 was contradicted by the alternative CPI figures, which yielded a 35 percent increase instead of a 9 percent decrease. Irwin M. Stelzer, "Lies, Damned Lies, and Statistics Revisited," *Weekly Standard*, December 23, 1996, at http://www.aei.org/article/16905 (December 2, 2009). In contrast, the website Shadow Government Statistics argues that this change was a convenient government ploy. They make the case that payments to Social Security recipients should be doubled from current levels because "inflation, as reported by the Consumer Price Index (CPI) is understated by roughly 7% per year...due to recent redefinitions of the series as well as to flawed methodologies, particularly adjustments to price measures for quality changes." Walter J. Williams, "The Consumer Price Index," Shadow Government Statistics, updated October 1, 2006, at http://www.shadowstats.com/article/consumer_price_index (December 2, 2009). Which of these is "correct" is debatable. Either way, inflation was calculated in one way for decades and then in a significantly different way after

that for at least a decade. Whether such a thing as generalized inflation can ever be accurately calculated is debatable.

10. William F. Warde, "The Progress of Inflation," *Fourth International*, Vol. 4, No. 10 (October 1943), pp. 305–307, at http://www.marxists.org/archive/novack/1943/10/inflation.htm (December 2, 2009).

11. Garrett, *Salvos Against the New Deal*, p. 37.

12. Karl Marx, *Capital*, Vol. III, *The Process of Capitalist Production as a Whole* (New York: International Publishers, 1894), chap. 36, at http://www.marxists.org/archive/marx/works/1894-c3/index.htm (December 3, 2009).

13. Ted Grant, "Campbell Somersaults — The Communist Party and the Slump," *Socialist Fight*, Vol. 1, No. 2 (February 1958), at http://www.marxists.org/archive/grant/1958/02/campbell.htm (December 3, 2009).

14. A good introduction to the Austrian analysis of the business: Richard Ebeling, *Austrian Theory of the Trade Cycle and Other Essays* (Auburn, AL: Ludwig Von Mises Institute, 1996).

15. Marx, *Capital*, Vol. III, chap. 36.

16. V. I. Lenin, "The Impending Catastrophe and How to Combat It," *Collected Works*, Vol. 25, at http://www.marxists.org/archive/lenin/works/1917/ichtci/04.htm (December 3, 2009) (original emphasis).

17. Leon Trotsky, "The Transitional Program," 1938, at http://www.marxists.org/archive/trotsky/1938/tp/tp-text.htm (December 3, 2009).

18. Rexford G. Tugwell, "Planning and the Profit Motive," pp. 38–39, in *Socialist Planning and a Socialist Program*.

19. Karl Kautsky, *The Labour Revolution* (1924), at http://www.marxists.org/archive/kautsky/1924/labour/ch03_c.htm (December 3, 2009).

20. Victor Serge, "Year One of the Russian Revolution," *New International*, Vol. XIV, No. 6 (August 1948), chap. 4, pp.186-191, at http://www.marxists.org/archive/serge/1930/year-one-ni/part04.html.

21. Anna Louise Strong, *The First Time in History* (Boni & Liveright, 1925), chap. 4, at http://www.marxists.org/reference/archive/strong-anna-louise/1925/first_time/index.htm (December 3, 2009).

22. *Ibid.*

23. John Maynard Keynes, *The General Theory of Employment, Interest and Money and Essays in Persuasion* (New York: Classic Books America, 2009), p. 128.

24. Eighth Congress of the Russian Communist Party, "Political Program of the CPSU," March 22, 1919, *International Socialist Review*, Vol. 22, No. 4 (Fall 1961), pp. 115-124, at http://www.marxists.org/history/ussr/government/1919/03/22.htm (December 2, 2009).

25. Leon Trotsky, *The Revolution Betrayed*, chap. 2.

26. *Ibid.*, chap. 4.

27. M. N. Krestinsky, "Russia's New Financial Policy," *Soviet Russia*, Vol. 5, No. 6 (December 1921), p. 267.

28. Waldemar Gurian, *Bolshevism: Theory and Practice* (New York: Sheed & Ward, 1935), pp. 129-130.

29. V. I. Lenin, letter to S. Y. Chutskayev, November 30, 1920, in *Collected Works*, Vol. 45 (Moscow: Progress Publishers, 1976), p. 58, at http://www.marxists.org/archive/lenin/works/1920/nov/30b.htm (December 3, 2009).

30. A speech on the ideological justification for the tax in kind explains that "we do not want the peasants' products to be delivered to the workers' state as appropriations of surplus grain, or a tax. We want them in exchange for all the goods the peasants need delivered to them by our transport system." In other words, the tax in kind was the first step toward socialist exchange without money. V. I. Lenin, "Report on the Tax in Kind," April 9, 1921, *Lenin's Collected Works*, Vol. 32, 1st English Edition, (Moscow: Progress Publishers, 1965), pp. 286-298, at http://www.marxists.org/archive/lenin/works/1921/apr/09.htm.

31. Gurian, *Bolshevism*, p. 98, note 1.

32. Pipes, *The Russian Revolution*, pp. 701-702.

33. S. S. Katzenellenbaum, *Russian Currency and Banking, 1914–1924* (London: P. S. King, 1925), pp. 98–99.

34. Leon Trotsky, "If America Should Go Communist," August 1934, at http://www.marxists.org/archive/trotsky/1934/08/ame.htm (December 3, 2009).

35. Barbara Wootton, *Plan or No Plan*, p. 57. Soviet officials felt the need to apologize for the use of money in the socialist economy. Officials explained that the existence of finance and credit at that time was due to the fact that under socialism (the lower state before communism) there was necessarily still commodity production and commodity circulation. Hence, with two forms of socialist ownership (state and collective) plus personal ownership, there must be exchange between them, "Moreover similar inter-relations also arise within the State sector," as state firms must exchange between themselves. Hence, there is a "need for money as a universal equivalent or, in other words, the need for a monetary form of expressing the value of goods." K. N. Plotnikov, *Banking in the USSR: The Financial and Credit System of the USSR*, pp. 43–44, in S. S. Katzenellenbaum, *Russian Currency and Banking, 1914–1924*. Yet would not exchange be required between socialized firms under any system? How could this dissolve under communism? The answer expressed by Soviet officials was that, under the first phase, "social production does not reach a level of development that can ensure an abundance of consumer goods for distribution to members of society according to their requirements." But this was expected to occur under communism. Because this "abundance" did not yet exist, officials explained that "there must be the strictest accounting and control by the State over the measure of labour and the measure of consumption," which is only possible using money. V. A. Vorobyev, *Banking, Planning of Money Circulation and Credit in the USSR*, p. 110. in S. S. Katzenellenbaum, *Russian Currency and Banking, 1914–1924*. Soviet officials learned that any kind of cost accounting, by firms or by the state, requires money. Money emerges naturally from exchange, and with free exchange, prices emerge and allow for cost accounting. This was imagined to not be necessary in the future communist society after great abundance allowed goods to be taken freely or distributed according to needs alone. Of course, such a society has never come to be.
36. J. Wilczinski, *The Economics of Socialism* (London: Allen & Unwin, 1977), p. 143.
37. For a detailed study of the Soviet wage system in the Stalin period, see Abram Bergson, *The Structure of Soviet Wages*.
38. Robinson, *An American in Leningrad*, p. 124.
39. E. A. Preobrazhensky, *From NEP to Socialism: A Glance into the Future of Russia and Europe*, trans. Brian Pearce (London: New Park Publications, 1973), Lecture 9, at http://www.marxists.org/archive/preobrazhensky/1921/fromnep/index.html (December 3, 2009).
40. Nove, *Political Economy and Soviet Socialism*, p. 178.
41. *Ibid.*, p. 219.
42. Wilczinski, *The Economics of Socialism*, pp. 147–148.
43. L. Gatovsky, *Ekonomicheskaya Gazeta*, No. 48 (December 1965), in *Soviet Economic Reform* (Moscow: Novosti Press Agency, 1967).
44. Alec Nove describes the other ways that a soft budget constraint affects the firm's willingness to share true costs. "For firms and control over their spending and investment, a further problem occurred in obtaining resources with the money allocated. Inputs were centrally coordinated, but it often occurred that those firms with the money to purchase inputs could not obtain them, while those firms which were able to locate materials did not have the necessary funds. When an enterprise was lucky enough to have both, it would often 'hoard' resources, purchasing more than it needed so as to have reserves in case of later shortage. For this reason, the claimed level of inputs needed was often much higher than the actual amount the firm required" (Alec Nove, *Political Economy and Soviet Socialism*, p. 183).
45. Nove, *The Soviet Economy*, p. 219, makes this case.
46. O. Nekrasov, *Voprosi Ekonomiki*, No. 11 (1965), in *Soviet Economic Reform* (Moscow: Novosti Press Agency, 1967).
47. Germain, "Soviet Management Reform," pp. 77–82.
48. Nove, *The Soviet Economy*, p. 223.
49. *Ibid.*
50. Kornai, *The Socialist System*, p. 545.
51. Nove, *Political Economy and Soviet Socialism*, p. 179.
52. *Ibid.*, p. 181.
53. Rockoff, *Drastic Measures*, p. 94.

54. Because one can feel more free sometimes by ceasing to desire greater material wealth, this is sometimes overlooked. The free feeling still depends on having one's basic needs met, allowing one to forget the most urgent material needs and enjoy the freedom from concern over accumulating more. If these basic needs were not met, instead of feeling free, one would feel the fear and hardship of the struggle for survival.

55. Nove, *The Soviet Economy*, p. 292.

56. Rudolf Hilferding, *Finance Capital: A Study of the Latest Phase of Capitalist Development* (London: Routledge & Kegan Paul, 1981), chap. 1, at http://www.marx.org/archive/hilferding/1910/finkap/index.htm (December 3, 2009).

57. See, for example, George Selgin, *Good Money: Birmingham Button Makers, The Royal Mint, and the Beginnings of Modern Coinage* (The Independent Institute, 2008). Also see Steven Horwitz, "Complementary Non-Quantity Theory Approaches to Money: Hilferding's Finance Capital and Free-Banking Theory," *History of Political Economy*, Vol. 26, No. 2 (Summer 1994), pp. 221–238.

58. Dick K. Nanto, "The 1997-98 Asian Financial Crisis," Congressional Research Service *Report for Congress*, February 6, 1998, at http://www.fas.org/man/crs/crs-asia2.htm (December 3, 2009).

59. CNNMoney.com, "Mint: Don't Melt Money," December 14, 2006, at http://money.cnn.com/2006/12/14/news/melting/index.htm (December 3, 2009).

60. Adam Smith, *An Inquiry into the Nature and Causes of the Wealth of Nations* (London: Methuen & Co., 1904), Book 5, chap. 3, at http://econlib.org/library/Smith/smWN22.html#B.V,%20Ch.3,%20Of%20Public%20Debts (December 3, 2009).

61. Austrian economists have focused on this problem probably more than any other school. See, for example, Richard Ebeling, *The Austrian Theory of the Trade Cycle and Other Essays*. As mentioned earlier, this is similar to the arguments made by Marx about the causes of "crises" under capitalism.

62. Rajshree Agarwal, Jay B. Barney, Nicolai J. Foss, and Peter G. Klein, "Heterogeneous Resources and the Financial Crisis: Implications of Strategic Management Theory," Copenhagen Business School, Center for Strategic Management and Globalization *Working Paper* No. 6/2009, July 28, 2009, at https://openarchive.cbs.dk/bitstream/handle/10398/7906/SMG%20WP%202009-06.pdf (December 4, 2009).

63. Nicolai J. Foss and Peter G. Klein, "Management Theory Is Not to Blame," *Mises Daily*, March 19, 2009, at http://mises.org/story/3375 (December 3, 2009).

64. Kenneth E. Boulding, "Samuelson's Foundations: The Role of Mathematics in Economics," *Journal of Political Economy*, Vol. 56, No. 3, (June 1948), p. 189, at http://ideas.repec.org/a/ucp/jpolec/v56y1948p187.html (December 3, 2009).

65. Similarly, an article from 1948 in *Voprosi Ekonomiki*, a Soviet economics journal, remarked about the absurdity of making such assumptions and then applying the conclusions to the real world. The author declared, "[The mathematical economist] has 30 pages of mathematics, and at the end there emerge the assumptions he put in at the beginning." The following statement is attributed to Nobel Prize-winning mathematical economist Wassily Leontief, a major early founder of input-output techniques and equilibrium modeling: "We move from more or less plausible but really arbitrary assumptions to elegantly demonstrated but irrelevant conclusions."

66. Milton Friedman, "The Methodology of Positive Economics," *Essays in Positive Economics* (Chicago: University of Chicago Press, 1953). Part of the essay can be found online at ttp://www.marxists.org/reference/subject/philosophy/works/us/friedman.htm.

67. For example, John B. Taylor (of the "Taylor Rule"), Joseph E. Stiglitz (a left-wing economist), Steven Gjerstad, Vernon L. Smith, Juliusz Jablecki, and Mateusz Machaj make this argument. See Jeffrey Friedman, "Introduction: A Crisis of Politics, Not Economics: Complexity, Ignorance, and Policy Failure," *Critical Review*, Vol. 21, Nos. 2–3 (2009), p. 138.

68. Lawrence H. White, "Federal Reserve Policy and the Housing Bubble," *Cato Journal*, Vol. 29, No. 1 (Winter 2009), p. 119, at http://www.cato.org/pubs/journal/cj29n1/cj29n1-9.pdf (December 3, 2009).

69. *Ibid.*, pp. 118–119.

70. For example, see Ianthe Jeanne Dugan and Alistair Macdonald, "Traders Blamed for Oil Spike," *The Wall Street Journal*, July 28, 2009, at http://online.wsj.com/article/SB124874574251485689.html (December 3, 2009).

71. Jon Birger, "What Onions Teach Us About Oil Prices," *Fortune*, June 30, 2008, at http://money.cnn.com/2008/06/27/news/economy/The_onion_conundrum_Birger.fortune (December 3, 2009).

72. In a letter to *The New York Times*, economics professor Donald Boudreaux humorously suggested to the Obama Administration that, rather than "reining in" speculators to address oil price volatility as they were contemplating, they should become speculators themselves. "Not only will these brilliant public servants earn personal fortunes in the oil market, they'll also, in the process, mute the allegedly excessive price fluctuations," Boudreaux quipped. "And because Mr. Obama & Co. would use their own resources, we the public will be better assured that their actions aren't driven by opportunistic politics." Don Boudreaux, "A Win-Win," Cafe Hayek, July 8, 2009, at http://cafehayek.com/2009/07/a-winwin.html (December 7, 2009).

Chapter 8. Regulation and the Institutions of a Dynamic Economy

Introduction

There are many debates in the policy world about why regulation does or does not achieve its intentions and whether deregulation has caused market failure. Often, new regulations are piled on top of failed regulations in an attempt to stem problems that seem to be inherent in certain industries.

Once enacted, policies are notoriously difficult to reverse. Even failing policies often remain in force for decades. When deregulation appears to make a situation worse, there is often a return to tighter rules. Yet the regulations imposed on firms are not the primary factor motivating behavior. It is the core institutions that firms face that drive them—the institutions of private property in a market economy, or of public property in a socialist economy.

In modern market economies, the institutions of private property are often compromised by policy. For example, subsidies attenuate the "hard budget constraint" that firms face when strict private property laws are enforced. Price controls violate the right of a firm to sell its own property to willing buyers at a privately agreed price. Other policies shield firms from losses or prevent them from profiting in certain kinds of transactions.

These ameliorations of the harsh competition that private property institutions create may drive certain kinds of behavior by firms. When policymakers attempt to control this behavior with regulation it often fails. Soviet planners learned that externally imposed controls or directives upon firm behavior are not effective. Only a reform of the basic institutions within which the firm acts can alter behavior; regulations will simply be evaded.

THE SOCIALIST ARGUMENT

As discussed in the introduction, the socialist experiment was an experiment in altering the entire institutional structure of the economy. This was not an accident. It was a purposeful change intended to produce better results. Socialists believed that the institutional structure they were putting in place would produce equality and abundance. This would be achieved in part through the well-known means of creating incentives for production: worker control over the economy would lead to greater enthusiasm for and ownership of work. "Wealth will then grow at a still faster rate because the workers will work better for themselves than they did for the capitalists; the working day will be shorter; the workers' standard of living will be higher; all their conditions of life will be completely changed."[1]

The primary institution of importance in the socialist economic system is the public ownership of the means of production. The protection of public property replaces the protection of private property.

> We must repeat that we are Marxists and that we take as our basis the *Communist Manifesto*....
>
> From capitalism mankind can pass directly only to socialism, i.e., to the social ownership of the means of production and the distribution of products according to the amount of work performed by each individual. Our Party looks farther ahead: socialism must inevitably evolve gradually into communism, upon the banner of which is inscribed the motto, "From each according to his ability, to each according to his needs."[2]

Lenin here indicated that the social ownership of production characterized socialism, Engels similarly said:

> In fact, the abolition of private property is, doubtless, the shortest and most significant way to characterize the revolution in the whole social order which has been made necessary by the development of industry—and for this reason it is rightly advanced by communists as their main demand.[3]

After the revolution, Bukharin and Preobrazhensky agreed, saying that "[t]he basis of communist society must be the social ownership of the means of production and exchange."[4]

Protection of private property was replaced by protection of public property; the inviolability of one's own property was replaced by the inviolability of common property. The protection of exchange and contract between two persons was replaced with the protection of exchange and contract between an individual and the state and between two state entities. What was once protected—contracts, investments, the right to open a business—was suddenly against the law. Instead there were new rights: the right to employment and the right to proceeds from all the commonly owned enterprises.

THE SOVIET EXPERIENCE

Once in power, the Soviet government put in place the institutions that they had advocated. As he attempted to implement this program in 1919, Lenin argued:

> In Russia, labour is united communistically insofar as, first, private ownership of the means of production has been abolished, and, secondly, the proletar-

ian state power is organising large-scale production on state-owned land and in state-owned enterprises on a national scale, is distributing labour-power among the various branches of production and the various enterprises, and is distributing among the working people large quantities of articles of consumption belonging to the state.[5]

The 1918 Soviet constitution enumerated the new institutions which would govern Soviet society. All land was now owned by the state. Factories, mills, and transport would soon be owned by the state. Once the new socialist society was fully in place, no object that could be used as a means of production would be privately owned. Hence, no contract could be made or enforced that bought or sold such objects. Nor could any person privately hire another person for work, except in extremely limited circumstances.

War communism was a failure. The Soviet government saw its power slipping away as famine, terror, and outrage took hold. Some of this was due to the civil war, which followed on the heels of Russia's involvement in World War 1, but some of it was due to the policies enacted by the new government. Lenin and the other true believers did not change their minds about the coming socialist society, but they decided that they needed to step back and reintroduce limited markets in order to increase output. They would then be able to introduce the planned society on top of a larger capitalist base.

When the Soviet government introduced the New Economic Policy, which was a return to a largely market-driven economy, they realized that certain institutions must be in place for it to flourish. The Communist Party understood that "the restorative qualities of private enterprise would not be felt on the nation's economy unless there was developed a set of laws defining civil relationships. A buyer and seller had to know what would be the expected result of a contract."[6]

Contracts between private parties would need to be enforced to allow investment, exchange, and employment. The buyer and seller would need to know that the contract would be upheld in court, if it came to that. A lender of money would need to know that the debt would be recoverable through the courts. Property owners would need to know that their property would be protected against theft or damage. These were the institutions that the market economy required—Lenin understood this, so he was ready to reintroduce these laws.

However, Lenin was also concerned about the power of the capitalist and his ability to exploit the worker, and about the use of private property against the interests of the society as a whole. Lenin's compromise for the New Economic Policy was to introduce laws to enforce contracts and to protect property against theft, but limited by the clause that these property rights were not to be protected in any case in which the state or society would be injured. Property must be used in the interest of society. For example, a house would not be protected for a property owner who allowed it to waste away in disuse, while some in society went without houses. This was deemed to be against the interests of society and thereby voided the property right.[7]

Another part of the code voided any contract in which one party took advantage of the "extreme want" of the other; thus if a poor man sold his house to a rich man at a very low price, the courts might not enforce the contract for the sale if it was ruled to be out of desperation. The relative wealth of the parties was also taken into account when suits for damages were tried. If a poor party injured a wealthy party, the courts were to take his income level into account and not enforce damages. If a wealthy party caused damage to a poor man's property, he was to owe damages even if there was no fault. The code also instituted a "presumption of state ownership," a policy of assuming state ownership in the event of an ownership dispute.

> In 1925, for instance, the Supreme Court of the RSFSR established the rule of the so-called "presumption of state ownership," i.e., that in case of a dispute between state agencies and private persons on the right of ownership to property, such property is always presumed to belong to the state and the burden of proving the opposite always rests upon the private party. This rule was widely used in the conduct of the policy of limiting and eliminating capitalist elements.[8]

The New Economic Policy was extraordinarily successful. The economy, which had sunk in many areas to levels below those of 1913, finally rebounded. Yet, the Communist Party saw it as a temporary retreat, and wanted to contain "the capitalist" and slowly nationalize private business and agriculture. The compromises made on property rights, and the uncertainty caused by shifting and changing rules, made investors wary. Small business flourished, but large-scale investment was limited by fears that the state would appropriate the business and its profits. A spokesman for a private textile firm wrote in 1926 that

> The main factor, from which private trade and industry suffer a great deal, is that up to now there is no straight and protracted policy with regard to private capital. It would be easier to adapt one's activity to the harshest system than to be dependent on completely arbitrary and unanticipated developments.[9]

This risk and confusion created by changing policy is called "regime uncertainty," and it threatened to destroy the growth created by the New Economic Policy. When business flourished, the Communist Party responded with harsher measures to "combat the Nepman" and "contain the capitalist class." As the 1920s wore on, the policies became stricter and the controls began to take their toll on the economy. The state retained ownership and control over areas of agriculture and heavy industry, and the attempts to set prices in these areas were causing shortages (see Chapter 6). Partially for these reasons, the push to collectivization took hold at the end of the 1920s.

Under Stalin, the original institutions of socialist intent, which were initially enforced under war communism, were reintroduced. Public ownership of all the means of production was the centerpiece. The method of organizing production with these resources was the plan. Therefore, public property protection, plan enforcement, protection of planned employment, and planned product pricing and exchange contracts replaced private property protection, private contract enforcement, freedom to hire and fire workers, and freedom to buy and sell products. Stalin described the new institutions in 1933 and explained how the protection of public property—like the protection of private property in market societies—was inviolable:

> The basis of our system is public property, just as private property is the basis of capitalism. If the capitalists proclaimed private property sacred and inviolable when they were consolidating the capitalist system, all the more reason why we Communists should proclaim public property sacred and inviolable in order to consolidate the new socialist forms of economy in all spheres of production and trade. To permit theft and plundering of public property—no matter whether it is state property or co-operative or collective-farm property—and to ignore such counter-revolutionary outrages means to aid and abet the undermining of the Soviet system, which rests on public property as its basis. It was on these grounds that our Soviet Government passed the recent law for the protection of public property. This enactment is the basis of revolutionary law at the present time. And it is the prime duty of every Communist, of every worker, and of every collective farmer strictly to carry out this law.[10]

Common ownership and public property produce a different set of possible legal arrangements than does private ownership and private property rights. If something is privately owned, the person owning it makes all decisions about its use, including the sale of it, and reaps all rewards and suffers all losses relating to it. Basic private property rights protect this situation: laws against theft, the breaking of contracts, and fraudulent contracts. In contrast, public property must be administered by the "public" somehow, whether democratically or by a representative elite. Decisions made by the "public" are then enforced as law.

Businesses could not be privately owned in the Soviet Union after the end of NEP. Managers running publicly owned firms had certain rights and responsibilities over them. The civil legal code restricted "operative administration" of state property by the following: (1) The Purpose of Its Activity, (2) Planned Tasks, and (3) The Purpose of the Property. The first of these limits the state firm to its intended function: "[A] steel mill may not produce candy; a pharmacy may not sell postcards; etc." The second limitation is even stricter: The firm must produce and sell goods according to the planned inputs and output, and nothing else. The third limitation regards the different "funds" that the state firm may use for production, such as the investment funds and the wage fund—these must be used for their intended purpose.[11]

Hence, in a socialist economy the law is not broken when one firm breaks a promise to another (a violation of contract), but when a firm breaks a promise to the state. Each firm has a different set of promises it has made to the state, because each firm has a different set of plan targets and production funds. The intricate set of promises between a given firm and the state is written up in a huge annual plan book and accompanying documents, and it is these promises that the firm manager aims not to break if he wants to avoid prison and advance his career. Failing to meet targets may only reduce the firm's bonuses and "premiums," but use of funds or resources for unplanned purposes or damage of state property could carry a prison sentence.[12]

Soviet law did not make every plan transgression a criminal (or even administrative) offense. Soviet law recognized that sometimes violations of the plan were inevitable. However, what if a Soviet firm manager was negligent, lazy or intentionally sabotaged an order? In a market economy this would be prosecuted as violation of contract. If one firm promised another 100 tons of cement and only delivered 65, the other firm could sue to recover this property. In the Soviet Union, the firm failing to deliver the goods was only held responsible if it was found to have acted with negligence; otherwise, the loss was born by the state. This was only natural: the state owned all the resources and determined how they were to be used. Failure on the part of one firm might easily have been triggered by a failure upstream of that firm.

However, this centralization of responsibility affected the incentives of the individual actors. "Attorneys from conflicting industrial units are always ready to agree that no one is to blame and that the loss must be borne by the entire Soviet people," remarked the American law student Logan Robinson. "Given the possibility of reaching such a 'no fault' result, it is not surprising that industrial and commercial losses in the Soviet Union are staggering." Knowing that they can avoid responsibility for their actions, the people may lose their sense of moral culpability. "Rather than looking for ways to safeguard against loss, individuals and factories would spend their time dreaming up excuses as to why they personally were not to blame."[13]

Although workers and managers may have tried to evade responsibility, it was true that in general they were not responsible for the supply problems, inefficiencies, and poor quality of production at their firms. Because of the hierarchical organization of a planned economy, even economic ministers usually lacked the power to improve production. Much of this book recounts the inefficiencies and failures of the Soviet attempt at planning. Every economy has failures, and every government enacts reforms. Soviet planners attempted several kinds of reform to eliminate the inefficiencies that they saw—inefficiencies that stemmed from the institutional structure. Of course, they did not change the institutional structure itself: The Soviet economy remained a planned economy. It is also worth remembering that they could not completely reform—or privatize—some sections of the economy and not others. As the Sovietologist Alec Nove explained:

> [T]he system has an inner logic that resists partial change. Thus if one frees an industry—say clothing—from central control, then what would happen to the industries that provide it with inputs? Unless they too responded to market stimuli (i.e., based their production on orders from the clothing industry), there would be acute problems in ensuring that they produce what is needed.[14]

Reaping the benefits of allowing some to have freedoms would require giving these freedoms to all enterprises.[15] The Soviet state resisted giving all firms these freedoms because it would mean fully turning to the market economy. They could also not alter the institutions of socialism and remain socialist. Thus, the reforms that they did enact had to be regulations or additional commands on top of the existing structure or reforms of the structure that did not affect the core institutions.

One kind of reform that planners tried was "economic reorganization." Planners reorganized the governmental hierarchy, not to reduce the scope of control by planners, but to increase the efficiency and effectiveness of their control over enterprises.[16] Several reforms over the long Soviet period were taken to improve the efficiency of the hierarchical planning bureaucracy: Commissariats became ministries, ministries were organized (as *sovnarkhozi*) by location instead of function and then reorganized by function again, and power within the hierarchy was alternately centralized or decentralized depending on the latest reform program. Yet none of the reforms was satisfactory:

> Measures of a purely technical nature can undoubtedly overcome some of the most flagrant contradictions in bureaucratic management; but they can only bring this about by simultaneously provoking or exacerbating other contradictions. Thus, introductions of the *sovnarkhozes* unquestionably eliminated some of the major flaws of extreme centralization; steel was no longer shipped from Leningrad to Vladivostok, while being simultaneously shipped from Vladivostok to Leningrad. But in place of this defect, another appeared; each "autonomous economic region" having a *sovnarkhoz* tried to "duplicate" enterprises existing in other regions as much as possible. Instead of wasting means on useless transportation, they were wasted on superfluous investments. "Regional egoism" supplanted "ministerial egoism."[17]

Changes in the hierarchy of the planning apparatus could not change the planning institutions. They could only better organize the implementation of the plan. If the planning institutions caused "contradictions," due to the nature of command, these reorganizations could not resolve them. The specific problem of shipping from one region to another while simultaneously shipping along the reverse route reflected the particular hierarchical structure of the bureaucracy, but the institutional structure was the underlying cause. Public ownership requires centralized planning and removes the decentralized profit and loss incentives of the firm. Neither of these factors was affected by the rearrangement of the hierarchy. Any reorganization would have the same underlying problem. The particular expression of the contradictions caused by distorted incentives might change, but they would still find an outlet.

A second kind of reform involved altering the number of targets planned at the higher levels. Planners realized that bureaucracy was clogging the planning apparatus and that the plan indicators were causing distortions. Soviet economists suggested reducing the number of plan indicators. Reform economists suggested that "Only the key indices, the decisive indices, should be handed down to enterprises, whose directors should be given greater rights and opportunities for economic manoeuvring within their scope."[18] The Central Committee of the party took this advice, determining that:

> A serious shortcoming of industrial management is that administrative methods have superseded economic necessity.... The powers of enterprises with regard to their economic activity are restricted.
>
> The work of enterprises is regulated by numerous indices which restrict the independence and initiative of the personnel of enterprises, diminish their sense of responsibility for improving the organisation of production....
>
> It has been found expedient to put a stop to excessive regulation of the activity of enterprises, to reduce the number of plan indices required of enterprises from above.[19]

This reform did not reduce the number of commodities planned at the top of the hierarchy, but it did reduce the level of detail planned at this centralized level, giving ministries more control over how they fulfilled these plans. Ministers, in turn, were to leave each enterprise with more control over how to fulfill their plans. Ministers would keep the broad targets in place, but give firms more flexibility on the details of fulfilling those targets. While the reorganization of the hierarchy aimed at tightening control over planning, target reform was arguably an attempt at loosening or decentralizing the planning process.

Yet this "deregulation" of the enterprise was dangerous, given the institutions in place. With private property, targets are not needed. Profit drives firms to serve the customer. With public property, the firm requires guidance. As discussed in Chapter 3, when the plan targets were set as precisely as possible, critical information was already missing. Firms had to fill a certain list of targets and product variations, and they found the most expedient way of doing so. Planners could not holistically encompass all the potentialities and ensure that the firms would please the customer. But they tried to do so by providing firms not only with output targets covering specific variations of the product, sometimes numbering in the hundreds, but also with targets for quality, cost, labor usage, and other factors for each variation.

The "deregulation" that reduced the number and specificity of targets actually took the firms further from the goal of a "holistic target" that could guide the firm to please the customer. The targets were set centrally, so they might be an inaccurate representation of customer desires, or they could be impossible to fulfill. Yet they could at least tell the firm something about the mix of products that planners thought were required. With reduced target specificity, firms had even more leeway to produce only the easiest of their planned production. Firms did not even need to underfulfill targets to create a massive imbalance because it was perfectly acceptable to produce whatever mix the firm preferred.

If firms were producing for profit, this freedom would allow the firm to produce for the customer, but Soviet firms were not allowed to produce for profit. They were only given fewer, less specific targets. The institutional structure remained the same: Loss was subsidized, profits were not left with the firm, prices and supplier contracts were chosen by planners, and the firm and its property were not privately owned. Within this institutional structure, the smaller number of targets did decentralize the decision, but without using profit as a guide and loss to curb waste, the reform produced the opposite of the intended effect. The institutional structure meant that the decentralization, which intuitively sounds like it should help firms produce what their customer wanted, only encouraged firms to "simulate" plan fulfillment, cut corners, and produce more lopsided combinations of products.[20]

Planners recognized this early on and supplementary targets were passed down through the ministries to many firms. Planners understood that if firms had too much leeway in their production assortment they would not be assured that inputs required at other firms would actually be produced. Planners could not allow this reform to be fully implemented because it would make planning impossible.

Hence, planners were forced to make the targets more specific again.[21] In fact, these sorts of reforms changed little. Targets were increased and decreased with detail requirements added and removed, but ministers were still given the complete plan instruction and inevitably guided the firm essentially as they had before the reform.

Campaigns were also used to reduce costs and to direct production toward specific high-priority industries. During a "campaign," the managers of firms were encouraged to pay greater attention to the specific targets associated with the campaign. For example, raw materials, labor productivity, or capital costs would be targeted. The campaigns did somewhat increase the attention given to the particular goals, but they could not alter the underlying incentives of the factory. Most often, the enterprise would exert effort to appear as if they were conforming to the goals of the campaign, rather than honestly conforming to them. Similar to the "simulation" of plan fulfillment, firm managers "simulated" prioritizing the campaign targets above other targets.

A third kind of reform was implemented in 1955. Committees were established to ensure that firms reduced costs and directed production toward the addition of new product lines—both ongoing problems facing the planners. However, because the new committees did not change the underlying incentives, they were similar to permanent campaigns:

> [Two committees] were established in the middle of 1955 to cope with special problems the new regime found particularly troublesome.... From the published discussions, however, it is clear that the approach is essentially the familiar "campaign" technique with a new departure in the establishment of high-level committees to give permanence to the campaign.... The past failure of campaigns to yield desirable results, however, has been due only partly to their impermanence. It has also been due to the fact that a campaign is essentially a way of exerting *external pressure* upon the enterprise. It does not attempt to *change the basic features of the economic system which generate the practices under attack....* Judging from past experience, managers will react to the new barriers by finding new ways of protecting their interests.... Thus the new committees may alter the details of enterprise operation, but are not likely to change the principles governing managerial behaviour.[22]

Berliner was right to doubt the efficacy of these new committees. Adding additional layers of bureaucracy to externally pressure firms in the areas of cost and new product development did not alleviate the problems. Instead, managers—as Berliner predicted—found ways around the campaign targets or ways to "simulate" compliance. Once again, the incentives of the enterprise managers remained because the institutions remained, and external pressure could not fundamentally affect the outcome. New products were usually essentially the same as old products, but were introduced as "new," just as they already had been to obtain higher prices under the plan. Innovation remained low. Costs still ballooned because the planners could not know if the higher costs were justified. Budgets were still soft.

The reforms that planners reintroduced multiple times are especially instructive because they show the laws of economics that were so necessary that planners kept returning to them to try to improve the outcome of the Soviet economy. A Western textbook on Soviet economics explains the "recurring themes" of Soviet economic reform.[23] Each of them highlights a major lesson that helps to illustrate the fundamental importance of basic economic laws for society and policy, and the institutions necessary to accommodate these laws. The textbook recounts: "First, there is the idea that Soviet enterprises should have more autonomy. There should be less "petty tutelage" (*opeka*) on the part of ministries and state committees; enterprises should have increased freedom to make their own output and input decisions."[24]

This reform concept brings up several interesting questions:

- Is it consistent with central planning?

- Under what conditions is it possible to introduce, in whole or in part, and what other reforms may it depend on?

- What insights about economic systems can be learned from it?

With public ownership, enterprises cannot make these decisions completely on their own. The state must determine the required inputs for each firm based on the plan for the overall economy and the budget for the state sector. If individual firms have the freedom to determine which inputs they desire, how much to purchase, and from where to obtain them, then the state not only has no control over that firm, it also has no control over the resources being used to produce those inputs. Those resources would have to be mobilized on the basis of what the firm required, not on the basis of the plan, otherwise the firm does not have "increased freedom to make [its] own output and input decisions." In fact, these are two sides of the same coin: one firm's input decision is another firm's output decision. Yet, at this point, the state has lost control over the economy. Firms would produce for each other, or for the consumer, and the plan would have to be discarded. The state must make these determinations if it is to plan the economy, and publicly run the firm.

Yet, Soviet reformers kept returning to this theme, because centrally planning the inputs was not possible. The state did not have the information necessary to set targets well, and the targets could not aid firms in responding to actual demand by the customer. Planners came to the conclusion that firms know what inputs they require better than planners can. It is telling that "petty tutelage" became known as a bad thing even though directing industry was a core part of ideology.[25]

Planners realized that they were incapable of determining the right kind or amount of inputs or directing firms to produce the appropriate outputs. This indicates a basic inability of planning to fulfill its function: allocating resources across the economy and responding to consumer demand. Centralized knowledge was insufficient to determine the requirements. Planners simply did not have the necessary *information*. It does not, however, tell us precisely why. The second recurring theme helps to fill in the details.

A second recurring theme is that enterprises should be held responsible for their final results. The enterprise that cannot make a profit should not count on an automatic bailout by higher authorities.[26]

The second reform type indicates the problem with a soft budget constraint and brings us back to the notion of profit as a guiding force and loss as a necessary corollary. However, a central tenet of the doctrine of planning holds that profits are *not* a guide to efficiency, and failure of firms to generate profits does *not* indicate that they are not socially useful. Socialists argued that many socially useful sectors may be unprofitable, and the plan itself would determine allocation. Individual firms, industries, and sectors that could not generate profit would be supported by those that could. This recurring reform theme shows that planners learned the problems with this approach, and is instructive for market economies that also engage in bailouts of firms or subsidies for loss-making enterprises.

Even if planners wanted to introduce profit and loss as a guiding force, it was not possible to reconcile this with planning. Profit is only a useful signal when prices are decentralized and determined by supply and demand. "Planned losses" were common in the Soviet Union for two reasons.[27] First, prices were based on *average cost across an industry*, because this was the only cost that could be determined. Hence, the true profit or loss of a given firm could not be known. The use of "planned losses" in this regard was to make a workable plan possible with *less information*.

Second, profits were used to subsidize socially necessary, but unprofitable firms. However, it became clear that subsidizing unprofitable firms was inefficient and ultimately unworkable. Thus, planners kept returning to the theme that socialist enterprises were not to be subsidized when they made losses, and that what is profitable for society should be profitable for the individual enterprise. However, in the planned economy losses may not be the fault of a given firm or its products. It may be due to shortages or supply problems, plan errors, low-quality inputs, or any number of other circumstances. So this reform was also not workable alone.

A third recurring theme—often termed "direct links"—is the notion that enterprises should be tied more closely to their customers. An enterprise that produces for the consumer should know what the consumer wants. An enterprise that produces materials for other enterprises should deal directly with its customers to learn what they want and when they want it.... Tying enterprises to their customers implies a reduction in tutelage from above.[28]

Planners saw that the state-run firm could not respond to the customer and wanted to change this. Their proposed remedy was to give the firm more control over its own resources and to allow contracts between firms and between the firm and the (individual) consumer. This is a clear admission that the idea of consumer sovereignty in the market is correct. This reform taken to its natural conclusion would have the consumer, not the plan, decide what should be made. "Direct links" where firms have the freedom to determine what the final consumer wants and then contract with other firms for inputs would lead to market-driven, not plan-driven, production.

This reform is also difficult to do halfway. If planners tie firms to each other, then "direct links" between them will not lead to greater accountability to the customer, particularly if the firms are given instructions from above on what to produce. The only way to make use of "direct links" is to allow firms to compete for contracts with other firms. However, this still cannot work if output is determined by a plan. If firms can "compete for business" by trying to better produce for a customer to win a contract with them (and form a "direct link"), but the enterprise's output is centrally set, then there can be no real response to the customer and no real competition between firms. Losing firms cannot lower their price or change their product to win the contract. Winning firms cannot increase production in response to greater demand until the plan allows it. There can be no competition unless firms have the freedom to alter their prices, output, and products. True competition also requires that firms retain ownership over profit and be responsible for loss. Hence, the "direct links" program was unable to achieve what planners had hoped, but it is telling that they kept returning to this theme.

Another indication that these reforms were addressing issues fundamental to the institutional structure, and not simply problems that happened to occur in the particular cultural context or circumstance, is that these same themes were debated and addressed in other socialist countries; for example, in China:

> Ever since 1956, we were told, the Liu Shao-ch'i revisionist line had had some influence upon factory procedures. State planning levels were seriously affected by the policies of Liuist Po I-po, and there were a number of Liu's "agents" in the factory. The reality behind these political labels seems to have taken the following form: The State plan imposed strict controls on budgeting. *Within tight budget restrictions*, individual factories were permitted *some* flexibility to plan production according to the criterion of profit.... State requirements were met by manipulation of available resources at the factory level. *There was a tendency to produce those goods which could be turned out most cheaply and quickly, or for which materials were readily available.*[29]

Just as in the Soviet Union, the profit criterion was introduced by Chinese reformers, but it was limited by planned budgets. Because the Chinese factories could not respond directly to the customer, and were not constrained by market competition, this led to "simulation" rather than efficient production. The responses by Soviet and Chinese firms were the natural outcome of having to fill targets, and not having the feedback from the customer or the constraints imposed by the profit and loss system. Although numerous reforms attempted to correct the incentives created by public ownership, they could not get to the crux of the issue. Private ownership and the ability to retain profits and suffer losses create the basic environment from which the behaviors that planners desired are derived. Until this basic institutional environment was restored, no reforms or regulations would succeed. Planners had depended upon ideological persuasion to replace this institutional structure, but it cannot fulfill this function. As János Kornai described the situation,

> The official ideology suggests that every functionary should manage the activities entrusted to him or her "like a proprietor." In fact, it is impossible for a truly proprietorial motivation to develop at any level of the bureaucracy. Neither the

> director of a firm nor his or her superiors can pocket the residual income. They are neither able nor willing to bear full responsibility for their decisions, since they are instructed from above, and there is constant interference in the way once given the instructions are carried out.... "Proprietorial" motivation cannot develop from persuasion if the actual social position of the official in the bureaucracy is not proprietorial in nature.[30]

Thus, it is a feature of the institutional structure. Individuals are encouraged to care for property both by the gains and by the losses they incur personally. Common ownership, and the socialist ideal that a worker should feel a sense of ownership over shared resources, could not replace this. The constant external pressure and various new regulations could not overcome this basic problem.

Many of the later reforms were couched in market rhetoric, but did not alter the core institutions either. As long as the state owned the property of the firms, these reforms were often nothing but accounting wizardry. For example, some reforms "cut subsidies" to state firms. This kind of reform might sound like it would reduce the problems of the soft budget constraint and move toward a profit-and-loss-driven system. However, closer scrutiny reveals that these reforms only shifted the numbers in the accounting books. For example,

> The Soviets also cut subsidies to key staple goods, and that is partly why people saw this as a promarket reform. But under state ownership, in effect, all goods produced are subsidized, that is, not tested by the competitive market. Instead of directly financing production out of the state budget, they did it by arbitrarily increasing the prices for monopoly goods.[31]

Whether a firm is directly subsidized or just given a high price and protected from competition, the result is the same. Many "privatizations" and "deregulations" are just a change in accounting if the state maintains control over some of these factors. For the firm to truly face a hard budget constraint, and therefore competition and the guidance of profit and loss, the firm must be accountable for all of its own costs, prices, and choices. It must not be shielded from competition and innovation.

The owners must also know that the property and contracts are protected from theft and fraud by private or public parties. Only then will the firm truly be driven by profit, loss, and competition. In the Soviet Union, even when markets *were* given more freedom, the benefits of the market could not be realized because private property was not protected.

Many former communist countries and developing countries have faced this problem. Without private property protection and with regulations that can be used to arbitrarily attack businesses and extract bribes, the benefits of the market remain elusive. Strong protection of property rights allows individuals and firms to invest in new enterprises and in expansions and upgrades of existing ones. This means that they can chase profits, and are limited by loss. This in turn means that the "out of equilibrium" state in which one firm earns massive profits and looks like a monopoly will tend not to last long. Consumers will be sovereign and suppliers will respond to changes in demand and scarcity.

However, if the state maintains ownership or control, but releases one aspect from its control, it is likely to unravel the economy and worsen the situation. To ensure an improvement in the situation, the socialist economy needed to move to a strong protection of property rights. This must include the ability to own and run businesses, control operations and budgets, and own profits and losses. It also requires enforcement of all contracts made with other individuals and businesses. Instead, even the later reforms tended to fall short of this and focus instead just on prices:

> The outlook for the economy continued to look worse and worse. This is not because Yeltsin had not applied the advice from Western academics and World Bank bureaucrats. The problem was he took them at their word when they said flexible prices, not private property, were what the Russian economy needed.
>
> Contrary to all the promises and beliefs of Russian Keynesians, headed by the Yeltsin economic minister Yegor Gaidar, we watched a simultaneous increase in prices and a fall-off in production. Because the essence of socialism is public ownership, without dismantling this system, none of Yeltsin's "reforms" will work. Like Gorbachev before him, Yeltsin's government is directed at "restructuring the state regulatory mechanism."[32]

If prices were free, but costs were covered by the state, then firms selling to other firms could raise prices arbitrarily high without losing any customers. If wages were fixed high and prices free, prices would rise to cover wages so that firms would not have to economize in other areas, knowing that they faced no serious competition. All other firms could do the same, and losses would be subsidized.

LESSONS

> [T]he most perilous moment for a bad government is when that government tries to mend its ways. — Alexis de Tocqueville[33]

The institutions of the socialist program were based around public ownership of the means of production. Although socialists had described some of the advantages that they believed would come from this institutional arrangement, they had not based these advantages on explicit economic theory because they did not believe that "bourgeois" economic laws would apply under the new conditions and did not predict what the new laws would be. Socialists believed that formal laws and legal institutions would wither away just as the state would ultimately wither away under the new institutional arrangements. This meant that, unlike private property institutions, the new institutions of public property would not need laws to enforce them.[34]

However, they soon learned that the commonly owned property would be abused if it was not protected by law, and hence the new institutional arrangements were based on protection of public property. There is one well known problem with the institutional arrangement of commonly owned property. If everyone owns something, it is as if nobody owns it. In this "tragedy of the commons,"[35] nobody wants to maintain the property because they can let someone else care for it. Each person will "free ride" off the other owners. The legal nature of ownership of property directly affects the incentives of those who use the property. As economist Eugen Bohm-Bawerk pointed out in 1884:

> If standing lumber is a relatively rare natural resource at all, then it follows from the very nature of things and irrespective of any provision of law, that any wastage of rare natural resources affecting weal or woe, must proceed from persons. The legal provisions are concerned only with the question of *which specific persons suffer the deprivation.* Under a system of private ownership of land the proprietor is the person interested, and the one who feels the loss; under a system of socialized property in land, the entire circle of society would be the persons concerned; in the absence of any system of law and order it would be the incumbent in actual control, be he the first or the strongest.[36]

The change in the institutional nature of the economy from private ownership to public ownership changed incentives in the economy because it changed which persons felt the loss when resources were abused. If one person personally owns property, then he has an interest in protecting it, caring for it, and investing in it. If a broad community owns it, then no one individual personally feels the loss when it is damaged, and the community members may shirk their responsibility to maintain and care for it. This is the "tragedy of the commons."

Any personal investment in commonly owned property will reward the whole group, but it will cost the individual his own energy and time. This creates a "free riding" problem, in which many individuals do not bother to invest their own time, knowing that it will be unlikely to make a difference in the total output of the group or in their own share of the proceeds. Additional problems arise if the group owners need to make decisions about the use of the property.[37]

This is the most obvious and well-known change that occurs with the move from private to public ownership. Yet even though it is well known, not all of its consequences are immediately obvious. When regulations affect just some of the property rights of a firm owner, then only some of her incentives will be affected. For example, controlling the price of a product, protecting a firm from competition, or regulating the details of a product will not create a pure case of the "tragedy of the commons," but it will affect the incentives of the firm. Private property ownership is defined by a complete set of property rights and ownership. Economist Ludwig von Mises describes the effects of partial curtailment of property rights:

> Carried through consistently, the right of property would entitle the proprietor to claim all the advantages which the good's employment may generate on the one hand and would burden him with all the disadvantages resulting from its employment on the other hand. Then the proprietor alone would be fully responsible for the outcome. In dealing with his property he would take into account all the expected results of his action, those considered favourable as well as those considered unfavourable. But if some of the consequences of his action are outside of the sphere of the benefits he is entitled to reap and of the drawbacks that are put to his debit, he will not bother in his planning about all the effects of his action. He will disregard those benefits which do not increase his own satisfaction and those costs which do not burden him. His conduct will deviate from the line which it would have followed if the laws were better adjusted to the economic objectives of private ownership. He will embark upon certain projects only because the laws release him from responsibility for some of the costs incurred. He will abstain from

other projects merely because the laws prevent him from harvesting all the advantages derivable.[38]

This may seem obvious; in fact many policies rely on such incentives when they tax the activities of firms deemed socially undesirable, or subsidize ones with positive effects. Yet, it can become hidden within the complex policy arrangements of modern economies. Policies aimed at helping the consumer or increasing competition may release firms from some of their property obligations, but the effects of this change may be muddied by the interactions of other policies and regulations. A firm's behavior may be wrongly blamed on other regulatory and legal requirements it faces, or on the character of the firm owner or manager. If character is blamed, often laws banning certain behaviors are introduced instead of looking for an institutional cause. When consequences of the institutional structure are not traced to the original cause, regulations enacted to alleviate the problems may mask the cause further. If they are unsuccessful, additional regulations may be added on top, making it difficult to identify the underlying problem.

This may be especially true when regulations and policies persist for long periods, and the public forgets what it was like without them. Perhaps the most obvious reason that policies are difficult to reverse is because the regulators, benefiting parties, and bureaucrats have vested interests in maintaining the status quo.[39] This is evidenced by the recurring lobbying by industries that receive subsidies. Although this reason is intuitive and supported by clear empirical evidence, it is not always modeled by economists when evaluating temporary policies. Even when the goal of a subsidized program is not met, the lobbying, and often campaign contributions to committee members by those lobbying, help to ensure that the program persists.

However, this is not the only reason that policies remain, even when their success is questionable. A policy may appear useful when it is not, and deregulation may prove troublesome, even though the industry would be better off with fewer regulations.

Economist Vernon Smith studied deregulation in the electric energy market in the United States.[40] Deregulation in the market was undertaken with "numerous political compromises," he argued. Those compromises meant that the energy market was regulated on one side, but not on the other, making prices and incentives more imbalanced than when the entire market was guided by regulation. In the wholesale market prices were deregulated, but retail prices were still fixed at hourly rates and over seasonal cycles. "Because of the regulatory mandate that all demand must be served at a fixed price, the planning did not allow for the early introduction of demand responsive retail prices and technologies to enable peak consumption to be reduced." Smith argues that this led to the California energy crisis of 2000 and 2001. This is similar to the problems faced by the Soviet government during the New Economic Policy, when price controls led to the "scissors crisis," and shortage of industrial goods. (See Chapter 6.) Facing the crisis, the Soviet government responded by increasing control over the firms in the market, ultimately taking them all under public control. Similarly, the California energy crisis led to calls for increased regulation and even nationalization.[41]

Just as Alec Nove said of the Soviet economy, that "[T]he system has an inner logic that resists partial change," deregulation of controlled industries might cause serious new distortions. Many policymakers have noted this in other industries as well, whether aiming to increase or decrease governmental involvement. During a recent health care summit in the United States, several policymakers argued that health care reform defies an "incremental approach." One Senator said that "You can't get from one point to the next incrementally unless you deal with it holistically."[42]

Very heavy-handed regulations, such as controls over price or output or subsidies that relieve the firm of cost considerations, alter the basic institutional incentives a firm faces. Property rights are a package, and the loss of some of these rights alters the basic incentives of a firm. After changing these incentives and seeing a negative outcome, policymakers may respond with further controls or regulations over the operations—external pressure. Loosening these controls would constitute "deregulation," but would not change the basic incentives the firm faces.

The institutional structure providing incentives to the firm is the best route to affect the behavior of the firm. As Soviet planners learned, external pressure is usually futile in changing the behavior of economic actors, but private property institutions do not even require external pressure (as the Soviet economist Strumulin observed, "Economic laws take their own revenge on those who break them"[43]), only the enforcement of rights.

While adding layers of regulation to subsidized firms that have anti-social incentives rarely works (because, as Soviet economist Norozhilov noted, "Fear is a less effective stimulus than economic or moral interest"[44]), no regulations are necessary when incentives are in place for firms to act in the public interest. In contrast, removing regulations from *subsidized* firms may make things worse if the incentives are still aligned so as to encourage anti-social behavior.

Considérant and other socialists argued that market competition and the drive for profit led to "adulteration of products." This is not a common complaint about market economies today, given the incredible advance of quality and technology in most industries (except where price has fallen instead).[45] However, this is a common problem in industries in which firms have no profit motivation or attenuated property rights. If the government fixes prices or regulates profit in an industry, it may then find that it must add more layers of regulations to prevent the firms from reducing the quality of their product or engaging in other unpleasant activities. For example, during World War II, price controls led to deteriorating quality of items including necessities such as food. Lowering quality was one way of attempting to evade the controls:

> Quality deterioration became a problem in many foods where it sometimes went under the old name of "adulteration." Fat was added to hamburger, the but-

terfat content of milk was reduced, cornstarch was added to spices, and coffee was stretched with fillers.[46]

Instead of competing by either raising quality or reducing price, firms had to keep prices low, constant, and equal to their competitors, and therefore reduced quality to retain enough profit to continue to compete. In response to the deteriorating quality, clearly driven by the inability to set prices at a profitable level, authorities resorted to further regulations:

> The OPA tried various ways of meeting this problem. One regulation required butchers to grind hamburger in the presence of the customers. Other regulations specified the amount of fat that could be left to border a given cut of meat. In 1944, the OPA filed a number of injunction suits in cases of improper fat trim, an adumbration of what might be expected with a permanent set of controls on the World War II model.[47]

While this is a common occurrence under a price control regime, it is rare under usual market circumstances. Far from the "race to the bottom" in quality and "adulteration" cited by Considérant and other socialists, competition in the market drives improvements in quality and advances in technology.[48] Still, it is sometimes argued that the profit motive drives fraud in the banking industry, and this must be attenuated with regulation.

> Joseph Stiglitz, a Nobel Prize winner in economics and other economists say one of the tenets (greed) that propels capitalists to invest or produce at their highest potential is the same motive that spurs rampant corruption. As US former President Herbert Hoover stated, the problem of capitalism is that capitalists are very greedy. Or to put it simply, the desire to make profits usually puts pressure on good people to break ordinary rules of decency.[49]

According to this view, the drive for profit (and hence the institutional structure of private property) leads to corruption. This natural feature of market economies must be tempered with regulation. It is not enough, it is argued, to prosecute fraud when it occurs: Regulations must be in place that make it more difficult to engage in such activity. However, many "capitalists" in market economies are not within an institutional structure of complete private property protection—as described by Mises in the passage above, they are not subject to the complete set of rewards and burdens that the profit and loss system provides.

The particular institutions that help the actor to channel his greed make all the difference in its result. Regulations will not be effective if the institutions drive fraud, while regulations will not be necessary (only prosecution of fraud) if the institutions do not. This was the lesson that planners faced when they attempted to correct the socialist firms' behavior with campaigns and reforms.

Some have argued that the Glass–Steagall Act, by prohibiting banks from offering investment, commercial banking, and insurance services, helped to prevent fraud in the U.S. financial sector. Its repeal, with the Gramm–Leach–Bliley Act, is cited as a cause of the 2007–2008 financial crisis.[50] The argument is that the new financial securities firms, which combined insurance and securities companies into a single company, had the incentive and ability to create new financial instruments that hid risk from customers. Essentially, it is argued that banks were allowed to gamble with the people's money, and huge bonuses drove executives to take huge risks. The regulations had been necessary to prevent this, and when lifted Wall Street went mad.

This implies that firms in the financial sector wanted to take advantage of this insurance-securities combination to hide risk from the customer—which is to say, to commit fraud against investors. Yet under what conditions would it make sense for financial firms to defraud their customers? Without special oversight, would the financial sector become a "market for lemons"?[51] In other words, would all financial firms defraud the customer? If financial firms did this, would there not then be an opportunity for an innovative firm to reap massive profits by offering private oversight (for example, an alternative rating system) or more transparent and trustworthy financial products? If there is significant fraud in any market, one must wonder what has prevented such innovations.

In a market economy, if the customer is not satisfied and the firm is not protected by government from competition, a competitor or entrepreneur can expose fraud or low quality, offer a better product, and take their business and their profit. Unfortunately, the U.S. government had a monopoly on ratings, so this prevented any entrepreneur from offering this service.[52] In addition, the rising speculative boom in the mortgage market, driven by low interest rates and other measures, could have contributed both to the short-term outlook of firms (putting immediate profit above the loss of customers over the longer-term) and to a lack of competitive pressure.

Housing prices were rising every year, and demand was insatiable. In this climate, it must have seemed like any loan could sell, and immediate trading was more important than the long-term satisfaction of the customer. Furthermore, it was not necessary for firms to expose the feckless dealings of their competitors. It was more important to make money in the short term on the rising house prices. Speculative frenzies are just that—frenzied buying and selling that does not concern itself with the long term.

This may have made stricter regulation necessary. The market itself may not require such regulation absent these policies. One article written at the height of the crisis argued that the core problem was, "The failure of US regulators to tighten capital and lending standards when abundant capital inflows combined with loose Fed policies ignited a furious credit boom."[53] Capital inflows (e.g., from Asia) may create a boom, but are unlikely to cause the kind of bust that occurred because the projects undertaken with the new capital should have been sustainable. However, loose monetary policy drove down interest rates, and was able to create this speculative frenzy, driving money into projects that would become worthless once the interest rates inevitably rose again. (See Chapter 7.)

Banks were responding to the incentives they faced given the institutional environment: The level of interest rates acted as a subsidy for borrowing, offsetting some of the burden of loss that firms should have faced. The subsidies that were driving prices up in the housing market offered additional unearned reward, and other policies similarly distorted behavior. Given this environment, policymakers attempted to impose external controls on the behavior of bankers, and later removed some of those regulations, possibly making things worse. Economist Richard Posner argued:

> Because the Federal Reserve under Alan Greenspan pushed interest rates too low and kept them low for too long, and because regulation of financial interme-diaries had over the years dwindled and became especially lax during the Bush Administration, the bankers were allowed, and competition forced them, to take risks that could have and have had disastrous results. If the government thinks that shaming the bankers and capping their pay will prevent future banking disas-ters, it will be distracted from making the regulatory changes that are necessary to restore effective public supervision of a vital industry.[54]

Yet these regulations that were removed may not have been necessary if the inter-est rates had not been set artificially low. The more fundamental cause of the bank-ing disaster is the incentive environment of the speculative bubble—not the effect of removing layered-on regulations. The speculative bubble arguably was created by wearing away the property rights of firms in the industry, through subsidies and in-flationary policy. This is a more fundamental issue than what regulations are imposed upon the industry after this environment is created.

A regulatory environment may itself create bad incentives that lead to the need for more regulation, if firms are not held responsible for their own actions. Arguably, in the financial sector this traces back all the way to regulations enacted prior to the 1929 stock market crash and the regulatory response that followed. Some economists have argued that policies in place in America, but not in Canada, made the 1929 crash much worse:

> [D]eposit-insurance legislation was thought, in 1933, to be necessary to guard against banking panics such as had just been seen across the United States. That theory may have been wrong. "Historically it does not appear that panics are an inherent feature of banking generally." "The United States experienced panics in a period when they were a historical curiosity in other countries." [References omitted] And this unfortunate case of American exceptionalism may, in turn, have been due to a series of earlier American regulations, dating back to the Civil War, which impeded bank-note issuance and prohibited branch banking and nation-wide "clearing houses."
>
> While at the onset of the Great Depression, the United States underwent the greatest "contagious" banking panic in history, Canada experienced no panics or bank failures at all. Like the United States, Canada did not have deposit insurance; but Canada also lacked the American laws that inhibited flexible banking. Thus, the institution of deposit insurance, hence capital minima, hence the Basel rules, might all have been a mistake founded on the New Deal legislators' and regulators' ignorance of the fact that panics like the one that had just gripped America (not for the first time) were the unintended effects of previous regulations.
>
> But having reached the conclusion that deposit insurance was needed to fore-stall bank panics that they thought were endemic to capitalism, the rule-makers had little choice but to institute capital requirements to guard against the risky behavior in which they thought that bankers, now insulated from the threat of runs on their banks, would be even more likely to engage.[55]

According to this story, regulations that stifled competition and diversification of currency may have led to a contagious and therefore catastrophic nationwide bank

panic in the United States, which did not occur in Canada. The response by U.S. policymakers was to provide state-backed insurance to banks, which freed them somewhat from the fear of loss, and created greater incentive for risk-taking. Once banks
were encouraged to be excessive risk-takers, regulators added layers of external rules
and regulations to contain the beast they had created.

During the 2007–2008 financial crisis, Canada also fared better than the United
States. This was arguably because stronger regulations were in place, including higher capital requirements.[56] However, in the period between these two crashes, Canada
introduced deposit insurance. This might have made those capital requirements necessary. It is not clear that the optimal solution is to have both state-provided deposit
insurance and capital requirements. If the underlying incentives of the firms were the
same in the two countries, both driven by monetary policy, the limitations on competition, and state-provided deposit insurance, Canada's more stringent regulation may
have only limited the consequences of an entirely preventable crisis.

An article in the *Financial Times* touched on the limited liability of modern corporations, another core institutional concern. As the quote above by Ludwig von Mises
emphasized, the institution of private property only works at its best if *all* profit and
all loss belong to the property owner.

> The place to start is with the core of modern capitalism: the limited liability,
> joint-stock company. Big commercial banks were among the most important prod-
> ucts of the limited liability revolution. But banks are special sorts of businesses:
> for them, debt is more than a means of doing business; it is their business. Thus,
> limited liability is likely to have an exceptionally big impact on their behaviour.
>
> ...In a highly leveraged limited liability business, shareholders will rationally
> take excessive risks, since they enjoy all the upside but their downside is capped:
> they cannot lose more than their equity stake, however much the bank loses. In
> contemporary banks, leverage of 30 to one is normal. Higher leverage is not rare.[57]

It should not be surprising that firms that can retain all profit, but are shielded
from the full burden of loss, will take excessive risk. This was an even more obvious
problem with respect to Fannie Mae and Freddie Mac, two government-sponsored
enterprises in America. These institutions fully reflect the concept of "privatized
profit and socialized loss." They took on even more risk than most other banks, although some of this risk was mandated by law.

After the 2007 financial crisis and the subsequent bank bailouts, some commentators were discussing the bonuses received by executives in these failed banks. One
commented that "we didn't realize there were huge incentives to cheat and to mis-
report things, and that's what seems to have occurred." The question the commentator did not address is why these companies had such an incentive—not only to cheat
regulators but to need such regulation to begin with. Another commentator replied
that the answer is to "pay the top regulators substantial salaries to make it a fair
fight."[58] Yet regulators in this environment will always face an uphill battle because
these companies have strong incentives to avoid regulation.

This environment existed before the most recent crisis. One article points out
that, "GE's ability to live in the best of both worlds—capitalizing on the federal safety

net while avoiding more rigorous regulation—existed well before last year's crisis, because of its unusual corporate structure."[59] Many firms have been shielded from loss in one way or another by government, and this has led them to grow excessively large and take excessive risk. Regulations are then added to tame this risk-taking. When the inevitable crisis occurs, they may then be labeled "too big to fail" and bailed out, yet again teaching them that they need not fear loss.

As a solution, President Obama has called for new regulations including limits on the size and scope of banking operations, so that he can promise: "[n]ever again will the American taxpayer be held hostage by a bank that is too big to fail."[60] Instead of considering repeal of the policies, such as the limits on competition and government-backed deposit insurance, which may have created the problems seen in the financial markets, Obama is responding to the excessive risk with additional layers of regulation. Yet, he seems to recognize the problems caused by these policies:

> As part of these efforts, today I'm proposing two additional reforms that I believe will strengthen the financial system while preventing future crises.
>
> First, we should no longer allow banks to stray too far from their central mission of serving their customers. In recent years, too many financial firms have put taxpayer money at risk by operating hedge funds and private equity funds and making riskier investments to reap a quick reward.
>
> And these firms have taken these risks while benefiting from special financial privileges that are reserved only for banks.
>
> Our government provides deposit insurance and other safeguards and guarantees to firms that operate things. We do so because a stable and reliable banking system promotes sustained growth, and because we learned how dangerous the failure of that system can be during the Great Depression.
>
> But these privileges were not created to bestow banks operating hedge funds or private equity funds with an unfair advantage.
>
> When banks benefit from the safety net that taxpayers provide, which includes lower cost capital, it is not appropriate for them to turn around and use that cheap money to trade for profit. And that is especially true when this kind of trading often puts banks in direct conflict with their customers' interests.
>
> The fact is, these kinds of trading operations can create enormous and costly risks, endangering the entire bank if things go wrong. We simply cannot accept a system in which hedge funds or private equity firms inside banks can place huge, risky bets *that are subsidized by taxpayers* and that could pose a conflict of interest. And we cannot accept a system in which *shareholders make money on these operations if the bank wins, but taxpayers foot the bill if the bank loses....*[61]

Arguably, there were two options to resolve the crisis, given Obama's analysis: remove the special privileges and state-backed deposit insurance, or restrict banks from privately trading this taxpayer-backed money. President Obama chose the latter because he saw deposit insurance as vital to the stability and security of the American economy. However, deposit insurance can be provided privately, in which case banks would likely have to prove their trustworthiness to the private providers. Furthermore, many economists have argued that the new regulations limiting the scope and size of an institution's investments would make the system less, not more, stable.[62] Banks would be less diversified, and still have the incentive, and some (although reduced) ability to take risks.

If the former option was chosen, and the special privileges given to banks were repealed and deposit insurance left to the private sector, banks would no longer have the incentive to take these excessive risks. Private deposit insurance agencies would keep the banks' risk-taking in check by charging more to insure riskier banks. With the latter option, banks would still not be responsible for their own risk-taking; but now they would have fewer options for diversifying their risk, and in addition to having partly socialized losses they would have restrictions on their profit-making.

After the financial crisis, the Bush and Obama administrations in the United States enacted policies to bail out companies in several industries, including mortgage and banking, and the automobile industry. In exchange for government funds, the Obama administration took a partial stake in some American car companies, including General Motors. Although the government stated clearly from the start that it would not interfere in the running of these companies, the new institutional structure—the public ownership in the company—changed the incentive structure again and forced the government to intervene further and regulate the companies, capping executive pay and changing the management structure and the board of directors.[63] If the taxpayer is asked to support these firms, like any stockholder they will want to make decisions about how the company is run. If the firm can depend on taxpayer subsidy, it no longer is forced to keep costs low and quality high for the customer, so these interventions become necessary.

When the institutions of private property are completely removed and replaced with common ownership, regulations become critical. When property is publicly owned across the whole society, there must be a plan for production and distribution because individual and decentralized decisions are no longer protected by law, but now violate "public property" institutions.[64] Yet a plan is really just a long list of commands that must be imposed on the economic actors.

While the institution of private property exists to protect individuals, who then trade freely with each other in decentralized actions, the plan centrally coordinates these decisions (whether democratically, or by an elite committee – for this, see Chapter 9) and then imposes directives on the actors. Hence, a planned economy is a very large book of economic regulations. The plan lists the prices, output, wages, benefits, budget, and other considerations of every firm in the economy and (ideally) coordinates them with each other. It also lists the duties of and provisions for every worker in the economy. Even private exchanges, to the extent allowed, must be subject to regulation. Yet as Soviet planners learned, regulations can never do the job that basic institutions can do.

The basic institutions that guide an individual to make choices within his private sphere—whether or not to work, invest, care for property, take intelligent risks, etc.—will always be stronger than the rules and regulations layered on afterward to curb his most outrageous actions. Removing these externally imposed rules, which is usually called "deregulation," may make things worse, but the core problem cannot be solved with regulation, only with a good set of initial institutions.

CONCLUSION

Although deregulation is sometimes blamed for anti-social behavior of business, with strong private property institutions the incentives released might not lead to negative outcomes. Soviet planners learned that layering regulations on top of an institutional structure cannot effectively change the behavior of firm managers. The underlying institutions are stronger.

The benefits of a market economy can only be realized if the institutions of private property are well enforced. Compromise of these institutions creates an environment in which self-interest no longer works for the social good. Rather than piling regulations on top of compromised institutions and faulting the removal of regulations when things go wrong, it would be wise to consider the ways in which the basic institutions may have been undermined by prior policy.

ENDNOTES

1. V. I. Lenin, "To the Rural Poor," May 1903, in *Collected Works*, Vol. 6 (Moscow: Progress Publishers, 1964), chap. 2, at http://www.marxists.org/archive/lenin/works/1903/rp/2.htm (December 4, 2009).
2. V. I. Lenin, *The Tasks of the Proletariat in Our Revolution*, 1917, in *Collected Works*, Vol. 24 (Moscow: Progress Publishers, 1964), p. 84, at http://www.marx.org/archive/lenin/works/1917/tasks/ch12.htm (December 4, 2009) (emphasis added).
3. Frederick Engels, "The Principles of Communism," 1947, in *Karl Marx and Frederick Engels: Selected Works*, Vol. 1 (Moscow: Progress Publishers, 1969), pp. 81–97, at http://marxists.org/archive/marx/works/1847/11/prin-com.htm (November 28, 2009).
4. Bukharin and Preobrazhensky, *The ABC of Communism*, chap. 3.
5. V. I. Lenin, "Economics and Politics in the Era of the Dictatorship of the Proletariat," November 7, 1919, in *Collected Works*, Vol. 30 (Moscow: Progress Publishers, 1965), pp. 107–117, at http://www.marxists.org/archive/lenin/works/1919/oct/30.htm (December 4, 2009).
6. Hazard, *The Soviet System of Government*, p. 149. The following examples also can be found in *ibid.*, pp. 150–151.
7. *Ibid.*, pp. 150–151.
8. Evgeny Pashukanis, "A Course on Soviet Economic Law," *Selected Writings on Marxism and Law* (London: Beirne & R. Sharlet, 1980), pp. 304–345, at http://www.marxists.org/archive/pashukanis/1935/xx/sovlaw.htm (December 4, 2009).
9. Quoted in Alan Ball, "NEP's Second Wind: 'The New Trade Practice,'" *Soviet Studies*, Vol. 37, No. 3 (July 1985), pp. 371–385.
10. J. V. Stalin, "The Results of the First Five-Year Plan," January 7, 1933, in *Works*, Vol. 13 (Moscow: Foreign Languages Publishing House, 1954), pp. 213–214, at http://www.marxists.org/reference/archive/stalin/works/1933/01/07.htm (December 4, 2009).
11. Olimpiad S. Ioffe and Peter B. Maggs, *The Soviet Economic System: A Legal Analysis*, (Boulder, CO: Westview Press, 1987), pp. 70–71. A firm may not even use its own product, i.e., a paper factory may not use the paper it produces in its management offices, unless it is written into the national economic plan. "To use its own product, the economic entity must transfer the requisite portion of it from goods produced to production or other funds. If the goods produced are subject to planned distribution, then, in order to acquire its own product, the producer must be included in the plan of distribution issued by planning agencies. Violations of this rule lead to legal sanction," (p. 73).

12. *Ibid.*, pp. 290–294.

13. Robinson, *An American in Leningrad*, pp. 167–168.

14. Nove, *The Soviet Economic System*. Other economists also recognized this problem. In a discussion on the 1965 Soviet reforms, economist and Sovietologist Warren Nutter said, "Naturally, the reforms have to take place in a gradual way if they're going to take place at all, but I think we have to be alert for problems arising because this approach that they're taking may mean that the cure is worse than the disease. Let's just take one area — the experiment in producing to order in one part of the consumer goods industries. Now, this sounds very good and makes pretty good sense if we think in the context of an economy we're accustomed to, but suppose that we start, as in Russia, with shoes, and you let the shoe factory produce to order. How many orders it gets presumably depends upon how good a shoe it produces. Well, suppose that the shoe factory produces very good shoes. The prices are fixed from above. Presumably its orders will increase. Now, if it has to meet orders, it has to get leather to produce the shoes, but presumably the leather isn't produced to order—it's produced to plan. And so you face the dilemma that the factory that is producing bad shoes presumably will still get its leather, and the factory producing good shoes can't get the extra leather, so shortages in good shoes will still remain. There's a very grave question in my mind as to how possible it is to introduce these kind of reforms piecemeal." Economist and Sovietologist Abram Bergson responded that this problem "is posed again and again" by Western economists and that he agreed that it was likely difficult, especially if prices do not reflect supply and demand conditions. He explained that some in Eastern Europe liken it to a traffic reform in which 90 percent of drivers stay driving on the right, and 10 percent are told to start driving on the left. The other Sovietologists in the discussion agreed, although Herbert Levine argued that the consumer goods industry was easier to separate, and therefore some reform was possible in it. Abram Bergson, Alexander Erlich, Herbert S. Levine, G. Warren Nutter, Stanislaw Wellisz, and Henry L. Roberts, "Soviet Economic Performance and Reform: Some Problems of Analysis and Prognosis," *Slavic Review*, Vol. 25, No. 2 (June 1966), pp. 222–246.

15. Some have argued that the reforms during the transition to a market economy in the Soviet Union and other communist countries should not have been taken incrementally, because this led to distortions and corruption. One article argued that "In a partially reformed economy, distortions beget distortions. Segments of the economy that are freed from centralized control respond to the rent-seeking opportunities implicit in the remaining distortions of the economy." --Alwyn Young, "The Razor's Edge: Distortions and Incremental Reform in the Peoples Republic of China," *The Quarterly Journal of Economics*, Vol. 115, No. 4, (Nov., 2000) pp. 1091–1135. --Also see Guinevere Nell, "Rent-Seeking, Hierarchy and the Centralization: Why the Soviet Union Collapsed So Fast and What it Means for Market Economies," *Critical Review*, forthcoming 2010

16. Berliner, *Factory and Manager in the USSR*, p. 303.

17. Germain, "Soviet Management Reform," *International Socialist Review*, Vol. 26, No. 3 (Summer 1965), pp. 77–82, at http://www.marxists.org/archive/mandel/1965/03/sovreform.htm (November 20, 2009).

18. E.G. Liberman: "Planning Production and Standards of Long-term Operation," in *Voprosy Ekonomiki*, No. 8, 1962, in Myron E. Sharpe, ed., *Planning, Profit and Incentives in the USSR*, Vol. 1, *The Liberman Discussion; A New Phase in Soviet Economic Thought* (White Plains, NY.: International Arts & Science Press, 1966), pp. 65–66, at http://www.oneparty.co.uk/html/book/ussrchap1.html (December 4, 2009).

19. Communist Party of the Soviet Union, Central Committee, "On Improving Management of Industry, Perfecting Planning and Enhancing Economic Incentives in Industrial Production," September 1965, in "The Soviet Economic Reform: Main Features and Aims," Moscow, 1967, p. 147, in William B. Bland, *The Restoration of Capitalism in the Soviet Union*, 2nd ed. (1995), at http://www.oneparty.co.uk/html/book/ussrchap1.html (December 4, 2009).

20. Berliner, *Factory and Manager in the USSR*, pp. 304–305. Of course, this would also make the extreme case of a plant producing one humongous nail even more possible, as in a certain *Krokodil* cartoon.

21. The 1965 reforms reduced the number of targets, but then they were increased again. Gregory and Stuart, *Soviet Economic Structure and Performance*.

22. Berliner, *Factory and Manager in the USSR*, p. 307 (emphasis added).

23. Gregory and Stuart, *Soviet Economic Structure and Performance*, p. 467.

24. *Ibid.*

25. For example, Stalin said of planning during his time: "Our plans are not forecast plans, not guess-work plans, but *directive* plans, which are *binding* upon the leading bodies and which *determine* the trend of our *future* economic development on a *country-wide* scale." Yet reformers argued: "These norms have largely become obsolete; they have turned into petty tutelage, binding the manager's activities.... The time has come to discard the obsolete forms of economic management based on directive norms." J. V. Stalin, "Political Report of the Central Committee to the 15th," December 1927, in *Works*, Vol. 10, p. 335, at http://www.marx2mao.com/Stalin/Index.html (December 4, 2009), and V. Trapeznikov, "For Flexible Economic Management of Enterprises," *Pravda*, August 17, 1964, in Sharpe, *Planning, Profit and Incentives in the USSR*, Vol. 1, pp. 193–194, at http://www.oneparty.co.uk/html/book/ussrchap1.html (December 4, 2009).

26. Gregory and Stuart, *Soviet Economic Structure and Performance*, p. 467.

27. Nove, *The Soviet Economic System*, and Gregory and Stuart, *Soviet Economic Structure and Performance*, p. 211.

28. Gregory and Stuart, *Soviet Economic Structure and Performance*, p. 467.

29. Mitch Meisner, "The Shenyang Transformer Factory, A Profile," *The China Quarterly*, No. 52 (October–December 1972), pp. 717–737 (pp. 719-720) emphasis added.

30. János Kornai, *The Socialist System: The Political Economy of Communism* (Princeton, N.J.: Princeton University Press, 1992), p. 120.

31. *Ibid.*

32. *Ibid.*

33. Alexis de Tocqueville, quoted in Marshall I. Goldman, "Diffusion of Development: The Soviet Union," *American Economic Review*, Vol. 81, No. 2 (May 1991), p. 280.

34. This is implied in all the writings on the withering away of the state and explicitly mentioned in a fair number of them. See Rudolf Schlesinger, *Soviet Legal Theory: Its Social Background and Development* (London: Oxford University Press, 1945).

35. The phrase comes from the experience of England's commons, which were exploited without inhibition until they were destroyed, because no individual making use of them had a personal stake in protecting them, seeing as every other person would likely continue to abuse them. For a full account, see Garrett Hardin, "The Tragedy of the Commons," *Science*, December 13, 1968.

36. Eugen Von Bohm-Bawerk, *Exploitation Theory of Socialism-Communism* (ISI Books, 1975 [1884]), p. 28 (emphasis added).

37. Political scientists James Buchanan and Gordon Tullock analyze democratic procedure with the example of a vote to fund public roads. They describe how individuals living along certain sections of the road may band together and form interest groups and vote to have their sections funded at the expense of the others. In many instances, it is not obvious that majority voting or any other particular democratic (non-unanimous) procedure is fair for spending collective money in ways that advantage different portions of the populations differently. James Buchanan and Gordon Tullock, *The Calculus of Consent: Logical Foundations of Constitutional Democracy* (Liberty Fund Inc., 1999), at http://www.econlib.org/library/Buchanan/buchCv3c10.html.

38. Mises, *Human Action*, 4th ed. (Irvington: Foundation for Economic Education, 1996), p. 655, at http://mises.org/resources/3250 (December 4, 2009).

39. Peter Boettke cited this obstacle as one of the major hurdles in reform of the Soviet economy after the fall of the communist government, although as we have seen there were other reasons. Peter Boettke, *Why Perestroika Failed: The Politics and Economics of Socialist Transformation* (New York: Routledge, 1993).

40. Vernon L. Smith, "Constructivist and Ecological Rationality in Economics," *The American Economic Review*, Vol. 93, No. 3 (June 2003), pp. 465-508 (pp. 472-473).

41. See, for example, William Pfaff, "The Privatization of Public Utilities Can Be a Disaster," *International Herald Tribune*, February 22, 2001, at http://www.commondreams.org/views01/0222-04.htm.

42. "Highlights from Obama's health care summit," *CNN*, February 25, 2010, at http://edition.cnn.com/2010/POLITICS/02/25/health.care.summit.updates/index.html

43. Cited in Nove, *The Soviet Economy*, p. xviii.

44. Novozhilov, quoted in Nove, *The Soviet Economic System*, p.354.

45. One exception is the argument that we have become a nation of cheap, disposable goods of low quality. For example, some argue that cars, appliances, and consumer goods have deteriorated in quality over the years, are made of plastic, and are designed to break; therefore, the cheap price tag is an illusion. Unfortunately, for those who make this claim, the facts are precisely contrary.

46. Hugh Rockoff, *Drastic Measures*, p. 147.

47. *Ibid.*

48. For some data on consumer durables owned by the US population in 1992 and 2005, see The U.S. Census Bureau, Extended Measures of Well-being: Living Conditions in the United States, 2005, detailed tables at http://www.census.gov/population/www/socdemo/extended-05.html and U.S. Census Bureau, Extended Measures of Well-Being: 1992, at http://www.census.gov/hhes/www/poverty/beyond/index.html.

49. J. Yanqui Zaza "Capitalists Trickle Down, Not Profits, Corruption on Wall Street, in Liberia, Everywhere," *Perspective*, November 13, 2008, at http://www.liberiaitech.com/theperspective/2008/1113200802.html (December 4, 2009).

50. For a roundup and discussion of books on the financial crisis, most of which contain this argument, see William Dixon, "Failure to Moderate Excess: A Round-Up of Crisis Chronicles," *Mute*, October 21, 2009, at http://www.metamute.org/en/content/failure_to_moderate_excess_a_round_up_of_crisis_chronicles (December 4, 2009).

51. The idea of a "market for lemons" is that, in some circumstances (with the used car market as a famous example), customers will consider the risk of doing business on the basis of the reputation of a whole market rather than an individual firm, and in such cases firms will no longer protect their own reputation, and will begin to defraud their customers (giving them "lemons") in pursuit of profit. "There are many markets in which buyers use some market statistic to judge the quality of prospective purchases. In this case there is incentive for sellers to market poor quality merchandise, since the returns for good quality accrue mainly to the entire group whose statistic is affected rather than to the individual seller " -- George A. Akerlof, "The Market for "Lemons": Quality Uncertainty and the Market Mechanism," *The Quarterly Journal of Economics*, Vol. 84, No. 3 (Aug., 1970), pp. 488-500 (p. 488).

52. Economists recognize the potential advantages of self-regulation (private market-driven regulation and private ratings agencies), especially with strong market competition. Competing ratings agencies and the reputation mechanism in a free market may outperform centralized regulatory mechanisms, even in markets in which customers have informational disadvantages. Yet this was not permitted in the U.S. financial sector.

53. Barry Eichengreen, "Anatomy of a Crisis," Daily News Egypt, September 19, 2008, at http://dailystaregypt.com/article.aspx?ArticleID=16596 (December 4, 2009).

54. Richard Posner, "Against the Pay Caps," Becker-Posner Blog, February 8, 2009, at http://www.becker-posner-blog.com/archives/2009/02/against_the_pay.html (December 4, 2009).

55. Friedman, *A Crisis of Politics, Not Economics* (parenthetical references omitted).

56. For example, see James Flaherty, "'Boring' Canada's Financial Tips for the World," *Financial Times*, November 12, 2008, at http://us.ft.com/ftgateway/superpage.ft?news_id=ftoll1220081503251801 (December 4, 2009). The article cites Canada's high capital requirements, transparency, and risk prevention schemes. Yet would these have been necessary if bubbles had not been fueled by easy monetary policy and subsidies to buyers and sellers?

57. Martin Wolf, "Reform of Regulation Has to Start by Altering Incentives," *Financial Times*, June 23, 2009, at http://www.ft.com/cms/s/0/095722f6-6028-11de-a09b-00144feabdc0.html (December 5, 2009).

58. "Questions Remain on Fate of Disputed Exec Bonus Pay," *PBS NewsHour*, transcript, April 10, 2009, at http://www.pbs.org/newshour/bb/business/jan-june09/clawback_04-10.html (December 4, 2009).

59. Jeff Gerth and Brady Dennis, "How a Loophole Benefits GE in Bank Rescue," *The Washington Post*, June 29, 2009, at http://www.washingtonpost.com/wp-dyn/content/article/2009/06/28/AR2009062802955.html (December 4, 2009).

60. Barack Obama, "Obama statement on limiting bank risk-taking," Reuters, at http://www.reuters.

com/article/idUSTRE60K5D820100122.

61. *Ibid.* (emphasis added).

62. The Gramm–Leach–Bliley Act arguably reduced risk in the economy. Individuals tend to invest in the stock market more when the economy is doing well and to save more in savings accounts when the economy is bad. If one firm can offer the customer both savings and investment, the firm is better protected from the cyclical nature of the economy. Hence if firms can do this, arguably fewer bankruptcies would occur when the economy is weak. Firms may do better to hedge against the downturns by diversifying their products, just as individual investors do. Many economists have argued that Glass–Steagall, by preventing this crossover, reduced competition in the banking industry and led to greater instability and risk in the financial markets. — Robert E. Litan, "Reuniting Investment and Commercial Banking," *Cato Journal*, Vol. 7, No. 3 (Winter 1988), at http://www.cato.org/pubs/journal/cj7n3/cj7n3-12.pdf.

63. In a May 31, 2009, report, *The Boston Globe* summarized the administration's position with regard to government interference in the management of GM and other companies. "The government will not interfere with or exert control over day-to-day company operations. No government employees will serve on the boards or be employed by these companies." Jason Tuohey, "Details of the GM Restructuring Plan Released," *Boston Globe*, May 31, 2009, at http://www.boston.com/news/politics/politicalintelligence/2009/05/details_of_the.html (December 4, 2009). On June 1, 2009, President Obama stated, "What we are not doing—what I have no interest in doing—is running GM." Jim Puzzanghera, "U.S. Role at GM to Be Passive, Obama Vows," *Los Angeles Times*, June 2, 2009, at http://articles.latimes.com/2009/jun/02/business/fi-gm-reax2 (December 4, 2009). In the same speech in which he claimed not to want to run GM, the first steps were taken— the government had to reject the initial business plans submitted by the company, deeming them unworthy. "The original restructuring plans submitted by GM and Chrysler earlier this year did not call for the sweeping changes these companies needed to survive—and I couldn't in good conscience proceed on that basis. So we gave them a chance to develop a stronger plan that would put them on a path toward long-term viability." One part of the new and improved plan, as accepted by the Obama administration, was a promise to employ American workers building a new and "environmentally friendly" small car. Another move the administration immediately made was to prevent the company from moving its headquarters. After several conversations with the Mayor of Detroit, President Obama called to reassure him that GM would not move to Warren, Michigan, which had been courting the company, but would stay in Detroit. One senator, Jeff Sessions (R–AL), summed the problem up succinctly: "The more we proceed with policies whereby the government owns 80% of the stock of a private insurance company— having poured $170 billion of our wealth into it—the more we are inevitably compelled to direct how the company operates, to the point of deciding who their executives should be, what the company's salary scale should be, or what aircraft it can or cannot have or where or what kind of corporate retreat they may have, and whether or not it can pay bonuses." *Congressional Record*, March 16, 2009, p. S3099.

64. Other forms of "public" decentralization, such as democratic decisions at the factory level, must still be coordinated across the economy. With private property, this can occur in a market through exchange, but this is not possible without market prices. Market prices are not possible when all property is owned by the same central institution. (See Chapter 6.)

CHAPTER 9. DEMOCRACY AND FREEDOM

INTRODUCTION

Socialists understood freedom differently from classical liberals. Freedom was a freedom of ownership over the society and economy, with worker control. Socialists argued that the "free" in "free markets" was not real freedom because only the wealthy could make use of it. It was only the freedom of the strong to exploit the weak. Real freedom would exist when all workers could choose to run a newspaper without depending upon capitalist funding, when production was commonly owned and democratically run, and when workers could own the full product of their labor and not depend on the capitalist. Real freedom would come when all things were free and the economic system was run as a democracy. "Positive liberty," based on a material assurance of the opportunity to exercise freedoms, is still popular, as is the notion that true freedom comes with free access to resources and democratic control over their use.

Socialism and democracy were closely connected ideologies at one time. Before the Russian Revolution, proponents of Marxism, known as social democrats, were considered the most democratic of all parties. Democracy at this time was mostly a privilege for the landowners: Most states reserved the franchise for a small subset of nobility and landlords or capitalists (property owners). Even many liberal intellectuals believed that the franchise must be restricted—often because they foresaw that popular vote would bring more redistribution.[1]

Therefore, equality and democracy were closely linked. Both advocates and critics of socialism saw the egalitarian distribution and the democratic government as tied together. Not all liberals felt this way—there were advocates of limited representative government with a broad franchise. However, they were often still presented as defenders of the privileged classes. For true democracy, one looked to the socialists.

Socialists promised a break from the old class system, in which capitalists had real freedom and democratic choice, while workers had none. The socialist system was to be a massive extension of democratic rule by the people. The evidence shows that, once in power, the Bolshevik socialists did attempt to implement economic democracy and the classless system that they believed would allow for true freedom and the withering away of the state. Believers in this system continued to see it as more democratic than capitalism for decades, despite mounting evidence of its authoritarian nature. An understanding of why the positive freedom and economic democracy of the socialist system did not deliver true freedom is critical to a better understanding of alternative institutional arrangements, and the nature of public ownership of media and other resources.

THE SOCIALIST ARGUMENT

> Fine freedom, where the proletarian has no other choice than that of either accepting the conditions which the bourgeoisie offers him, or of starving, of freezing to death, of sleeping naked among the beasts of the forests! A fine "equivalent" valued at pleasure by the bourgeoisie! — Friedrich Engels[2]

> The oppressed are allowed once every few years to decide which particular representatives of the oppressing class shall represent and repress them in parliament. — Lenin[3]

Socialists disparaged the freedom of the press and freedom of contract that people in capitalist countries enjoyed. It was not real freedom because the workers had no monetary control or bargaining power. Capitalists owned the press and hence determined public opinion. Only socialism could offer real freedom because only socialism would give them the economic power to exercise their supposed "freedom of the press." The same was true, argued the socialist, in all realms of life. Freedom of contract was freedom of the rich to exploit the poor, of the beast to devour his prey.

In the ABC of Communism, Bukharin and Preobrazhensky described the socialist view of the capitalist system in this way:

> The workers wish to publish a newspaper, and they have the legal right to do so. But to exercise this right they need money, paper, offices, a printing press, etc. All these things are in the hands of the capitalists. The capitalists won't relax their grip. Nothing doing! Out of the workers' paltry wage it is impossible to accumulate adequate funds. The result is that the bourgeoisie has masses of newspapers and can cheat the workers to its heart's content day after day; whereas the workers, notwithstanding their legal "rights", have practically no press of their own.

> Such is the real character of the workers' "freedom" under bourgeois democracy. The freedom exists solely on paper. The workers have what is termed "formal" freedom. In substance, however, they have no freedom, because their formal freedom cannot be translated into the realm of fact. It is the same here as in all other departments of life. According to bourgeois theory, master and man are equals in capitalist society, since "free contract" exists: the employer offers work; the work-

er is free to accept or refuse. Thus it is upon paper! In actual fact, the master is rich and well fed; the worker is poor and hungry. He must work or starve.[4]

Not only could the worker not afford what he desires in the capitalist state, but he was made to consume whatever the capitalist produced because the capitalist held the reins of power. Socialists argued that the people should have a say in pro duction and distribution. The way to give everyone a democratic say would be to have the government represent the people and to allow the people to use democracy to allocate resources. Economic democracy over production would ensure free use of all resources and an equal vote for each worker over what is produced.

Socialists ridiculed the idea that consumers decide what is made in a capitalist economy. Barbara Wootton argued, "The statement that the unplanned economy gives us what we want often amounts to little more than saying that it makes us want what we are given."[5] For socialists, it was not a voluntary trade of money for goods, it was an exploitation of the worker and consumer by the capitalist. The capitalist soci ety was a hierarchy of money. The proletariat—the masses—was the majority class of exploited workers, and the bourgeoisie—the capitalist class—was the smaller ruling class of exploiters. To end this exploitation, the socialist revolution would replace this dominance of capital with common ownership over resources by all the people. Under socialism, the state would act as a representative of the people to ensure that the people's democratic will was done. The socialists promised an incredible exten sion of democracy:

> [Communist revolution] means replacing what in fact is the dictatorship of the bourgeoisie (a dictatorship hypocritically cloaked in the forms of the demo cratic bourgeois republic) by the dictatorship of the proletariat. This means re placing democracy for the rich by democracy for the poor. This means replacing freedom of assembly and the press for the minority, for the exploiters, by freedom of assembly and the press for the *majority* of the population, for the working people. This means a gigantic, world historic *extension* of democracy, its transformation from falsehood into truth, the liberation of humanity from the shackles of capital.[6]

The democratic allocation of resources through economic democracy and the promise of free use of those resources would bring true positive freedom and an ex tension of the democratic ideal to all people. This would liberate the worker from the chains of his master, and would liberate man from the chains of nature:

> With the seizing of the means of production by society production of com modities is done away with, and, simultaneously, the mastery of the product over the producer. Anarchy in social production is replaced by systematic, definite or ganisation. *The struggle for individual existence disappears.* Then for the first time man, in a certain sense, is finally marked off from the rest of the animal kingdom, and emerges from mere animal conditions of existence into really human ones.... Man's own social organisation, hitherto confronting him as a necessity imposed by na ture and history, now becomes the result of his own *free action....* Only from that time will man himself, with full consciousness, make his own history—only from that time will the social causes set in movement by him have, in the main and in a constantly growing measure, the results intended by him. *It is the humanity's leap from the kingdom of necessity to the kingdom of freedom.*[7]

Bolsheviks were not the only ones to see a connection between freedom from necessity and a new sort of true freedom. Many had argued that true freedom and true individuality, would come with the release of the individual from property ownership. Oscar Wilde said:

> With the abolition of private property, then, we shall have true, beautiful, healthy Individualism. Nobody will waste his life in accumulating things, and the symbols for things. One will live. To live is the rarest thing in the world. Most people exist, that is all.[8]

Thus, socialists believed that freedom from want, which they argued would come with a free provision of socialized resources, would allow for true freedom. There are two distinct potential problems with this argument that they did not foresee or did not fully answer. One is that all needs might not be met if abundance was not achieved: there might still be scarcity. The second is that resources, even when offered free to the consumer, must be administered. The power that allocates the goods must be guided by some mission—if not economic then political—and the rest of society must follow the plan set forth.

Socialists foresaw only the common will guiding production for the good of the people. A new society would be born, and man would be emancipated. Under communism, the worker would enjoy work, and it would lead to a new level of consciousness within him and within society as a whole. Labor would become "life's prime want," and scarcity would be eliminated. This would bring freedom from necessity— a true freedom to just live.

THE SOVIET EXPERIENCE

> [Soviet power] gives those who were formerly oppressed the chance to straighten their backs and to an ever-increasing degree to take the whole government of the country, the whole administration of the economy, the whole management of production, into their own hands. — Vladimir Lenin[9]

Socialism was to bring freedom to the people by allowing the people to organize and direct production, providing all the means for survival and prosperity. Both necessities and the means for making use of the old bourgeois formal rights would be provided by the state. No longer would workers be exploited and repressed by their status. The Soviet Constitution enumerated the rights of the people and the obligation of the state to ensure that these rights were not merely formal rights, but that the people had the means to take advantage of the rights:

> 14. In order to secure for the workers actual freedom of expression of opinion, the Russian Socialist Federative Soviet Republic abolishes the dependence of the press upon capital, and puts into the hands of the working class and the poor peasantry all the technical and material means for the publication of newspapers, pamphlets, books, and all other products of the printing press, and provides for their free distribution throughout the country.
>
> 15. In order to secure for the workers the actual right of assembly, the Russian Socialist Federative Soviet Republic gives to all citizens of the Soviet Republic the unrestricted right to hold meetings and congresses, to march in processions, etc., and puts into the hands of the working class and the poor peasants all the

buildings suitable for the purpose of holding public meetings, together with the provision of light, heating, etc.

16. In order to secure for the workers actual freedom of combination, the Russian Socialist Federative Soviet Republic, having overthrown the economic and political power of the possessing classes, and having removed all the hindrances which hitherto in bourgeois society have prevented the workers and peasants from effectively realizing the freedom of organization and activity, furnishes to the workers and poor peasants every kind of assistance, material and moral, requisite for their combination and organization.

17. In order to secure for the workers effective access to knowledge, the Russian Socialist Federative Soviet Republic makes it its duty to provide the workers and poor peasants with a complete, many-sided, and gratuitous education.[10]

As *The ABC of Communism* explained, "Herein we see the enormous difference between the spurious freedoms of bourgeois democracy and the effective freedoms of proletarian democracy."[11] The Soviet state was ensuring that workers had the freedoms that the bourgeois state had promised, but never delivered. "In the Soviet Republic, on the other hand, freedom really exists for the working class. It exists because it is a freedom which can be translated into the realm of fact."[12] It would also offer a vast extension of democracy, which would ultimately lead to the true freedom only possible with complete freedom from necessity.

The socialists would achieve the vast extension of democracy through democratic administration of the economy. The Soviet state was tightly connected with the trade unions and other worker organizations so that workers could help determine what their factories would produce and how they would be managed. As explained in *The ABC of Communism*:

> The soviet institutions are based on the Communist Party, the trade unions, the factory committees, and the cooperatives. These organizations comprise many millions of workers, who all combine to support the Soviet Power. Through the instrumentality of these organizations, the toiling masses take an active part in the State administration. The Communist Party and the trade unions appoint their most trusted members to fill all the posts and to carry out all the functions. In this way the best among the workers are delegated, not merely to talk, but actually to administer. In the so-called democratic republic, nothing of this kind happens. There the working class elector drops his ballot paper into the box, and then his part in the affair ends. The bourgeoisie assures him that he has fulfilled his "duties as a citizen"; he need trouble himself no longer about affairs of State.[13]

Many other measures were taken to expand democracy in the new society. In fact, democratic groups permeated the society.[14] It was a core part of socialist theory that all the people would become part of the political process. Regardless of income or their parents' trade, young people were offered a chance to become politically active. Youth could join the political process by joining the Komsomol and later the Communist Party. All workers had the right to take part in the democracy of the enterprise. Trade union membership was ubiquitous, and about 28 million trade union members were considered "activists," meaning that their participation went beyond mere membership.

In addition to these more traditional outlets, many groups of mass-participation gave direct democratic control to the workers and community members. To ensure economic democracy, People's Control Committees checked on the work of governmental and economic administrators and relied on volunteers. Meetings and conferences were arranged in the factories and farms to enable workers to directly participate in decision making. "Permanent production conferences" and other committees and subcommittees were extensive, involving 64 percent of employees of 16 important enterprises surveyed, according to a 1972 study.[15]

Finally, there were also decentralized community groups, called organizations of "public self-administration," which included street and apartment house committees, "comrade courts," auxiliary police, library councils, and so forth. There were also theater clubs in nearly all factories and in many other organizations. All of these groups were there to help foster a feeling of community, involvement, and democracy at the individual level. Mass participation would bring communism, and communism would bring true freedom.

The sense of freedom was a significant promise of socialism, in which many intellectuals strongly believed. There were many accounts of capturing this democratic spirit and the feeling of true participation. The book *How the Soviets Work* describes the sense of ownership over society that a child was (purportedly) raised with in the early 1920s:

> The child attains the dignity of a worker in the mill at sixteen years of age. That phrase in some lands rings with bitter irony. In Russia the words "worker and peasant" are used much as old-fashioned Englishmen will talk of the "nobility and gentry." They are titles of honor. The child who is born into these ranks has the sense that he is growing up with power and opportunity before him. There are no barriers to cross; the road stands smooth and open in the factory and the State, in the army and even in the learned professions, if he has the ambition to serve his fellows. The children who have seen life opening before them since the Revolution, acquire instinctively this sense of power. I was talking in 1920 with a group of quite little children in a wood outside Moscow. A bright boy asked why England was blockading Russia. I answered the embarrassing question, and then came another: "Why do the English workers allow it?" The little fellow could not realize that there could be any limits to the power of a working class. To enter the mill is for these lads and girls their initiation into great rights and duties.[16]

This sense of power and ownership may have existed for children even at later dates, but did it withstand growing up? It did seem to, at the start. Many memoirs of the early days recall a newfound sense of freedom and control over one's life. *How the Soviets Work* relates the following discussion:

> "Yes," he continued, "it is quite true that in those days we were better off in some ways materially. Our wages in the last years before the war would buy rather more than they will buy today. But what is it that the Scriptures say? 'Man does not live by bread alone!' We were dark and ignorant in those days...."
>
> "Yes," said his wife, "we live in an age of progress. Why, Ivan was working at twelve years of age and there was no school for him. And [now] we're free; we can say what we like. There's no flogging now. Why, I can remember when a man was flogged if he got drunk and stayed away for a day from work. And now, even in our village, the peasants want to learn. You see newspapers in every cottage, and even the women go to the village library—yes, and they carry books home and read them."[17]

Yet by the 1930s (and before, but perhaps not as widespread or well known), there was much worse than just flogging. Those who were to bring freedom had brought tyranny. A memoir by a Soviet air force officer, Peter Pirogov, recounts his own dismay at this turn of events, as he became the oppressor. Pirogov's family had feared the Soviets during the 1917 revolution, but a decade and a half later he had become one of them.

> Sixteen years—and nothing had changed. But instead of Sashnev and his "activists," the cursed state was personified by me and my sergeants. They called us "the Soviets"—a name to frighten children at night; it was what made their mothers weep; it was the "Soviets" that took the last horse from their father's farm and their favorite pet from the rabbit cage. It was the word that condemned little ones to starvation and slow death.[18]

The first decree calling for harsh measures against counterrevolutionaries and saboteurs came by December 1917, barely two months after the revolution. Lenin drafted the decree in a letter to Felix Dzerzhinsky. The Cheka, the precursor to the KGB, was created shortly thereafter on the basis of this communication, and Dzerzhinsky was appointed its chairman.[19] Despite being created to handle temporary problems of revolution, it was never disbanded.

When planning took hold in earnest in 1928, private property was outlawed and many normal kinds of exchanges were banned. The plan also failed to produce as much output as expected. Because all property was owned by the state and the government was attempting to increase the productive use of it, punishments were necessary for "crimes against state property." Otherwise, the people—who did not personally own the property—might fail to care for it, and might abuse it, or even steal it.

Lenin argued that when "the people" owned the means of production, work would become a joy because the workers would feel ownership over production. This feeling of ownership would extend over all state property, and all property would be state property, the property of the people:

> Communism begins when the *rank-and-file workers* display an enthusiastic concern that is undaunted by arduous toil to increase the productivity of labour, husband *every pood* [a pood is a measure similar to acres] *of grain, coal, iron* and other products, which do not accrue to the workers personally or to their "close" kith and kin, but to their "distant" kith and kin, i.e., to society as a whole, to tens and hundreds of millions of people united first in one socialist state, and then in a union of Soviet republics (italics in original).[20]

The worker was supposed to see the factory and the state as his own property. Therefore, all property, as property of the state, should be treated as his own. A "model workingwoman" is reported as saying, "The most important thing is that I myself am the owner of the factory. The factory is mine. The state is mine.... I am part of all Soviet power."[21] This feeling of ownership combines with the feeling of community and togetherness sparked by working together on a common project and collectively owning the resources and the results. Selfishness succumbs to common ownership, and altruism becomes identified with self-interest. Then the state could wither away because no crimes against it would ever be perpetrated—because the people self-identified with it. This is the ideal.

A Soviet bulletin informed the workers of their need to maintain this mindset: "All the population...must understand that the abolition of all types of labor desertion and self-seeking, lateness to work, carelessness, indolence, and misuses are problems of life and death for all the country."[22] Misuse of public property was seen as a problem of life and death to the country because making the best use of this public property was the only way to increase the wealth of the people. The state's role was to ensure that all the people worked together to do this. Hence, Lenin argued, "it is not fully appreciated that...it is *those* who violate labour discipline at any factory, in any undertaking, in any matter, who are *responsible* for the sufferings caused by the famine and unemployment, that we must know how to find the guilty ones, to bring them to trial and ruthlessly punish them" (italics in original).[23]

As long as the people were unable to completely become one with the collective and treat common ownership as if it were private ownership and the state as if it were oneself, laws against abuse of state property would be necessary. The less that the people were able to care for state property as their own, the greater the sentences would need to be to deter abuse of it. Unfortunately, the people were not able to care for state property as their own, so harsh punishments continued to be used for some time.

The *Cheka* were mobilized against counterrevolutionaries. Also, "bourgeois" political parties and any non-communist parties were banned.[24] It is not necessarily a unique feature of the economic system that bourgeois parties were banned: Market societies have also banned communist parties because the system itself cannot be sustained if those who wish to undermine it are voted into power.[25]

However, the limitations on political parties and policies must be more extensive in a socialist system than a mixed-market society. As Marx and Lenin both argued, building socialism requires a political dictatorship. The "dictatorship of the proletariat"[26] would be necessary to institute the socialist economy, root out the entrenched interests of the old ruling class, and organize the new society. It would be led by the "vanguard of the proletariat," the Communist Party.

Political democracy must be subordinate to building socialism, which would lead to a democratic society impossible within the old bourgeois political structure. The socialist belief in a "pure democracy" was based on the idea of economic, not political, democracy. Pure economic democracy would mean democracy over production and would lead to a truly democratic ownership over resources. A one-party state, as long as the state was representative of the people, was more compatible with socialist goals than competing political parties. Competing parties, by virtue of their division, must not be united in the common goal of building socialism according to a plan.

Socialists argued: Why should we allow a party that does not represent the people compete with the party that does?[27] This is similar to the socialist argument that a single supplier, if that supplier is the benevolent government that represents the people, is preferable to competing capitalists. However, it hardly mattered in practice whether socialists believed this. In practice, even if another political party was allowed to form, the Communist Party's de facto ownership of society's resources would ensure an unequal fight. Even "democratic control" would not resolve this problem. For example, democratic ideals were in place for newspapers in the early years, while other parties were still legal. Yet this economic democracy allowed the Communist Party, the incumbent party, to control the media:

> There was a great scarcity of paper in Russia and they argued that a just arrangement would be to limit the amount of press-paper, ink, etc., to the proportion of votes cast by each political party. A decree was passed to this effect which cut down the papers of the conservatives to a large extent.[28]

The state owned the media and all the resources to create media.[29] Hence, it had complete control over which parties and groups could publish their message. This usually meant that the message came from the Communist Party, which according to socialist theory was the vanguard of the proletariat and the representative of the people.

This is the same problem seen in dictatorial countries all over the world when elections are allowed, but the dictator suppresses the message of his rivals. Even the sympathetic observer of the Soviet political process could see that this ownership power made competition between political parties impossible:

> There is no organization which could compile any alternative list of candidates.... It might be contended that in theory this possibility does exist, but without the right to issue rival newspapers freely, or to print controversial leaflets, of what value would such a right be?[30]

"Democratic centralism," the guiding concept of Soviet-type democracy, meant that the Party would act as the vanguard and guide the state apparatus. Every function of the state (industry, agriculture, education, cultural affairs, etc.) had a mirror in the Communist Party apparatus. The number of Party officials assigned to the task was much smaller than the number in the state body, so it could act as the vanguard. It could guide the state, and thereby guide production for the common interest. The Party official's decision on any matter was final.[31]

The Party was only to act as vanguard until the people learned to govern the common resources on their own. The state would wither away and the Party would no longer be necessary once socialism came to its apex and became communism. This would usher in complete individual freedom in all material, spiritual, and intellectual ways. Party officials periodically announced that the day when the state would wither away was near,[32] but the day obviously never arrived.

Until that time, the one-party state would give the workers true democracy: economic democracy. For this, political democracy was unnecessary and indeed not possible. This is because, with worker control, the people must come together with one mind and make economic choices that serve the common good. One of socialism's selling points was the unity of working toward a common goal. In the Soviet elections,

[The people] are not consciously settling big issues of national policy, nor are they even directly choosing legislators. They are choosing average, trustworthy citizens, who will see that the administrative machine of the city runs efficiently for the common good of the working population. The atmosphere of the election and, indeed, of debates in the Soviets themselves, is strangely remote from "politics" as Western democracies conceive them. *A big family, animated by a single purpose, sits down on these occasions to administer its common property.*[33]

These one-party "democratic" events have a certain appeal, but they also have significant side effects that mirror those seen in the economics of state monopoly. Even the description by a true believer in the system reveals how a mass psychology may prevail or simply usurp decision making, potentially leading to unpleasant results. *How the Soviets Work* gives the following account:

First came a deputation from the biggest textile mill in Moscow, the Three Hills Factory. A woman announced that it had elected the Communist list unanimously, and she urged us to do likewise and so give Sir Austen Chamberlain his answer. The band played, the audience cheered, and it was obvious that no further eloquence was needed.

The chairman then asked us if we had all read the [manifesto]. Our hands said "Yes." Did we agree with it? "Why, yes, of course," again said all the hands. Did we want to add anything to it? It seemed that we did. The textile factory wanted us to demand more tramway lines, and to insist that more room should be found for workers by limiting the number of "Nep men" (profiteers) who might inhabit any tenement, by ten percent. Why not?[34]

Even to obtain a majority, let alone unanimity, socialist planners required a single party to vote on these decisions about production. Similar to the problems of a production monopoly, there are problems of a political monopoly. A political party that feels the threat of opposition, even if it holds all the power at a given moment, behaves fundamentally differently than one that is protected by law as the only recognized party. Without the potential check from another party, who will represent the minorities, and who will check the excesses? Furthermore, how can a single party represent *everyone*? In a Utopian vision, will there not be any disagreement whatsoever? In fact, many early observers and believers did imagine such a situation. The same memoir also recounts how the party offered a unified vision of progress and order that was accepted:

And then at last came the election. The Works Council (the standing council of shop stewards) had a list to propose to us. The name of Vorosilof headed it in an honorary capacity, and then came four workers of the factory. We all cheered. We all assented. No one wanted to make any other nomination....

A little startled, I began to realize that the election was over. It was exactly like what we call at home an "eve-of-the-poll rally." But with us, when we hold such a demonstration, we have the uncomfortable knowledge that at the same moment, in another hall, our opponents are holding an exactly similar meeting. In Russia it has been discovered that the other meeting is superfluous.[36]

If there were unanimity, indeed the other party might be superfluous. Socialists had argued that other parties did not represent the people as the Communist Party did, but the minority within the single party always represents another point of view—another potential party—unless the vote is unanimous. So long as there is any disagreement, another meeting would not be superfluous. Just as their Utopian vision depended upon common ownership leading to the end of scarcity, it also depended upon unanimous agreement on how to govern the commonly owned resources.

Yet there is a good reason for having a single party come together to vote unanimously for policy in a planned economy. A struggle between two different parties would make planning extremely difficult. Even voting on what to produce would make reconciliation of planned output nearly impossible. Officially, the plan was produced on "a broad basis of democracy" involving thousands of local meetings and millions of participants, and the detailed plans produced in the meetings (on the basis of control figures given from above) formed the basis of the economy-wide plans.[37] In reality, local sessions merely rubber-stamped the plans provided by Party officials.

Although discussion can exist in the early part of the planning period, at some point the discussion must stop and a plan must be written down. The different parts of the plan must then be coordinated. Once the plan is determined, it must be "disaggregated" and handed down to local level officials. For example, "first the planning office breaks down the national economic plan for its ministries. Then each ministry breaks it down for its directorates...and finally, the directorate disaggregates its own plan for the firms belonging to it." These plans are then compulsory. "The plan a lower level receives from a higher is a *command*, not a recommendation." The "democratic" period during the creation of the plan exists within this hierarchy when "the subordinate institution makes proposals and comments on the initial drafts."[38]

Comments and suggestions can ascend the hierarchy, but a fully democratic process would be unworkable. This is clear when the process of plan construction is viewed from the perspective of consistency. If a democratic vote had resulted in a choice, for example, to increase tramways, this would need to be reconciled with the planned output of fuel, steel, regional employment, and much more. Or if the voters determined not to cut down any more trees than last plan period in order to save the forests, but to increase the amount of paper produced by a large amount, these two decisions would need to be reconciled.[39]

It may not be possible to reconcile every decision by taking another vote because each decision is likely to produce further contradictions. These are problems of collective choice, decisions made by groups, and they are not easily solved.[40] In practice, material balances were used (see Chapter 6), with all final decisions being made by a small group of planners in charge of them. For each plan period, about two thousand material balances were created by the central planning agency Gosplan, and "several tens of thousands more" by the supply agency Gosnab and the economic ministries.[41] Once the plan was reconciled and written up, it had about sixty thousand separate headings.[42]

In a planned economy, all political representatives must agree not only on the goals and means generally but also on the economic plan in total. Soviet economists generally agreed that efficient planning requires the whole economy to act "as an administrative whole."[43] This is the "centralization" part of democratic centralism; the democracy is in the participation at each level. A Polish economist named four condi-tions for the superiority of planning over the market: the state has perfect knowledge of all available options and means at its disposal, the ability to enforce its preferences, the ability to create motivation of all actors, and the ability to respond to changes in condition. He named the first three as only possible with a full political hegemony.[44] It is arguable whether the first three are possible even with such hegemony,[45] but without it, they are certainly impossible. Socialists understood this from the start, and the Soviet government was organized with this in mind:

> No large issues of policy are ever settled at a Soviet election. When necessity does require a sharp change of policy, it is invariably within the ranks of the Com-munist Party, and not at the elections for the Soviets, that the controversy is fought out. The business of an election is rather to choose persons who will carry out the day to day work of administration. The entire structure of the Soviet system lends itself naturally to this limitation. Only the local Soviets (the word, of course, means simply "Council") at the basis of the pyramid are directly elected by the masses of the citizens. The national and federal Soviets at the apex of the system are chosen by indirect election, and to these alone belong legislative functions and the right to approve or reject any large change in national policy.[46]

This was consistent with the purpose of the elections according to Soviet ideolo-gy. It was the "direct" democracy that socialists had sought: A young person could be-come involved in politics through local elections and functions at the factory simply by joining the one Party, which was represented there. They could become engaged with politics, and help to determine the fate of their common property—the day to day work of administration—easily. The ambitious could then ascend the ranks of the single political channel if they wished.

However, the Party was hierarchical, and the elections were themselves in a sense embedded in this hierarchy. The Party determined the nominees for every election, and often the winner. As Waldemar Gurian explained in his book *Bolshevism: Theory and Practice*, "The Bolshevik party draws up the lists of electors and candidates alike. The electors must accept by acclamation the lists presented to them."[47] Many times there was only one nominee.[48] When there were more, the Party could nullify any results that it did not like: "An obnoxious Soviet can be immediately dissolved on one pretext or another—for example, that the masses did not take sufficient part in the election."[49]

The Party also controlled legislation and judicial proceedings: "There is no separa-tion between the executive, the legislature and the judiciary. It is therefore perfectly possible to alter sentences of the courts on political grounds," and, "[t]here is no pos-sibility of invoking legal safeguards against political decisions."[50]

The highly centralized political system may have been the natural outcome of economic planning. Waldemar Gurian made the case that "A system of government which in practice is absolute," because it is the owner of all economic resources and thereby determines the use of all resources, "excludes the possibility of an organised and public political opposition." Without such opposition, the state and the party become unified, and the structure of the party becomes the structure of the state.[51]

Without external competition, both become hierarchical because this hierarchy is necessary to carry out their tasks. Gregory T. Grinko, vice chairman of the planning commission (Gosplan) and one of the authors of the first five-year plan identified the "essential foundations on which the planned organization of Soviet economy develops in spite of colossal difficulties."[52] They included:

> [T]he ability peculiar to the Soviet system, to concentrate at any given moment, under the guidance of a single thought and will, on the most important sectors of the general line of economic construction virtually all the combined resources of the State, the monopolistic political party, the trade unions, the peasant organizations, the state trusts, syndicates, banks, the co-operatives, the press, schools, etc.[53]

Probably the only way to mobilize resources in this way is to have a strong authoritarian figure leading a hierarchically organized state. There must be someone in a powerful position who can ensure these separate groups are all mobilized, and their actions coordinated. Even when, for example during wartime, a non-dictatorial country mobilizes all resources under one authority, it is a temporary dictatorial power that is assumed for that purpose.

Socialists had predicted that economic planning would allow for the withering away of the state. In fact, perhaps for these reasons, the state did not wither away but instead became more powerful. It was the most powerful and brutal during the early period of comprehensive planning, under Stalin. Trotsky described the progress of the withering away of the state in 1939:

> The gist of the Soviet constitution, "the most democratic in the world," amounts to this, that every citizen is required at an appointed time to cast his ballot for the one and only candidate handpicked by Stalin or his agents. The press, the radio, all the organs of propaganda, agitation and national education are completely in the hands of the ruling clique. During the last five years no less than half a million members, according to official figures, have been expelled from the party. How many have been shot, thrown into jails and concentration camps, or exiled to Siberia, we do not definitely know. But undoubtedly hundreds of thousands of party members have shared the fate of millions of nonparty people. It would be extremely difficult to instill in the minds of these millions, their families, relatives and friends, the idea that the Stalinist state is withering away. It is strangling others, but gives no sign of withering. It has instead brought the state to a pitch of wild intensity unprecedented in the history of mankind.[54]

Many Marxists saw the Stalinist version of planning and of Party democracy as authoritarian; and they argued that there were better ways to achieve socialism that might still bring true economic democracy and the withering away of the state. One Marxist writer, Max Shachtman, pinpointed the lack of democracy in planning as the major cause of what he saw as a slave state in the Soviet Union:

> The workers did not do the planning; they did not organize production; they did not manage production; the plan was not worked out with any consideration for the workers' welfare or freedom. Just the opposite. *That is why*, as the Plan went ahead, the workers were turned into totally disfranchised state-slaves, the peasants (in their mass) into equally disfranchised state-serfs, the Bolshevik Party wiped out root and branch, its traditions flouted and new ones invented in their place, the trade unions turned into a slave-driving apparatus, the Soviets gagged,

gutted and finally read out of existence, the national republics deprived of their autonomy and all other rights.[55]

Shachtman blamed this lack of freedom on the disenfranchisement of the worker within economic planning. However, he does not confront the fundamental paradox inherent in freedom and planning: leaving economic decisions to the workers while simultaneously planning production for the whole economy. Western "market socialists" have recognized this contradiction. Economists Saul Estrin and David Winter explain that, although plan construction may incorporate democratic input:

> [I]t is hard to envision effective plan implementation that allowed or encouraged a wide diversity of views among the participants. Central plan implementation naturally takes place within an essentially authoritarian hierarchy. Unless the tasks are so simple that one or two people can perform them all, teams will have to be formed and their activities coordinated. It is difficult to see how such teams can operate on a genuinely democratic basis to implement predetermined targets.[56]

The value of the democratic process, to the extent that plan construction is able to be democratic,[57] must be weighed against the hierarchical implementation portion. For the minority that loses out during the democratic phase, the much longer period of implementation will consist of activities that are against their will. Because the plan coordinates the whole economy, this means that an individual's entire economic life is planned—whether by democratic will or dictatorial decision—and is not freely determined herself.

Marx envisioned a worker-centered economy, where individuals could become involved in economic democracy through their factory or place of work. Labor was to become "life's prime want," so the factory became the center of one's life in the Soviet Union. The factory was like a microcosm of the state and society as a whole. As a microcosm of the state, it could offer opportunity to the regular worker, the "positive liberty" of an equal start. At the same time, it could as easily take all freedom and opportunity away. "The workshop can be the launching pad for a career leading as far as a seat in the legislature or a post as minister, but it can also land someone on a nationwide blacklist."[58]

If a worker wanted to obtain outside income, apply for a passport to travel to another town, apply for a telephone, or get a divorce, she needed permission from the firm where she worked.[59] Housing was generally provided by the firm. For those workers living in common workplace housing, family, friends, and social activities all revolved around the workplace. Political activity occurred at the firm, as did child rearing and entertainment.

From this microcosm, the workplace, there were direct connections all the way through the hierarchy of the planned economy. Because it was against the law not to work, and because the state owned virtually all resources, nearly every Soviet citizen worked for the state. Yet, as Max Shachtman argued, if the individual does not take part in creating the plan—in fact, if he does not agree with it, regardless of whether he took part—then he becomes a slave of the state. One economist argued in 1875 that "The freedom to decide on one's own needs is surely the fundamental basis of all freedom." About the planned economy, he asked:

> What are the criteria according to which labour is to be distributed throughout the broad field of production? Will it consent to be moved around, resettled, and retrained by economic bureaucrats?... Any advantages will turn into their opposites in a mechanically organised system of forced labour, if freedom of individual movement is not fully preserved... If every one had their needs laid down by a central authority then such a state would represent the apogee of slavery and boredom.[60]

Although all labor was not planned (as discussed in Chapter 2) it was certainly not all free either. The plan and all of the related laws and decisions, and thus most life choices, came down from the top. A law or a decree based on plan instructions directed nearly every aspect of an individual's life—because, as the economist F. A Hayek observed, "Economic control is not merely control of a sector of human life which can be separated from the rest; it is the control of the means for all our ends."[61]

Any action that requires scarce resources is economic. If posting a letter takes resources, then it is economic. Visiting a friend, caring for an ill relative, pursuing a personal goal, or viewing entertainment all require resources and are therefore economic. One may argue that visiting a sick relative is not economic because the relative does not offer payment for the visit—just as love may be said to be outside economics because one does not pay for it—but it is economic because it requires time, and often other resources. Because resources are scarce, every activity is potentially economic. Use of time itself is economic because time is scarce.

Any activity or goal that one may have in life, even love, is tied to the economy because the means of achieving it are economic and because the means of life, of survival, are economic. Economists have long realized that economics is not merely the study of the material sphere, such as incomes and purchases. Economic life and regular life are not distinguishable.[62]

One of the goals of socialism was to remove this economic factor from everyday decisions and actions—to remove necessity and thereby enhance freedom. If the people could freely dip into a common pot for food, for the means of producing media, for the necessaries and luxuries of life, then the people would be free in action and in mind. Yet despite Oscar Wilde's argument that the abolition of private property would lead to a true individualism, common property required administration. The hierarchy and coordination necessary for planning and for mobilizing forces to administer the economy made the withering away of the state impossible.

Collective action, the allocation of common resources, and the distribution of proceeds required a plan. The plan must be followed. Yet, the plan, which was centrally determined, meant that people were not left free to live with true individualism. They were left obeying orders from the center. This also meant that the central authority had incredible power over the lives of the people. It had the ability not only to determine *where* someone worked and lived, but *whether* they worked and lived. For example, the politically unreliable could be deprived of food when food was rationed by the state:

> The streets presented a strange appearance to one who had become accustomed to throngs of peasant pedlars. For the first time since the introduction of the rationing of food the population became almost wholly dependent upon the supply of food obtainable on their ration cards at the governmental and co-operative shops. The plight of those people who were deprived of electoral rights, and consequently of the right to have ration cards, was difficult indeed.[63]

Although rationing was repealed, the state's control over resources still allowed it to determine where an individual could travel, work, and live. It also meant that any action a person took might need to be sanctioned by a state bureaucrat. Any activity requiring resources had to be included in the plan, and once planned the choices involved were no longer made by the individual.

Is art to be planned in a planned economy? The Soviets felt that art was part of the enlightenment of the proletariat and hence should express certain sentiments. Soviet art and literature (at least that which was to receive funding) all had to follow one form: constructivism, or socialist realism.[64] Despite Oscar Wilde's dream, freedom from economic necessity did not lead so much to individualism as to conformism directed by the state.

LESSONS

> Free software is a matter of liberty, not price. To understand the concept, you should think of free as in free speech, not as in free beer. — Richard Stallman, founder of the Gnu operating system.[65]
>
> There is much talk about the "dangers to liberty," and professed readiness to "defend" it against the wicked designs of sinister interests. But are we certain we know exactly where the danger to liberty lies? Ought we not at least to pause and ask whether the menace may not have its roots in our own ambitions and endeavours? — F. A. Hayek[66]

Socialists believed that positive liberty was more important and more real than the "negative," or "formal," liberty of the free market. Without the ability to pay for something, the freedom to obtain it was worthless. Furthermore, under capitalism workers had no control over their work, the management of their factory, or their wages. They were completely dominated by the owner of the capital. Socialism was to provide the people real democracy by giving the workers economic control over the means of production. Economic democracy, together with the positive liberty that it would provide, would mean real freedom and a truly democratic society.

However, public ownership gives those in power the right and the ability to control all of the resources of the economy and, hence, the people who depend on those resources. Although the harsh punishments imposed upon the Soviet people were often seen as abuses of power, public property had to be defended just as private property is defended in a free market system.

Economist Murray Rothbard has argued that rights such as free speech are actually not rights in and of themselves but are part of one's property rights, and cannot exist without them:

> In short, a person does not have a "right to freedom of speech"; what he does have is the right to hire a hall and address the people who enter the premises. He does not have a "right to freedom of the press"; what he does have is the right to write or publish a pamphlet, and to sell that pamphlet to those who are willing to buy it (or to give it away to those who are willing to accept it)....[67]

Furthermore, couching the analysis in terms of a "right to free speech" instead of property rights leads to confusion and the weakening of the very concept of rights. The Soviet constitution protected the right to "freedom of speech" and "freedom of the press," yet denied individuals the right to hire a hall or publish a pamphlet because the state and not the people were granted these property rights. Instead of individually and privately making transactions with the private owner of the theater, use of the theater would be decided "democratically" through the workers' government.

Socialists claimed that their constitution was the most democratic, protected the most human rights, and would offer the greatest freedom to the people. Many Western intellectuals agreed, and defended the Soviet Union on this basis.[68] All evidence suggests that it was the sincere desire of the socialists to protect these basic rights once in power. However, rights like freedom of speech meant nothing in practice in the Soviet Union. Why? Rothbard demonstrates the confusion that protecting the right of "freedom of speech" rather than the right of property can cause:

> The most famous example is [the] contention that no one has the right to shout "Fire" falsely in a crowded theater, and *therefore* that the right to freedom of speech cannot be absolute, but must be weakened and tempered by considerations of "public policy." And yet, if we analyze the problem in terms of *property* rights we will see that no weakening of the absoluteness of rights is necessary. For, logically, the shouter is either a patron or the theater owner. If he is the theater owner, he is violating the property rights of the patrons in quiet enjoyment of the performance, for which he took their money in the first place. If he is another patron, then he is violating both the property right of the patrons to watching the performance *and* the property right of the owner, for he is violating the terms of his being there.[69]

Freedom of speech need not be diluted or restricted by law in a private property economy. Any abuse of it is an abuse of the basic institution of property. So long as property is fully protected, both for its gains and for its losses (see Chapter 8), freedom can extend until it breaches this right. There need be no restrictions on speech written into law.

Of course, socialists saw the problem as economic. Although one was free to speak, one was not able. However, if private property is not protected, the right of free speech is meaningless according to Rothbard. The Soviet experience provides support for this idea. Although earning the money for the "positive freedom" of speech was seen as a hurdle to socialists, the hurdle of access to state property turned out to be much greater.

The capitalist control of newspapers was one of the sins of the capitalist economic system that idealistic socialists had promised to end. Even today we hear of "corporate media" and how big business tells us what to think. Public support for art-ists is very popular, and many people would like to see permanent public funding for artistic movements. However, experience in market economies has also shown that this can lead to politicization of artistic content: the state determines what is made politically, rather than upon the basis of consumer demand. For example, the Works Progress Administration of President Roosevelt's New Deal extensively funded pro-New Deal artwork and theatre. As one 1941 article on the new propaganda of the Roosevelt government put it, "W.P.A. makes use of every device of publicity-exhibits, dramas, radio programs, moving pictures-to arouse the sympathy of a public reluc-tant to support it." [70]

Similarly, public ownership and control of the school system make possible a po-liticization of the curriculum, one-sided histories, or religious indoctrination. Once again, vouchers for the disadvantaged may provide a better answer than social own-ership: Private ownership and competition would force schools to better serve their pupils, and would allow free choice and experimentation rather than centralized one-size-fits-all decisions about what is appropriate to teach children.

Although democratic control over the media was the honest intention of the new socialist society, even when resources were shared based upon votes this led to an advantage for the state and for the incumbent political party. The minority could not be protected by pure democracy based on majority rule. Well-meaning Marxists also protected the state with censorship to ensure no deviation from the road to socialism. Even after this experience, although he felt the revolution had been "betrayed" in the Soviet Union, Trotsky argued for extending democracy to the media as part of the road to socialism. He explained that if America were to go socialist:

> Soviet America will have to find a new solution for the question of how the power of the press is to function in a socialist regime. It might be done on the basis of proportional representation for the votes in each soviet election.
>
> Thus the right of each group of citizens to use the power of the press would depend on their numerical strength—the same principle being applied to the use of meeting halls, allotment of time on the air and so forth.
>
> Thus the management and policy of publications would be decided not by in-dividual checkbooks but by group ideas. This may take little account of numeri-cally small but important groups, but it simply means that each new idea will be compelled, as throughout history, to prove its right to existence. [71]

Yet is this a better solution? Today, if someone finds a monetarily cheap way to reproduce his ideas through his own efforts or finds a kind benefactor or a hopeful in-vestor, he can publish a magazine or newspaper. Under a socialist system, the need to secure the group's approval before publication would seem to put the minority idea at a far greater disadvantage. Marx only needed to convince one person—Engels—that his ideas were worth funding. If he had required "numerical strength," he might never have published his ideas.

Economists distinguish between "exit" and "voice." A market offers the chance of exit (and entry), while the political system offers the chance to express oneself with a vote. If a majority votes for something, all the minority can do is express themselves through their vote. Democracy gives them a voice, but not an opportunity for action. The majority must be persuaded before any action can take place. There is only one supplier, and the supply is determined by votes, so exit is not possible.

The entry and exit that the market offers are actions: voting with one's feet or dollars. This is possible because there are competing options (because there is free entry). Economist Arnold Kling has argued, "The exercise of voice, including the right to vote, is not the ultimate expression of freedom. Rather, it is the last refuge of those who suffer under a monopoly."[72]

Perhaps not everything should be decided democratically. For things that are truly public—that affect everyone—it makes sense to vote. It makes far less sense for everyone in the country to vote on what I can eat for breakfast or where I should go on my vacation. In the Soviet Union, the workplace often did vote on such things because they were communally owned and funded. Yet what if your co-workers always want to go skiing, but you have a bad back, hate the cold, or just want to get away from them? What if the majority wants a meat dish in the cafeteria, but you are a vegetarian?

When democracy replaces private transactions and the goods are communally funded, you may have to spend your money in ways you do not want. One recent example of the unrest this can create is the debate about whether taxpayer-funded health insurance should cover abortions.[73] Even short of such controversial procedures, democratically choosing might leave the taxpayer paying for many services she would rather not. It may be more democratic, but it is less free.

The market system is inherently based on freedom of the individual, both buyer and seller, while political systems are not. Buying a book or a newspaper that criticizes the political leaders depends not only on the freedom to buy, but also on the freedom to sell. It depends on the publisher being able to own a publishing house or the printing press to produce the newspapers, buy paper and ink, and sell copies of the final product. Free speech depends critically on the freedom to buy *and* sell, including buying and selling mundane items, such as ink cartridges, building space, and batteries.

The market is made up of voluntary transactions agreed upon as they take place. Laws, even those democratically enacted, have only the agreement of the voting majority. When these laws regulate economic choices, they are banning a consensual transaction. As transactions between willing adults, economic crimes are crimes that have no victim, unless that victim is identified as "society as a whole" or some similar party.

In fact, voluntary transactions are the basis of an economic system and banning them is bound to create conflict. These economic "crimes" were often difficult to avoid committing in Soviet society because the plan was unable to fill the needs of the people (See Chapter 5). This resulted in the absurdity that society as a whole was committing crimes against society.

Although such laws must be part of a planned society, laws that ban voluntary transactions may exist in all kinds of societies. Democracy may itself create a momentum toward more restrictions on consensual acts: the "tyranny of the masses." For example, since 1994, federal law in the United States has withheld some funding from any state that did not create a "sex offender registry," and a number of lawmakers have apparently engaged in an escalating contest to pander to the public's desire to punish sex offenders. The number of registered "offenders" has climbed to 674,000.[74]

In addition to any jail time, offenders must register—sometimes for life—and this information is available online. Offenders may be banned from living near a school or even a bus stop, and from working at a church. They may find it difficult to obtain employment. Essentially, offenders are ostracized. Yet some of the acts (depending on the state) that may brand a person as a sex offender are not crimes against another person at all. In addition to the very serious crimes of rape and molestation, the legal definitions include a series of "crimes" in which no other individual is harmed. These include consensual "sodomy," visiting a prostitute, urinating in public, "streaking," and sex acts between two consenting teens near the cut-off age of 18, one of whom is a few months older.[75]

Economic crimes are like any crime that has no victim. They are a crime only because a law bans a consensual act. When enforced, these laws may be experienced as absurd, harsh, and even totalitarian, regardless of the political system that voted them in. Imagine that you go to the shop to buy a bag of onions, and you are arrested for "engaging in an illegal exchange." The freedom to buy and sell is not usually questioned, but when these freedoms are abridged it becomes clear how fundamental they really are. The freedom to spend the fruits of one's labor is fundamental. The freedom to exchange one good for another, such as a pair of pants for a tea kettle, is a fundamental freedom.

If, in order to feed one's family, one must first bring the pants to the market and earn some cash from them, and then go to another market to buy the tea kettle or a bag of onions, it is just as fundamental a freedom. Yet the economic laws of the Soviet Union, as well as President Roosevelt's New Deal in the United States and other regulatory regimes in other countries, have banned or restricted such exchanges.

Because economic laws have no victims and violation can be so widespread, they may be enforced arbitrarily upon "enemies of the state." The thousands of economic "crimes" that central direction of the economy created in the Soviet Union were often used for leverage and discretionary purposes. In a similar manner, the "crimes" of jaywalking, resisting arrest, tax evasion, and minor drug and prostitution violations may be used in a discretionary manner when the police cannot find evidence of another crime. Even if not used for such purposes, enforcement of crimes with no victim, including economic crimes, may become brutal as individuals find that they need to break the laws just to survive.

Market socialists have come to realize this, and their new programs tolerate "small-scale capitalist acts between consenting adults [rather] than to endorse the levels of state surveillance and discretion that would be required to prevent them."[76]

Economic sanctions have led to increased surveillance and even authoritarian measures not only in a fully planned economies, but also in Western countries. John Flynn described what occurred under Franklin Roosevelt's New Deal:

> But, little by little, the spell began to fade. In spite of all the fine words about industrial democracy, people began to see it was a scheme to permit business men to combine to put up prices and keep them up by direct decree or through other devious devices.... But the [National Recovery Administration] continued to exhibit its folly in a succession of crazy antics which could only proceed from people who had lost their bearings and their heads. A tailor named Jack Magid in New Jersey was arrested, convicted, fined and sent to jail. The crime was that he had pressed a suit of clothes for 35 cents when the Tailors' Code fixed the price at 40 cents.
>
> ...The NRA was discovering it could not enforce its rules. Black markets grew up. Only the most violent police methods could procure enforcement. In [the] garment industry, they employed enforcement police. They roamed through the garment district like storm troopers. They could enter a man's factory, send him out, line up his employees, subject them to a minute interrogation, take over his books on the instant. Night work was forbidden.
>
> ...[p]olice went through the district at night, battering down doors with axes, looking for men who were committing the crime of sewing together a pair of pants at night. But without these harsh methods many code authorities said there could not be compliance because the public [did not support the law].[77]

Of course, some might say this policy should be ended if the American people were not behind it,[78] and continued if they were—this is real democracy. If the people were rebelling then they would vote it down, and it would end, unless an authoritarian figure usurped democratic control. The NRA was struck down as unconstitutional, so it will never be known if this would have occurred. The fact that the Supreme Court could strike down these laws might strike some as undemocratic.

Socialists argued that they wanted to extend democracy and that bourgeois democracy was a sham. Under socialism everything—the workplace, the political arena and even the choices over production—would be truly democratic. In this view, limitations on democracy, such as the U.S. Constitution, which limits what voters can ask their representatives to do, are limitations on democracy, and by extension, freedom. The voters should be able to set the prices that tailors charge, when workers can be employed to work, and any other production decision.

However, economic democracy not only requires regimentation for enforcement, but also a centralization of government. For various projects that the public might want to be reconciled, and for decisions to be made in a timely manner, strong authority is required. It is not a coincidence that socialist governments had no checks and balances, but liberal governments did.

When he introduced the New Deal, President Roosevelt took some actions that centralized power in the executive branch. In *The Roosevelt Myth*, John Flynn recounted how "Under our system, Congress holds the purse strings," however, "early in Roosevelt's first term the NRA Act provided an appropriation of $3,300,000,000 which the President was given to be spent for relief and recovery at his own discretion. He now had in his hands a sum of money equal to as much as the government had spent in ten years outside the ordinary expenses of government." With this single stroke of his pen, Roosevelt had taken this function of Congress out of their hands, and put it in his own. "If a congressman or senator wanted an appropriation for his district, instead of introducing a bill in Congress, he went up to the White House with his hat in his hand and asked the President for it."[79]

Planning, or the spending of a vast sum of money at the discretion of the executive, which is the same thing, requires executive orders, or decrees. Just as Stalin issued thousands of decrees, Roosevelt issued vastly more executive orders than any prior U.S. President. In 1941 an article on the growth of the power of the executive argued that "it is significant that President Roosevelt has issued such orders at a rate more than twice that of his most prolific predecessor. The question may legitimately be raised whether the influence and authority of the executive on legislation and in the issuance of regulations having the force of law has not reached a point where the traditional understandings of government by consent have been altered."[80]

After the Supreme Court struck down the NRA, Roosevelt introduced his "court packing plan," an attempt to give the President more control over the courts. Flynn wrote about Roosevelt's views on the courts:

> His conception of the structure of government was never really clear. The independence of the courts is something which all parties had accepted as a matter of course. Yet Roosevelt could suggest to Chief Justice Hughes that it might be well if Hughes discussed controversial constitutional decisions with him while he would discuss proposed legislation with the Chief Justice. The veriest law tyro would see the impropriety of this. Yet Roosevelt, in telling of the incident, described Hughes' coolness to his suggestion as evidence of the Court's "unwillingness to cooperate."[81]

It is difficult to plan an economy if the plan is struck down as unconstitutional. Yet does this "extension of democracy" that ensures the Supreme Court goes along with the policies of the voter (or of the executive) actually extend freedom? Or does it just give more power to the executive and legislative branches and reduce checks and balances? In the most extreme case, the Utopian vision of a common will carried through with a unanimously agreed-upon plan, would require no checks and balances at all.

Those who believe that the government's job is to plan and coordinate the economy will want the government to have great leeway to do this. If checks and balances of the republican style of government hinder the government from doing this, they will give up the checks and balances one by one rather than back down from this goal. This is only natural: the plan would only be struck down as unconstitutional in a system in which this "extension of democracy" was seen as illegitimate. If economic planning is legitimate, then the courts should be directed to conclude this.

Conversation among the President, the legislators, and the courts would alleviate obstructions and allow government to fulfill these functions. Roosevelt complained that the Court was uncooperative and prevented him from doing his job. A hierarchically structured government is much more efficient for getting things done. An enormous number of decisions must be made every day when the government is planning economic activity, and they must be coordinated with each other.

A planned economy is a lot like a firm. Lenin said that under socialism, "The whole of society will have become a single office and a single factory, with equality of labor and pay."[82] It is not easy to run a factory democratically. There have been few examples of successful democratically run firms. Although many market socialists favor an "extension of democracy into the workplace," market socialists frequently criticize worker-managed firms for their tendency to devolve toward traditional hierarchy. This happens because of "the inevitable emergence of managerial elites" and because "organizational imperatives create a thrust toward oligarchy."[83]

Firms are engaged in a common goal of planned production. This requires coordinating a multitude of different actors toward a common goal. In such a situation, a leader with a particular stake in the outcome who can coordinate these actors tends to emerge. Anyone who has attempted to use democratic or anarchic procedures to achieve a set goal can attest that such coordination, even with a small group, is incredibly difficult. Across a whole economy, it necessarily becomes more difficult. In contrast, a government that solely protects the rights of the citizens has no set goals to achieve. Production in a market economy results from the "anarchy" of the system—individuals interacting without guidance from a central leader (though with protection of property rights, as discussed in Chapter 8.)[84]

When economic decisions are made through the political process a small group of elite may need to reconcile the decisions. The voter cannot be deeply involved if the complexity of the economic choices becomes too great. "It will be of little avail to the people that the laws are made by men of their own choice," wrote James Madison in Federalist Paper No. 62, "if the laws be so voluminous that they cannot be read, or so incoherent that they cannot be understood."[85]

The necessity for a strong executive branch for economic planning is well known. In 1947, in *The Keynesian Revolution*, Lawrence R. Klein described the trade-off which would be necessary were true Keynesian policy solutions to be enacted—a trade-off which he supported. He argued that although a planning board with strong executive powers would be necessary, "[t]he regimentation of unemployment and poverty is infinitely more severe than the regimentation of economic planning."[86] Klein admitted that the planners would have to have "complete control over government fiscal policy so that they can spend when and where spending is needed to stimulate employment and tax when and where taxation is needed to halt upward price movements."[87] The Congress would have to delegate its legislative power in the area of economic policy entirely to the planning board.

The pressure for more centralization is seen even when the state does not attempt to guide production explicitly through a plan. In mixed economies with populist public sentiment, "partisan bickering," "obstructionism," and "gridlock" are often targets. The unspoken assumption is that both parties should just come together, put disagreements aside, and push through new legislation (generally to place more of the economy under public control). This sentiment is reminiscent of the socialist ideal of coming together to "administer our common property."

For example, in the United States, Senate Majority Leader Harry Reid (D-NV) recently called 2009 one of the most "productive spans of legislative work since the Great Depression." He argued for working together "as Americans" to fight the economic downturn. "Only by working together—not as Democrats or Republicans, but as Americans—can we put the jobless back to work, make sure everyone can afford to stay healthy and create a clean-energy economy for this new century," Reid wrote. "Only if we work as partners, not as partisans, can we preserve the American dream for so many Nevadans who fear losing their homes."[88]

However, public support for the initiatives of the Congress and President began to fade mid-2009, and in early 2010, *The New York Times* reported that "With much of his legislative agenda stalled in Congress, President Obama and his team are preparing an array of actions using his executive power to advance energy, environmental, fiscal and other domestic policy priorities."[89]

Despite the popular criticism of "partisan bickering," checks and balances play an important role, and competition between parties is a significant part of checks and balances. It does not make sense to "come together" on policy unless the policy is correct—efficient and capable of fulfilling its proposed ends. If, for example, a policy hurts the minority badly, but aids or does not affect the majority, it is more likely to pass if there is not long and healthy debate.

Some market socialists have argued that democracy in the corporation and over corporations, much like Lenin's vision of a worker-controlled society, would represent a more democratic society than the capitalist one, even if there were no democracy in the political sphere. The market society is hierarchically organized in its own way, they argue. Only the wealthy have power and control over production.

Many market socialists, indeed many people of all political views, would probably agree with the characterization of corporate shareholder democracy in *The ABC of Communism*:

> It is easy to understand how the great capitalist shareholders have been able to make the small shareholders their hodmen. The small shareholder often lives in another town from that in which the enterprise is centred, and cannot travel a hundred miles or more to attend a shareholders' meeting. Even when some of the ordinary shareholders turn up at the meeting, they are unorganized, and merely jostle one another like blind puppies. But the big shareholders are organized. They have a common plan; they can do what they please. Experience has shown that it suffices the great capitalist to own one-third of all the shares, for this gives him absolute control of the whole undertaking.[90]

It is difficult to argue with this. Certainly, someone with only $100 of shares is going to exert less effort, even as part of a group, to control the management of a firm than someone who has invested millions of dollars in the firm. However, the small shareholders express themselves in another way: These shares are sold on the market. Although it is not a political voting process, the contribution by those buying and selling on the market is like a vote. Even if a small shareholder does not attend a meeting, she can influence the management by selling or holding the stocks. Her individual contribution may be small, but the worker-control by an organized group of shareholders exists in fact, although not as envisioned by the socialists: They are organized by the market, and they exert control by affecting the price of the stock.

These shareholders express their opinion through the market, just as individuals express themselves as customers in a market economy when they buy from one shop or another and sell their labor power to their preferred employer. Democracy was limited in the planned economy because the plan directed resources, and the Party and state enforced the plan. Private ownership limits the power of the state because it decentralizes the command over resources. This then allows the individual a greater power to express his own preferences, as consumer, worker, "capitalist," and entrepreneur. This expands the arena for a democracy "of the dollar" and for personal freedom.

This conclusion has been implicitly accepted by political scientists and historians discussing socialist countries. Socialist countries that were less centralized retained private ownership in certain spheres. Those with little or no private ownership were the most centralized and least democratic. Poland was officially designated as a "popular democracy," different from a dictatorship of the proletariat, "and this difference was to consist, partly, in the continued existence of private farming and some forms of private enterprise in non-agricultural activities."[91]

It has also been recognized by market socialists. In an article titled "A Case For Market Socialism," David Miller and Saul Estrin argued that "Markets tend to dissolve personal power...they free people from dependence on particular individuals such as petty bureaucrats. This is not because markets have a directly ennobling effect on human nature, but because competitive pressures tend in the long run to favor the survival of the helpful."[92] The right to own a business, to print a newspaper, and to make contracts with others enables free speech and the freedom to choose where to work and where to live. As János Kornai succinctly stated, "the indivisibility of power and the concomitant totalitarianism are incompatible with the autonomy that private ownership entails."[93] However, they are not incompatible with public ownership—and, in fact, extensive public ownership may require a certain amount of authoritarianism in order to pursue the objectives agreed upon.

Even in such free societies as the United States and Great Britain the extension of planning or public ownership may require more bureaucracy and hierarchy, and less freedom. British Prime Minister Margaret Thatcher argued that this was beginning to occur in Britain:

> We started off with a wish on the part of the people for more government intervention in certain spheres. This was met. But there came a time when the amount of intervention got so great that it could no longer be exercised in practice by government but only by more and more officials or bureaucrats. Now it is difficult if not impossible for people to get at the official making the decision and so paradoxically although the degree of intervention is greater, the government has become more and more *remote* from the people. The present result of the democratic process has therefore been an increasing authoritarianism.
>
> Recently more and more feature articles have been written and speeches made about involving people more closely with decisions of the government and enabling them to participate in some of those decisions.
>
> But the way to get personal involvement and participation is not for people to take part in more and more government decisions but to make the government reduce the area of decision over which it presides and consequently leave the private citizen to 'participate', if that be the fashionable word, by making more of his own decisions. What we need now is a far greater degree of personal responsibility and decision, far more independence from the government, and a comparative reduction in the role of government. [94]

Thatcher was arguing the distinction between positive liberty and democratic control over public resources and the freedom of individual choice and negative liberty. Rather than having the people become more involved democratically over commonly owned resources, she argued that the better solution would be to return some of these resources back to private control.

Socialists theory argued that the state would wither away once social ownership of the means of production led to abundance. Yet, even earlier some classical liberal thinkers had predicted a day when markets would allow for a self-governing economy, and true freedom. Yet, for these thinkers, freedom was the freedom to make private contracts, open a business, and live free from coercion of the state. Gareth Stedman-Jones, of Cambridge University, described these thinkers' view on the relationship of liberty, markets, and morality:

> According to this theory, man was a creature of needs with the faculty to fulfil them. Liberty was the power to use one's faculties, to live by work and to obtain the product of one's work. Evil was identified with any force which prevented man from fulfilling this law. Man followed his interest, there was no place for morality and any supposed conflict between duty and interest was based upon ignorance of the laws of economics. Since these were the laws of man's being, he had but to follow them to be happy. [95]

These thinkers argued that the free market was bringing liberty and prosperity to the world, and that economics could illustrate how the market was capable of doing this. Some of the arguments of these thinkers about the withering away of the state were similar to Marx's. Both argued that free trade was non-antagonistic, but the state, by imposing tariffs, could raise revenue, and this gave it the incentive to expand its territory and clash with other states. Both argued that the state gave monopoly power to businesses which helped them to exploit the people. Although Marx concluded that the workers should take control and govern resources democratically, these classical liberal thinkers concluded that limitations should be imposed upon the state. These distinctions form the basis of Chapter 10.

CONCLUSION

Socialists promised a more equal, democratic and free society. The socialist system would offer a massive extension of democracy by giving workers a democratic say over what they produced. Socialism would also extend freedom to all people because money would no longer be necessary to make practical use of basic rights like free speech and assembly. For many years it was widely believed that socialism would bring great democracy and freedom to the people.

However, a planned economy is much like a firm. The people in it must work together to produce to specified goals and targets. While a system of private property allows for spontaneous coordination as individuals make voluntary exchanges with their own property, commonly owned property precludes such decentralized solutions. Without private ownership there can be no real exchange. Instead, property must be administered and coordination between actors requires a plan.

First the plan must be chosen, and then it must be implemented and administered. Just as with collective action in a firm, a leader tends to emerge to take charge and ensure that the output goals are met. Hence, democracy and freedom did not emerge in the Soviet Union. Instead authoritarianism and totalitarianism resulted.

ENDNOTES

1. Hutchison, *The Politics and Philosophy of Economics*.
2. Frederick Engels, *The Condition of the Working Class in England* (London: Panther Books, 1969), at http://www.marxists.org/archive/marx/works/1845/condition-working-class/index.htm (December 5, 2009).
3. Lenin, *State and Revolution* (1917), chap. 5, at http://www.marxists.org/archive/lenin/works/1917/staterev/ch05.htm.
4. Bukharin and Preobrazhensky, *The ABC of Communism*, chap. 6.
5. Wootton, *Plan or No Plan*.
6. Lenin, "Democracy' and Dictatorship," January 3, 1919, in *Collected Works*, Vol. 28 (Moscow: Progress Publishers), pp. 368–372, at http://www.marxists.org/archive/lenin/works/1918/dec/23.htm (December 5, 2009).
7. Frederick Engels, *Anti-Dühring: Herr Eugen Dühring's Revolution in Science*, trans. Emile Burns, part 3, *Socialism* (Moscow: Progress Publishers, 1947), chap. 2, at http://www.marxists.org/archive/marx/works/1877/anti-duhring/index.htm (December 5, 2009) (emphasis added).
8. Oscar Wilde, *The Soul of Man under Socialism* (Boston: John W. Luce, 1910) (emphasis added).
9. V. I. Lenin, "What Is Soviet Power?" March 1919, in *Collected Works*, Vol. 29 (Moscow: Progress Publishers, 1972), pp. 248–249, at http://marxists.org/archive/lenin/works/1919/mar/x08.htm (December 4, 2009).
10. Constitution of the Russian Soviet Federated Socialist Republic, art. 2, paras. 14–17 (1918).
11. Bukharin and Preobrazhensky, *The ABC of Communism*, chap. 6.
12. *Ibid.*
13. *Ibid.*
14. For a description, see Jerry F. Hough and Merle Fainsod, *How the Soviet Union Is Governed*, 2nd ed.

(Cambridge, MA: Harvard University Press, 1979), pp. 302–303.

15. Study cited in *ibid.*

16. H. N. Brailsford, *How the Soviets Work* (New York: Vanguard Press, 1927), pp. 18–19, at http://www.marxists.org/history/archive/brailsford/1927/soviets-work/index.htm (December 5, 2009).

17. Ibid., pp. 27–29.

18. Peter Pirogov, *Why I Escaped* (Duell, Sloan and Pierce, 1950), p. 205.

19. V. I. Lenin, "Note to F. E. Dzerzhinsky with a Draft of a Decree on Fighting Counter-Revolutionaries and Saboteurs," December 7, 1917, in *Collected Works*, Vol. 26, pp. 374–376.

20. V. I. Lenin, "A Great Beginning: Heroism of the Workers in the Rear, 'Communist Subbotniks,'" July 1919, in *Collected Works*, Vol. 29, pp. 409–434.

21. Frederick I. Kaplan, *Bolshevik Ideology and the Ethics of Soviet Labor 1917–1920: The Formative Years* (London: Peter Owen, 1969), p. 384.

22. *Ibid.*, p. 385.

23. V. I. Lenin, "The Immediate Tasks of the Soviet Government," April 28, 1918, in *Collected Works*, Vol. 27, pp. 235–277.

24. This was not only the method in Russia proper, but also in all countries into which the Bolsheviks spread. Lenin answered to A. M. Krasnoshchokov, the Foreign Minister of the Far-Eastern Republic, regarding the democratic socialist state for the Far-Eastern Republic, "Democracy [is] permissible with slight privileges for Communists." This meant that the communists were to ensure a majority in the parliament, but otherwise to go along with democracy. In response to the extent of the republic's authority, Lenin said "Obey the C.C., otherwise we'll sack you." V. I. Lenin, "Answers to Questions by A. M. Krasnoshchokov, Foreign Minister of the Far-Eastern Republic," July 1920, in *Collected Works*, Vol. 42, p. 204.

25. As one writer reminds us, "We are apt, I think, to exaggerate the extent to which they differ in their practice from the defenders of other systems, who profess an unlimited loyalty to democracy. Could the Declaration of Independence be made an issue at an American election? Save in minor matters of legal interpretation, can one conceive an extensive and fundamental alteration of the American Constitution without a civil war?" Brailsford, *How the Soviets Work*, p. 32.

26. "Between capitalist and communist society there lies the period of the revolutionary transformation of the one into the other. Corresponding to this is also a political transition period in which the state can be nothing but the revolutionary dictatorship of the proletariat." Karl Marx, "Critique of the Gotha Programme," chap. 4.

27. Indeed, the multi-party system requires compromise, and this was the same compromise that led so many social-democratic parties in other countries away from socializing all the means of production—allowed them to become bourgeois parties capable only of increasing the "welfare state," and remaining market economies.

28. Louise Bryant, *Six Red Months in Russia: An Observers Account of Russia Before and During the Proletarian Dictatorship* (New York: George H. Doran Company, 1918), chap. 22, at http://www.marxists.org/archive/bryant/works/russia/index.htm (December 4, 2009).

29. The socialist view of the private ownership of media was that capitalist control silenced the working class voice. Thus, in the socialist society, no private person could get his hands on the media. Instead, the workers' state would provide whoever asked for it the means to publish his story. The press was socialized so that no money was required in order to create a newspaper and so the newspapers would not be in the hands of the rich. There was no possibility of capitalist seizure of the media because ownership of printing outlets was banned. Not only was private ownership of any printing establishment that hired labor illegal, but licensing restrictions prevented even a cooperative from printing pamphlets because ownership and operation of a reproductive apparatus was forbidden. Hazard, *The Soviet System of Government*, p. 191.

30. Brailsford, *How the Soviets Work*, p. 31.

31. For example, see János Kornai, The Socialist System: The Political Economy Of Communism (Oxford: Oxford University Press, 1992), pp. 34–35.Robinson, *An American in Leningrad*, p. 36.

32. In 1926, a Bolshevik theoretician argued that this was already happening: "All our People's Commissariats are divided into two groups: economic organs (production and distribution) and organs of coercion (military, internal affairs, and judiciary).... It is quite apparent that the latter

are gradually withering away and that they undergo atrophy, while the former, directing the economic orchestra, are growing. This development may ultimately result even in an "orchestra without a conductor," but this is a matter of the distant future. One thing remains indisputable: the state, as well as the law in its class meaning, evaporates, i.e., withers away, together with the organs of coercion." P. Stuchka, *The Last Act of the State: It Withers Away* (1926), cited in Michael Jaworskyj, *Soviet Political Thought: An Anthology* (Baltimore: John's Hopkins, 1967), p. 243.

33. Brailsford, *How the Soviets Work*, p. 36 (emphasis added).

34. *Ibid.*, pp. 41–42.

35. Of course, there may be other kinds of democracy than majority-rule. However, many of the criticisms of democratic decision-making would apply to other forms of democracy.

36. Ibid., pp. 42–43.

37. P. S. Ivanov, "Development of the National Economy of the USSR," in *Banking in the USSR: Lectures Delivered at the 15th International Banking Summer School* (Moscow: State Bank of the USSR, 1962), p. 27.

38. Kornai, *The Socialist System*, p. 113.

39. Plan reconciliation in this case and others would be much easier if planners could depend upon foreign trade. Foreign trade relieved pressure on Soviet planners as well. Some have argued that the Soviet Union would have achieved its promise had the revolution spread – that communism needed to be international – and that trade embargoes were a major cause of its failure. However, the way that foreign trade can best relieve pressure on plans is when it can occur spontaneously: when it is a market transaction. For example, in this case the plan could be democratically determined, and then planners could make orders for any output for which the inputs are lacking. If the other countries had also undergone a socialist revolution, then instead of a simple market transaction, the missing inputs would have to be written into the plan for the other country, and be reconciled with what the voters of the country want to produce, etc.

40. For an introduction to the problems of collective choice, including "cycling" and other inconsistent and inefficient outcomes, as well as an analysis of market and state solutions to social needs, see Joe B. Stevens, *The Economics of Collective Choice* (Boulder, CO: Westview Press, 1993).

41. Kornai, *The Socialist System*, p. 112 (ft. 6).

42. *Ibid.*, p. 111 (ft. 4).

43. Philippe J. Bernard, *Planning in the Soviet Union* (Oxford, N.Y.: Pergamon Press, 1966), p. 69.

44. Bartołomiej Kaminski, *The Collapse of State Socialism: The Case of Poland* (Princeton, N.J.: Princeton University Press, 1991), pp. 32–33.

45. Perfect knowledge of all options is a highly unrealistic demand. Even if the planners knew all of the options, how could they decide among them? As stressed elsewhere in this book, without the market the planners cannot know the costs of the various choices. The last requirement, that planners could respond to change, theoretically could be a precondition for the planners to mimic the market and retain useful prices; however, this is an impossible precondition. The limited information at the center would not allow perfect market imitation.

46. Brailsford, *How the Soviets Work*, pp. 32–33.

47. Waldemar Gurian, *Bolshevism: Theory and Practice* (London: Sheed & Ward, 1932), p. 85.

48. Bohdan Harasamiw, "Nomenklatura: The Soviet Communist Party's Leadership Recruitment System," *Canadian Journal of Political Science*, Vol. 2, No. 4 (December 1969).

49. Waldemar Gurian, *Bolshevism: Theory and Practice*, p. 85.

50. Gurian, *Bolshevism*, p. 86.

51. *Ibid.*, pp. 86–87.

52. G. T. Grinko, *The Five-Year Plan of the Soviet Union*, p. 13.

53. *Ibid.*, pp. 13–14.

54. Leon Trotsky, "The Bonapartist Philosophy of the State," *The New International* [New York], Vol. 5 No. 6 (June 1939), pp. 166-169, at http://www.marxists.org/archive/trotsky/1939/05/bonapartism. htm.

55. Max Shachtman, *The Struggle for the New Course* (New York: New International Publishing, 1943), at http://www.marxists.org/archive/shachtma/1943/fnc/index.htm (emphasis added).

56. Saul Estrin and David Winter, "Planning in Market Socialist Economy," in Julian Le Grand and

Saul Estrin, eds., *Market Socialism* (Oxford: Clarendon Press, 1989), pp. 122–123.

57. Estrin and Winter make the point that political democracy may not be more democratic than market "voting" because, although markets allow those with more wealth to "vote" more times with their dollars, in a political process there are also strong interest groups that may pressure more for their ends. Furthermore, a minority will still lose out in the democratic process. Those groups and individuals whose votes are in the minority must still fulfill their part of the plan.

58. Kornai, *The Socialist System*, p. 221.

59. *Ibid.*, pp. 221–222.

60. Schlaffe quoted in T. W. Hutchison, *The Politics and Philosophy of Economics*, p. 171 (ft 2).

61. Friedrich August Hayek, *The Road to Serfdom* (Chicago: University of Chicago Press, 2007), p. 127.

62. For example, see Lionel Robbins, Essay on the Nature and Significance of Economic Science (London: Macmillan and Co., 1952 [1932]), p. 14.

63. Calvin B. Hoover, "The Fate of the New Economic Policy of the Soviet Union," Economic Journal, Vol. 40, No. 158 (June 1930), p. 187.

64. Constructivism was the early school of socialist art, which saw art as a practical tool to be used for political and social purposes. After about 1934, Constructivism was replaced by Socialist Realism, a school based on the same premise. See, for example, James von Geldern and Richard Stites, Mass Culture in Soviet Russia, (Bloomington, IN: Indiana University Press, 1995).

65. Richard Stallman, "The Free Software Definition," at http://www.gnu.org/philosophy/free-sw.html (December 5, 2009). This distinction is not always made, even today. For example, 3 Doors Down, a popular musical group, recently released a song called "Duck and Run," which asked whether it was really a "free country" if "it costs so much to live?" This may be just a play on words, but it is a crucial distinction. A free country, like free speech, means that one can do or say as he pleases, while a "free beer," or a country in which income is ensured, means that—under the particular conditions set by the person offering the gift—the thing is free of direct cost. A free gift from the state may come with many strings attached.

66. F. A. Hayek, *Freedom and the Economic System* (Chicago: University of Chicago Press, 1939).

67. Murray N. Rothbard, "'Human Rights' as Property Rights," Mises Daily, May 18, 2007, at http://mises.org/story/2569 (December 5, 2009).

68. For example, Beatrice and Sidney Webb, Soviet Communism: A New Civilization?

69. Rothbard, "'Human Rights' as Property Rights."

70. Harold W. Stoke, "Executive Leadership and the Growth of Propaganda," *The American Political Science Review*, Vol. 35, No. 3 (June 1941), pp. 490–500. -- See also, Steven C. Dubin, "Artistic Production and Social Control," *Social Forces*, Vol. 64, No. 3 (March 1986), pp. 667-688. -- Posters created during the New Deal are available online at http://lcweb2.loc.gov/ammem/wpaposters/wpahome.html.

71. Leon Trotsky, "If America Should Go Communist," August 1934, at http://www.marxists.org/archive/trotsky/1934/08/ame.htm (December 3, 2009).

72. Arnold Kling, "What Is Real Freedom?" EconLog, August 10, 2009, at http://econlog.econlib.org/archives/2009/08/what_is_real_fr.html (December 5, 2009).

73. James Rowley and Catherine Dodge, "Democrats Seek Votes on Health-Care as Delay Possible," Bloomberg.com, November 6, 2009, at http://www.bloomberg.com/apps/news?pid=20601087&s id=a5gDY7q4FTgc (December 5, 2009).

74. "Unjust and Ineffective Sex Laws," *The Economist*, August 6, 2009.

75. *Ibid.*

76. Christopher Pierson, *Socialism After Communism: The New Market Socialism* (University Park, PA: Pennsylvania State University Press), p. 98.

77. Flynn, *The Roosevelt Myth*.

78. One should note that a majority may agree to something, such as an economic regulation, and brutal measures may still be required for enforcement upon the minority. Flynn adds, "The American people were not yet conditioned to regimentation on such a scale. It could not have been operated successfully on Americans by angels." *Ibid.* Arguably, the same could be said of Russians or of any society. Human nature does not take well to strict regimentation. It requires authoritarian methods. Even then, force must be applied consistently, or it will unravel.

79. *Ibid.*, p. 289.
80. Harold W. Stoke, "Executive Leadership and the Growth of Propaganda," *The American Political Science Review*, Vol. 35, No. 3 (June 1941), pp. 490–500, at http://www.jstor.org.mutex.gmu.edu/stable/pdfplus/1948763.pdf.
81. John Flynn, *The Roosevelt Myth*.
82. V. I. Lenin, *The State and Revolution* (1918), chap. 5, in *Collected Works*, Vol. 25, pp. 381–492, at http://www.marxists.org/archive/lenin/works/1917/staterev/ch05.htm (December 5, 2009).
83. Robert Dahl, quoted in Pierson, *Socialism After Communism*, p. 167.
84. Whether the protection of these basic rights—the right of property, along with rights of life and liberty—can be provided privately as well, leaving no role for government, is a question explored by some economists. See, for example, Edward P. Stringham, Anarchy and the Law: The Political Economy of Choice, Independent Institute, 2006.
85. James Madison, *The Federalist No. 62: The Senate*, Independent Journal, February 27, 1788, at http://www.constitution.org/fed/federa62.htm.
86. Lawrence R. Klein, *The Keynesian Revolution*, 1947, quoted in Richard M. Ebeling, *Monetary Central Planning and the State*.
87. *Ibid.*
88. Harry Reid, "Senate Working Swiftly to Right Nevada's—and Nation's—Course," *Las Vegas Sun*, August 2, 2009, at http://www.lasvegassun.com/news/2009/aug/02/active-senate-working-swiftly-reverse-nations-cour (December 5, 2009).
89. Peter Baker, "Obama Making Plans to Use Executive Power," *The New York Times*, February 12, 2010, at http://www.nytimes.com/2010/02/13/us/politics/13obama.html.
90. Bukharin and Preobrazhensky, *The ABC of Communism*, chap. 6.
91. Adolf Sturmthal, "The Workers' Councils in Poland," *Industrial and Labor Relations Review*, Vol. 14, No. 3 (April 1961), p. 380.
92. David Miller and Saul Estrin, "A Case For Market Socialism," in Franklin Roosevelt and David Belkin (eds), *Why Market Socialism? Voices From Dissent*, M. E. Sharp, 1994 (p. 227) See also "A Vision of Market Socialism" in the same book, pp. 248–253.
93. Kornai, *The Socialist System*, p. 362.
94. Margaret Thatcher, "What's Wrong with Politics?" October 11, 1968, Margaret Thatcher Foundation, http://www.margaretthatcher.org/speeches/displaydocument.asp?docid=101632 (February 13, 2010).
95. Gareth Stedman-Jones, 'Saint Simon and the liberal origins of the socialist critique of Political Economy' in La France et l'Angleterre au XIXe siècle. Échanges, représentations, comparaisons, eds. Sylvie Aprile and Fabrice Bensimon, Créaphis, 2006, pp. 21–47 at http://www-sul.stanford.edu/depts/hasrg/frnit/pdfs_gimon/stedman_jones.pdf (p. 21)

Chapter 10. Corporate Capitalism or the Free Market

Introduction

Many socialist arguments against capitalism concerned the power of the capitalist. They criticized the power of the corporation to extract "surplus value" from the worker and to swindle the consumer with high prices. Socialists also pointed out that these capitalists were protected by the capitalist state. They criticized trade barriers, exploitative central bank policy, and periodic crises driven by inflation. Yet the capitalist's power does not stem from the nature of markets: it is that power granted to them by the state. Even the richest capitalist, Bill Gates of Microsoft, cannot force you to purchase his product without the help of the state; nor can he force you to work for him rather than his competition; nor can he redistribute your wealth to another through inflationary policy. When corporations do leverage state power they can exploit the consumer, the worker and the taxpayer, but without this power they can only offer you their products at a competitive price.

Although socialists advocated planning to end the "anarchy of production" (as they described the market) and "commodity fetishism," the primary *ills of the system* that they criticized were not a result of market forces, but of a corporate capitalism that depended on state power. Hence, socialists might have set their aims at the wrong target. Perhaps the real power that should have been under scrutiny was that of the state.

The solution that socialists presented should be seen in this light: Socialism offers *more* power to the state, and nationalization of the corporations ties them even more closely to the government and its politics. Socialists viewed this positively because they believed that, with workers in power in the socialist government, the outcome would be beneficial. However, changing the faces of the political class may not produce different results if it is the structure and not the individuals that drives the outcome.

"Market socialists" have recognized this distinction and offer a new program that attempts to leverage the value of markets while still striving for the same socialist goals. The means they offer differ, but they aim to achieve the same ends as traditional socialists. Others argue for market systems free of government influence altogether, which they claim puts an end to the ills cited by socialists even better than a market-based socialism would because the market socialist solution still offers government too much power and influence on the allocation of investment.

The distinction between markets and corporate power is important. Traditional socialist arguments were against a "capitalism" in which the "ruling class" was business—in which business held the reins of government and used that power against the people. They did not argue against a market system in which business had no help from the state. Once this distinction is made, many of the socialist arguments make much more sense. It also becomes clear why their solution was misguided. Their solution was to strengthen this interference, enhance state power, and then simply to change the face that heads the system.

Some socialists could see this. Lenin, and especially Bukharin, warned of the dangers of "state capitalism," a highly concentrated form of "corporatism," and yet both spoke of how it was also the last step on the road to socialism. They explained that the system of planning would already be in place, and the only step left would be to replace the ruling capitalists with the new rulers, the proletarian class. Yet, this means that the system they feared and the one they advocated were essentially the same. If the system itself is repressive, unable to respond to the needs of the people, or dysfunctional in some other way, then it matters little who rules the system. Although socialists hoped that the state could wither away, and therefore the system itself would change, this turned out to be a Utopian dream.

In hindsight, it is easy to be cynical and say that they knew what they were doing—consolidating power and then taking the reins—but the evidence does not support this. Book after book was written supporting the theory that once the worker took the reins of power the need for control would dissolve: The people would find true freedom. Once in power, it appears that an attempt was made for democracy, equality, and liberty. However, power was necessary to run the economy based on a plan and to distribute the proceeds, so the state could not wither away. Of course, even if the Bolsheviks did know what would happen, surely the many intellectuals who followed them did not.

The Soviet experiment to cure the ills of corporatism with increased power to the state offers a useful case study, and helps to shed light on the distinction between free markets and corporate capitalism.

THE SOCIALIST ARGUMENT

Socialists argued that they could end the periodic crises of capitalism, the power of the ruling class of capitalists, and the expropriation of the workers through worker control of the planned economy. Their arguments were often directed against state intervention on behalf of the capitalists. The following passage from *The ABC of Communism* begins as if it is written by an advocate of free markets. It describes intervention commonly known as interest-seeking, or rent-seeking, and "trusts," which cannot survive without aid from government:

> Here the "democratic" administration of President Wilson is nothing more than a servant of the trusts. Congress merely carries out what has previously been decided at secret conclaves of trust magnates and bankers. The trusts spend vast sums in buying congressmen, in financing electoral campaigns, and the like. Myers, an American writer, reports that in the year 1904, the great life insurance companies spent the following sums in bribes: the Mutual, $364,254; the Equitable, $172,698; the New York, $204,019. The minister for finance, McAdoo, Wilson's son-in-law, is one of the leading bank and trust magnates. Senators, ministers of State, congressmen, are merely the henchmen of the great trusts, unless they themselves hold large interests in these bodies. The State authority, the governmental machinery of the "free republic," is nothing more than a workshop for the fleecing of the public.
>
> We can therefore say that a capitalist country under the dominion of financial capital is as a whole transformed into an immense combined trust. At the head of this trust are the banks. The bourgeois government forms its executive committee.[1]

Yet, this is structurally identical to what the socialists themselves proposed. The system that the communists were arguing against, they also proposed as the solution. The only difference is that their system was to be run in the name of the people. Lenin himself described socialism as a system unified as if in "a single office and a single factory,"[2] and Bukharin and Preobrazhensky described it as "one vast people's workshop."[3]

Wall Street and the bankers of "financial capital" held sway over the "trusts" engaged in production, but socialists saw this as a step in the right direction. They only wanted to replace the executive committee of the capitalist government with the executive committee of the Soviet government. (As we saw in Chapter 7, the Soviet government did become the executive committee of the single central bank.) Socialists saw that the first step toward planning under socialism would be to put an end to the "anarchy of production," which they saw as a feature of the system they despised: capitalism. Control over banking could help them to achieve this end.

> In individual countries the effect of the sway of financial capital is, in a certain measure, to put an end to the anarchy of capitalist production. The various producers, who have hitherto been fighting one another, now join forces in a State capitalist trust.[4]

The socialist system would be the same, but with worker control. As Lenin said, "socialism is merely state-capitalist monopoly *which is made to serve the interests of the whole people* and has to that extent ceased to be capitalist monopoly."[5] In order to allow the people to have the reins of power, the economy had to be in the power of the state.

The difference would be who controlled the reins of power. As Bukharin explained in *Economics of the Transition Period*:

> [T]he same method is formally necessary for the working class as for the bourgeoisie at the time of state capitalism. This organizational method exists in the coordination of all proletarian organizations with one all-encompassing organization, i.e., with the state organization of the working class, with the *Soviet state of the proletariat*.... Thus, the system of state capitalism dialectically transforms itself into its own inversion, into the state form of worker's socialism.[6]

So, if socialism was structurally identical, what was the purpose of revolution? The difference lay in whom the state represented. Capitalist control meant exploitation of the people, while worker control would mean a fair and just distribution of the proceeds of society. In Marxist terminology, the consolidation of the capitalist system would reach its peak with a state-capitalist planned economy and then dialectically transform into a socialist economy, which would allow the state to wither away. The evils of state capitalism were outlined first by Marx and later by Lenin and Bukharin. Marx described it in military terms, with the people enslaved in a vast authoritarian factory:

> Modern Industry has converted the little workshop of the patriarchal master into the great factory of the industrial capitalist. Masses of labourers, crowded into the factory, are organised like soldiers. As privates of the industrial army they are placed under the command of a perfect hierarchy of officers and sergeants. Not only are they slaves of the bourgeois class, and of the bourgeois State; they are daily and hourly enslaved by the machine, by the overlooker, and, above all, by the individual bourgeois manufacturer himself. The more openly this despotism proclaims gain to be its end and aim, the more petty, the more hateful and the more embittering it is.[7]

This vision of capitalist society, with "corporate hierarchy" extending throughout society pitted the worker against the capitalist, who was seen as enslaving him. It was the vision of a caste society, divided into two distinct classes that did not overlap or mix. Marx believed that the continuing consolidation of capitalist power would drive the wages of the workers lower and lower until class warfare became revolution.

Bukharin went further than Marx in his description of the totalitarian nature of the bourgeois planned economy. He described the capitalist-run planned economy and the evils that it would contain in 1928, at the start of the first 5-year plan, in his book *Imperialism and the World Economy*:

> [W]e would have an entirely new economic form. This would be capitalism no more, for the production of *commodities* would have disappeared; still less would it be *socialism*, for the power of one class over the other would have remained (and even grown stronger). Such an economic structure would, most of all, resemble a slaveowning economy where the slave market is absent.[8]

Socialists argued that class domination would end when the workers took control. The workers would be in charge, and workers were the majority. Soon, because production would be owned commonly, all citizens would be workers. Ultimately, all of the people would be in control both of the state and of production. At that point the state would no longer be required, and would dissolve away.

Bukharin saw the danger in the concentration of power that planning requires. Yet he believed that, as long as socialists succeeded in their revolution, they could ensure the dialectical transformation and the dissolution of the state and its powers. When the plan was under the control of the bourgeoisie, he described this "slave-state" as a "New Leviathan":

> Thus emerges the finished type of the contemporary imperialist robber state, the iron organization, which with its tenacious, raking claws embraces the living body of society. This is the New Leviathan, beside which the fantasy of Thomas Hobbes looks like a child's toy. For the time being there is no force on earth that might be its equal — *Non est potestas super terram quae comparetur ei.* [There is no power on earth that can compare with it.][9]

However, under rational economic planning guided by the workers, this power would be put to good use. Bukharin imagined an abundance that the socialist planners could distribute widely and freely to all the people. Greater productivity and equality would bring prosperity to all. Furthermore, at that point there would no longer be need of the state. Marx explained that "the chief function of state power is the guaranteeing of the process of exploitation."[10] Thus, the state itself would not be necessary once socialism reached its higher stage. It would "wither away."

Thus the primary difference between the slave-state of planning under capitalist control and the Utopian vision of planning under socialist control was that socialists could ensure that production was democratic and distribution was egalitarian. Bukharin emphasized how the structure of the system itself was not different: "[In state-capitalism] a planned economy exists, organized distribution not only in relation to the links and interrelationship between the various branches of production, but also in relation to consumption." Furthermore, just as in a socialist planned economy, "The slave in this society receives his share of provisions, of goods constituting the product of the general labor." In both kinds of planned economy the plan directs all of production and consumption, and the "slave" or citizen follows the commands of the plan, and receives a portion of the proceeds of the total output. "He may receive very little, but all the same there will be no crises," Bukharin added. There would be no crises because Marxists argued that crises were driven by banks driving overproduction in a market society, and would not occur in a planned economy.[11]

Another difference is that although state capitalism was structurally identical to socialism, it contained seeds of its own "barbaric demise." Bukharin explains the historical path to destruction: Because capitalist consolidation ends competition within a country, "it gives rise to a fierce and embittered competition between the various states," in other words, to imperialist war. The planned economy under socialists was to be international, and socialists could put an end to war.

The evidence that socialists pointed to of these "seeds of demise" within capitalism were all incidences of state intervention. Socialists admitted that "When two manufacturers compete with one another, they do not attack one another with knives, but attempt to steal one another's custom by peaceful methods."[12] The explanation for why this "fierce competition" between states must become violent is found elsewhere. Socialists found it in tariffs, syndicates, and trusts, and the collaboration of business and government. Bukharin explained in his book *Imperialism and the World Economy*:

> When we now survey the world economy as a whole, there appears before our eyes the following picture. Cartel tariffs and the dumping system practiced by the foremost countries provoke resistance on the part of the backward countries which raise their defensive tariffs; on the other hand the raising of tariffs by the backward countries serves as a further stimulus to raise the cartel duties that make dumping easier....
>
> ...England, that citadel of free trade, is in a period of transition; there is an increasing number of ever sharper and more persistent voices demanding fair trade instead of free trade, i.e., the introduction of a protectionist system.[13]

The protectionist system, as Marxists understood, could be used to protect the power of the state and of the big corporations. This power in the hands of a few—the vast riches and the control over policy together—was very dangerous because it could lead to war. Socialists cited the "syndicates" that were protected by the state as a leading cause of consolidation of industry and tying of business to state, ultimately leading to wars between capitalist countries. Syndicates were not simply companies that banded together or formed merger agreements; they were industries or groups of firms protected from competition by government. Bukharin explained that the syndicates could enhance their profits by eliminating competition:

> The syndicated capitalists kill two birds with one stone. In the first place they free themselves from foreign competition. Secondly, to the buyers of their own land, they are able to raise prices by an amount nearly equal to that of the tariff.... *If the industry were not syndicated, the internal competition between the capitalists of the country we are considering would immediately lead to price cutting.* But if there is a syndicate in control, it has no difficulty in raising prices, for the foreigner is kept out of the market by the customs barrier, and *owing to the syndication of the industry* there is no competition in the homeland. Insofar as there are any imports, the State revenue benefits, while the syndicated manufacturers secure additional surplus value in consequence of the enhanced price. *This can only take place where there is a syndicate or trust.* But that is not the end of the affair. Thanks to these surplus profits, the syndicated manufacturers are able to introduce their goods into other countries and to sell them there below cost price simply in order to supplant all competitors in those countries. [Emphasis added.][14]

Without the aid of the state, businesses could not engage in this power-grabbing, monopolization, or exploitation. But together, both firm and state could benefit: The syndicates gain monopoly profits, and the state gains revenue. This collaboration of business and government in violation of free market principles then leads to war—because revenue can only be collected within the area that the state controls:

> Now, the customs area usually coincides with the area administered by the State. How can this latter be enlarged? By grabbing some foreign territory, by annexing it, by including it within one's own frontiers, within one's own governmental area. But this means war.[15]

It is this collusion between the state and business that socialists cite as the cause for imperialist wars. Business alone could not trigger war, nor extract the monopoly profits, and the state, if restrained from laying tariffs or protecting cartels, would not have this incentive to go to war.

Bukharin goes on to explain how these same policies lead to foreign investment that is also protected by the state, the protection brings higher prices and revenues and a rush for new territory.[16] In addition to war, socialists argued that "periodic crises" were inherent to capitalism and that they would ultimately ruin the economy. Every seven years or so, a crisis would strike the economy and impoverish the people.[17]

Economists call these business cycles and are not in agreement on their cause, but as discussed in Chapter 7, there are good arguments to be made that government entanglement in the economy, through inflationary monetary policy and other policies, helps to trigger or inflate the bubbles that precede each crash. Socialists also pointed to inflationary monetary policy as the cause of the periodic crises. As Marx said, "Banking and credit thus become the most potent means of driving capitalist production beyond its own limits, and one of the most effective vehicles of crises and swindle."[18]

Marxists saw the power that centralized monetary policy had in the hands of the capitalist government and argued that it hurt the workers. "The government slashes into the real income of the workers by its monetary measures and policies,"[19] they argued, but their proposed solution was to increase state power over banking, by putting it entirely under "worker control." As Lenin said, "[O]nly control over the banks, over the centre, over the pivot and chief mechanism of capitalist circulation, would make it possible to organise real and not fictitious control over all economic life."[20]

For all the above reasons, the socialists argued that the capitalist system would have to crumble and end in chaos, unless it was replaced by the rational planning of socialism. Yet this "rational planning" was only an enhancement of the state control that they despised. The link between corporations and the state that they criticized led to an "immense combined trust" with bankers and politicians at its head. It led to monopoly corporate prices and the taxes from them that drove the state to war; and it led to monetary policy that caused financial crises and impoverishment of consumers. In all these cases, it was state control and combination with business that allowed these ills, yet the socialist solution was to enhance—not reduce—state control and combination.

Perhaps they believed that the state could keep the corporations in check, that it was that half that caused the ills. But what is a corporation? It is only a decentralized actor, given whatever power it has by the state or by the consumer. If the firm has no power given by the state, can it exploit the consumer? Can it form a trust and dominate the market? Can it wage war? Can it control prices and money and cause periodic crises? Or can only the state produce these things? Socialists themselves pointed to protectionism and government policy as their cause.

And what is the government? Even if run by well-meaning socialists, the state is a monopoly. It is a centralization of power able to cause all the ills that socialists described, and when given enough power can become "the iron organization, which with its tenacious, raking claws embraces the living body of society."

The Soviet Experience

> Who's the Boss: we or the law? We are masters over the law,
> not the law over us—so we have to change the law; we have to
> see to it that it is possible to execute these speculators! — Nikita
> Khrushchev[21]

How was it that this workers' state, so promising for socialists in theory, became so powerful, and ruled with such an iron fist? It turns out that the theory itself endorsed the high level of power. Socialists recognized the need for such power to stamp out the evils of capitalism—the bad elements (profiteers) that would fight against their program. They saw that this power would be necessary to ensure the implementation of the workers' program and to direct the economy. Marx described the "dictatorship of the proletariat," arguing that

> Between capitalist and communist society there lies the period of the revolutionary transformation of the one into the other. Corresponding to this is also a political transition period in which the state can be nothing but the revolutionary dictatorship of the proletariat.[22]

Yet this could be seen as temporary, and the power was to be used for the good of the people, to set up a state that would serve the interests of the people, not dominate them. The new state was not supposed to bow to moneyed or powerful interests. Worker control over production, wielded for the good of all the people, was to replace the interest-seeking bourgeois political process. The moneyed interests were powerful; hence, a powerful force would be required to quash them. *The ABC of Communism* reminded the workers how it was under capitalism:

> [L]et us remember the enormous financial resources of the trust magnates, which enable them to corrupt the workers' representatives—however honest these may have been at the outset—by offering comfortable jobs, by flattery in the daily press, and so on. Then we can understand why it is that even in such parliaments the majority always consists of the secret or declared agents of the bourgeoisie, of financial capital, of the bank kings.[23]

The new workers' republic would not allow this because the capitalists, while there were still any left, would have no power. The socialist revolution had replaced "capitalist" control with worker control. This was not an empty promise—the Soviet government did, in fact, introduce new powers for the worker. The state represented the interests of the workers because only workers and poor peasants could vote. As *The ABC of Communism* reminded the people:

> Here the parasites—the traders and the factory owners, the prelates and the landlords, the military officers and the rich peasants—have no right to the vote. They can neither elect nor be elected. On the other hand, the exercise of the franchise by the workers and the poor peasants is simple and easy.[24]

Yet the corruption, through promise of "comfortable jobs" and "flattery in the daily press," remained. The individuals giving and receiving flattery and jobs changed, but the power to give and receive remained. In fact, it was enhanced. With the state now able to control every position within the economy, the possibility for "corruption" of the workers' representatives and the use of political power as a device to trade favors for monetary and other rewards were vastly expanded. However, it all ran through the political hierarchy.

The flattery, rent-seeking, and corruption of the bourgeois economy were replaced with flattery and bribery within the planned economic system of the socialist economy. Firm managers in the planned economy could still seek to influence the political powers to give them favors. The economic and the political had just united under the plan into one hierarchy.

In a corporatist economy the two are distinct. Firms are privately owned but the property right is shared with the state through subsidies, regulations and taxes. Firm owners, or "capitalists," in Marxian terms, can bribe politicians for favors. In the Soviet economy, the firm owner had no actual property rights over the firm, hence he had no economic power with which to sway the political actor, but his position was still the same. If he could win the favor of the political actor he was given advantage: Promotions in all areas of economic life were tied to political connections.[25] "No significant economic appointment, whoever is nominally responsible for making it, can in fact be made without at the very least the approval of a party committee."[26]

Without economic power the best way to gain favors from the politician was by doing what the politician desired. One had to prove his allegiance to the Party line and to the Party in order to gain favors and to be promoted.

This hierarchy ran through all areas of industrial and rural economic life. Political power ascended through the Communist Party in a rigid hierarchy. The most important posts were filled by top Party officials through a system known as the *nomenklatura*.

> The term "nomenklatura" literally means nothing more than "nomenclature": it is a list of positions, arranged in order of seniority, including a description of the duties of each office. Its political importance comes from the fact that the party's nomenklatura—and it alone—contains the most important leading positions in all organized activities of social life. Other intermediate positions are contained in institutional nomenklatury, but these are subject to supervision, if not specific approval, by the party. Rank-and-file cadres are managed by institutional authorities; the party oversees this work as well.[27]

The commands of the plan and the will of the "vanguard of the proletariat," which was embodied in the Party,[28] replaced the "bourgeois" concept of "equality before the law." According to socialist theory, equality before the law was not true equality. Instead, the will of the people should be law. Hence, the vanguard of the Party, which led the building of the new system, was shielded from the law, and the Nomenklatura were also beyond the reach of socialist law.[29]

As mentioned in Chapter 9, it was not only appointed state firm positions, but also elected positions that came under this economic-political hierarchy.

> In the Communist party and in other organizations the *nomenklatura* system governs not only appointive positions but also elective ones. This applies to many personnel mentioned in the foregoing discussion (for example, kolkhoz and soviet executive committee chairmen, party secretaries, and heads of non-party organizations), as well as to the delegates selected for every kind of congress (party, soviet, trade union, Komsomol, writers', and those of other professions). As well as con-

trol over personnel, of course, this gives the secretariat of the CPSU tremendous control over policy in all spheres of Soviet public life. The slate of an organization's executive up for election consists of names approved beforehand by the corresponding or higher party body, and hardly ever contains more candidates than there are posts to be filled. What often happens is that a party secretary or a union leader is a complete stranger to the organization that "elects" him. Very rarely such a person is rejected by the local people—to the undoubted consternation of his sponsors. Cases of such overt manipulation of elections are frequently criticized, but they seem inevitable where reliability is more important than the democratic element in "democratic centralism."[30]

Hence, the state or the Party, which was in control of the state,[31] as its vanguard, although not "capitalist" because it was not influenced by private economic actors, was in control of every aspect of economic and social life, just as in Bukharin's "New Leviathan." The Party was the representative of the "workers" which ran the state, and it used political control to keep the economic actors in line.

[P]arty organizations are expected to supervise the management of personnel in every public organization and, where necessary, to interfere and offer "guidance." Instructions to this effect are clear: "There is not in the economic, cultural and social life of the [district] a question such as would not interest the Party body. There is no such enterprise or *kolkhoz*, no soviet, economic or other institution for whose work the Party organization does not bear responsibility."[32]

This control was supposed to ensure that the will of the workers was done. However, as discussed in Chapter 9, planning required hierarchy and often conflicted with the will of individuals in the society. The desire for power also did not dissolve after the revolution.

Although the enhancement of state power was intended to ensure that production be directed for the good of the people, it resulted in authoritarian governance and an economy guided by political and uneconomic motives. In 1943, one socialist lamented, "The past fifteen years of economic progress and political transformation in Russia are the years of the rise and consolidation of a new type of slave-state, with a new type of ruling class."[33] This was precisely what Bukharin had predicted would occur if capitalists were in charge, but it appeared not to matter that his socialist Party had taken control.

The state was expected to wither away once the economy reached abundance. The socialists promised to deliver equality and an end of scarcity in return for greater power. But this was not something they could deliver. Planners, whatever their intentions, were not capable of guiding the economy efficiently. Just as the "slave state" described by Bukharin offered the slave a portion of the society's proceeds—but very little—so under the socialist government the worker received only very little. Their idealized society depended on abundance, but the system could not produce abundance. The result was simply the pre-dialectical-transformation system of Leviathan described by Bukharin.

The end to the business cycle arguably also did not materialize. Socialists had been sure that the chaos, "periodic crises" or business cycles, and recessions would end. Instead, the entire economy was dragged into a permanent depression, and there were still recessions[34] within this depression. The underlying problems of inflation and "malinvestment" also remained. As described in Chapter 7, control over monetary policy did not allow planners to prevent "bubbles" forming due to low interest rates—even after they reintroduced capital charges. Low interest charges still drove unsustainable, uneconomic projects, and planners could not determine what interest rate was necessary to prevent this. Inflation persisted in a hidden form and continued to eat away at the living standards of workers.

Finally, worker control over the economy did not prevent the state from engaging in protectionism, or from expanding its territory. Disarming the corporation but not the state arguably did not end any of the major ills of "capitalism" that Marx criticized. Worker controlled or capitalist controlled, the state remained the state.

LESSONS

Socialists were concerned about the power of government, and its misuse by Hitler and others in Europe. Yet their remedy was to provide government with even more power in order to put the socialists' program into practice. Even if property owners were not averse to the program, the government would need to assume additional powers. Economic centralization and planning required far more power, and concentration of power, than the market-based system. (See Chapter 9.) In fact, the precise powers of the state that socialists criticized became central to the socialist system.

This lesson is important when considering criticism of concentrations of power and remedies to it in market economies. An article written by a Marxist in 1934 about Franklin D. Roosevelt complained about the additional powers that Roosevelt was assuming:

> The "Europeanization" of America has reached a new stage with President Roosevelt's Labor Day message to Congress. Government by decree—the kind of authoritarian government conducted in Germany by Bruening and Von Schleicher, the immediate predecessors of Hitler; in France by Daladier, the organizer of France's defeat—is on the order of the day, Roosevelt declared, in the following words: "In the event that the Congress should fail to act and act adequately, I shall accept the responsibility, and I will act." Unless Congress, before an October 1 deadline, changes its parity legislation on farm products, Roosevelt would violate the existing law....
>
> Roosevelt has followed up his Labor Day threat with a few examples of presidential decrees. On September 9 he decreed the abolition of all premium pay for weekends and holidays, thereby abrogating with a stroke of his pen the many provisions in existing union contracts providing for such overtime pay. On September 14 he decreed that the 2,300,000 federal employees could henceforth be transferred from job to job, into factories or other work, as Manpower Commissioner McNutt sees fit; thereby in effect he abrogated all existing civil service legislation. Likewise on September 14 he ordered that workers in the lumber and non-ferrous metals industries in twelve western states may not leave their jobs without permits, on pain of reclassification and drafting into the army; this decree put teeth in a September 7 order by McNutt freezing to their jobs the workers in these industries.[35]

Decrees, of course, were the primary instrument of the Soviet government. Stalin, during the same period as the above actions by Roosevelt, issued thousands of decrees each year.[36] The power was similarly used—to set prices and to change contracts set by workers' unions. Workers were forcibly kept in their jobs in the Soviet Union as well. The socialist remedy was not of the sort that could stop centralization of power and use of decrees.

The article on Roosevelt goes on to name the socialist demands: an automatically rising scale of wages as prices rise, democratic committees on prices and rationing, nationalization of the war industries under workers' control, and a "Workers' and Farmers' Government." In other words, they wanted to put the "workers" in charge and represent them with "democratic committees," but keep the government powerful enough and positioned to set prices, direct industry, change contracts, and ration goods. This was in fact identical to the experiment in Russia that led to Stalin's government, but under Stalin these ills were enhanced, not eliminated.

The criticism of Roosevelt was that he was seizing too many powers, issuing decrees, and changing contracts made independently by workers and unions. Yet the proposed solution would leave this power intact and simply replace Roosevelt with a central "democratic" committee (in Russian, a "soviet"). In the Soviet Union, power was supposed to be based on a broad democracy as well, yet the structure of the government and the logistics of planning led to dictatorial control instead. (See Chapter 9.) It should not have been surprising that this would occur. One economist made a similar case regarding Lenin's proposed solution to capitalism, which like the proposal of the socialists criticizing Roosevelt, handed more power to the state:

> The elected deputies are to be civil servants, ministers and representatives of their constituents at one and the same time. They have to make the laws, carry them out *and* criticize them.... If [Lenin] is accepting that there are dangerous potentialities in the roles of a representative, of a legislator, of a civil servant and of a minister, his answer to those dangers borders on the absurd: conflate all these roles into one, embody them in a single individual.[37]

If one criticizes the power of the state it makes no sense to propose giving it more power. Even if those that head the new state are well intentioned and believe in democracy and freedom, they may find themselves ruling dictatorially. Economist Don Lavoie argued that Lenin expected "the bureaucrat to respond both to democratic pressures from below and to a coordinated plan being received from above," but by assuming this, Lenin just "evaded the real problems of bureaucracy."[38] Even with the best intent, if a plan is at the top of the hierarchy, democracy and freedom may be consumed by the plan. Similarly, it seems unlikely that a democratic committee on prices and rationing, combined with nationalization, is a good program to replace the "capitalist" system of price setting and rationing that Roosevelt had put in place.

The assertion that the people in charge—democratic committees of workers—are the primary issue at hand is not convincing. Democracy of the plan was not realistic in the Soviet Union because the plan required a select few at the top of the hierarchy to ensure consistency, and the minorities and individuals affected were forced to fulfill commands with which they disagreed.

Whether the firm or the state is nominally in charge, the results may be identical. If advantages to businesses that let them ignore consumers are bad, then why would it be better to completely remove the profit and loss constraints that force firms to serve the consumer? If subsidizing firms produces bad results, is the best answer to nationalize them?

The proposal by socialists of a planned economy is much closer to the system they criticized than is a market economy. Rudolf Hilferding, a socialist and contemporary of Lenin, on whose work Lenin and Bukharin based much of their analysis, wrote about the planned economy. Like Bukharin and Lenin, he wrestled with the notion of "state capitalism" and the difference between a totalitarian planned economy and the socialist Utopia that they all hoped would emerge from the revolution. Yet he viewed capitalism as incompatible with planning—perhaps he took a more "free market" view on the nature of capitalism:

> The concept of "state capitalism" can scarcely pass the test of serious economic analysis. Once the state becomes the exclusive owner of all means of production, the functioning of a capitalist economy is rendered impossible by destruction of the mechanism which keeps the life-blood of such a system circulating. A capitalist economy is a market economy. Prices, which result from competition among capitalist owners (it is this competition that "in the last instance" gives rise to the law of value), determine what and how much is produced, what fraction of the profit is accumulated, and in what particular branches of production this accumulation occurs. They also determine how in an economy, which has to overcome crises again and again, proportionate relations among the various branches of production are re-established whether in the case of [consumer goods or investment].
>
> A capitalist economy is governed by the laws of the market (analyzed by Marx) and the autonomy of these laws constitutes the decisive symptom of the capitalist system of production. A state economy, however, eliminates precisely the autonomy of economic laws.... It is no longer price but rather a state planning commission that now determines what is produced and how. Formally, prices and wages still exist, but their function is no longer the same; they no longer determine the process of production which is now controlled by a central power that fixes prices and wages.... While maintaining the form, a complete transformation of function has occurred.[39]

Indeed, just as Lenin and Bukharin claimed, socialism was the same form of "state economy" that they despised, yet as Hilferding points out here, this is not what a market economy is. Hilferding also indicated in this passage that a market economy, if it undergoes a crisis, has an automatic mechanism for recovering: market prices ensure that "proportionate relations among the various branches of production are re-established." Prices do this in a market economy, but this function was not reproducible in the socialist economy because prices were set centrally.

Although it is unpopular to say so today, socialism is more similar to fascism than to a free market economy. In the 1940s, an economist described the similarity in the *American Economic Review*, a prestigious economic journal:

> Communists say of German national socialism and Italian fascism that they represent no fundamental change in the economic order.

> ...I believe, indeed, that there are perhaps greater resemblances between national socialism and fascism on the one hand and the soviet system on the other than there are between national socialism and fascism and old style capitalism.
>
> ...It is my belief that the laissez faire aspect of modern capitalism has been perhaps its most determinative characteristic. Whenever laissez faire is abandoned, something drastic has happened to the capitalist system.
>
> ...[T]he essence of both national socialism and Italian fascism is opposed to laissez faire. Italian fascism insists that the interests of the nation must be placed before those of the individual or his property. Thus an owner of agricultural land may be compelled to raise wheat instead of sheep and employ more labor than he would find profitable.
>
> ...The paramount interest for German national socialists is the race rather than the nation, but from the economic point of view this difference is of small moment.[40]

Socialism was more centralized than the "corporatist" economy that Marx saw emerging in the Western capitalist countries and was even more centralized than the Nazi economy, which socialists saw as representing a sort of "state capitalist" economy. The state was never able to "wither away," so the "New Leviathan" described by Bukharin remained the nature of the socialist planned economy.

Western "capitalist" governments never reached this level of power concentration, despite the trend that socialists perceived. Perhaps this is because the "class" power that socialists argued was inherent in capitalism, and which explained the need for government to be intimately tied to corporations, was mistaken. Socialists never theorized about the rise of the entrepreneurial class, although this class was rising in Russia at the time of the revolution, and was far more advanced in "capitalist" countries. In a free market, the small business owner or "entrepreneur" can challenge big business. If big business is not protected—as Marx assumed that they were—by the state, then this factor can transform the economy and the standard of living of the entire population. "Class warfare" is only possible if individuals are not mobile between classes—but an entrepreneurial economy is one in which workers daily become capitalists.[41]

However, the more government protects the interests of big business, as Marx had argued, the less this is possible. This is a crucial distinction in an analysis of modern capitalist economies. While the pre-revolution socialists had argued that capitalism was consolidating and leading to "state-capitalism" and that the state was acting in the interests of the capitalists as a class, a more subtle distinction later emerged from socialist analysis.

The second edition of the official Soviet textbook, *The Political Economy of Contemporary Modern Capitalism*, written in 1974, stated the mainline position of the Communist Party on this matter. The first edition had stressed only that the capitalist state reflected the "class interests" of the capitalist class, but the second edition was more refined. It informed readers that some capitalist concerns could have greater use of government power than others. It reads much like the criticisms by "public choice" economists about the interest-seeking (or "rent-seeking") of modern corporatist economies.

> Depending on the force of these pressures [of the different business groups]...
> the concrete goals of governmental regulation can reflect the demands of monop-
> olistic capital for a maximization of current profits to a greater or lesser degree.
> It can to a certain extent favour the interests of some groups of monopolies over
> others.[42]

More recently, "market socialists," recognizing the benefits of the market, have
made this distinction more explicitly.[43] It is far less common to hear this sort of argument within the public discussion of government regulations: that government uses
its regulatory power to protect certain businesses from competition, making them
monopolies and preventing competition and innovation, and that in return these
businesses offer favors and perks to government officials.

Many critics of the heavily regulated U.S. mortgage industry, including of the
government-sponsored enterprises, have suggested nationalization as a cure. Yet nationalization may not reduce the political exchanges and cannot reduce the government protection from competition or the distortions from subsidies. Instead, as in the
Soviet Union, it simply becomes institutionalized.

Still, few critics of capitalism distinguish explicitly among these problems. Instead, many conflate the problems of corporate power with perceived problems of
the market. A recent article in *Forbes* magazine written by economists Art Carden
and Steve Horwitz made this case while critiquing another writer, Jane Smiley, for
confusing these two systems:

> Some notable exceptions notwithstanding, it is—as Smiley writes—"human
> nature to cheat, monopolize and buy off others." But *we see this as a reason to distrust
> politics rather than markets*. Political incentives exacerbate knavery. Centralizing
> power in the hands of the state, which is Smiley's implied alternative to free mar-
> kets, will not make things better. It will put more power in the hands of the sorts
> of people Smiley fears.
>
> ...Smiley, like so many others, confuses "capitalism" with "corporatism." Being
> in favor of capitalism, in the sense of free markets, does not mean we support
> whatever is in capitalists' interests. We support competitive markets, which often
> work against the interests of capitalists who would generally prefer cozy monopo-
> listic relationships with the state, such as those likely to result if the state gets
> more power.[44]

Some market socialists, like Oskar Lange mention in Chapter 1, have argued that
free markets would be desirable if perfect competition were possible. In the absence
of perfectly free competition, they argued that market socialism is preferable to corporatism.[45] Some others on the left today also make this distinction and see the recent
bank and automobile company bailouts in the U.S. and Europe as corporatist, and
hence worse than free markets.

Michael Hudson, an economist and author of *Super-Imperialism: The Economic Strategy of American Empire*, and chief economic adviser to Representative Dennis Kucinich
during his 2008 presidential campaign, argued against these policies:

> [Government bailouts are] the worst possible move, and [they] puts the class
> war back in business with a vengeance. Wall Street has been preparing for this
> for years, because every financial analyst knows that the debts can't be paid. And
> the question that Wall Street has, if you're going to take a gamble on bad debts

> that can't be paid, how are you going to come out a winner? And there's only one way of coming out a winner, and that's to make the government bail you out. This has been known for years.... Every banker I know knew that the loans they were making were going to go bad. They were trying to sell them to somebody else, ultimately expecting them to end up with some sovereign wealth fund.
>
> ...When the debts exceed the ability to pay, there's only one thing any economy can do, and that's wipe them out. Instead, the government is trying to keep the fiction alive.[46]

Bailouts are not free market policy. They compromise the institutions of private property. They are a policy of corporatism, and the discretionary government aid is what economists call "rent-seeking." Socialists were against corporatism, or state-capitalism as they called it. Yet their solution was to nationalize these companies, putting them on permanent government subsidy. This made the companies even less responsive to consumers and completely dependent on government. Compared to state-capitalism, the balance of power may have been shifted from the corporation to the government, but the political class and the managerial, or capitalist, class were still tied together, often so closely as to be indistinguishable. On paper, profits accrued to the state under socialism, while they accrued to the capitalist under state-capitalism, yet under both the profit and power were shared by a small group of economic and political elite, and the population was enslaved.

Similarly, nationalizing the banks or mortgage companies would not resolve the problems that Hudson identified. Only forcing them to submit to the consumers' will (letting them "wipe out") would. Putting these firms on permanent government subsidy would only exacerbate the problem. For the power to return to the people the consumer must have control, not the state-firm monopoly that subsidies or "corporatism" creates. The firms need to face a hard budget constraint, and the state must be restrained to just protecting these property rights. The basic institutions of property, the free market, must be reintroduced.

Another author from the left, Naomi Klein, author of *The Shock Doctrine: The Rise of Disaster Capitalism*, has similarly written that there is danger in bailing out companies:

> We're really heading to a future where there will be, you know, three or four large banks, all of them too big to fail, which means that if they take more—they take more and more risks, which nobody is asking them not to. It's important to understand that in exchange for the bailout money, the banks are not being told that they can't carry the incredible leverage rates that we saw, for instance, at Bear Stearns, thirty-three to one. They aren't being told that they can't invest in these high-risk, complex financial instruments. They can still do whatever they want, but now they're even bigger, which means that if they get themselves into trouble again, they will be bailed out again.[47]

For many of these critics, though, nationalization would offer a good solution: Then government could force the banks to reduce their leverage and not to invest in risky assets. Then it would not be "privatized profit and socialized loss." Profit would be socialized, too. The bankers had exploited the bubble and profited, nationalization would remove this profit motive. The Revolutionary Communist Group criticized Fannie Mae and Freddie Mac with many of the same arguments made in this book, pointing out the way that subsidies distort the incentives of the management, create bubbles, and allow political favoritism to replace economic decision making. Yet they conclude, "The only workable solution to the problem is to cancel all residential mortgages and to implement a housing program which ensures that people are housed on the basis of need, not wealth."[48]

Yet, that would be a simple extension of what is already occurring. *The Wall Street Journal* reported that on Christmas Eve, the U.S. Treasury announced that it was "lifting the $400 billion cap on potential losses for Fannie Mae and Freddie Mac as well as the limits on what the failed companies can borrow." The article explained that,

> The loss cap is being lifted because the government has *directed* both companies to pursue money-losing strategies by modifying mortgages to prevent foreclosures. Most of their losses are still coming from subprime and Alt-A mortgage bets made during the boom, but Fannie reported last quarter that loan modifications resulted in $7.7 billion in losses, up from $2.2 billion the previous quarter.[49]

Mainstream economists made the argument for nationalization too. Nationalization, some said, would allow government to contain risk. This was much like the socialists' argument. More power and control would allow the workers to direct resources—choose what loans are worth the risk. The imbalance seen as causing the crisis was that profit was privatized but loss was socialized. This can be corrected one of two ways: privatize both or socialize both. The Soviet experience is informative here. The state bank in the Soviet Union took "too many risks" as well. It undertook many of its investments without full consideration for the true cost of capital. Many projects had to be abandoned. Interest rates were negligible if even positive, and this caused mass inefficiencies across the economy.

The lesson here is not about the Soviet government making a mistake that future governments can learn from, by setting interest rates appropriately.[50] It is not simply a lesson about politics or how best to control an economy. Even if politics is put aside, and rationality, foresight and democratic control over choices reign supreme, nationalization may exacerbate these issues not resolve them.

Planners, economists and central banks might think that they know that less lending must occur, for example, but nationalizing means that they will from that moment forward need to know the changing conditions of supply and demand without the guides of profit and loss. Any advantage in risk-reduction potentially gained by socializing the profit is voided by the inability of a nationalized bank to judge risk and reward.

Those on the left sometimes criticize central banking in more sophisticated ways than mainstream economists, often drawing on the work of socialist theory: Central banking fails because the center cannot know the appropriate prices, best investments, or the appropriate interest rate. It cannot prevent inflation or efficiently redistribute wealth. Yet too often the proposed solution to its failures is to enhance political control. Journalist William Greider of the magazine *The Nation* recently named six reasons why the Federal Reserve should not be granted more power. He then went on to endorse at least the same amount of power for the Federal Reserve—if not more—so long as it was "democratized."[51]

Greider argued that the bank has been "a central force in destabilizing the US economy" and "cannot examine 'systemic risk' objectively because it helped to create the very structural flaws that led to breakdown." He said that the Federal Reserve would continue with a policy of "too big to fail" and that this will lead to the "corporate state," which he defined as a "fusion of private and public power." Yet despite this list of grievances, Greider's conclusion is that the Federal Reserve should be "democratized" and put in the hands of Congress rather than stripped of its powers.[52]

Democratizing the Federal Reserve would not reduce its power. The democratic guidance of it—if it could be achieved—would not prevent it from interfering in inefficient ways and thereby destabilizing the economy. It could not prevent political, rather than economic, direction of the economy, and policies such as "too big to fail." It could not ensure that the bank would be able to judge systemic risk or even judge risk at all. Socialists thought that proletarian control of monetary policy could do all of these things, but the Soviet state bank was even less capable of judging risk and was under even more political control.

Another area in which political control was criticized by socialists was foreign policy. The dangers socialists perceived regarding expansion and foreign entanglements were based on tariffs and subsidies that would protect companies and reduce international competition. The socialist solution did not reduce these dangers, but instead gave the state more of a direct interest in production and expectation of revenue from firms, and therefore a more compelling reason to desire expansion. Instead of having an interest equal to a tax rate of twenty percent, for example, the state has an interest in the entire revenue of the firm after nationalization.

Just like protectionism, nationalization has the potential to introduce expansionist foreign policy. Even General Motors, which the U.S. government only very recently took a stake in, has had to contend with foreign policy questions.[53] GM has a German division, and German politicians apparently fear that under a U.S.-owned GM, German jobs at Opel would be at risk. Hence, they favor selling a subsidiary of the company to a Russian-Canadian consortium. GM's board rejected the plan, and the German foreign minister raised the issue with U.S. Secretary of State Hillary Clinton. Although this may be a minor foreign policy question, it already indicates that increased state control may make this kind of nationalistic concern more prominent to the company.

General Motors, now leveraging the power of the state, need not compete on a level playing field and can use the entire bureaucratic apparatus in its own favor. The tax and regulatory treatment of General Motors' competition is now made by General Motors: The same individuals on the GM executive board, with the largest stake in GM, also staff the regulatory agencies and determine tariffs on foreign car manufacturers and subsidies for auto parts industries. If it is politically expedient for the nationalized company to survive (even if it is less efficient), then these executive-politicians can kill off competitors through any of these means. Hence, nationalization is not a solution to the problem of tariffs and company leverage of political power—it only makes those more likely.

Another industry in the United States in which political leverage is widespread and nationalization is proposed as a solution is the health care industry. The health care bill currently before the US Congress (the "Patient Protection and Affordable Care Act") would mandate that insurers purchase a large number of specific health care products and services, most of which were lobbied for by the producers of these products and services. Already existing state law was created in a similar fashion. These companies have a far easier time making profit and winning against their competition if purchase of their product is required.

Although the public often views advocacy of mandates favorably (as moral) or neutrally (as harmless), this sort of advocacy should be scrutinized. If a company can go to Congress or Parliament and convince lawmakers to subsidize or mandate purchase of their product, why would they try to serve the customer instead? One trip to Washington could save massive amounts of actual productive work. (See Chapter 4.) Politicians and bureaucrats gain through increased power and wealth. (See Chapter 9.) This sort of maneuvering can also help to inflate the pocketbooks of those who invest heavily in these companies—those lucky individuals who gain by the uniting of political and economic interests.

An example of the exploitation of this corporatist unity of interest can be found in the alternative energy industry. Each alternative energy is quite distinct and has only a few leading companies. Securing a mandate for electricity companies to purchase one of them (or for gas companies to use ethanol) could send the stock prices of one of these companies skyrocketing. If "insider trading" is wrong within the private-sector corporate world, shouldn't it be seen as problematic for an individual to invest in one of these companies and then secure a governmental mandate for purchase of that specific technology?

Even if a technology is a good idea—leaving aside whether "picking winners" (as discussed in Chapter 4) among different technologies is a good idea or not—when government offers subsidies and tax breaks, it opens the door for this sort of "insider trading" within government. John Stossel recently pointed out a case of this on his show on Fox Business Network. The "stimulus bill" chose energy efficient windows as an investment plan. One firm, Serious Materials, seems to have reaped the primary benefit. It was visited by both the President and the Vice President of the United States, and cited in a tax bill as an "energy efficient" company to receive a significant tax credit. Serious Materials' main competitors were not so lucky, and as a result Serious Materials' stock rose dramatically, and the CEO was featured on the cover of *Fortune* and *Inc.* magazines.

Coincidentally, the vice president of policy of Serious Materials (their in-house lobbyist you might say) is married to a top Department of Energy government official, specializing in "weatherization," and responsible for choosing the "green" firms that are to receive government aid. Unsurprisingly, the company also invested heavily in the Obama campaign.[54] Watchdog.org also wrote about this case of crony capitalism:

> Last year Congress passed the American Recovery and Reinvestment Act (ARRA or the so-called Stimulus Bill). The US Department of Energy's office of Energy Efficiency and Renewable Energy (EERE) received $16.8 billion of those ARRA funds to be used to promote green energy and conservation programs including the popular $1,500 tax credit for homeowners who install energy-efficient windows. The Assistant Secretary of Energy, Cathy Zoi, is responsible for oversight in disbursing these stimulus funds.
>
> Ms. Zoi is married to Robin Roy, a top executive at Serious Materials, a privately held manufacturer of "sustainable green building materials" located in California. On the Executive Branch Personnel Public Financial Disclosure submitted by Ms. Zoi to the White House Ethics office as part of her confirmation, Ms. Zoi disclosed ownership with her spouse of 120,000 vested and unvested stock options in Serious Materials, a company her office regulates and that she may profit from.
>
> According to several news reports and the trade magazine *Window & Door*, Serious Materials was "[A] company, and a man, virtually unknown in the window and door industry just a short time ago." Yet this small California manufacturer suddenly burst on the scene in Washington as what Vice President Joe Biden called the "poster child" for green jobs and economic recovery. For the past several months, the White House has repeatedly praised and promoted Serious Materials.... "On the surface, this appears to be another case of government using tax dollars to pick winners and losers," said Annette Meeks, CEO of the Freedom Foundation of Minnesota. "Yet upon closer examination, it appears to be a bit more than that. Our research suggests that one window manufacturer that has very close ties to this Administration has received lavish attention and special tax breaks.[55]

If this company was unknown before being bestowed with special tax favors and subsidies that sent its stock price soaring, and the government official in charge of bestowing these favors was married to a top executive at the firm, this is little different from embezzlement of government (taxpayer) funds. Arguably it is even worse than one-time embezzlement, as the privilege granted the firm may be long-lasting. However, because Ms. Zoi reported her stock holding on her financial disclosure forms, this was probably entirely legal

Because he is a well known figure, it is also worth considering the example of former U.S. Vice President Al Gore. Gore already owned a large amount of stock in the Silver Spring Network, a company that produces "smart energy grids," when the Energy Department announced new "smart energy grid" grants. *The New York Times* reported:

> The deal appeared to pay off in a big way last week, when the Energy Department announced $3.4 billion in smart grid grants. Of the total, more than $560 million went to utilities with which Silver Spring has contracts. Kleiner Perkins and its partners, including Mr. Gore, could recoup their investment many times over in coming years.[56]

This subsidy will almost certainly boost the stock price of Silver Spring because it will be assured of demand at whatever price it sets for some time. Although Gore may not have specifically campaigned for smart grid grants—that would have called attention to this potential conflict or unity of interest—he has been a strong advocate of this sort of grant. He has called attention to the potential problem of global warming (and some say in the role of an alarmist), using his celebrity to spotlight the issue. He also maintains strong connections within Congress and the executive branch departments. It would not have been difficult for him to all but ensure that the company in which he invested benefited from grants of this sort.

Gore's defense is that he ought to be able to invest however he wishes. "Do you think there is something wrong with being active in business in this country?" the article quotes him as asking. "I am proud of it. I am proud of it."[57] This defense, however, conflates investing in companies subject to market competition with investing in companies that need only respond to political imperatives. It conflates investing and then working toward efficiency and customer satisfaction with investing and then requesting political favors that will boost the profits of the company without it having to serve the customer (and usually without having to please the voter, either). It conflates private property and free markets with crony capitalism, or "corporatism."

On the "other side" of the issue, there are oil company executives who lobby Congress for subsidies and protections for oil companies.[58] Some of them may personally invest and reap millions as well. It is the nature of corporatism that this "rent-seeking" behavior will occur, and individuals will gain at the expense of the public, as economic and political interests merge. Some have played both sides of the climate debate. United Nations Intergovernmental Panel on Climate Change chairman Rajendra Pachauri stands to gain from the policies that he helps to push through, but he had previously fought for oil subsidies.

> No one in the world exercised more influence on the events leading up to the Copenhagen conference on global warming than Dr Rajendra Pachauri, chairman of the UN's Intergovernmental Panel on Climate Change (IPCC) and mastermind of its latest report in 2007.
>
> Although Dr Pachauri is often presented as a scientist (he was even once described by the BBC as "the world's top climate scientist"), as a former railway engineer with a PhD in economics he has no qualifications in climate science at all.
>
> ...Today, in addition to his role as chairman of the IPCC, Dr Pachauri [acts] as director or adviser to many of the bodies which play a leading role in what has become known as the international "climate industry."
>
> It is remarkable that only very recently has the staggering scale of Dr Pachauri's links to so many of these concerns come to light, inevitably raising questions as to how the world's leading 'climate official' can also be personally involved in so many organisations which stand to benefit from the IPCC's recommendations.
>
> ...The original power base from which Dr Pachauri has built up his worldwide network of influence over the past decade is the Delhi-based Tata Energy Research Institute, of which he became director in 1981 and director-general in 2001. Now renamed The Energy Research Institute [TERI].
>
> ...In India, Tata exercises enormous political power, shown not least in the way it has managed to displace hundreds of thousands of poor tribal villagers in the eastern states of Orissa and Jarkhand to make way for large-scale iron mining and steelmaking projects.

> Initially, when Dr Pachauri took over the running of TERI in the 1980s, his interests centred on the oil and coal industries.... He was, for instance, a director until 2003 of India Oil.... In 2005, he set up GloriOil.[59]

Now heavily invested in alternative energy technologies, the Tata group and TERI have extensive lobbying organizations in addition to their UN position. The article describes TERI's Washington-based North American offshoot, TERI-NA. Dr. Pachauri is president of this group. It is a lobbying organization, aiming to "sensitise decision-makers in North America to developing countries' concerns about energy and the environment." TERI-NA is funded by governmental and corporate sponsors, including the UN, U.S. governmental agencies, oil companies such as Amoco, two leading U.S. defense contractors, the corporate agricultural company Monsanto, and the environmental group World Wildlife Federation (which itself is partly funded by the EU). The group has more than $1 trillion worth of assets.

This lobbying has recently been aimed at promoting carbon trading schemes. Not only does the group have a huge amount invested in alternative energy technology which could benefit from policies that mandate or promote its use, it also can gain from carbon limitation, as it creates a scarcity in "carbon credits," and drives up the price for these companies to sell that scarce good. It is a UN carbon trading policy that is "enabling Tata to transfer three million tonnes of steel production from its Corus plant in Redcar to a new plant in Orissa, thus gaining a potential £1.2 billion in 'carbon credits.'"[60] It should come as no surprise that the group is willing to spend a great deal on lobbying for more such policies.

The answer to this is not to nationalize the utilities or direct all energy investment publicly. As the Soviet experience shows, this would only increase the problem. At that point, profit and loss would not direct investment choices, the customer would not be served, and political motives would replace economic cost-benefit analysis— and those with economic power and those with political power will both still benefit.

When government has some power to regulate the prices set by firms, or the profits they are allowed or the losses they must face, through subsidy, tax, and regulation, those firms may influence policy toward these favors, offering politicians reward for passing the bills. Nationalizing the firms to address this rent-seeking by firms gives all power of profit, loss and production to the state. This does prevent private individuals from teaming up with politicians for personal benefit, but it replaces this collusion with a stronger and more hierarchical economic-political collusion. Consumers and worker preferences are still subordinated to political decisions, often driven by personal gain. This distinction can also help to reconcile the arguments made by some of those on left, including Naomi Klein and Michael Hudson, with free market or libertarian critics of government involvement, and to relate these critiques to both Austrian and market socialist economic theory. I have argued in previous chapters that voucher programs or income support programs may achieve some of the ends that nationalization or subsidy schemes have aimed at better than those policies are able. Market socialists have also made this argument,[61] often citing failures of Soviet planning in their analysis. Market socialists recognize many of the problems inherent in central planning that I have outlined in this book. They have offered many interesting alternatives to planning, which in turn can be considered individually as alternative policy solutions to nationalization of individual firms or industries.

Conclusion

Socialist arguments for enhancing state power and bringing it under worker control failed to solve the problems that they saw in the "capitalist" economy. This is because they failed to distinguish between problems of the market and problems of state-supported firms. The power that they saw "capitalists" exerting over the economy, and over the people, were powers that the firms obtained from government. Each of the major ills that they wished to combat was caused by this tight linkage between corporations and the "capitalist" government. Their answer was to replace this "capitalist" government with a "worker" government, yet the "worker" government was even more powerful and therefore increased the tight linkage between state and producer.

The increase in the state power only enhanced the problems that they outlined. Similarly, policy proposals that aim to cure the failures of the market system that stem from subsidies, tariffs and protectionism, bailouts, or monetary policy with nationalization or enhanced state power will also tend to exacerbate rather than relieve the problem. It is crucial to distinguish between the free market and the problems that may exist based only on markets and free exchange and problems caused by the protection and support of individual companies by the state.

The Soviet experience makes clear why the best arguments of socialists against "capitalism" are fitting arguments against "corporatism" but not against free markets. Socialist arguments also make a good case against traditional socialism, which is, as Lenin and Bukharin could see, just an extremely centralized sort of corporatism. Finally, the Soviet experience puts in perspective the arguments for market socialism and for a more free market system, taking the political debate away from a right-versus-left dichotomy that sometimes masks the more important distinction of centralization by the state versus decentralized ownership by individuals.

Endnotes

1. Bukharin and Preobrazhensky, *The ABC of Communism* (original emphasis omitted).
2. V. I. Lenin, "The State and Revolution: The Marxist Theory of the State and the Tasks of The Proletariat in the Revolution," *Collected Works*, Vol. 25, chap. 5, pp. 381-492, at http://www.marxists.org/archive/lenin/works/1917/staterev/ch05.htm.
3. Bukharin and Preobrazhensky, *The ABC of Communism*, chap. 3.
4. *Ibid.*, chap. 4.
5. V. I. Lenin, "The Impending Catastrophe and How to Combat It," October 1917, in *Collected Works*, Vol. 25 (Moscow: Progress Publishers, 1977), pp. 323–369 (original emphasis).
6. Nikolai Bukharin, *Economics of the Transition Period* (1920), quoted in Lewis H. Siegelbaum, *Soviet State and Society Between the Revolutions, 1918–1929* (Cambridge: Cambridge University Press, 1992),

pp. 11–12 (original emphasis).

7. Karl Marx and Friedrich Engels, *Manifesto of the Communist Party*, chap. 1, at http://www.marxists.org/archive/marx/works/1848/communist-manifesto/ch01.htm.

8. Nikolai Bukharin, *Imperialism and World Economy* (International Publishers, 1929), chap. 13, note 22, at http://www.marxists.org/archive/bukharin/works/1917/imperial/index.htm (December 5, 2009) (original emphasis).

9. Nikolai Bukharin, "Toward a Theory of the Imperialist State," 1915, at http://www.marxists.org/archive/bukharin/works/1915/state.htm (December 5, 2009).

10. Nikolai Bukharin, *Marx's Teaching and its Historical Importance*, chap. 4, at http://www.marxists.org/archive/bukharin/works/1933/teaching/index.htm (December 5, 2009).

11. Nikolai Bukharin, *Imperialism and World Economy*, quoted in Stephen F. Cohen, "Bukharin, Lenin and the Theoretical Foundations of Bolshevism," *Soviet Studies*, vol. 21, no. 4 (April 1970), pp. 436–457.

12. Bukharin and Preobrazhensky, *The ABC of Communism*, chap. 4.

13. *Ibid.*

14. *Ibid.*

15. *Ibid.*

16. "When the German capitalist has a factory in Russia, and when he too becomes a member of the 'Russian' syndicate, of course the Russian tariff helps him to earn surplus profit. The import duties are just as useful to him in fleecing the Russian public as they are to his Russian colleagues.... The various powerful States begin to compete for the possession of those territorial areas or lesser States to which they wish to export capital.... With the growth of syndicates and the introduction of tariffs, the struggle for markets becomes greatly intensified." *Ibid.*

17. "[S]o long as big industry remains on its present footing, it can be maintained only at the cost of general chaos every seven years, each time threatening the whole of civilization and not only plunging the proletarians into misery but also ruining large sections of the bourgeoisie; hence, either that big industry must itself be given up, which is an absolute impossibility, or that it makes unavoidably necessary an entirely new organization of society in which production is no longer directed by mutually competing individual industrialists but rather by the whole society operating according to a definite plan and taking account of the needs of all." Frederick Engels, "The Principles of Communism," in *Selected Works*, Vol. 1 (Moscow: Progress Publishers, 1969), pp. 81–97, at http://www.marxists.org/archive/marx/works/1847/11/prin-com.htm (December 2, 2009).

18. Karl Marx, *Capital*, Vol. 3, *The Process of Capitalist Production as a Whole* (New York: International Publishers, n.d.), chap. 36, at http://www.marxists.org/archive/marx/works/1894-c3/index.htm (November 20, 2009).

19. William F. Warde (William F. Warde was a pseudonym of George Novack.), "The Progress of Inflation," Fourth International, Vol.4, No. 10, October 1943, pp. 305–307.

20. V. I. Lenin, "The Impending Catastrophe and How to Combat It," *Collected Works*, Vol. 25, at http://www.marxists.org/archive/lenin/works/1917/ichtci/04.htm (December 3, 2009).

21. Nikita Khrushchev (1961), quoted in Konstantin M. Simis, *USSR: The Corrupt Society: The Secret World of Soviet Capitalism* (New York: Simon and Schuster, 1982). The Supreme Soviet did then issue a decree introducing the death penalty (again) for the crime of speculation. *Ibid.*, pp. 29–31.

22. Marx, "Critique of the Gotha Programme."

23. Bukharin and Preobrazhensky, *The ABC of Communism*, chap. 6.

24. *Ibid.*

25. "In these economies, promotions retained all of the capitalist advantages of increased power and income with the additional attractions of providing desirable goods and services for oneself and one's family." Jone L. Pearce, Imre Branyiczki, and Gyula Bakacsi, "Person-Based Reward Systems: A Theory of Organizational Reward Practices in Reform-Communist Organizations," *Journal of Organizational Behavior*, Vol. 15, No. 3 (May 1994), p. 263.

26. Nove, *The Soviet Economy*, p. 101.

27. Bohdan Harasamiw, "Nomenklatura: The Soviet Communist Party's Leadership Recruitment System," *Canadian Journal of Political Science*, Vol. 2, No. 4 (December 1969), p. 494.

28. "If there is one commonplace which cannot be too strongly emphasized, it is that *the communist*

party is the organizational expression of the revolutionary will of the proletariat. It is therefore by no means bound to embrace the whole of the proletariat from the very outset; as the conscious leader of the revolution, as the embodiment of the revolutionary idea, its task is rather to unite the most conscious sections, the vanguard, the really revolutionary and fully class-conscious workers." Georg Lukács, "The Moral Mission of the Communist Party," in *Political Writings* (1972), at http://www.marxists.org/archive/lukacs/works/1920/moral-mission.htm (December 5, 2009) (original emphasis).

29. *Ibid.*, p. 495.
30. Harasamiw, "Nomenklatura," p. 508.
31. *Ibid.*
32. *Ibid.*, p. 506.
33. Max Shachtman, *The Struggle for the New Course* (New York: New International Publishing, 1943), at http://www.marxists.org/archive/shachtma/1943/fnc/index.htm (December 5, 2009).
34. The biggest drops in output occurred during the major pushes toward socialism: war communism and collectivization. Yet the Soviet economy was not immune to downturns. Higher growth, at least as measured with aggregate indices, characterized the 1940s and 1950s, but began to drop off in the 1960s. There are several possible explanations for this. The best explanation is probably that growth had been based on bringing new workers and equipment online ("extensive growth"), and these avenues had been exhausted by the 1960s. The only way to continue to grow would be through innovation, cost-reducing technologies, and other improvements in productivity ("intensive growth"). However, these were not easy for the planned economy to produce. —The reforms of the 1960s aimed to resolve these problems. There were other "disturbances" in growth (recessions), such as a slowdown in the 1970s, and these were becoming increasingly common. Underlying growth continued to decline thereafter. See Robert C. Allen, "The Rise and Decline of the Soviet Economy," *Canadian Journal of Economics*, Vol. 34, No. 4 (November 2001), pp. 859–881; Gregory and Stuart, *Soviet Economic Structure and Performance*; and Mark Harrison, "Coercion, Compliance, and the Collapse of the Soviet Command Economy," *Economic History Review*, Vol. 55, No. 3 (August 2002), pp. 397–433.
35. Editorial Comment, "Roosevelt and the Farm Bloc," *Fourth International*, Vol. 3, No. 10 (October 1942), pp. 291–295, at http://www.marxists.org/history/etol/newspape/fi/vol03/no10/editorial.htm (December 5, 2009).
36. P. R. Gregory and M. Harrison, "Allocation under Dictatorship: Research in Stalin's Archives," *Journal of Economic Literature*, Vol. 43, No. 3 (Sep., 2005), pp. 721–761. Between 1930 and 1941 Stalin issues 32,000 decrees, of which 4,000 were published. The other 28,000 were secret, of which 5,000 were only known to a few high level officials.
37. A. J. Polan, *Lenin and the End of Politics* (London: Methuen & Co., 1984), p. 81.
38. Don Lavoie, "Political and Economic Illusions of Socialism," *Critical Review*, Vol. 1, No. 1 (Winter 1986).
39. Rudolf Hilferding, "State Capitalism or Totalitarian State Economy," *Modern Review*, June 1947, pp. 266–271, at http://www.marxists.org/archive/hilferding/1940/statecapitalism.htm (December 5, 2009).
40. Calvin B. Hoover, "The Paths of Economic Change: Contrasting Tendencies in the Modern World," *American Economic Review*, Vol. 25, No. 1, supplement (March 1935), pp. 13–15.
41. A lower level of regulation, nationalization and subsidies and preferential treatment should offer individuals greater opportunity for entrepreneurship. The Global Entrepreneurship Monitor reports that the United States consistently maintains at least fifty percent higher rates of entrepreneurship than the average of all high income countries; and the correlation between economic freedom and entrepreneurship has been studied with the Index of Economic Freedom. GEM reports the rate of entrepreneurship in the United States as about 12 percent, or 1 in every 8 individuals. In addition to the chance to open one's own business, a free market economy offers the individual the chance to own a piece of a business through stock market investment. The Survey of Consumer Finances reports that in 2004 (some of these numbers fell in 2007 due to the financial crisis) 20.7 percent of families owned individual stocks directly, 15 percent owned pooled investment funds (such as mutual funds) and 49.7 percent owned private retirement accounts (despite the state's provision of Social Security). Although the percentage of families

owning stock predictably rose by income class, from 5.1 percent in the lowest quintile to 55 percent for the top quintile, the breakdown by age is also revealing because both income and stock ownership tend to rise with age. For those under 35, the rate of stock ownership was 13.3 percent, while for age 55–64 it was 29.1 percent. In other words, one in every eight Americans is a capitalist and about one third own capital by the time they reach retirement (about half do, if retirement accounts are included). --"Changes in U.S. Family Finances from 2004 to 2007: Evidence from the Survey of Consumer Finances," *Federal Reserve Bulletin*, February 2009, at http://www.federalreserve.gov/pubs/bulletin/2009/pdf/scf09.pdf. --See also, Global Entrepreneurship Monitor, at http://www.gemconsortium.org Index of Economic Freedom at http://www.heritage.org/index/

42. Jerry F. Hough, "The Evolution in the Soviet World View," *World Politics*, Vol. 32, No. 4 (July 1980), pp. 509–530.

43. "Capitalism places economic power in the hands of capital and its owners. Traditional socialism gives power exclusively to labour: the dictatorship of the proletariat, preferably exercised through a centralized authority. And the New Right—actually better characterized as traditional liberalism—claims to locate power in the hands of the individual—particularly, the individual citizen and consumer. Since we are all citizens and consumers, since most of us are (or have been or will be) workers, and since the majority own, or would like to own, capital in some form (a house, savings account, pension rights, insurance policies, stocks and shares), it is not surprising that none of these traditional "models'" of how the economy should be organized finds universal favour. Full blooded capitalism is unattractive because it exploits labour through its monopoly of employment and because it exploits consumers through monopolizing goods markets. Traditional socialism expropriates capital and subordinates the interests of the consumers to the interests of the workers. Indeed, with its penchant for centralization, it is far from clear that even the interests of workers are properly taken care of. Liberalism puts people's livelihoods and their savings at the mercy of consumer taste and fashion; its emphasis on the narrow rights of individuals jeopardizes the collective activities of the community, and hence the community itself." Julian Le Grand and Saul Estrin, eds., *Market Socialism* (New York: Oxford University Press, 1989), p. 23.

44. Art Carden and Steven Horwitz, "Everything You Always Wanted to Know About Economists," Forbes.com, September 12, 2009, at http://www.forbes.com/2009/09/11/economists-free-market-jane-smiley-opinions-contributors-capitalism.html (December 5, 2009) (emphasis added).

45. As described in Chapter 1, Oskar Lange argued for a market socialism that could mimic perfect competition (see Lange and Taylor, *On the Economic Theory of Socialism*), arguing that perfect competition in a free market system cannot be realized. More recently, market socialists have offered new analysis. For example, see Le Grand and Estrin, *Market Socialism*. In this argument, market socialists mirror some free market proponents of anarchy who argue that a state of any size will ultimately lead to rent-seeking and the emergence of a strong and corporatist state.

46. Missing Footnote

47. "Naomi Klein on the Bailout Profiteers and the Multi-Trillion-Dollar Crime Scene," Democracy Now, November 17, 2008, at http://www.democracynow.org/2008/11/17/naomi_klein_on_the_bailout_profiteers (February 21, 2010).

48. Steve Palmer, "Adventures of Freddie and Fannie in the Land of Make-Believe," *Fight Racism! Fight Imperialism!* April 14, 2009, at http://www.revolutionarycommunist.org/index.php/capitalist-crisis/236-adventures-of-freddie-and-fannie-in-the-land-of-make-believe--frfi-204-aug--sep-2008.html (December 5, 2009).

49. "The Biggest Losers: Behind the Christmas Eve taxpayer massacre at Fannie and Freddie," *The Wall Street Journal*, January 4, 2010, at http://online.wsj.com/article/SB1000142405274870415280457 4628350980043082.html.

50. There is a running theme to note here: economists have debated what the central bank should target (inflation, unemployment levels, size of the money supply) in order to stabilize the economy, assuming that the central bank simply needs to learn best how to control the money supply; economists have debated the best targets for the NHS and other centrally directed industries to use, again assuming that the state must simply learn how best to direct firms in

the absence of profits; economists have also debated how best to set prices to benefit the social good, and so forth. In each of these cases, the assumption is that a technical mistake was made in determining *the* price or target that should be used. What if it was not a matter of a flaw in determining the right price or target, but something more fundamental: What if the price changes more often than the state can change it? What if the state cannot know the right price or target because it lacks the necessary information to do so? What if by setting the price or target, the government changes the circumstances and makes gathering this information impossible?

51. William Greider, "Dismantling the Temple," *The Nation*, July 15, 2009, at http://www.thenation.com/doc/20090803/greider/single (December 5, 2009).

52. *Ibid.*

53. Christine Tierney and David Shepardson, "Future of Opel Is Hot Topic in Germany," *Detroit News*, August 26, 2009.

54. John Stossel's take on Fox Business Channel, first aired 8pm EST January 14, 2010, relevant video clip at http://stossel.blogs.foxbusiness.com/2010/01/14/a-little-company-praised-by-president-obama/ (January 15, 2010).

55. Jason Stverak, "A Serious Conflict of Interest?" January 15, 2010, at http://watchdog.org/2010/01/15/%E2%80%9Ca-serious-conflict-of-interest%E2%80%9D/.

56. John M. Broder, "Gore's Dual Role: Advocate and Investor," *The New York Times*, November 2, 2009, at http://www.nytimes.com/2009/11/03/business/energy-environment/03gore.html (December 6, 2009).

57. *Ibid.*

58. President Obama's recent budget proposal for 2011 includes the repeal of $45 billion worth of tax credits and subsidies to the oil industry, in addition to "cap and trade" carbon emissions taxes. Obama proposed a smaller set of cuts to oil industry subsidies the year before but Congress did not pass it. Some of the groups that have fought against cap and trade have received money from the oil and gas industry. Former Congressman Dick Armey is the chairman of the group FreedomWorks, which orchestrated simultaneous protests against cap and trade, as well as other policies the group says give government too much power and hurt competition. While in Congress, Armey received $245,000 in campaign funds from oil and gas industry executives. —Simon Lomax and Daniel Whitten, "Energy Companies Face $45 Billion in Costs in Budget," Bloomberg.com, at http://www.bloomberg.com/apps/news?pid=20601072&sid=amN07lqk7V sw, and Media Matters, "Fact Check: Oil and Gas Industries Fuel Unruly Townhall Meetings," August 6, 2009, at http://mediamattersaction.org/factcheck/200908060005.

59. "Questions over business deals of UN climate change guru Dr. Rajendra Pachauri," *The Telegraph*, December 20, 2009, at http://www.telegraph.co.uk/news/6847227/Questions-over-business-deals-of-UN-climate-change-guru-Dr-Rajendra-Pachauri.html.

60. *Ibid.*

61. See, for example arguments to this effect in Le Grand and Estrin, *Market Socialism.*

Conclusion: Lessons for Economic Modeling

Adam Smith spoke of the invisible hand of the market, which guides the self-interested actor to benefit others around him. Economist F. A. Hayek described the market as a spontaneous social order that emerges out of voluntary actions, coordinating the desires and needs of individuals with the available resources around them. The two concepts are similar in that they describe the actions of individuals and the way they coordinate together, creating a good society.

A spontaneous order emerges when individuals take actions and interact in society and in the market, and produce an outcome that cannot be planned in advance. Central direction is not necessary because individuals interacting with each other will produce outcomes that are potentially beneficial to the whole of society.

The framework of spontaneous orders is useful for investigating questions about the economy. A market economy is a spontaneous order that emerges from the interaction between individuals within a framework of rule of law—basic rules of the game that apply equally to all. It is a spontaneous order because the allocation of resources across the economy is unplanned: It emerges from interactions between individuals who only plan their own exchanges.[1]

In contrast, a centrally planned economy is not spontaneous. Instead of broad rules, the society is organized according to a plan. The plan determines the allocation of resources across the economy. Although a socialist economy is bound by a framework of institutions—those protecting public property, rather than private property—there is no emergent order that has come of those institutions. Instead, the only way to allocate resources under a public-property system is through central planning, which must involve specific decrees.

Private property allows for the emergence of a spontaneous order because each agent within the system can make exchanges and build on her own property; hence, the outcome may not be known in advance and the decentralized actions and inter-actions of the individual agents can produce something unexpected. Public property institutions do not provide this possibility for decentralized action. Each agent has no right or ability to exchange her *own* property, as she owns no property.

Instead, the publicly owned property must be administered, and the agents must coordinate this in some way. For it to remain public property, individual agents can-not take ownership of parts of it and therefore cannot exchange them or privately build on them. The only way for the individual agents to build on the property is to coordinate common action. Private action is outlawed because private ownership is required to make private decisions. The coordination of common action is known as the economic plan. Whether it is democratically or otherwise coordinated, once it is decided upon, the agents carrying it out are subject to individual decrees rather than simply the broad framework of institutions. No emergent order is possible because all actions are planned ahead of time.

This important distinction points the way toward an approach to economic mod-eling and comparative systems analysis. Economists have often been criticized for as-suming profit maximization on the part of firms and utility maximization on the part of consumers. "Rational choice" and "public choice" theories assume that individuals perform rational cost-benefit analysis in each of their choices. This is not always, per-haps not usually, realistic. Self-interest is not the only motivation for decisions in the market or the public sphere.

While firm owners or managers may not consciously be maximizing their profit—using marginal cost and benefits—arguably, they may still behave precisely as if they were consciously doing so. The environment in which they exist may provide the incentives and pressures that make such behavior the only possible choice. How-ever, profit maximization is not the only conceivable behavior. It may not even be possible to discern exactly what behavior the pressure of the market produces. Each firm owner or manager may respond differently to the pressures of the market. Some may maximize profit, while others only avert loss. Yet others may be somewhere in between. However, there is a minimum that *can* be known for certain.

In a pure market economy, the hard budget constraint facing firms results in the outcome that, whatever their personal motivation, only those that make a profit sur-vive, and those that make a bigger profit tend to expand and overtake those that make a lower profit. As Jeffrey Friedman explains in a 2004 paper,

> For capitalism to work in the real world, producers need neither want nor know what the standard model assumes that they know and want. Acting from any conceivable motive, and without necessarily having any (accurate) idea of what they are doing, entrepreneurs under pure, laissez-faire capitalism would be impelled, as it were, to satisfy each other's wants—simply because if a consumer buys a product that turns out to be distasteful or not worth the price, he could Exit by not buying it again. If a producer offered a product from which enough con-sumers exited, she would go out of business. But afterwards, or in the meantime, she—or someone else to whom the resources previously under her control flowed

as she lost money—might either accidentally or deliberately hit on a better way to satisfy actual consumer "demand."[2]

This is the impersonal force of the invisible hand of Adam Smith. It is not the benevolence of the baker, nor his assumed profit maximization, but simply the pressure exerted upon him by the invisible hand that forces him to serve his fellow man. Profit maximization need not be assumed, yet selection in the marketplace will mimic some profit drive and loss aversion. This phenomenon can be labeled *profit guidance*.

This is not true in a planned economy with state production because the consumer arguably cannot exit (the state is a monopoly provider), and even if they do, this does not compel the state to shut down the producing firm or eliminate the product. The state need not compete with anyone else. There is no pressure to serve the customer, and the state may not even *know* whether the customer likes the product. This is especially true when both firms and consumers are forced to make substitutions along the way.

In the public sector, there may also be altruistic or self-interested motives. What is important is what the institutional constraints select for. Public choice economists often assume that bureaucracies want to maximize their budgets. A focus on the selection pressures on these bureaucrats may provide greater insight. It is well known that the "rules of the game," the formal and informal institutions of a given society, determine the behavior of the actors and hence the productive activity of the economy. As Douglas North pointed out, output is determined by "the characteristics of the basic institutional environment and the degree to which these basic ground rules are enforced."[3]

In the Soviet Union, most (arguably all) economic actors were also political actors, i.e., bureaucrats. Sovietologists have pointed to the self-interested behavior of Soviet firm managers, even likening it to budget maximization, as public choice economists argue bureaucrats in market economies do. Managers often argued that their costs were higher than they were and tried to get the plan with the lowest targets. They then tried to maximize premiums by overfulfilling their targets by cutting corners. As Soviet economists Treml and Gallic explain, revealing all of one's resources to planners would put managers in a "very difficult position" because the planners would press for greater and greater output. Instead, managers were encouraged to strive for the easiest possible plan in order to achieve overfulfillment "without special strain."[4]

Different Sovietologists assumed different "maximizations" by factory managers.[5] It may not be possible to know what motivated managers, or what motivates any individual. However, it may not be necessary to choose a motivating factor. One can instead use a model based on the constraints of the given economy. Rather than try to determine the behavior that the institutions induce in each system and then make a strong assumption of maximization by firm managers, it may be more appropriate to simply determine what the institutions select for, regardless of the individual motivation.

An evolutionary model relies only on the recognition that chronic underfulfill-ment of plan targets must lead to removal of the managers. As it was once summed up, "repeated failure to fulfill plans has the same effect on the career of a Soviet manager that repeated losing seasons have on a football coach in any country."[6] System struc-ture and institutional constraints compel the actors to behave in a certain way or lose their positions. Hence, remaining firm managers must be those that are plan-guided. They may have been altruistic believers in communism or jaded and selfish counter-revolutionaries. Only the selection of outward behavior is assumed. (It would be interesting, however, to see what motivation was selected for. F. A. Hayek argued that planning selects for brutal leaders; it may select for other attributes in factory managers.)

It is also well known that private property rights can lead to good social outcomes (the "invisible hand" of Adam Smith), while commonly owned property may be ex-cessively exploited (the "tragedy of the commons"). Traditionally, the reasons for this phenomenon have been described in terms of incentives. Private property creates an incentive to pursue profit because the earnings can be privately held, and profit is created by serving the consumer, leading to socially desirable outcomes. Commonly owned property, in contrast, provides an incentive for excess use and waste because the costs are not privately born, and any profit derived from efficient use or produc-tion cannot be retained by any given individual.

As alluded to above, one critique of this accepted wisdom pertains to altruistic motivation. Perhaps common property will not be excessively depleted or exploited if it is respected by the community. Perhaps workers of a cooperatively owned com-pany will work hard and efficiently if they believe in the values of the firm and the society. In fact, such motivations are common. Humans are not selfish and motivat-ed solely by the desire to maximize personal gain. Humans are complex, filled with many varied motivations both among us and within each of us.

An evolutionary approach offers insight in this respect. If we are not all greedy, but not perfectly altruistic either, then the institutional environment critically affects the outcome because it selects for certain behaviors, even if it does not induce them in an altruistic person. In general, if someone is greedy he will seek out a winning behav-ior that will allow him to ascend the social hierarchy (becoming rich or climbing the political power ladder, for example). If a single person is greedy and finds a behavior that gives him an advantage, then this behavior will begin to dominate because it is a winning strategy. Those who refrain from engaging in this behavior will lose and die out. If the behavior chosen by the "greedy" person produces socially beneficial results, then this selection process will lead the system to a good social outcome; if the be-havior produces socially negative results, the selection process will lead to a negative outcome. A great mixture of actual personal motivations may exist in both cases, but the selection process determines the predominant behavior.

A 1973 paper by economists Alchian and Demsetz recounted the story of the Canadian government's experience with communal rights and hunting. The government instituted a maximum number of animals that could be hunted, but allowed hunting on a first-come first-served basis. Unusually cruel practices of clubbing baby seals soon resulted.

It is unlikely that Canadian hunters enjoy clubbing baby seals more than hunters of other nations. Instead, one hunter must have determined that hurriedly killing young animals would give him an advantage in obtaining more animals before the quota was reached. Once he set this competitive bar, any other hunters who wanted to compete and obtain any kills would have to match this tactic. The system selected for more cruel and inhumane hunting methods. The authors of the paper explained that the institutional environment made "a condition for success the degree to which the hunter can be ruthless."[7]

Institutions do much more than provide incentives. They shape our worldview, select for certain behaviors, and shape our interactions:

> By specifying both the formal and informal "rules of the game" that guide most interactions, institutions determine what possibilities are productive and influence which possibilities are likely to be seen as such at any given time. Over time, institutions influence which deployments are even possible.[8]

The rules of the game determine which kinds of behaviors succeed and which fail. The rules of private property ensure that those guided by profit and loss succeed, and those firms that are wasteful and not afraid of loss, or do not produce products that are profitable, fail. This does not mean that firms that put something else ahead of profit cannot succeed. Non-profits and charities succeed by the rules of the game of the market economy because there many individuals that value charitable giving. Private property institutions allow the individuals in the economy to make voluntary agreements, and production and consumption come from this private individual trading and cooperation.

Socialists valued cooperation, and many socialists who have lost faith in the Soviet approach have proposed worker cooperatives or other sorts of cooperative arrangements for production, consumption, and living, at a national level. However, it is not clear why such a system should be imposed upon the whole society, rather than allowing shared resource organizations to co-exist with single-owner ones, within a private property society. In that case, the organization is run with common ownership, but the society is one of private property ownership.

Cooperative living and working arrangement like the kibbutz, the cooperative store, and the hippie commune, in which sharing is central, can and do exist in a market society. Although they are based on social property ownership, they can exist within a private property society if members choose to live or work in that community voluntarily. They do not require a socialist economy, with public property of all resources.

The private property society allows for charity and non profit production, communes and other kinds of shared living and consumption, and worker cooperatives and cooperative production such as anarchically coordinated artistic collaboration. All of these exist, and even sometimes thrive, in private property societies. Several of the most profitable industries in market societies include a significant amount of cooperative production: the film and music industries, although in the most profitable companies there is a "corporate hierarchy," often include collaborative writing, and other experimental kinds of production. Computer game development companies, and web search companies like Yahoo and Google, are very profitable and many of the companies have been experimental in production techniques and worker involvement. Non-profit completely decentralized development of software and operating systems such as Linux, as well as research tools such as Wikipedia, and media websites like YouTube, were created and have flourished in the private property institutional environment. These all involve collaborative work that diverges from the picture that socialists presented of dominant capital exploiting and repressing workers and consumers.

In a private property society, the ownership and management of resources within a firm can take any number of forms. There is no ban on individuals coming together to purchase resources and share them and use them cooperatively. In fact, a private property society makes this relatively easy. In the Soviet Union, even if the state did not actively prevent groups from forming cooperative organizations (which they frequently did, because the resources were owned by the whole society and already earmarked for another use, if not also for political reasons) social ownership would still mean asking permission to use resources. To the extent than any individual in a market economy can obtain some money either from working or from charity, resources to begin a small cooperative organization are relatively easy to obtain because they can simply be purchased. In an economy with social ownership securing permission may be more difficult.

The private ownership of resources allows the spontaneous pursuit of an infinite variety of inventive ideas, only bounded by our imaginations. These ideas become subject to the market test: the test of whether the consumer, be he a philanthropist or an egotist—finds it worthwhile. The market only fails to the extent that the consumer fails. The consumer may fail if he is immoral or if there is a good that he is unwilling to pay for privately, but that he would consume if others pay—public goods. Otherwise, the market produces for the consumer, and the consumer produces in order to consume. Production and consumption emerge from cooperation and exchange within these rules of the game.

That markets emerge from these "rules of the game" is well known. However, full property rights are necessary for many of the features of the market to emerge. If the institutional structure is compromised, rent-seeking may replace competition among firms. The framework of the spontaneous order is also useful for analyzing the tendency of rent-seeking to change the nature of the economy. The rules of the game that govern the emergent market order include private property rights and hard budget constraints. Yet the political order may allow some firms to obtain soft budgets or to violate the property rights of other firms. Of course, this changes the rules of the game. Meckling and Alchian describe it this way:

> [I]n trying to improve their lot individuals do more than merely adapt to given cost-reward relationships. They try to alter the schedule of prizes and costs to their own advantage. How? By changing the rules, especially through government. By pressing for advantageous legislative, administrative, or judicial action, individuals can and do use the power of government for personal gain.[9]

In this way, commands may replace rules of the game in the market order because favors from government that violate the basic rules of the game are simply commands, like those of an economic plan. When this occurs, a small number of politicians make the decisions that were previously made by the consumer through purchase and exit.

The market order becomes centralized through the workings of politics. The institutional structure determines whether rent-seeking is allowed and the momentum it may gain through a process of selection. As Meckling and Alchian point out, "the extent to which people attempt to change rules depends on the relation between the costs of changing rules and the potential rewards."[10]

Countries that inflict little or no punishment for buying political favors have little else directing the economy. In countries with at least some restraint on governmental power, as well as bans on outright bribery, the expansion of rent-seeking is certainly slower. But many kinds of rent-seeking can be sold as positive—as aid to the needy, protection of jobs, free or cheap medicines for the people, and so forth. Despite the centralized and political decision by which firms are chosen to receive the people's money, the policy is sold as a policy passed for the consumer.

The spontaneous order framework also sheds light on the limits of what government can do. When weighing any policy, we should recall that government is not omniscient: It cannot know all the information that individual actors in the economy know, and without a system that coordinates this information through prices, it can know very little. Nor is government omnipotent: Even if it knows what should be done, government can only convey its information through language and command.

The public may want the government to provide for the poor, provide health care to all, provide excellent schools, and provide low-income housing and retirement incomes. It may want government to boost competition or prevent greedy firms from getting too large, but government may not be able to do these things well or improve upon the outcome possible in a free market. Yet as the Nobel Laureate F. A. Hayek warned, "so long as the public expects more there will always be some who will pretend, and perhaps honestly believe, that they can do more to meet popular demands than is really in their power."[11]

The public may be willing to believe that government is super-powerful and benevolent and cede to politicians whatever controls over the people's lives that they require. There are dangers in this tendency:

In the physical sciences there may be little objection to trying to do the impossible; one might even feel that one ought not to discourage the over-confident because their experiments may after all produce some new insights. But in the social field the erroneous belief that the exercise of some power would have beneficial consequences is likely to lead to a new power to coerce other men being conferred on some authority. Even if such power is not in itself bad, its exercise is likely to impede the functioning of those spontaneous ordering forces by which, without understanding them, man is in fact so largely assisted in the pursuit of his aims. We are only beginning to understand on how subtle a communication system the functioning of an advanced industrial society is based—a communications system which we call the market and which turns out to be a more efficient mechanism for digesting dispersed information than any that man has deliberately designed.

If man is not to do more harm than good in his efforts to improve the social order, he will have to learn that in this, as in all other fields where essential complexity of an organized kind prevails, he cannot acquire the full knowledge which would make mastery of the events possible. He will therefore have to use what knowledge he can achieve, not to shape the results as the craftsman shapes his handiwork, but rather to cultivate a growth by providing the appropriate environment, in the manner in which the gardener does this for his plants.[12]

This appropriate environment Hayek spoke of is the enforcement of basic property laws and the right of life and liberty—the basic institutions that protect each person's rights and allow for exchange and the emergence of trade and the market. These basic institutions provide a maximum of freedom for each person within the social order, and the order is allowed to grow and develop. Society and traditions may evolve, and innovations and technological change can advance the economy and allow healthy progress.

Even Marx seemed to understand this. He spoke of the separation that the state should have from personal freedoms. "The state is based on this contradiction. It is based on the contradiction between public and private life, between universal and particular interests. For this reason, the state must confine itself to formal, negative activities."[13]

Socialists have actually been their own worst critics and made the best arguments for markets over planning, even if they have not recognized that they have done so. Although Marxists argued that socialism must be implemented on the back of a developed capitalist nation, and some have used this detail to excuse its failures, this demand is in fact a clear refutation of the practicability of socialism in any era short of a Utopian future, in which Heaven has already come to Earth. Socialist arguments make this clear. For example, Trotsky argued that the Soviet Union would have done better had it been built on a larger capitalist base. Yet, his arguments raise profound questions about the socialist economic system:

The Soviet Union, to be sure, even now excels in productive forces the most advanced countries of the epoch of Marx. But in the first place, in the historic rivalry of two regimes, it is not so much a question of absolutely as of relative levels: the Soviet economy opposes the capitalism of Hitler, Baldwin, and Roosevelt, not Bismarck, Palmerston, or Abraham Lincoln. And in the second place, the very scope of human demands changes fundamentally with the growth of world technique. The contemporaries of Marx knew nothing of automobiles, radios, moving pictures, aeroplanes. A socialist society, however, is unthinkable without the free enjoyment of these goods.[14]

By demanding an economy that has the innovations of capitalist countries on which to build socialism, Trotsky appears to be conceding that socialism cannot produce the growth and innovation to advance an economy to meet those needs. Yet there will always be new needs and new demands. How then could pure socialism ever succeed if it cannot create this development on its own? Socialism is "unthinkable" without the inventions and innovations of the capitalist world: "automobiles, radios, moving pictures, aeroplanes." Yet since Trotsky wrote those words, we have added color televisions, computers, digital music players and recording devices, and cell phones to the list, along with a world of Web technology and Internet commerce, to name just a few more obvious inventions. The list of new medicines would be perhaps more significant. Now, because "the very scope of human demands changes fundamentally with the growth of world technique," socialism is presumably unthinkable without those.

For socialism to be "thinkable" then, there would have to be a time in which the pinnacle of capitalist development was able to actually satiate the desires of human will and want, and the people would finally say, "There is no need for new medicines to live longer, new fashions and video games, new technologies for entertainment or communication, travel or accommodation. There is nothing new under the sun that I may ever desire to have or to create."

Will we ever come to that place? What has brought us this far? Markets, in general, have made these technologies possible.[15] If this were not so, we would have seen technologies like compact discs, mobile phones, and the digital cameras invented in the Soviet Union. Marx understood this. In the Communist Manifesto he wrote:

> [The market] has accomplished wonders far surpassing Egyptian pyramids, Roman aqueducts and Gothic cathedrals.... The bourgeoisie has through its exploitation of the world market given a cosmopolitan character to production and consumption in every country.... All old-established national industries have been destroyed or are daily being destroyed. They are dislodged by new industries, whose introduction becomes a life-and-death question for all civilised nations.... In place of the old wants, satisfied by the production of the country, we find new wants, requiring for their satisfaction the products of distant lands and climes.... National one-sidedness and narrow-mindedness become more and more impossible, and from the numerous national and local literatures there arises a world literature. The bourgeoisie, by the rapid improvement of all instruments of production, by the immensely facilitated means of communication, draws all, even the most barbarian, nations into civilization.[16]

What a wonderful eulogy for capitalism. The market brings forth these wonders by responding to the needs and desires of the people. It creates new industries that become such vital requirements for the civilized thenceforth. It is the market that dissolves nationalism and brings peoples together and that dissolves class and race divides. But a market depends on the basic protection of individual rights of property and contract so that decentralized exchange and choice can take place. The philosopher David Hume put it this way:

> [T]he stability of possession,...its transference by consent, and...the performance of promises. 'Tis on the strict observance of these three laws, that the peace and security of human society entirely depend; nor is there any possibility of establishing a good correspondence among men, where these are neglected. Society is absolutely necessary for the well-being of men; and these are as necessary to the support of society.[17]

This is what we must remember as we go about creating policies that attempt to shape and prune the results of decentralized actions and market exchanges. The policies themselves cannot create wealth, yet they can disrupt people as they go about creating wealth. The knowledge that we think we have may fall short of what is required to achieve the ends that are promised by politicians—politicians who will tend to benefit from the power they seek. Whatever our good intentions may be, we must learn from history the limits of our effective power over our social order. For these reasons, it is wise to learn the lessons of history, especially the lessons from those periods of history in which theory was best tested.

ENDNOTES

1. Whether the economic institutions themselves evolve in a similar process is an interesting question. Clark questions this, whereas Sungden provides evidence in favor of this assertion. Whether or not they do, certainly the market process itself may be seen as a spontaneous order, evolving within the necessary institutions. C. M. A. Clark, "Spontaneous Order versus Instituted Process: The Market as Cause and Effect," *Journal of Economic Issues*, Vol. 27, No. 2 (June 1993), pp. 373–385, and R. Sungden, "Spontaneous Order," *The Journal of Economic Perspectives*, Vol. 3, No. 4 (Autumn 1989), pp. 85–97.
2. Jeffrey Friedman, "Theory Gets a Reality Check: Philosophy, Economics, and Politics as if Verisimilitude Mattered," *Dissident*, No. 1, at http://www.the-dissident.com/theory.shtml (December 6, 2009).
3. Douglass C. North, "Institutional Change and Economic Growth," *The Journal of Economic History*, Vol. 31, No. 1, The Tasks of Economic History (March 1971), pp. 118–125 (p. 124).
4. V. Treml and D. Gallik, ASTE Bulletin, Vol. 7, No. 3 (Winter 1965), pp. 20–24.
5. Kornai, *The Socialist System*, cites "recognition by superiors" as a main guiding force for Soviet managers but also presents a list of additional motivating factors. Joseph Berliner, *Factory and Manager in the USSR*, cites maximization of "premiums," Portes models Soviet firms maximizing output, while Granick focuses on maximization by economic ministers. See Kornai, *The Socialist System*, pp. 264, 119; Joseph Berliner, *Factory and Manager in the USSR*; R. D. Portes, "The Enterprise Under Central Planning," *The Review of Economic Studies*, Vol. 36, No. 2 (April 1969), pp. 197–212; and David Granick, "The ministry as the maximizing unit in Soviet industry," *Journal of Comparative Economics*, Elsevier, Vol. 4, No. 3, (September 1980), pp. 255–273.
6. Ioffe and Maggs, *The Soviet Economic System*, p. 291.
7. Armen A. Aichian and Harold Demsetz, "The Property Right Paradigm," *The Journal of Economic History*, Vol. 33, No. 1, (March 1973), The Tasks of Economic History, pp. 16–27 (p. 20).
8. Peter Moran and Sumantra Ghoshal, "Markets, Firms, and the Process of Economic Development," *The Academy of Management Review*, Vol. 24, No. 3 (July 1999), pp. 390–412 (p. 394).
9. William H. Meckling and Armen A. Alchian, "Incentives in the United States," *American Economic Review*, Vol. 50, No. 2 (May 1960), pp. 55–61 (p. 56).
10. *Ibid.*, p. 56.
11. Friedrich August von Hayek, "The Pretence of Knowledge," Nobel Prize Lecture, December 11, 1974, at http://nobelprize.org/nobel_prizes/economics/laureates/1974/hayek-lecture.html

(December 6, 2009).

12. *Ibid.*

13. Karl Marx, "Critical Notes on the Article 'The King of Prussia and Social Reform. By a Prussian,'" *Vorwarts!* No. 63, August 7, 1844, at http://marxists.org/archive/marx/works/1844/08/07.htm (December 6, 2009).

14. Leon Trotsky, *The Revolution Betrayed: What Is the Soviet Union and Where Is It Going?* trans. Max Eastman (1937), chap. 3, at http://www.marxists.org/archive/trotsky/1936/revbet/index.htm (November 25, 2009).

15. This is true even if some of these technologies were thought up by military employees. First, these employees depended on the technology, information, and wealth of the market economy to invent these technologies. Second, the adaptation and innovation that has transformed, for example, the original computer into the vast array of modern computer-based technology was a product of market forces.

16. "Manifesto of the Communist Party," February 1848, chap. 1, in *Marx/Engels Selected Works*, Vol. 1 (Moscow: Progress Publishers, 1969), pp. 98–137, at http://www.marxists.org/archive/marx/works/1848/communist-manifesto/index.htm (December 6, 2009).

17. David Hume, *A Treatise of Human Nature*, Book III, at http://oll.libertyfund.org/index.php?option=com_staticxt&staticfile=show.php%3Ftitle=342&Itemid=27.

Appendix: Further Lessons for Economic Modeling

The economic science should be influenced by these lessons. Socialists believed in their ideas. They intended to rid the world of the cruelty and harsh oppression of what they saw as the greatest evil—possession. They learned that without this great evil, society could not function. They learned that this "evil" was just a device—a tool that individuals can use to make agreements and cooperate by exchanging parts of a whole social network of production.

Socialists wanted to create a shared social network of production, but they imagined it without exchange because abundance would make even exchange unnecessary. But abundance was just a dream. Instead, the plan that was to guide their production was left without information and without a tool to coordinate actions. The society could no longer come together without a leader, and the leader was blind, standing outside the social order that required him.

The lessons from the Soviet experience can help to illuminate the features of the market economy that economists should focus on in their models. One important lesson from this experience is that a model must account for the dynamic character of the economy. During the experiment with pure socialism, many economic models represented the economy in such a way that the socialist's vision looked promising. Unfortunately, recent models have not been updated to fully account for the faults that allowed those models to present an unrealistic picture.

There are five significant flaws in many mainstream economic models that the experiment with socialism in the Soviet Union highlights. The five are interconnected and form a whole problem, which may have a general solution. The problems are:

- Models sometimes represent the economy as *static*.

- Some economists depend on *aggregate* concepts or statistics about the economy.

- Models rarely account for the *interactions between the heterogeneous economic actors* of which the economy is made.

- Models rarely account for the *institutions and evolution within them* that drives the economy.

- Models do not recognize the new and unexpected *innovations* that entrepreneurs may devise if given sufficient incentive.

Competition cannot be measured in a market or an economy by comparing the price and profit levels of firms to some ideal or standard. This was proven in the Soviet Union when competition was eliminated and replaced with the ideal outcomes from these models. The static model of competition, still used by regulators and policymakers concerned with market power, is fatally flawed. If firms are pushed toward a more "competitive" outcome, innovation is likely to be stifled. Yet the benefits of market economies—the new technologies and higher living standards that they produce—are a result of innovation. Growth in the economy is tied to the dynamic nature of competition as entrepreneurs seeking profit compete and innovate. Market competition is an evolutionary process, always in a state of disequilibrium.

The problem of unemployment in a market economy is also often viewed statically. The idea that government can and should either protect jobs or employ the unemployed assumes that the actions government takes will have no other consequences on the economy. However, they always will. Employment is also not uniform. It is not something that can be aggregated, presented as a statistic, and compared. In the Soviet Union there was very high employment, but much of it was "unemployment on the job." It was inefficient because government did not know how to employ workers most efficiently. Workers and employers in a market economy form contracts based on their local knowledge and their particular skill sets and needs, just as entrepreneurs do. This heterogeneous interaction in a dynamic market, where individuals can respond to the particular needs and conditions around them, is what leads to efficient and productive employment.

Static models of profit, and moral outrage against self-interested pursuit of profit, have led many to disregard the role that profit plays in guiding a firm to serve the customer. Without profit as a guide and loss as a constraint, Soviet firms had to rely on instructions from superiors, handed down from central planners. In a market economy, the individual firm can engage with customers and determine what products are valued and what quality is expected for a given price. Knowing their own limitations and unique access to resources, these firms can contract with preferred suppliers and find cost-effective ways to produce the products. These interactions between heterogeneous economic agents are not modeled by most economists, and hence the true value of the guide of profit and loss is not captured.

Furthermore, static models of profit cannot capture the role that profit and loss play in allocating resources across the economy. Without the guiding force of profit and loss, investment in the Soviet Union was often misdirected. Unneeded projects were undertaken, wasteful ones extended, and useful ones bypassed. In a market economy, profit unites the self-interest of some with the requests of others, allowing voluntary exchange to coordinate resolutions to the continually emerging needs of society. Models that aggregate total investment, total consumption, and total output fail to distinguish between investment that fulfills demand and investment that produces unwanted goods. These aggregate numbers also do not reveal whether production was efficient or whether scarce resources were squandered unnecessarily.

The middleman in a market economy is often seen as wasteful. This again is a static analysis of his role because it does not account for why the middleman emerged (as he did even in the Soviet economy) or how efficient he may be at his job given the institutions he faces (which turned out to be less so in a planned economy). It disregards his specialized knowledge and hence the potential benefits of voluntary interaction between heterogeneous agents. Finally, it ignores any innovations that a middleman might produce given the right institutional incentives. The middleman forms another link in a decentralized system of exchange, adding flexibility and knowledge. This is most efficient with a complete set of property rights, an atomistic decentralization of production.

Prices are nearly always modeled statically, even though they are the most dynamic part of a market economy. The economy depends upon the information that they carry about local conditions where there have been individual exchanges. This information is aggregated into a single price, so that total conditions of supply and total amount of demand for the resource is conveyed. Each price is only the price for a single exchange, but the price interacts with every other price in the economy so that it represents society's valuation of the product with regard to all other potential uses of the resources. But this depends upon voluntary interactions of heterogeneous agents in a market, and any price that was set centrally will not convey this information. Hence, comparing aggregates that are based on prices not set by market exchange with ones that are is like comparing apples (that are valued) and oranges (that are not).[1] Yet many economic studies, including statistics the results of nearly every economic policy, include prices of both kinds.

Money emerges from the interactions between economic agents as they exchange. The idea that government can safely "stimulate" the economy by adding additional money to it ignores this fact because it ignores the way that money affects each interaction. It depends on a static picture of an aggregate price level, level of investment, and level of savings that can be boosted by an increase in the aggregate money level. It ignores the time component of investment: Money affects all prices including the interest rate as it connects buyers and sellers, investors and producers, and borrowers and lenders. The money level affects not only the aggregates of savings and consumption, but also the individual choices of heterogeneous agents planning their actions over time. Soviet planners discovered not only that money was necessary for coordination between agents, but also that it could not be efficiently controlled, because controlling money meant controlling every choice in the economy, and they did not have the knowledge to do this.

Blaming deregulation for inefficient actions or fraud assumes that the individual's actions are guided toward these ends from the beginning and that regulations are necessary to prevent such outcomes. An individual's original motivation is framed by the institutions he faces. The institutional structure of an economy allows for the evolution of that economy over time. Private property institutions bestow the guide of profit and loss. This system enables individuals to seek their self-interest and simultaneously, serendipitously, serve others and coordinate the social order. Institutions of public property do not provide this environment for the economic actors. Self-interest produces a different result because actors chase targets instead of profit. With a partial set of private property rights, actors may face incentives toward risky or misguided behavior. They may have potential for profit, but not loss, or they may earn profit based on prices that do not reflect true conditions of supply and demand. They may chase an aggregate that carries no true value.

The belief that freedom could come from freedom from want and the belief that the state could wither away rested on a vision of the institutions of public property in which plan and leader were not necessary. A system of decentralization and exchange does not require a leader—it is a spontaneous order—but a system that does not atomistically protect the rights of each individual agent within it and allow for free interaction between agents cannot self-organize as a spontaneous order can. To make use of property owned by all, a plan was necessary. Markets allow for voluntary interactions between heterogeneous economic actors. These interactions depend upon the institutions of private property. They are not possible under socialism. Although socialists had expected greater freedom and democracy with common ownership, neither was possible under that institutional regime.

It is also a static image of market economies that led socialists to blame markets, not government aid and intervention, for the ills that they perceived. Their solution contained none of the dynamic advantages of the market and was in fact an exaggerated form of corporatism, the system they despised. Aggregate figures and models do not distinguish between firms that face pure market conditions and those that receive aid from the state, yet the two are very different because the institutions facing a firm determine its available knowledge and create incentives that affect its behavior. The society that evolves within pure market conditions with full protection of private property rights differs dramatically from the society that evolves where these rights are compromised or absent.

If economic models are to be capable of representing life's true complexity and reveal the economy that is the result of the model in its full dimensions—the complete social system that actually emerges given the chosen economic institutions—they must allow for interaction over time between heterogeneous actors. As ambitious as this may sound, there is in fact a modeling approach capable of doing this. In the field of complex systems analysis, there is an approach called "agent based modeling."[2] With it, heterogeneous interactive agents can be computationally modeled, allowing social systems to emerge over time and allowing for continual, evolving social change. Interactions, contracts over time, exchanges and contract violations, and even social phenomena like herding behavior and butterfly effects can be modeled. Hierarchy and democracy can be compared. Plan and market can be compared.

With today's technology, simulations of the economy can be modeled as computer games. Whole virtual realities exist in cyberspace as complex as our interactions every day. Institutions of market exchange exist in multiplayer online games like EverQuest, World of Warcraft, and simulated worlds both online and off.

Current models of the economy, even those that are computational and aim to represent the economy dynamically, suffer from problems of aggregation and lack representations of individual economic exchange. Hence, the market dynamics of price and profit and loss are not modeled. Equilibrium assumptions are used, rather than evolutionary growth within institutions. Dynamic Stochastic General Equilibrium (DSGE) models were born out of the recognized problems with earlier general equilibrium models. The Lucas critique[3] was accepted—the problems of aggregation were supposedly understood. Yet even DSGE models cannot resolve the full problem indicated by Lucas and Hayek and by the experience of socialism.

Interactive agent models can potentially speak to these problems. Agent models also have the advantage because they model individual agents. They do not need to rely on an aggregate assumed behavior, such as profit maximization. Instead the institutions can be modeled, and the natural selection that occurs as the system evolves within the institutions can determine the outcome.

Economists often imagine that an assumption like profit maximization, even if unrealistic, is a close enough approximation for the purposes of a model. Yet society is like a growing, evolving being[4] with past consequences and interactions continually affecting current responses to policy. This is the "culture" and "path dependency," and "unknowable factors" that economists frequently admit exist, but that remain unmodeled. Individuals also have their own motives and influences that affect their behavior. Economic laws exist because individuals do react to institutions, but economic actors do not react like robots with a predetermined plan like "profit maximization" and complete information that allows them to fulfill it. Furthermore, when they do act they interact, they affect others in the economy. Hence, the aggregate result of their actions cannot be assumed from the beginning as an equilibrium condition. If it could, innovation would be impossible.

For a model to be realistic, innovation cannot be assumed or ignored. Time and uncertainty must be accounted for in a realistic model. Finally, coordination evolves and develops, but it is not a given. Coordination is not a static concept; it is an active force. The economic system as a whole, as well as the individual actors, must exist over time in a model capable of illustrating reality. This is asking a lot of a model, but modern simulation techniques are up to this task.

ENDNOTES

1. Or in a wonderful visual picture, comparing GDP of a market economy with GDP of a planned economy may be like comparing a 300-pound man with a muscular figure with a 300-pound man who is fat. The content of the aggregate is not included in the aggregate number (the 300-pound weight). I am indebted to Peter Boettke for this metaphor.
2. For an introduction to the use of agent-based modeling in economics, see J. Epstein, "Agent-Based Computational Models And Generative Social Science," *Complexity*, Vol. 4, No. 5 (1999), pp. 41–60. Also see Guinevere Nell, "Competition as Market Progress: An Austrian Rationale for Agent Based Modeling," *Review of Austrian Economics*, 2009.
3. Robert, Lucas, "Econometric Policy Evaluation: A Critique," *Carnegie-Rochester Conference Series on Public Policy*, Vol. 1 (1976), pp. 19–46.
4. One can almost think of it in biological terms: Institutions are like genes, but individuals have mutations, for example, when they innovate, but also through policy changes, mergers, and other kinds of interactions. The life form has a memory; the mutations change it the way that society changes in response to the social and political climate.

Bibliography

Armen A. Aichian and Harold Demsetz, "The Property Right Paradigm," *The Journal of Economic History*, Vol. 33, No. 1, (March 1973), The Tasks of Economic History.

Alan Ball, "Nep's Second Wind: 'The New Trade Practice,'" *Soviet Studies*, vol. 37, no. 3 (July 1985), pp. 371–385.

Janusz Bardach, *Man is Wolf to Man: Surviving Stalin's Gulag*, University of California, 1998

E. Belfort Bax, "Modern Socialism," *Modern Thought*, vol. 1, no. 8 (August 1879), pp. 150–153, at http://www.marxists.org/archive/bax/1879/08/socialism.htm

Joseph Berliner, *Factory and Manager in the USSR* (Cambridge, Mass.: Harvard University Press, 1957).

Peter Boettke, "Economic Calculation: The Austrian Contribution to Political Economy," *Advances in Austrian Economics*, vol. 5 (1999), at http://economics.gmu.edu/pboettke/pubs/pdf/Economic_Calculation.pdf

Eugen Von Bohm-Bawerk, *Exploitation Theory of Socialism-Communism* (ISI Books, 1975 [1884]).

Eugen von Böhm-Bawerk, "Karl Marx and the Close of His System," (New York: Augustus M. Kelley, 1949), at http://mises.org/books/karlmarx.pdf

Nikolai Bukharin, *Imperialism and World Economy* (International Publishers, 1929), chap. 13, note 22, at http://www.marxists.org/archive/bukharin/works/1917/imperial/index.htm

Nikolai Bukharin and Evgenii Preobrazhensky, *The ABC of Communism* (Penguin Books, 1969), http://www.marxists.org/archive/bukharin/works/1920/abc/index.htm

Richard Ebeling, *The Austrian Theory of the Trade Cycle and Other Essays* (Ludwig Von Mises Institute, 1996).

Michael J. Ellman, "The Use of Input-Output in Regional Economic Planning: The Soviet Experience," *Economic Journal*, vol. 78, no. 312 (December 1968)

Friedrich Engels, *The Principles of Communism*, 1847, online at: http://www.marxists.org/archive/marx/works/1847/11/prin-com.htm

Friedrich Engels, *Socialism*: Utopian and Scientific, *Marx/Engels Selected Works*, Progress Publishers, Volume 3, p. 95-151, 1880, online at: http://www.marxists.org/archive/marx/works/1880/soc-utop/index.htm

Chris J. Farrell, "How to Measure Innovation in the Products and Services of Firms and Use It to Explain GDP Growth for the Second Half of the 20th Century," U.S. Department of Commerce, at *http://www.techmatt.com/techmatt/Farrell0308.pdf*

John Flynn, *The Roosevelt Myth*, (San Francisco: Fox & Wilkes, 1998).

Burton Folsom Jr., *The Myth of the Robber Barons* (Young America's Foundation, 1987).

Garet Garrett, *Salvos Against the New Deal*, Caxton Press, 2002 [1934]

Marshall I. Goldman, "Retailing in the Soviet Union," *The Journal of Marketing*, vol. 24, no. 4 (April 1960), pp. 9-15.

Paul Gregory, Restructuring the Soviet Economic Bureaucracy, (Cambridge University Press, 1990).

Paul Gregory and Irwin Collier, "Unemployment in the Soviet Union: Evidence from the Soviet Interview Project," *American Economic Review* (September 1988).

Paul R. Gregory and Robert C. Stuart, *Soviet Economic Structure and Performance* (Harpercollins College Division, 1990).

Paul R. Gregory and Valery V. Lazarev, eds., *The Economics of Forced Labor: The Soviet Gulag* (Hoover Institution Press, 2003).

Gregory T. Grinko, *The Five Year Plan of the Soviet Union: A Political Interpretation* (London: Martin Lawrence Limited, 1930).

Waldemar Gurian, *Bolshevism: Theory and Practice* (London: Sheed & Ward, 1932).

F. A. Hayek, "Competition as a Discovery Procedure," *Quarterly Journal of Austrian Economics*, Vol. 5, No. 3 (Fall 2002), at http://mises.org/journals/qjae/pdf/QJAE5_3_3.pdf

Friedrich August von Hayek, "The Pretense of Knowledge," Nobel Prize Lecture, December 11, 1974, at http://nobelprize.org/nobel_prizes/economics/laureates/1974/hayek-lecture.html

Friedrich August Hayek, *The Road to Serfdom* (Chicago: University of Chicago Press, 2007).

John N. Hazard, *The Soviet System of Government* (Chicago: University of Chicago Press, 1968).

Marjorie L. Hilton, "Retailing the Revolution: The State Department Store (GUM) and Soviet Society in the 1920s," *Journal of Social History*, vol. 37, no. 4 (Summer 2004), pp. 939–964.

Steven Horwitz and Peter Boettke, "The House That Uncle Sam Built: The Untold Story of the Great Recession of 2008," Foundation for Economic Education, at: http://fee.org/wp-content/uploads/2009/12/HouseUncleSamBuiltBooklet.pdf

O. S. Ioffe and P. B. Maggs, *The Soviet Economic System: A Legal Analysis*, Westview Special Studies on the Soviet Union and Eastern Europe (Colorado: Westview Press, 1987), p. 165

Leonid Vitaliyevich Kantorovich, "Mathematics in Economics: Achievements, Difficulties, Perspectives," Nobel Prize Lecture, December 11, 1975, at http://nobelprize.org/nobel_prizes/economics/laureates/1975/kantorovich-lecture.html

Hiroaki Kuromiya, *Stalin's Industrial Revolution: Politics and Workers*, 1928-1931 (Cambridge University Press, 1990).

Karl Kautsky, The Social Revolution (Chicago: Charles H. Kerr & Company, 1916), at http://www.marxists.org/archive/kautsky/1902/socrev/index.htm

Karl Kautsky, *The Capitalist Class*, trans. by Daniel De Leon (National Executive Committee Social Labor Party, 1911), at http://www.marxists.org/archive/kautsky/1911/capclass/index.htm

John Maynard Keynes, *The General Theory of Employment, Interest and Money and Essays in Persuasion* (New York: Classic Books America, 2009),

Israel Kirzner, The Driving Force of the Market: Essays in Austrian Economics (New York: Routledge, 2000).

J. Kornai, *Contradictions and Dilemmas: Studies on the Socialist Economy and Society* (Massachusetts: MIT Press, 1986).

János Kornai, *The Socialist System: The Political Economy of Communism* (Princeton, N.J.: Princeton University Press, 1992).

Constantin A. Krylov, *The Soviet Economy* (Lexington, Mass.: Lexington Books, 1979).

Oskar Lange, Fred M. Taylor, "On the Economic Theory of Socialism," reprinted, (Minnesota: University of Minnesota Press, 1938).

V. I. Lenin, "The State and Revolution: The Marxist Theory of the State and the Tasks of The Proletariat in the Revolution," *Collected Works*, Vol. 25, chap. 5, pp. 381-492, at http://www.marxists.org/archive/lenin/works/1917/staterev/ch05.htm.

V. I. Lenin, "The Impending Catastrophe and How to Combat It," *Collected Works*, Vol. 25, at http://www.marxists.org/archive/lenin/works/1917/ichtci/04.htm

V. I. Lenin, Declaration of Rights of the Working and Exploited People, *Collected Works*, Progress Publishers, Moscow, Volume 26, 1972, pp. 423-425 at http://www.marxists.org/archive/lenin/works/1918/jan/03.htm

V. I. Lenin, "The Immediate Tasks of the Soviet Government," *Lenin's Collected Works*, Vol. 27, 4th English Edition, (Moscow: Progress Publishers, 1972) pp. 235-277, at http://www.marxists.org/archive/lenin/works/1918/mar/x03.htm#sec6

Karl Marx, "Critique of the Gotha Programme," 1875, at http://www.marxists.org/archive/marx/works/1875/gotha/ch01.htm

Karl Marx, *The Civil War in France* (1871), at http://www.marxists.org/archive/marx/works/1871/civil-war-france/index.htm

Karl Marx, Das Kapital, Chicago: Charles H. Kerr and Co., 1906 [1867], at: http://www.econlib.org/library/YPDBooks/Marx/mrxCpAl.html

Karl Marx and Friedrich Engels, *Manifesto of the Communist Party*, chap. 1, at http://www.marxists.org/archive/marx/works/1848/communist-manifesto/ch01.htm.

John Stuart Mill, *On Socialism*, Prometheus Books, 1987

Ludwig von Mises, *Human Action: A Treatise on Economics*, 4th revised ed. (San Francisco: Fox & Wilkes, 1996)

William Morris and E. Belfort Bax, "The Manifesto of the Socialist League," 2nd ed., 1885, at http://www.marxists.org/archive/morris/works/1885/manifst2.htm

Robert P. Murphy, "The Depression You've Never Heard Of: 1920-1921," *Freeman*, vol. 59, no. 10 (December 2009), at http://www.thefreemanonline.org/featured/the-depression-youve-never-heard-of-1920-

Guinevere Liberty Nell, "Competition as Market Progress: An Austrian Rationale for Agent Based Modeling," *Review of Austrian Economics*, published online June 23, 2009.

Guinevere Nell, "Rent-Seeking, Hierarchy and the Centralization: Why the Soviet Union Collapsed So Fast and What it Means for Market Economies," *Critical Review*, forthcoming 2010.

Alec Nove, *The Soviet Economic System* (London: Unwin Hyman, Inc, 1986)

Alec Nove, *The Soviet Economy: An Introduction* (New York: Praeger, 1966)

Henry Norr, "Shchekino: Another Look," *Soviet Studies*, vol. 38, no. 2 (April 1986), pp. 141–169.

Richard Pipes, *The Russian Revolution*, Vintage Books, 1990, p. 671-672

Amy E. Randall, "Revolutionary Bolshevik Work": Stakhanovism in Retail Trade," *Russian Review*, Vol. 59, No. 3 (Jul., 2000), pp. 425-441

Leonard Reed, "I Pencil," December 1958, at http://www.econlib.org/library/Essays/rdPncll.html

Logan Robinson, *An American in Leningrad*, New York / London, W. W. Norton & Company, 1982

Hugh Rockoff, *Drastic Measure: A History of Wage and Price Controls in the United States* (Cambridge, UK: Cambridge University Press, 1984).

Steven Rosefielde, "The First 'Great Leap Forward' Reconsidered: Lessons of Solzhenitsyn's Gulag Archipelago," *Slavic Review*, vol. 39, no. 4 (December 1980),

Peter. Rutland, *The Myth of the Plan: Lessons of the Soviet Planning Experience* (Essex: Open Court, 1985

Andrei Shleifer, "State Versus Private Ownership" *Journal of Economic Perspectives*, vol. 12, no. 4 (Fall 1998), at http://www.economics.harvard.edu/faculty/shleifer/files/state_vs_private.pdf

Adam Smith, *An Inquiry into the Nature and Causes of the Wealth of Nations* (London: Methuen & Co., 1904), Book 5, chap. 3, at http://econlib.org/library/Smith/smWN22.html#B.V,%20Ch.3,%20Of%20Public%20Debts

Leon Trotsky, *The Revolution Betrayed*, trans. by Max Eastman (1936), chap. 3, at http://www.marxists.org/archive/trotsky/1936/revbet/index.htm

Rexford G. Tugwell, "The Principle of Planning and the Institution of Laissez Faire," *The American Economic Review*, Vol. 22, No. 1, Supplement, Papers and Proceedings of the Forty-fourth Annual Meeting of the American Economic Association (Mar., 1932), pp. 75-92

Rexford G. Tugwell, "Planning and the Profit Motive," pp. 38–39, in *Socialist Planning and a Socialist Program*, (Falcon Press, 1932).

J. Wilczinski, *The Economics of Socialism* (London: Allen & Unwin, 1977).

Barbara Wootton, *Plan or No Plan* (New York: Farrar and Rinehart, 1935)

R

S

5386122R0

Made in the USA
Charleston, SC
07 June 2010